Legal Perspectives in Bioethics

Issues in bioethics often turn, at least in part, on the law and regulatory requirements. Consisting of chapters that address particular bioethics topics from the law's perspective, this fascinating book includes:

- an introduction to the intersection of law and bioethics
- papers identifying the principal ways in which the law influences discussions and decisions concerning each of the topics highlighted
- supplemental papers on certain areas that address the influence and status of the law in countries other than the United States.

Covering traditional topics in bioethics, such as determinations of death and health care decisions for vulnerable groups, the text also explores emerging areas such as conflicts of interest in research, genetics, and privacy and confidentiality in the electronic age.

Incisive and thought-provoking, this volume provides readers with a rich context for understanding the intersection between the law on bioethics and the central issues in bioethics.

Ana S. Iltis is Assistant Professor of Health Care Ethics at Saint Louis University. She is Assistant Editor of the *Journal of Medicine and Philosophy* and Co-Editor in Chief of *The Journal of Law, Medicine, and Ethics.*

Sandra H. Johnson holds the Tenet Endowed Chair in Health Care Law and Ethics at Saint Louis University. She holds faculty appointments in the University as professor of law and professor of health care ethics. Professor Johnson is a co-author of *Health Law – Cases, Materials and Problems* and the treatise *Health Law*, and is Co-Editor in Chief of *The Journal of Law, Medicine, and Ethics.*

Barbara A. Hinze is a doctoral student in the Center for Health Care Ethics at Saint Louis University.

Routledge Annals of Bioethics
Series Editors: Mark J. Cherry, St Edwards University, USA and Ana Smith Iltis, Saint Louis University, USA.

1 Research Ethics
Edited by Ana Smith Iltis

2 Thomistic Principles and Bioethics
Jason T. Eberl

3. Legal Perspectives on Bioethics
Edited by Ana S. Iltis, Sandra H. Johnson, and Barbara A. Hinze

4. The Ethics of Genetic Engineering
Roberta M. Berry

Previous titles:

Regional Perspectives in Bioethics
Edited by Mark J. Cherry and John F. Peppin

Religious Perspectives on Bioethics
Edited by Mark J. Cherry, Ana Iltis and John F. Peppin

Legal Perspectives in Bioethics

Edited by Ana S. Iltis, Sandra H. Johnson
and Barbara A. Hinze

Routledge
Taylor & Francis Group
NEW YORK AND LONDON

Published in 2008
by Routledge
711 Third Avenue, New York, NY 10017, USA

Simultaneously published in the UK
by Routledge
2 Park Square, Milton Park, Abingdon, Oxon OX14 4RN

First issued in paperback 2010

Routledge is an imprint of the Taylor and Francis Group, an informa business

Typset in Times New Roman MT by
Taylor & Francis Books

Library of Congress Cataloging in Publication Data
Legal perspectives in bioethics / edited by Ana S. Iltis, Sandra H. Johnson, and Barbara A. Hinze.

p. cm. – (Routledge annals of bioethics)

Includes bibliographical references and index.

ISBN 978-0-415-70148-8 (hardback : acid-free paper) 1. Medical laws and legislation–United States. 2. Bioethics–United States. 3. Medical laws and legislation. 4. Bioethics. I. Iltis, Ana Smith. II. Johnson, Sandra H. III. Hinze, Barbara A.

KF3821.L445 2007

British Library Cataloguing in Publication Data
A catalogue record for this book has been requested

ISBN13: 978-0-415-70148-8 (hbk)
ISBN13: 978-0-415-60751-3 (pbk)
ISBN13: 978-0-203-79935-2 (ebk)

Contents

Notes on Contributors

Roberta Berry, J.D., M.A., Ph.D., is Associate Professor and Director, Law, Science & Technology Program, Georgia Institute of Technology, School of Public Policy, Atlanta, Georgia, United States.

Bernard Dickens, Ph.D., LL.D., is the Dr. William M. Scholl Professor Emeritus of Health Law and Policy at the Faculty of Law, and cross-appointed to the Faculty of Medicine and Joint Centre for Bioethics, University of Toronto, Toronto, Canada.

Robert Gatter, M.A., J.D., is Associate Professor of Law and Associate Dean for Academic Affairs, Penn State University, Dickinson School of Law, Carlisle, Pennsylvania, United States.

Jesse Goldner, A.B., M.A., J.D., is John D. Valentine Professor of Law, Saint Louis University School of Law, and Professor of Law in Psychiatry and Pediatrics, Saint Louis University School of Medicine, St. Louis, Missouri, United States.

Diane Hoffmann, M.S., J.D., is Professor of Law, Associate Dean for Academic Programs, Director, Law and Health Care Program, and Maryland Health Care Ethics Committee Network, University of Maryland School of Law, Baltimore, Maryland, United States.

Marshall Kapp, J.D., M.P.H., is Garwin Distinguished Professor of Law and Medicine at Southern Illinois University School of Law. He also has a faculty appointment in the Department of Medical Humanities in the Southern Illinois University School of Medicine, Southern Illinois University, Carbondale, Illinois, United States.

Deirdre Madden, B.C.L., LL.M., Ph.D., is a lecturer in Medical Law at University College Cork, Ireland.

John Robinson, Ph.D., J.D., is Associate Dean and Associate Professor of Law, University of Notre Dame, Notre Dame, Indiana, United States.

Robyn Shapiro, J.D., is Ursula von Der Ruhr Professor and Director, Center for the Study of Bioethics, Medical College of Wisconsin, and Partner,

Health Law Department, Gardner Carton & Douglas, LLP, Milwaukee, Wisconsin, United States.

Udo Schüklenk, Ph.D., is Professor of Philosophy and Ontario Research Chair in Bioethics, Queen's University, Kingston, Ontario, Canada.

Peter Skegg, D.Phil., is Professor of Law, University of Otago, Dunedin, New Zealand.

Loane Skene, LL.B., LL.M., is a Pro Vice-Chancellor of the University, a Professor of Law in the Law Faculty, and an Adjunct Professor of Law in the Faculty of Medicine, Dentistry and Health Sciences, University of Melbourne, Victoria, Australia.

Bethany Spielman, J.D., M.H.A., Ph.D., is Director and Associate Professor of the Medical Ethics Program, Department of Medical Humanities, School of Medicine, Southern Illinois University, Springfield, Illinois, United States. She has a faculty appointment at Southern Illinois University School of Law, Carbondale, Illinois, United States.

Anita Tarzian, R.N., Ph.D., is a research associate at the Law & Health Care Program at the University of Maryland School of Law, Program Coordinator of the Maryland Healthcare Ethics Committee Network, Adjunct Professor at the University of Maryland School of Nursing, and an Ethics and Research Consultant in Baltimore, Maryland, United States.

Nicolas Terry, LL.M., is the Chester A. Myers Professor of Law and Co-Director, Center for Health Law Studies, Saint Louis University School of Law, Saint Louis University, St. Louis, Missouri, United States.

Susan Zinner, J.D., is Associate Professor in the School of Public and Environmental Affairs at Indiana University Northwest, Gary, Indiana, United States.

Acknowledgments

We wish to express our gratitude to the Center for Health Care Ethics, the Graduate School, and the Law School of Saint Louis University for their support of this project. We would like to thank Alan Sanders and Birgitta Sujdak for their editorial assistance on this volume.

Ana S. Iltis
Sandra H. Johnson
Barbara A. Hinze
Saint Louis University

1 Law and bioethics

Sandra H. Johnson, Ana S. Iltis, Barbara A. Hinze

This volume focuses on legal perspectives in bioethics. The "contribution" or "intrusion" of law, lawyers, and courts in bioethics has been controversial from the very inception of the field. While some find the power of the law essential to protecting patients, others have argued that the law is too blunt an instrument to deal with the delicate, intimate, and highly variable circumstances at the core of individual decisions concerning medical treatment. Some have argued that the intrusion of non-medical professions, including law, creates "strangers at the bedside," while others appreciate the accountability built into a legal approach.

In the United States, legal norms have emerged as central to discussions of bioethics. The particularly strong influence of law in bioethics in the United States is due in part to the self-identity of the country as a "nation of laws" and to its rather robust liability and regulatory systems that apply to the health care enterprise. Law is a product of a nation's culture, and so there is variability in the norms and influence of the legal system across nations. As the authors in this volume demonstrate, however, the relevance of law to bioethics is not confined to the United States alone.

Law and ethics often converge, perhaps leading to a mutuality of influence between the two perspectives. One point of convergence is evident in common methodologies. The common law system in many nations, for example, relies upon a methodology that has been prominent in bioethics discourse. The essential method of the common law approach is that law is developed one case at a time. A new situation is held up against the facts and circumstances of previously decided cases to see whether the latter situation is the same or different from earlier cases in relevant ways. Principles of the common law emerge from the analysis of commonalities and differences of diverse fact situations. This casuistry, a methodology with a long history and European roots, has been a keystone in bioethics scholarship and education in the United States and elsewhere as well.

Another point of convergence arises in instances in which the legal framework for bioethics issues has intentionally or self-consciously adopted ethical norms and ethical modes of reasoning. In most nations, for example, the legal norms applicable to research with human subjects are imbued with the Kantian framework of respect for persons even though nations may vary at the margins in what is permitted or prohibited. In the case of decisions at the end of life in the United States, the majority of the courts have explicitly adopted the principlist approach, referencing the mid-level ethical principles of patient autonomy, beneficence, nonmaleficence, and justice among others, in their resolution of conflicts over care.

Shared methodologies or values drive law and ethics toward convergence. In the United States, other forces operate as well to accomplish compatibility between law and health care ethics, at least as defined by the medical profession. U.S. law has a number of mechanisms that assure that law not directly contradict the demands of ethical behavior, especially on the part of health care professionals. It is common for courts and legislatures in the United States to adopt "professional custom" or "standards of the profession" as definitions or reference points for legal obligations so as to minimize conflict with professional practices. In malpractice liability, for example, the physician's behavior ordinarily is measured against the custom and standards of the profession as a whole rather than against a standard imposed upon the profession from without. In questions that have been particularly contentious, such as in the case of abortion and euthanasia, U.S. law has created some protections for individual health care providers or facilities who refuse to participate as a method for mediating the rights of the patient and the rights of the health care professional as moral agents.

Despite instances of shared methodologies of ethical analysis and adoption of specific principles of ethics, especially ethical principles adopted by the professions, the culture of law may itself contribute particular values to the debate. Law tends to emphasize consistency or fairness, for example, as primary principles. In the United States, in particular, the legal culture has contributed a very strong respect for process over specific outcome and an emphasis on analyzing conflicts in terms of individual rights and personal autonomy rather than in terms of a web of social relationships. Thus, the values in law may, in fact, cause friction with established ethical norms of professional practice. Deference to professional standards is not complete in the United States. The development by U.S. courts of the requirement of informed consent for medical treatment is an example of an exception to this general primacy of professional practice; and even there, some argue that the medical profession was moving in that direction without the push of the courts. Other nations strike a different balance than does the United States in conflicts between professional authority and other values, but all nations share the issue of the appropriate legal status of professional norms, custom, and practice.

The influence of law on the behavior of health care professionals certainly varies among nations and cultures and may even vary within a single system depending on the issue and the structure in place to enforce legal principles. It is tempting to assume that all substantial ethical obligations should be supported by the force of law. Paradoxically, however, the "legalization" of an obligation, like the "medicalization" of a personal or social problem, can have undesired consequences. The desired goals of establishing and enforcing legal duties and prohibitions include, for example, deterring bad behavior; encouraging good behavior; protecting those too vulnerable to protect themselves; and offering an effective nonviolent recourse for disputants. What one observes instead may include "gaming" of the system to seek out unintended benefits and exceptions; a defensive orientation toward the rules that results in a drive to the bottom; and inattention to the ethical foundations of the moral obligations now enforced by law causing a diminution of commitment to ethical behavior. Law is thus limited, as it is as well by the cost or intrusiveness of enforcement of legal standards, the variability of context, and lack of consensus on ethical norms. It is usually granted, then, that the obligations defined by law are not comprehensive of the moral obligations of the health care professional, the patient, or the family. The law states "minimal" ethical behavior, not ideal ethical behavior.

This volume explores the relationship between law and bioethics with two principal aims. One aim is to explore the relationship between law and bioethics in the United States, offering accounts of the development of particular areas in bioethics, such as human subjects research, ethics committees, privacy, genetic information and testing, reproduction, organ transplantation, end-of-life care, health care decisions for children and the elderly. In the first two chapters, Jesse A. Goldner and Robert Gatter analyze the U.S. legal response to ethical concerns inherent in human subject research and draw the reader's attention to the ever-increasing global and commercial nature of research. In "A Review of Current Issues in the Regulation of Human Subject Research in the United States," Goldner focuses on the structure of human subject research regulation – the institutional review board or IRB. This federally mandated structure places the responsibility of research regulation with the local institution. Each local institution establishes one or more IRBs to review research protocols and ensure compliance with federal regulations. Whereas there are definite advantages to placing the locus of regulatory review with the local institution, Goldner points to current challenges facing IRBs. Recent changes in the federal regulatory environment have altered the expectations of IRBs. Tort-based private litigation is expanding. Academic medical center involvement in human research is declining. Medical research focuses increasingly on the management of chronic conditions, requiring multiple centers of research and a large patient population, rather than on treatment of acute illness. As a result, research is as likely to be carried out in private medical offices and in foreign countries, as it is in traditional academic settings. Researchers increasingly turn to independent IRBs which may not be aware of local conditions. Perhaps one of the most crucial issues in research ethics is how the local IRB adapts to these challenges in protecting subject safety and privacy within the context of multi-center research.

A second important concern regarding regulatory challenges in human subjects research is financial conflicts of interest (COIs). In "Financial Conflicts of Interest in Human Subjects Research: Domestic and International Issues," Gatter analyzes these challenges, the U.S. legal response, and the need for international regulation. Providing background on drug development policy and the resulting increase in financial conflicts of interest in human subjects research, he examines U.S. policy that relies on an institution's regulation of its own conflicts of interest as well as those of its own researchers. Like Goldner, Gatter notes the implications of the increasing international nature of medical research. As pharmaceutical companies increasingly conduct trials in other countries, financial conflicts of interest in human subjects research becomes an international concern. Considering the absence of international COI standards, the potential for harm to human subjects in economically disadvantaged countries is a growing concern.

The next chapter also examines an intra-institutional review process in the United States. In "The Role and Legal Status of Health Care Ethics Committees in the United States," Diane E. Hoffmann and Anita J. Tarzian review both the history of U.S. health care ethics committees (HCECs) and their legal evolution. Although HCECs have been legally recognized as an alternative to the courts in resolving disputes over patient end-of-life care, their role remains somewhat unclear. In part, this may be due to their relative lack of legal status. Committees, for the most part, remain unregulated; and disagreements persist concerning the appropriateness of their regulation. There is also a lack of standardization in committee function and operation, as well as an inconsistent quality in their performance. However, a small number of state legislatures have given HCECs legal authority to make health care decisions for patients without medical decision making capacity and/or an available surrogate. Although the threat of malpractice may lead to improved HCEC performance, some jurisdictions protect these committees from liability. Considering that law suits are rare and that no published judicial opinions provide standards for committee performance, HCECs continue with minimal oversight and without substantive legal guidance.

Health privacy has become the focus of much discussion in recent years. Although the Health Insurance Portability and Accountability Act of 1996 (HIPAA) was intended to address concerns for privacy of medical information and patient autonomy, it has instead deepened disagreement concerning professionalism and health care regulation. In his chapter, "What's Wrong with Health Privacy?," Nicolas P. Terry analyzes this debate, describing the fragile nature of medical privacy, and identifying a paradigm built upon inconsistent terminology, an unpersuasive rationale, and general principles not easily conveyed to patients or to their providers. As such, misuse of terminology and the lack of a substantial rationale leave medical privacy open to consequentialist policy formation. Terry makes other important observations about the developments central to this debate. He notes that the "declining importance of the physician–patient relationship as the touchstone for obligations, particularly confidentiality, has created a 'rights' vacuum." Furthermore, he points out that the changes in health information management are truly revolutionary, both in their reach and their threat to patient medical privacy. As the federal government has increased its regulation of medical privacy and its support for more accessible electronic medical records, this issue becomes one of many battles in what Terry terms the "professionalism-market-regulation conflict" in the delivery of health care. It is a debate that will most likely become even more contentious before concerns over current health privacy protection are resolved.

Concerns over privacy also play an important role in discussions of genetic research and genetic testing. In the next chapter, author Roberta M. Berry explores various regulatory challenges involved in genetic research and testing. The phenomenal expansion in our understanding of the human genome and in related research endeavors and technology continue to challenge us with legal, social, and ethical controversies. In "Health Care and the Human Genome: Regulatory Challenge and Response," Berry examines current U.S. law on access to genetic information and on genetic research. Of special concern is the regulation of health insurance companies' access to and the use of genetic information. Berry also discusses the regulation of gene transfer research, genetic engineering, and reproductive cloning. In a later chapter, Loane Skene examines similar issues in the context of Australian law.

Advances in reproductive technology have not only increased the possibilities of assisted reproduction, but have also enabled physicians to perform preimplantation genetic diagnosis and to treat fetuses *in utero*. Along with the issues raised by these advances, the continued debate over birth control and abortion provokes ongoing bioethical and legal analysis. In her chapter, "Bioethics Issues Surrounding the Beginning of Life: Legal Aspects in the United States," Robyn S. Shapiro provides an overview of the key bioethical and legal questions and developments concerning the beginning of life. Her discussion covers birth control, abortion, sterilization, assisted reproduction technologies, mandates for health care services for pregnant women, posthumous reproduction, and cloning. She also considers significant legal and ethical challenges to health care providers, patients, and society, noting that as reproductive science and technology advance, bioethical and legal analyses become even more critical.

In the next two chapters, Bethany J. Spielman and John Robinson discuss the legal and bioethical implications of issues that concern questions concerning end-of-life matters – more specifically, the procurement and allocation of organs for transplantation and issues raised by advance directives. Human organ transplantation raises many legal challenges, particularly the support of important social values amidst a persistent organ shortage and continually changing technology. Spielman considers two questions central to the ethical and legal issues surrounding allocation and transplantation: How should organs be obtained for transplant? And how should they be allocated? In her chapter "Acquiring and Allocating Human Organs for Transplant: U.S. Law," the author summarizes how federal and state laws address these two questions. In the second part of the chapter, Spielman examines how organ allocation policies integrate considerations such as the ability to pay, medical factors, geography, and donor directives. She then describes recent developments toward market reforms, noting that modest financial incentives to donate sometimes are allowed or that financial disincentives are removed. Internet-based brokering of live donation, another example of these changes, poses a new challenge to regulating organ allocation. Another important change is that states are becoming more involved in the development of organ allocation policies, whereas before only the federal government and UNOS shaped policy. As current laws are revisited by the National Conference on Commissioners of Uniform State Laws, regulations on obtaining and allocating organs for transplant will continue to change.

Over the past century, sweeping changes in medicine and health care delivery have changed the way end-of-life choices are made. In his chapter, "End of Life Legal Issues in the United States," John Robinson identifies how modern medicine has changed the end of life. The number of early deaths has been dramatically reduced, and many now die in either a hospital or nursing home. Patients or their families/surrogates may at times make decisions that shape when and how patients die. Robinson discusses legal issues that arise when conflicts emerge over these end-of-life choices, and how legal mechanisms, mainly advance directives, serve to prevent such conflicts.

Medical decisions involving minors and elderly persons incapable of making their own decisions raise particular concerns. In the chapters by Susan E. Zinner and Marshall B. Kapp, our focus changes to those legal and bioethical issues concerning special populations. Traditionally, U.S. law has allowed parents to make all medical decisions for their minor children. However, this has changed somewhat as exceptions in both common and statutory law have been created. In her chapter, "Pediatrics, the Law, and Bioethics," Susan E. Zinner discusses the legal aspects of medical decision making for minors, as well as the roles of parents, children, and the state in these decisions. She concludes that the law sometimes, though not always, can help children as they face the medical system. She recommends that in cooperating with both providers and parents, children should be encouraged to develop cognitive reasoning skills by participating in choices about their own medical treatment. Whereas a child's choice may not always be appropriate, Zinner writes that a child's wishes should be considered at the very least.

Under normal circumstances the elderly make medical decisions, just as other adults do, within the ethical and legal framework of informed consent.

However, when persons are no longer able to make such decisions for themselves, particular problems emerge. In "Health Care Decisions for the Elderly," Marshall B. Kapp discusses the distinct legal and ethical concerns involved in making health care decisions for this special population. He gives particular attention to decision making capacity for both clinical care and participation in research.

A second aim of this volume is to explore the relationship between law and bioethics around the globe. Although the plausibility of a global bioethics – a shared, content-full understanding of ethical issues related to health and health care – is debated, bioethical issues are of global concern. Throughout the world, we see attention given to ethical issues concerning clinical care and research on humans as well as health policy and access to health care. The bioethics literature increasingly is international in scope. As we seek to understand international bioethics, we must recognize the relationship among the judicial system, laws and regulations, and the bioethics literature that emerges from particular countries. Bioethical analyses are offered in light of background conditions that shape specific clinical, research, and health policy concerns. Legal structures are an important part of those background conditions. This volume offers insight into the relationship between the law and bioethics in the United States and other nations and highlights the importance of understanding the law as it relates to issues in bioethics. Several chapters in this volume address the relationship between law and a particular area of bioethical concern around the globe.

The desire for genetic information can result in conflicts between the interests of individuals and the interests of society as well as between the interests of individuals and those of other family members. In "Legal Regulation of Genetic Testing: Balancing Privacy and Family Interests," Loane Skene discusses this balance that must be struck between the protection of individual privacy and the protection of other interests, arguing that the interests of family members should be considered. Skene describes debates in Australia over the legal regulation of genetic testing, noting that the debates have involved doctors and genetic counselors, and that they have focused on the clinical aspects of genetic conditions. An important aspect of these debates has been widespread community consultation. Skene notes that many people who suffer from genetic conditions, as well as their families, have urged that research be continued. Concern does remain about the possible harm to genetic privacy; however, the author suggests that within the Australian debates, the privacy interests of the individuals and the medical interests of family members in terms of sharing genetic information are fairly balanced.

While Shapiro provides a discussion of reproductive issues within the United States earlier in the volume, Deirdre Madden turns our attention to reproductive issues within the context of Irish law. In "Assisted Reproduction in Ireland," Deirdre Madden provides an overview of the legal context for assisted human reproduction (AHR) treatment services in that nation and includes a brief discussion of how AHR is regulated under British law. She concludes with a discussion of attempts within the European Union to introduce some level of coordination in relation to bioethics regulations generally, as well as the likelihood of achieving consensus among the European Union member states on AHR issues, in particular.

In the final three chapters of this volume, Bernard M. Dickens, P.D.G. Skegg, and Udo Schüklenk provide surveys of various international perspectives on bioethics and the law. In "Canadian Legal Perspectives in Bioethics," Dickens discusses the distinctive history of Canadian law regarding issues of bioethical concern. In particular, he analyzes more recent cases which reflect a departure from English law, including cases involving informed consent to medical treatment, restrictions on abortion, and macro-allocation of health care resources. Although Canadian law is historically founded in English law (the law in Québec is founded in French law), and Canadian judges have considered court rulings in the United States, the United Kingdom, Australia, and New Zealand, among others, Canadian courts have marked Canada's own unique path according to the values predominantly important to its citizens.

In "Bioethics and New Zealand Health Law," Skegg describes two features unique to New Zealand health law, as compared to health law of other countries. One element is the relatively limited role of civil actions for damages for personal injuries. A second is the role of codes and commissioners in New Zealand. Skegg notes that within health law contexts, they have helped fill some gaps left by the accident compensation scheme and the related statutory bar on civil actions for compensatory damages. Especially important is the Code of Health and Disability Services Consumers' Rights which provides a beginning point for the consideration of patient rights and provider duties. The author also discusses legal and ethical issues concerning reproduction, end-of-life research, resource allocation, organ and tissue donation, and pediatrics. In conclusion, Skegg notes that the New Zealand Government is in the process of establishing a Bioethics Council, which will consider matters beyond the more narrow scope of human biomedical ethics. As a result, a much broader concept of bioethics will likely become established in New Zealand.

Finally, a chapter on bioethics in the developing world considers some of the areas of bioethical concern in developing nations and the relationship between law and bioethics throughout this area. We do not mean to suggest that developing nations share legal systems, or cultural, or religious identities. However, there are some common needs and interests among them that play out in bioethics. In "Bioethics in the Developing World," Udo Schüklenk identifies common themes that concern bioethicists in the developing world and explores the impact laws and regulations concerning bioethical issues in the developed world have on the developing world. It also underscores the contrast between developed nations, where much that is of concern in bioethics has been subject to law and regulation, and developing nations, where typically fewer laws and regulations concern issues in bioethics.

This volume explores the relationship between law and bioethics, reflecting the convergence and divergence of the two perspectives and suggesting ways in which each approach has influenced the other. Chapters consider the legal context of the United States as well as a number of other nations. In the United States and throughout the developed world, law and legal reasoning have had significant impact on the bioethics literature and matters related to bioethics have been addressed repeatedly in the courts. The law also has been informed by bioethics, and bioethicists have had a growing influence in shaping public policy and regulation. An early example of philosophers, theologians, and other first generation bioethicists having substantive influence in modern day regulation in the United States is the Belmont Commission, which developed reports that shaped the regulations that govern human subjects research in the United States. Since the time of the Belmont Commission in the late 1970s, numerous government panels have included bioethicists to consider serious matters of health law and policy, including the definition of death (President's Commission for the Study of Ethical Problems in Medicine) and stem cell research and human cloning (National Bioethics Advisory Commission and President's Council on Bioethics). The relationship between law and bioethics is less defined in the developing world, a theme also explored here. Both the mutuality and tension between law and bioethics contribute to the development of legal and ethical norms and to bioethics as a scholarly endeavor, a public policy concern, and an area of professional practice. This volume provides the legal perspective for this exchange.

2 A review of current issues in the regulation of human subject research in the United States

Jesse A. Goldner

Introduction

The United States has developed an extensive, nationally mandated structure to regulate research with human subjects at the local institutional level. While emphasis on local institutional control has been and remains the source of some unique strengths, nonetheless it has some problematic implications. Institutional Review Boards (IRBs) established by individual hospitals, universities, and research institutions review research protocols and determine compliance with federal regulations. But the role of IRBs is changing in the face of recent developments in the federal regulatory environment, the expansion of tort-based private litigation, and the regrettably declining role of academic medical centers in human research.

Human experimentation and the National Research Act of 1974

Regulation in the United States of research using human subjects is based upon bioethical principles born out of discomfort with and even outrage at unethical treatment of vulnerable patients used in scientific studies both abroad and domestically. The system of American regulatory controls on research with human subjects originated, in part, from an awareness of the "experiments" conducted by Nazi physicians during World War II, and the resulting *Nuremberg Code*. These doctors, in various studies, exposed "volunteers" to malaria, jaundice, and typhus; injected them with poisons; sterilized them; forced them to breathe mustard gas or drink seawater; froze them in ice water; and subjected them to dangerously low atmospheric pressure until they died. In some cases, the physicians allegedly believed that the experiments were consistent with the Hippocratic Oath, done with the idea of healing disease or hastening the end of the war.

The *Nuremberg Code* itself actually was part of the decree of the court of American judges in the Doctor's Trial held in Nuremberg.[1] It is a statement of principles to determine when medical experimentation on human beings is appropriate. Those ideas were later used as a basis for the *Declaration of Helsinki,* developed by the World Medical Association in 1964.[2] The

American Medical Association (AMA) endorsed the *Declaration* in 1966 in its *Ethical Guidelines for Clinical Investigators,* part of the *Principles of Medical Ethics.*[3] Unfortunately, the AMA's *Ethical Guidelines* were vague, unenforceable, and had little effect on American research practices.

In a series of government-sponsored projects in the 1950s, American researchers exposed subjects to nuclear radiation, administered LSD to uninformed subjects, and studied uranium miners for increased risk of cancer and lung diseases without informing them of the suspected risks. Dr. Henry Beecher made an important contribution to public awareness of unethical research in the United States with his article "Ethics and Clinical Research," published in 1966 in the New England Journal of Medicine. It detailed over twenty published, but highly unethical, examples of post-World War II medical experiments conducted by American physicians where patients were not informed of risks or even of the fact that they were participants in medical research. Shortly thereafter came a series of medical research scandals uncovered in the early 1970s. The infamous Tuskegee Syphilis Study investigated the natural course of untreated syphilis in 400 indigent African-American men between 1932 and 1972, despite the development of penicillin during the course of the study that could cure the disease.[4] The subjects were not informed of their participation in the study, and most did not know they had the disease. They thought they were receiving ordinary medical care. In another episode, three physicians injected twenty-two patients with live cancer cells without the patients' informed consent at the Jewish Chronic Disease Hospital in Brooklyn, New York in 1963.[5] Developmentally disabled children at Willowbrook State School in New York were infected with hepatitis in the mid-1950s through the early 1970s.[6]

The publicity given to the research scandals led to hearings by U.S. Congressional committees, resulting in the passage of the federal National Research Act of 1974.[7] The Act established the National Commission for the Protection of Human Subjects of Biomedical and Behavioral Research, which issued the *Belmont Report* in 1978.[8] To protect the rights of potential subjects, the Report mandated review of proposed research, which it defined as "an activity designed to test an hypothesis, permit conclusions to be drawn, and thereby to develop or contribute to generalizable knowledge."[9] It authorized combining research with the practice of accepted therapy, but asserted that any "radically new procedure" had to be part of a formal procedure to determine its safety and effectiveness.[10]

The *Belmont Report* articulated the three basic bioethical principles for the conduct of research: respect for persons, beneficence, and justice.[11] Respect for persons incorporates two ethical convictions: that people should be treated as autonomous agents, and that persons with diminished autonomy were entitled to protection. These convictions lead to moral requirements to acknowledge autonomy and protect those with diminished autonomy. An autonomous person deliberates and acts accordingly; to repudiate a person's judgments, to deny a person the freedom to act on those judgments, or to withhold necessary information shows a lack of respect for an autonomous agent. The Report acknowledged that not all people were capable of autonomy. The immature and incapacitated must be protected, the extent of which depends on the risk of harm and likelihood of benefit. Some people may even need to be excluded from harmful activities. In most cases, respect for persons requires that human subjects participate in research voluntarily and with adequate information.[12]

Beneficence is an obligation that persons be protected from harm, and that affirmative efforts be made to maximize possible benefits and minimize possible harms. The Report recognized the dilemma that learning what will be beneficial may require exposing people to risk. That is, "even avoiding harm means learning what is harmful."[13] To mitigate this problem, the principle of beneficence is applied to both particular research projects and the enterprise of research as a whole. Researchers must plan how to maximize benefits and reduce risks to human subjects, and society must consider the long-term risks and benefits of improved scientific knowledge. In this way, beneficence justifies many areas of research involving human subjects.[14]

The principle of justice requires the appropriate consideration of who should receive the benefits and bear the burdens of research. "An injustice occurs when some benefit to which a person is entitled is denied without good reason or when some burden is imposed unduly."[15] Historically, the Report noted, burdens in scientific research were borne by poor ward patients, prisoners, and racial minorities. Research subjects, it declared, must be chosen based solely on reasons directly related to the problem being studied, rather than on easy availability, compromised position, or manipulability. Additionally, when research supported by public funds produces new therapies or devices, the principle of justice demands that the advantages be shared with those who cannot afford them and that research should not disproportionately involve groups who will not likely benefit from subsequent applications.[16] Ultimately, the *Belmont Report* mandated three requirements of ethical research based on these principles of respect for persons, beneficence, and justice: informed consent, risk/benefit assessment, and equitable selection of research subjects.[17]

Establishment of Institutional Review Boards at the local level

In addition to establishing the National Commission, the National Research Act also mandated the establishment of Institutional Review Boards, known as IRBs. It required what now is the federal government's Department of Health and Human Services (DHHS) (formerly known as the Department of Health, Education and Welfare (DHEW)) to develop, through a formal administrative rulemaking procedure, the federal regulations on human subject research.[18] Now called the "Common Rule," seventeen federal departments and agencies have adopted the regulations to govern research conducted or funded by these agencies. Essentially, all federally funded research is now covered by a common set of regulations that requires (1) review of research by an IRB, (2) application of substantive standards for the treatment of human subjects of research, including risk assessment and informed consent of subjects, and (3) institutional assurances of compliance with the federal regulations.[19]

In addition to the *Belmont Report*, the National Commission also issued a much lesser known Report in 1978 entitled *Report and Recommendations: Institutional Review Boards.*[20] The Report considered how best to balance society's interest in protecting subjects' rights against developing knowledge that can benefit the subjects or society as a whole. It concluded that this determination should not be left to investigators alone, who, by virtue of their concern with the pursuit of knowledge, have conflicts of interest on the issues. Rather, people who are independent of the research need to share the responsibility. While the Commission considered alternatives such as regional or national governmental review processes, ultimately it recommended the creation of "local review committees operating pursuant to federal regulations and located in institutions where research involving human subjects is conducted." The rationale was that such local committees would have the advantage of greater familiarity with the actual conditions surrounding the conduct of research, including the individual researchers themselves. Regulations governing IRB conduct were based on the recommendations of this Report, while regulations concerning protections for specific populations of human subjects were based on earlier reports by the National Commission.

Institutional Review Board responsibilities

The regulations issued under the National Research Act by what is now the DHHS dictate the general composition of an IRB, its role, and IRB procedures. Technically, the Act and regulations apply only to research studies that are either funded by the federal government, or are in contemplation of a pharmaceutical or medical device company's plan to seek governmental approval to market a drug or device. But nearly all institutions conducting research with human subjects have chosen to apply the rules to all research conducted at the institution or by its agents.

IRBs are local boards appointed by officials at the particular hospital, university, or research institution. Institutions have wide discretion in establishing the structure, procedures, and membership of the IRB. Typically, they are predominantly comprised of employees or others affiliated with the institution or facility. IRBs are charged with reviewing all research involving human subjects (unless they present no more than minimal risk and meet other established requirements), in an effort to protect the rights of the subjects, regardless of the source of funding for the research.[21] The federal government's Office for Human Research Protection (OHRP) provides some public oversight for this process. Until 2000 this office was called the Office for Protection from Research Risks (OPRR).

An institution whose research is covered by the regulations must provide "written assurances" that it meets all the requirements mandated by the federal government. Those assurances minimally must include (1) a statement of ethical principles for protecting the rights and welfare of research subjects; (2) the creation of at least one IRB; and (3) procedures for reviewing research methods and reporting violations to the government. By federal regulations, an IRB must be comprised of at least five persons whose expertise allows review of protocols from both scientific and ethical perspectives. At least one IRB member must not be affiliated with the institution, and at least one member must have a nonscientific background. The IRB's responsibilities include: (1) evaluating the risk/benefit ratio of proposed research based on its scientific design, including the necessary monitoring of the research as it proceeds; (2) ensuring that subject selection is equitable; (3) seeing that informed consent is appropriately sought and documented; (4) determining whether the research plan requires and, if so, adequately provides for data monitoring; and (5) protecting subjects' privacy and confidentiality of personal data. Moreover, under the regulations, institutions do not have the authority to overturn IRB decisions. IRB determinations are final and there is no opportunity to appeal either to other institutional bodies or to the courts. Theoretically, an institution could relieve all IRB members of their responsibilities and name a new Board to review and approve a previously disapproved study, because, as noted, the institution has the authority to appoint Board members, but such action would be the extent of an institution's power. Moreover, given federal regulatory oversight, such action would be unlikely.

In many respects, this entire regulatory approach is quite unusual, in that the government's granting of such significant and unreviewable powers to private citizens is rare. The U.S. Supreme Court has held that delegation of governmental regulatory power to private parties is unconstitutional in some circumstances,[22] and continues to impose strict limits on such delegation.[23] But delegation of power to private citizens is sustainable if proper safeguards are provided. The test is whether the delegation is reasonable under the circumstances; that is, the legislature itself must have decided the fundamental policy questions, and the exercise of power by private parties must be accompanied by adequate standards or safeguards against arbitrary or self-motivated action.[24] Generally, the delegated authority is limited to defining general standards for technical areas, such as wiring and electrical codes.[25] But IRBs do not seem to fall under this general scheme. First, IRB members generally are not appointed by governmental authorities (other than when the research is being conducted directly by or within governmental agencies such as the National Institutes of Health), but rather by private or public universities, hospitals, and research institutions. Second, an individual IRB does not establish general standards. These are found in the applicable federal regulations. Rather, fundamentally, the IRB makes the regulations' very broad standards more particular by acting as a quasi-judicial fact-finder on the questions of whether a particular proposed research protocol and the contents of consent documents are accurate and appropriate. It is quite clear, however, that different IRBs evaluating essentially the very same protocol often come to different determinations about these critical questions.[26] Third, researchers who are subject to an adverse IRB determination do not have recourse to the otherwise traditional judicial review that typically characterizes American governmental due process requirements. A researcher cannot appeal an IRB's decision in the courts and an institution cannot approve a study that has been rejected by its IRB.[27] The National Commission, in fact, did not recommend a mechanism for appeal from IRB determinations, since it believed that "an IRB should have the final word at its institution regarding ethical acceptability of proposed research involving human subjects."[28]

The Food and Drug Administration (FDA), another agency within DHHS, determines whether or not pharmaceutical, biological, and medical device manufacturers can market their products. The FDA has extensive regulations regarding the obligations of sponsors and investigators seeking such authority to market these products. These include requirements for IRB approval of study protocols and obtaining informed consent from study subjects. The FDA does not use the assurance process described above as a source of regulatory control, but rather the agency may audit a particular drug or device study, a given institution's conduct of the study, or the functioning of its IRB. Much of this history and the content of the regulations are fleshed out in greater detail elsewhere.[29]

Previously relaxed enforcement

Until relatively recently, American governmental regulatory authorities provided practically no oversight regarding the functioning of IRBs. The FDA conducted a few audits, but essentially there was a period of "sleepy" enforcement between the promulgation of the regulations in the 1970s and the mid-1990s. During this period, apart from being sure that they were drafting the language of their assurances properly, few involved in the process worried about the "regulatory environment" and the government's supervisory role. Federal regulatory authorities rarely took any kind of disciplinary action with respect to how research was conducted at institutions and how IRBs functioned. On the few occasions that they did so, minimal publicity was given to such interventions.

While Boards no doubt acted to minimize risks to subjects by requiring changes in protocols and insisting that consent documents be simplified so as to be better understood by potential subjects, essentially their roles were limited to such tasks. Moreover, little or no effort was made to encourage IRBs to have any involvement in the monitoring of ongoing research or in reviewing conflicts of interest. At times key researchers, upon learning that particular Board members were too demanding in their review of protocols, might complain to institutional officials. Soon thereafter those Board members might be informed that their previously unlimited terms on the Board were coming to an end. Others, arguably more "friendly" to research, would then be appointed in their places. In all probability, however, those asked to leave the Board gave little thought to the possibility of contacting governmental regulatory authorities about what had occurred. Moreover, apart from the development of additional regulations dealing with research on subjects falling within certain special population groups (pregnant women, human fetuses, neonates, prisoners, and children) the regulations have remained essentially the same for nearly twenty-five years. What *has* changed, however, is how the relevant federal agency, DHHS acting through what is now the OHRP, has interpreted them.

Similarly, during those same times of sleepy enforcement, that is, until quite recently, there was very little in the way of litigation in this area. Occasionally, medical malpractice lawsuits alleged violations of the federal regulations, but irrespective of the success of the malpractice case, such instances were more likely viewed as innovative therapy and the lack of IRB review was not seen as a factor in the outcome of the case.

The current regulatory environment

Reinterpretation of the regulations

The sleepy regulatory atmosphere of the 1970s through mid-1990s was followed by the tumultuous late 1990s. Official reports issued first by the President's Committee on Human Radiation in 1995 and then by the Office of the Inspector General (OIG) of DHHS in 1998 stated that IRBs were overworked, understaffed, and not adequately protecting subjects. The reports indicated that IRBs were functioning inadequately because they were overwhelmed with an increasing number of research proposals. Apparently, inexperienced Review Boards were judging too many research proposals too quickly. IRB workloads had increased an average of forty-two percent within five years, while IRB size and budgets had remained the same.[30]

The reports recommended, among other things, a series of revisions to the federal regulations designed to increase subject protections, require educational programs for investigators and IRB members, increase involvement by community members on Boards (including nonscientists and institutionally unaffiliated individuals), insulate Boards from conflicts of interest, require adequate IRB resources, and re-engineer the federal government's oversight processes. Surprisingly, the regulations have not been revised and, sadly, practically none of those recommendations have been put into effect in any way. The OIG issued another report in 2000 and concluded that only "minimal progress" had been made in improving IRBs.

It also criticized the failure to simplify federal regulatory provisions to decrease the workload on IRBs.[31]

There was also a great deal of new publicity in the public media, let alone that of the research community, given to research oversight failures, inadequate monitoring by IRBs, and lack of informed consent in some studies.[32] But these instances simply were representative of a much larger issue, which was the belief by many in the public that IRBs and researchers were running wild and not carefully reviewing the science and ethics of studies. The publicity was indicative of the whole matter of a lack of public confidence in research.

Institutional suspensions for noncompliance

Among other issues, there were concerns in the mid-1990s about the fact that OPRR was housed within the National Institutes of Health (NIH), the same larger government agency that itself conducts research on human subjects. While a draft of a DHHS Committee report circulated, recommending the transfer of the OPRR from the NIH to the Office of the Assistant Secretary of Health and Human Services to give the OPRR more independent clout, the OPRR conducted a series of investigations and for-cause site visits at a variety of hospitals and academic medical centers. The FDA similarly seemingly increased its enforcement efforts. Rush Presbyterian-St. Luke's Medical Center in Chicago was one of the first large research centers to have its assurances suspended. The OPRR or the FDA thereafter sanctioned the Veterans Affairs Medical Center in West Los Angeles, Duke University Medical Center, the University of Illinois at Chicago, St. Jude's Children's Research Hospital, Virginia Commonwealth University, the University of Alabama at Birmingham, the University of Colorado Health Sciences Center, the Institute for Human Gene Therapy of the University of Pennsylvania, the University of Oklahoma College of Medicine in Tulsa, the University of Texas Medical Branch at Galveston, the University of Miami, and Johns Hopkins University. Ultimately, approximately twenty institutions had significant restrictions placed on their abilities to conduct research on human subjects for varying periods of time. In a number of situations, regulatory authorities suspended the assurances that institutions had given to the government, which in effect halted nearly all of their human-subject studies and caused significant negative financial and public relations consequences, as described below.[33]

The range of problems uncovered with this more aggressive oversight was quite broad. IRBs had acted improperly by (1) approving inadequate protocols or informed-consent documents; (2) requiring insufficient information regarding plans for subject recruitment and enrollment prior to approval; (3) allowing inequitable selection of subjects; (4) approving protocols deficient in protecting subject privacy and confidentiality; (5) lacking quorums at IRB meetings; (6) maintaining minimal documentation in

Board minutes and files of Board actions and activities; (7) inappropriately granting exemptions from IRB review; (8) omitting required elements in informed consent documents and failing to provide adequate detail regarding other elements; (9) allowing inappropriately complex consent documents; and (10) operating while totally overburdened. In most institutions where assurances were suspended, a number of these findings were made.

Generally, one or more of three elements were present at every institution that was suspended: (1) a lack of institutional support, in terms of financing and manpower, that is, understaffed IRB offices and undermanned Boards had neither the time nor the inclination to take their obligations seriously; (2) institutional foot-dragging or refusals to comply with regulatory requests to conduct investigations of allegations of noncompliance or to alter procedures found to be noncompliant; and (3) a failure in institutional leadership in the area of human subjects protection – an attitude of benign neglect by those in power. What is unclear is how many or what combination of findings would warrant a suspension of the institution's assurances. There can be little doubt, however, that at least some of these problems existed and many still exist at every institution.

Federal legislation historically has not gone into any detail about institutions', Boards', and investigators' duties. In fact, the limited enabling federal legislation simply reads as follows:

> The Secretary shall by regulation require that each entity which applies for a grant, contract, or cooperative agreement under this Act for any project or program which involves the conduct of biomedical or behavioral research involving human subjects submit in or with its application for such grant, contract, or cooperative agreement assurances satisfactory to the Secretary that it has established (in accordance with regulations which the Secretary shall prescribe) a board (to be known as an "Institutional Review Board") to review biomedical and behavioral research involving human subjects conducted at or supported by such entity in order to protect the rights of the human subjects of such research.[34]

Certainly the statute does not address matters as detailed as what should be included in Board minutes. Theoretically, this is left to the regulations issued by the relevant executive/regulatory agency. But many of the deficiencies identified by regulatory agencies in the suspensions involved requirements that by no means were clearly set out in those federal regulations, let alone in any other document issued by those agencies. Thus, it might have been argued that those should not have served as bases for suspending the institutions' assurances or otherwise placing restrictions on their abilities to conduct research. Yet significant compliance actions were taken as a result of the agencies' – DHHS through the OHRP, and the FDA – interpretations of the meaning of those regulations.

Competing or unclear interpretations of laws are often the basis of lawsuits, and the negative actions taken by government agencies against institutions could have been challenged by these institutions in the courts. This never happened for four reasons. First, and most significantly, serious problems existed at practically every institution sanctioned. While a court might overturn some of the findings of noncompliance, others, probably quite justifiably, could stand alone as the basis for the suspension. Second, challenging the suspensions takes time, during which government funding of research would likely have ceased and that would be enormously expensive to the research institutions. Third, litigation costs themselves are significant. Finally, courts give great deference to agency interpretations of their own regulations, which is one of the basic principles of American administrative law, placing a heavy burden on those challenging agency action.

What were the consequences of a suspension? First, the bad publicity was incredibly harmful in today's competitive health care delivery atmosphere. Second, the suspension of federal funding, even for brief time periods, sometimes accompanied by similar actions by other funding sources, was extremely expensive; essentially millions of dollars were lost. Finally, IRBs and their staffs had to be reconstituted and upgraded in terms of personnel. For example, funding for Duke University's IRB jumped from $100,000 to $1,000,000 in one year. Then, in many instances, the newly reconstituted IRBs had to reconsider each protocol that was reviewed under noncompliant conditions.

Tort-based litigation

In addition to the OIG reports in 1998 and 2000 and suspensions or restrictions for noncompliance with regulations, institutions have faced the additional pressure of lawsuits brought by subjects harmed by unsafe research practices.[35] There is little doubt that the publicity given to government action fueled the fires of litigation. In a number of these instances IRBs and the individual Board members were sued. These suits had the effects of causing some competent members of IRBs to resign from Boards and to deter other potential members from serving, lest they needlessly be drawn into such suits in exchange for participating in what is generally viewed as a thoroughly thankless and unrewarding task. Also, in some cases the mere threat of naming IRB members individually as defendants in lawsuits precipitated settlements at sums arguably substantially greater than the case might otherwise have been worth, to avoid significant resignations by Board members or cause an inability to find new Board members in the future.

Some examples provide insight into the litigation process here and its connection with governmental actions. In 1998, eighteen-year-old Jesse Gelsinger died as a result of his participation in a gene therapy study at the University of Pennsylvania that after investigations by government agencies proved to be rife with violations of human subject regulations. Thereafter, the family filed a highly publicized lawsuit against the university, the research team, three other doctors, and two hospitals, alleging negligence and fraud in recruiting the young man for the study. The case subsequently settled, reportedly for a significant amount.[36] In 2001, *The Seattle Times* published a five-part investigative report describing "Protocol 126," a blood cancer experiment conducted from 1981 to 1993 at the Fred Hutchinson Cancer Research Center. The study initially had been shown to have an unusually high graft failure rate in their subjects, but the study continued nonetheless. As a result, in 2001, families of subjects who died filed two lawsuits that were later consolidated. The court found in April 2004 that the patients gave informed consent and that the researchers were not negligent in the deaths of four of five study subjects. The fifth plaintiff, however, was awarded just over $1,000,000 in damages for negligence.[37] Also in 2001, Ellen Roche, a healthy volunteer, died following her participation in an asthma study conducted by Johns Hopkins University. A settlement was reached with the young woman's family before any suit could be filed.[38] In the same year the Maryland Court of Appeals issued its decision in *Grimes v. Kennedy Krieger Institute*, involving human subject research on children.[39] That decision resulted in the reversal of a judgment in favor of the defendants, an affiliate of Johns Hopkins. The appellate court recognized the right of subjects of research to bring private lawsuits and remanded the case for trial on the issue of whether the defendants were liable to low income children and their families who had participated as subjects in a lead paint poisoning study it conducted. This suit was also subsequently settled.

Negative impact on IRBs of suspensions and litigation

The effect of these events on IRB members and chairpersons was significant. On the one hand, the suspensions brought some blessings to the human subject protection community. Hospital and university Boards of Trustees suddenly were interested in hearing from IRB chairpersons, most often about the institution's vulnerability to suspension. In many places, some additional funding for education and IRB support was forthcoming. One of the most significant effects, however, was that for substantial periods of time IRBs redirected much of their focus *away* from protecting subjects and *toward* avoiding suspensions and worrying about how to craft consent documents so as to minimize the likelihood of liability.

On the regulatory side, Boards and their members were like the proverbial Talmudic scholars, spending far too much time searching for the "true meaning" of the words in the text – the federal regulations. IRB members realized then that often the only way to learn what was expected was to read in the press either about what was found to be unacceptable during a site visit that resulted in a suspension of assurances, or to learn about an FDA audit that had significant negative consequences. Later, IRB members might glean something more by reading compliance letters that were posted on OHRP's website, or learn important new information by attending professional meetings and conferences where regulatory agency staffers gave presentations.

Continuing issues in the post-suspensions era

The most recent instance in which federal authorities suspended an institution's assurances for noncompliance with regulatory requirements was in 2001 at Johns Hopkins University, having arisen out of the Ellen Roche death described above. Since then there has been a rather remarkable change on the part of federal regulatory authorities; actions taken by them have been far less severe where instances of noncompliance have been found.[40] These authorities have largely transformed their general approach, increasing efforts to educate institutions and, through them, individual investigators, about how to best conduct research studies using human subjects.[41] At the same time, in many respects, the entire landscape for the conduct of human subject research has changed in a variety of ways.

Declining dominance of Academic Health Centers

Academic Health Centers (AHCs) "perform nearly thirty percent of all the health care research and development in the United States and more than fifty percent of research supported by the National Institutes of Health." They also serve as the principal training ground for preparing clinicians to conduct biomedical research.[42] Yet, while it is true that AHCs conduct a great deal of research, there has been a significant shift in research from AHCs to private hospitals and physicians in private practice.

Previously, the pharmaceutical industry needed the cooperation of academic physicians to perform drug trials for three reasons: the companies did not possess the expertise to devise studies themselves, hospitals affiliated with AHCs could provide subjects, and industry wanted the cachet of academic publications to promote their products. The situation has changed. Pharmaceutical and device companies have hired competent research physicians to develop and analyze clinical studies. Physicians in private practice have become interested in participating in trials and recruiting their patients to be subjects and may be attracted by the substantial compensation offered to them by the pharmaceutical firms for engaging in these trials. As a result, the pharmaceutical industry is increasingly relying on for-profit contract research organizations (CROs) to assist in conducting studies. In 1991, eighty percent of the dollars spent by the drug industry for clinical trials were directed to AHCs, while by 1998 that figure had dropped to forty percent. Another reason for the movement away from AHCs is that much of the pharmaceutical industry's business is now focused on the prevention and treatment of chronic conditions rather than acute infections. While FDA requirements for the latter types of medication rarely require large populations and lengthy studies, clinical trials for medications that treat chronic diseases must include many subjects over a long period of time and at many study sites.[43]

The trend away from traditional AHCs and toward private biomedical research has complicated, and perhaps compromised, the protection IRBs can provide human subjects. First, researchers often submit proposals to multiple IRBs, and then agree to conduct research only at those institutions where the proposals were accepted without revisions. If an IRB is too demanding, a researcher can "shop around" until he or she finds one that is more "sympathetic." There is no requirement that a researcher disclose that a proposal was previously rejected. Second, IRBs at AHCs, due to the bureaucracy common to large academic hospitals, are often perceived as too slow to suit the needs of pharmaceutical companies conducting drug trials at multiple centers. Thus, drug manufacturers have begun using independent IRBs that are not affiliated with any AHC or other research institution. This movement may facilitate research based on large populations in multiple sites, but it also has weaknesses. Most importantly, it negates the principal strength of the traditional IRB: namely, that the IRB has personal knowledge of the local circumstances and of the researchers themselves.

The growth of multi-center trials

When the federal regulations were first promulgated, a very significant portion of biomedical research occurred primarily at the local institutional level. This has changed for a variety of reasons. Purely "local" research now represents a smaller proportion of total research because of the predominance of very large multi-center clinical trials of pharmaceuticals. Many drugs being tested today are designed to treat chronic conditions and are expected to be used in a larger and much more diverse patient population.

As a consequence, studies must include a much larger number of research participants. Initial testing for safety and efficacy in the population for which the drug is expected to be used typically requires several hundred subjects; then the next level of testing requires the enrollment of several thousand patients. Research sponsors typically turn to a large number of institutions to work simultaneously to answer questions that may have been raised in the initial studies or posed by regulatory bodies, to insure that minor differences in the conduct of a study do not have significant differences in outcomes, to establish potential differences that make a particular drug stand out in its class in the highly competitive market and, most importantly, to recruit an adequate number of subjects to gain regulatory approval. Similarly, sponsors conduct clinical studies when seeking a new indication or a new dosage method for an already approved drug. Typically, these studies must be approved by multiple IRBs; and this often leads to the situation described earlier in which sponsors seek researchers at institutions whose IRBs do not conduct what the sponsors perceive to be "overly strict" reviews of protocols.

Data safety monitoring

Though IRBs are required to receive and review adverse events that occur as studies are conducted, it is increasingly recognized that they are not adequately qualified to do the types of analysis needed to evaluate the significance of these events. Such analysis typically requires a very high level of knowledge about the medical problem being studied, significant training in statistics and much time and effort to do the necessary calculations. These tasks are more commonly assumed by entities known as data or safety monitoring boards or committees (DSMBs or DSMCs). The use of such groups has increased substantially for a variety of reasons, including an increase in the number of trials with end points such as death from any cause or death due to cardiovascular disease; the fact that more trials are sponsored or funded by government agencies requiring such boards as part of their study design; and most critically, the increased awareness of methodological issues in trial design. Unlike IRBs, which generally review all studies being conducted at a particular institution, a separate DSMB is usually created for each study that requires one. In appropriate instances, IRBs can require investigators to develop alternative plans for data safety monitoring, such as the use of a qualified monitor who is independent of the study being conducted.

The rise of accreditation organizations

The public and political outcry over serious adverse events that occurred during research between 1997 and 2001 and the resulting government suspensions of some of the facilities involved have led to the development of a private accreditation movement. Two non-profit organizations emerged to offer accreditation services: the Association for the Accreditation of Human Research Protection Programs (AAHRPP)[44] and the Partnership for Human Research Protection (PHRP).[45] (The PHRP was dissolved as of November 15, 2005.) Each developed and began to apply somewhat similar standards, beyond the minimum required by federal regulatory authorities, which are designed to evaluate the adequacy of human research protections in hospitals, academic medical centers, and other settings seeking the organization's approval. The former group was founded by bioethicists, patient advocates, medical investigators, and research institutions, while the latter was a joint effort of two existing organizations that had previously been involved in various other healthcare accreditation activities outside the human subject research arena.

AAHRPP provides, and PHRP provided, to interested institutions a variety of educational programs that are designed to improve institutions' existing human-subject protection programs. AAHRPP requires organizations seeking accreditation to begin with a self-assessment process using the accrediting agencies' standards. A site visit conducted by peer reviewers follows, and then the accrediting body reviews the self-assessment and site visit report. The ultimate goal of the process is to improve the institution's human-subject protection program such that accreditation can be granted.

International research

Again in an effort to recruit quickly the required number of study subjects for clinical trials, and perhaps to decrease the likelihood of encountering what may be perceived as overly protectionist IRBs, sponsors have begun conducting a number of clinical trials outside of the United States. The roles of international research organizations and American researchers conducting studies abroad have often been called into question, given the different and allegedly fewer regulatory hurdles that exist for these studies. One example involved a series of studies done in Africa and Asia in the mid-1990s on prenatal HIV transmission.[46] In these countries there is a great need to treat HIV-positive pregnant women, as the HIV infection rate is far higher than in developed countries. In the United States, HIV-positive pregnant women typically receive a combination of drugs including AZT during the final six months of pregnancy, intravenous medication during delivery and, not infrequently, caesarian section deliveries. This is followed by six weeks of AZT treatment for the baby. The protocol, which decreases the transmission rate to about eight percent, would cost over $500 per birth in developing countries. Consequently, studies were undertaken in which HIV-positive women were randomly selected to receive much less expensive courses of treatment, including some placebo arms, in an effort to determine if there were less expensive but safe ways to treat HIV-positive pregnant women in poor countries. Questions were raised both about the validity of the consent process used as well as larger issues concerning whether the entire study design was ethically acceptable both in the United States and in the developing countries where the research was conducted.[47]

Concerns about conflicts of interest

A number of the research "scandals" of the late 1990s, such as the one involving the death of Jesse Gelsinger at the University of Pennsylvania noted above, raised issues regarding both investigators' and institutions' financial conflicts of interest. An entire chapter in this volume is devoted to the topic, and it should be noted that the matter remains one of great contention.[48] A variety of reports discuss conflicts of interest in research.[49] Different institutions have taken differing approaches to the issue, both substantively and procedurally. Some have proscribed the existence of any actual or potential conflicts and required investigators, for example, either to cease conducting research where a potential or real conflict exists or to sell any financial interests they may have in the entity sponsoring their research. Others have allowed such investments as long as their value does not exceed stated amounts or ownership percentages, and/or required that management plans be developed and approved. Procedurally, most institutions have established conflict of interest committees to review individual situations in the first instance. Alternatively, the IRB itself evaluates the actions needed to deal with conflicts. Even where separate committees are in operation, the IRB still has the responsibility for insuring that subjects are not inappropriately put at risk because of a potential conflict.

Conclusion

The conduct of human subject research in the United States has been defined over time by the competing aims of increasing generalizable knowledge and preserving the health and safety of individual patients. Until the 1970s, the value of improved scientific knowledge prevailed and American researchers had great discretion in conducting their studies. Unfortunately, this freedom led to numerous ethical abuses. The federal government reacted by promulgating rules that sought to temper scientific inquiry with respect for the autonomy and dignity of the subjects who participated in the research. The touchstone of the regulations was a reliance on local Institutional Review Boards, which have the distinct advantage of familiarity with actual research conditions when reviewing research protocols. However, for many years the regulations went largely unenforced, so researchers continued to enjoy a relatively free hand in the conduct of their research. In the 1990s the pendulum swung toward greater attention to patient autonomy when the OPRR and FDA suspended multiple institutions for noncompliance. The publicity surrounding these suspensions may have inspired tort-based litigation brought by injured subjects, which increased sharply in the following years. This powerful combination of governmental and private action had a strong impact on research institutions and changed the focus and culture of IRBs. Boards sometimes received more attention and funding, but they also became more concerned with shielding the institution from suspension and liability rather than protecting human subjects from harm.

Institutional suspensions and lawsuits have cooled recently, but IRBs now face a new set of challenges. Due to an increased focus on managing chronic conditions rather than treating acute illness, research is being conducted in multiple centers using large patient populations. Research is now diffused, taking place in private offices and in foreign countries rather than in traditional academic settings. Local IRBs are not favored by this type of study design, and researchers are increasingly turning to independent IRBs, which may not have knowledge of local conditions. How local IRBs manage to protect patient safety and privacy in the face of multi-center research may become the defining issue in the continuing effort to balance societal needs for greater scientific knowledge against individual human subject autonomy.

Notes

1 Office of the Judge Advocate General, U.S. Dept of the Army, Trials of war criminals before the Nuernberg Military Tribunals no. 10 vol. 2, 181–82 (U.S. Government Printing Office 1946–49).
2 George J. Annas, Leonard H. Glantz & Barbara F. Katz, Informed Consent To Human Experimentation: The Subject's Dilemma 8 (Ballinger 1977).
3 Cf. Jay Katz (with the assistance of Alexander Morgan Capron and Eleanor Swift Glass), Experimentation with Human Beings: The Authority of the Investigator, Subject, Professions, and State in the Human Experimentation Process, 845 (Russell Sage Foundation 1972) [hereinafter Katz, Human Beings].
4 James H. Jones, Bad Blood: The Tuskegee Syphilis Experiment 2–5, 6–17, 22–24, 29 (rev. ed., Free Press 1993).
5 Jesse A. Goldner, *An Overview of Legal Controls on Human Experimentation and the Regulatory Implications of Taking Professor Katz Seriously,* 38 St. Louis U. L.J. 63, 94 (1993) [hereinafter Goldner, *Legal Controls*]. *See* Katz, Human Beings, *supra* n. 3, at 9–65.
6 Goldner, *Legal Controls*, *supra* n. 5, at 94. *See* Katz, Human Beings, *supra* n. 3, at 1007–10.
7 National Research Act of 1974, Pub. L. No. 93–348, 88 Stat. 342 (codified as amended at 42 U.S.C.A. §§ 201 nt, 218, 218 nt, 241, 241 nt, 242a, 300a-7 (2004)).
8 The Nat'l Comm'n for the Protection of Human Subjects of Biomedical and Behavioral Research, Pub. No. (OS) 78–0012, The Belmont Report: Ethical Principles and Guidelines for the Protection of Human Subjects of Research (DHEW 1978) [hereinafter Nat'l Comm'n, The Belmont Report].
9 *Id.* at 3.
10 *Id.* at 3–4.
11 *Id.* at 4.
12 *Id.* at 4–6.
13 *Id.* at 7.
14 *Id.* at 6–8.
15 *Id.* at 8.
16 *Id.* at 8–10.
17 *Id.* at 10.
18 45 C.F.R. § 46.101 *et seq.* (2004), *as amended by* 43 Fed. Reg. 53655 (Nov. 16, 1978), 48 Fed. Reg. 9818 (Mar. 8, 1983), 56 Fed. Reg. 28012, 28022 (June 18, 1991), 60 Fed. Reg. 56778 (Nov. 13, 2001).
19 Cynthia Mcguire Dunn & Gary L. Chadwick, Protecting Study Volunteers in Research: A Manual for Investigative Sites 23, 37 (2d ed., Thomson Centerwatch 2002).
20 The Nat'l Comm'n for the Protection of Human Subjects of Biomedical and Behavioral Research, Pub. No. (OS) 78-0008, Report And Recommendations: Institutional Review Boards (DHEW 1978) [hereinafter Nat'l Comm'n, Institutional Review Boards].

21 *See* Barry R. Furrow, Thomas L. Greaney, Sandra H. Johnson, Timothy S. Jost & Robert L. Schwartz, Health Law: Cases, Materials And Problems 1519–29 (5th ed. 2004) [hereinafter Furrow et al., Health Law].
22 Carter v. Carter Coal, 298 U.S. 238, 56 S.Ct. 855, 80 L.Ed. 1160 (1936).
23 Richard J. Pierce, Jr., Administrative Law Treatise vol. 1 § 2.6, at 93 (4th ed., Aspen 2002).
24 16 C.J.S. *Constitutional Law* § 141 (1984 & Supp. 2004).
25 Alfred C. Aman, Jr. & William T. Mayton, Administrative Law § 1.3.2, at 31–33 (2d ed., West 2001).
26 Carl H. Coleman, *Rationalizing Risk Assessment in Human Subject Research*, 46 Ariz. L. Rev. 1, 15–16 (2004).
27 45 C.F.R. § 46.112 (2004).
28 Nat'l Comm'n, Institutional Review Boards, *supra* n. 20, at 36.
29 Goldner, *Legal Controls*, *supra* n. 5, at 90–103.
30 Office of Inspector General, Pub. No. (OEI) 01-97-00190, Institutional Review Boards: Their Role in Reviewing Approved Research 9–11 (DHHS 1998).
31 Jesse A. Goldner, *Dealing with Conflicts of Interest in Biomedical Research: IRB Oversight as the Next Best Solution to the Abolitionist Approach*, 28 J.L. Med. & Ethics 379, 389 (2000) [hereinafter Goldner, *Conflicts of Interest*].
32 *See* William Speed Weed, *Guinea Pigs*, Wash. Monthly 31 (Nov. 1, 1999); Sheila Kaplan & Shannon Brownlee, *Dying for a Cure*, U.S. News & World Report 34 (Oct. 11, 1999).
33 *See* Goldner, *Conflicts of Interest*, *supra* n. 31, at 389.
34 42 U.S.C.S. § 289(a) (2005).
35 *See* E. Haavi Morreim, *Medical Research Litigation and Malpractice Tort Doctrines: Courts on a Learning Curve*, 4 Hous. J. Health L. & Pol'y 1, 6–13 (2003); *See generally* Alice Dembner, *Lawsuits Target Medical Research Patient Safeguards*, Boston Globe A1 (Aug. 12, 2002).
36 Rick Weiss & Deborah Nelson, *Penn Settles Gene Therapy Suit; University Pays Undisclosed Sum to Family of Teen Who Died*, Washington Post A4 (Nov. 4, 2000).
37 David Heath & Luke Timmerman, *Jury Finds Hutch Not Negligent in 4 Deaths, Family of 5th Patient Awarded Over $1 Million*, Seattle Times A1 (April 9, 2004).
38 Tom Pelton, *Hopkins Reaches Settlement with Family of Lab Tech, Medical School Pays Undisclosed Sum in Asthma Study Death*, Baltimore Sun 1A (Oct. 12, 2001).
39 782 A.2d 807 (2001).
40 *See* Office for Human Research Protection (OHRP), U.S. Dep't of Health and Human Servs. (DHHS), *Compliance Oversight*, http://www.hhs.gov/ohrp/compliance (accessed May 25, 2005).
41 Jeffrey Brainerd, *New Human-Subjects Chief Will Face Challenges and Controversies*, Chron. Higher Educ. A25 (Nov. 22, 2002).
42 Task Force on Academic Health Centers, Envisioning the Future of Academic Health Centers 3, 31 (Commonwealth Fund 2003).
43 *See* Thomas Bodenheimer, *Uneasy Alliance – Clinical Investigators and the Pharmaceutical Industry*, 342 New Eng. J. Med. 1539 (2000).
44 *See* AAHRPP, Association for the Accreditation of Human Research Protection Programs, http://www.aahrpp.org (accessed May 30, 2005).
45 *See* PHRP, Partnership for Human Research Protection, http://www.phrp.org (accessed May 30, 2005).
46 *See* Furrow *et al.*, Health Law, *supra* n. 21, at 1555.
47 *See e.g.* Marcia Angell, *The Ethics of Clinical Research in the Third World*, 337 N. Eng. J. Med. 847 (1997).
48 *See* Robert Gatter, chapter three. *See also* Goldner, *Conflicts of Interest*, *supra* n. 31, at 381–86.

49 *See e.g.* Office of Public Health and Science, Draft, Financial Relationships and Interests in Research Involving Human Subjects: Guidance for Human Subject Protections, 68 Fed. Reg. 15456 (DHHS 2003); Ass'n of American Medical Colleges (AAMC) Task Force on Financial Conflicts of Interest in Clinical Research, Protecting Subjects, Preserving Trust, Promoting Progress II: Principles and Recommendations for Oversight of an Institution's Financial Interests in Human Subjects Research (AAMC Oct. 2002), http://www.aamc.org/members/coitf/2002coireport.pdf (accessed Oct. 10, 2005); Ass'n of American Medical Colleges, Protecting Subjects, Preserving Trust, Promoting Progress: Policy and Guidelines for the Oversight of Individual Financial Interests in Human Subjects Research (AAMC 2001), http://www.aamc.org/members/coitf/firstreport.pdf. (accessed Oct. 10, 2005).

3 Financial conflicts of interest in human subjects research

Domestic and international issues

Robert Gatter

Introduction

Public policies designed to use free market incentives to organize health care systems are under constant scrutiny, most notably in the United States. There is no better example of both the success and danger of injecting the profit motive into health care than the system by which new medicines are developed and tested in humans. On the one hand, reliance on the free market to develop new drugs has attracted substantial private investment, which, in turn, has produced significant advances in medicine. On the other hand, physician-investigators and their research institutions have acquired unprecedented financial interests in the drug research they conduct on humans, interests which conflict with their responsibility to protect human subjects from unnecessary risks.

This chapter analyzes the regulatory challenge posed by conflicts of interest in human subjects research, the way in which U.S. law has responded, and the need for an international response.[1] The next section provides some background on drug development policy and the resulting increase in financial conflicts of interest in human subjects research, both in the United States and internationally. Then, the chapter examines U.S. policy that relies on research institutions to regulate their own conflicts of interest and those of their researchers. The final section criticizes the absence of international conflicts-of-interest standards and identifies the danger this creates for human subjects participating in clinical drug trials in relatively poor foreign countries.

Drug development and financial conflicts of interest in human subjects research

The development of new drugs is, to a great extent, privately financed. For example, U.S. pharmaceutical companies spent more than $33 billion in drug research and development in 2003.[2] They are willing to make such an enormous investment because they stand to profit considerably from the sales of new drugs that successfully reach the marketplace. For example, wholesale pharmaceutical purchases totaled more than $216 billion in the United States in 2003.[3] Moreover, there is a social value to making new drugs available to patients as quickly as possible. In 2003 alone U.S. drug companies introduced thirty-five new medicines.[4]

The private system of drug development has succeeded because of its efficiency. The incentive to profit from sales of new drugs drives private firms to cull through the results of laboratory research in universities, identifying those scientific discoveries that could be developed into new human medicines. It also encourages companies to invest in the development of new drugs from laboratory discoveries and to shepherd those new drugs through the process of human testing and government approval, a process that can take ten years or more.[5] A completely public system of drug development would be hard pressed to make such enormous annual investments and to operate as efficiently.

The success of private drug development in the United States is in part due to federal policy that attempts to harness market incentives to encourage the speedy creation of new medicines using private capital. It is well known, for example, that federal patent law rewards companies that create new products, including new drugs, by granting them exclusive rights to profit from the sale of those products for a multi-year period. Additionally, a lesser known federal policy concerning "technology transfer" encourages companies to invest in drug development at the stage when a new compound moves from laboratory testing to human clinical testing.[6] Early development of new compounds typically occurs in academic centers in the form of laboratory and animal testing, which is often funded by public research grants. If such testing is successful, then compounds move to the stage of human testing, which is much more likely to be privately funded. To encourage this "transfer" from the laboratory to the clinical setting, and from public to private financing, federal law provides that scientists who conduct, and institutions that house, publicly funded laboratory research own any resulting data or discoveries.[7] This empowers university scientists and their institutions to sell or license the results of their research to private firms for further development into commercial products, including new drugs. At the same time, this policy enables private developers to acquire exclusive rights to laboratory research, which, from a business perspective, is a prerequisite to investing in the development of laboratory research. Without it, firms fear that any investment they make will be wasted if a competitor, with equal access to the laboratory research, develops a new product more quickly and wins the race to the patent office and to market. Indeed, prior to the enactment of current U.S. technology transfer policy in 1980, when the results of publicly funded laboratory research were public property, drug companies were much less willing to invest in the development of new compounds and, as a result, laboratory discoveries languished.[8]

The profit incentive is evident at all stages of drug development, including at the human testing stage. A new drug cannot be distributed for human use in any of the three major drug-consuming markets – the United States, the European Union, and Japan – without prior approval by the governing authority,[9] and governments in these markets will not approve a new drug for sale without scientific proof from human testing that the new drug is both safe and effective.[10] Thus, clinical studies of new drugs on human subjects, commonly known as "clinical trials," are an essential step in drug development. They take place in research institutions, often academic medical centers, and are conducted by "investigators" who are physician-researchers affiliated with those institutions.

Today, investigators and research institutions conducting clinical trials in the United States always have a financial interest in the outcome of their research, but the kind of financial interest varies from case to case. First, they have an interest in obtaining grants from drug companies to conduct future research. Research institutions and their physician-researchers depend on such grants to help fund substantial portions of their operating expenses.[11] Additionally, they must compete for these grants not only against other academic institutions, but also against private outfits, known as clinical research organizations (CROs), which organize and conduct clinical trials for a fee.[12] Thus, an investigator running a privately sponsored clinical trial and the investigator's institution have an incentive to conduct the trial in ways, and to reach scientific conclusions, that encourage the sponsor to choose the investigator and the institution for future clinical trials.[13] Second, many investigators and institutions have an ownership interest in the material being tested. Because, under federal law, scientists and their institutions own the results of publicly funded research they conduct, they routinely create companies, known as "faculty start-ups," to patent their laboratory discoveries, hold the intellectual property rights to those discoveries, and market those rights to commercial developers.[14] When the scientist and academic institution that own and have licensed discoveries to a developer also conduct the clinical trials designed to test those discoveries on humans, they have an incentive to assure that the clinical trials proceed and come to favorable conclusions about the safety and effectiveness of the tested material. Third, clinical trial investigators and institutions have a similar incentive when they own equity in a drug company that is sponsoring the clinical trial they are conducting, equity which may have been "paid" by the drug company under a licensing agreement with a faculty start-up owned by an investigator and her or his institution. The best available data suggest that U.S. investigators and institutions conducting clinical trials own equity in the trial's commercial sponsor about one percent of the time.[15] Fourth, an investigator conducting a clinical trial may also have a paid consulting position with a drug company sponsoring the trial. These consulting relationships often arise from the company's desire to benefit from the knowledge of academic experts as the company proceeds in the development of a new drug. When the company's consulting researcher is also the investigator conducting a clinical trial for the company, which occurs in about 2.5 percent of cases,[16] the investigator's interest in maintaining a lucrative consulting position with the trial's sponsor introduces a bias into the investigator's oversight of the trial.[17] Fifth, and finally, investigators conducting clinical trials often receive fees from the sponsoring drug companies, which are paid for each human subject investigators recruit for those trials. Such recruitment fees for investigators are common[18] and substantial, reaching as much as $6,000 per recruit.[19] Private sponsors of clinical trials pay such fees as an incentive for investigators to quickly organize a sufficient number of human subjects and thereby avoid unnecessary delays in shepherding a new drug through the clinical trial process. This incentive, however, also introduces a bias into investigators' judgments about whether a human subject meets the clinical criteria for participation and about what and how to disclose information to a potential human subject as part of seeking that individual's consent to participate in the trial.

Such financial interests create potential conflicts of interest (COIs) not only because of the responsibility of investigators to conduct clinical trials with scientific objectivity, but also because investigators and research institutions are required by federal law in the United States to protect the safety of human subjects in the trials they conduct. Rather than regulate human subject safety directly, federal law deputizes research institutions to do so through institutional review boards (IRBs),[20] which are committees of researchers, administrators, and others who – with the exception of at least one institutionally unaffiliated member – are generally employees of the institution.[21] An institution's IRB must review every proposal to conduct a clinical trial at the institution, and no trial may be conducted without the IRB's approval.[22] Moreover, an IRB may not approve a study unless it determines that, among other things, the risk of harm it poses to human subjects is reasonable relative to its likely benefits and the importance of scientific knowledge to be gained from the research, and that those risks have been minimized.[23] Additionally, the IRB must assure that each human subject participating in a clinical trial is doing so voluntarily after having been adequately informed by investigators about the risks of enrolling in the study.[24] Finally, IRBs are authorized to stop clinical trials where injuries occur despite efforts to minimize risks to human subjects.[25]

It is suspected that human subjects participating in clinical trials in the United States have been unnecessarily harmed as a result of financial COIs. A notable example is the highly publicized death of Jesse Gelsinger while participating in a clinical trial in 1999 at the University of Pennsylvania.[26] The study's principal investigator owned a thirty percent share (worth an estimated $13.5 million) of Genovo, a faculty start-up that he founded and that owned the material and methods being tested in the trial.[27] Likewise, the university owned equity in Genovo worth $1.4 million, and it had a contract with the start-up, giving it rights to gene research discoveries made at the institution.[28] These financial interests allegedly caused the investigator to take unreasonable risks with Mr. Gelsinger's life that had not been disclosed to him, and they caused the University's IRB and its committee on faculty COIs to approve both the trial and the investigator's COI.[29]

Financial COIs in human subjects research are not just a phenomenon of the United States, however. For example, Japan – a major market for drug manufacturing – is experiencing a growth of COIs as Japanese technology transfer policy is liberalized to encourage private licensing of intellectual property rights from public university scientists to private developers.[30] Yet, countries need not produce new medicines to experience the risks of financial COIs in human subjects research. Increasingly, major drug manufacturers are conducting clinical trials in foreign countries where individuals with untreated disease exist in greater numbers and are eager to avail themselves of experimental therapies, where the cost to conduct a clinical trial is relatively low, where the regulatory barriers to human subjects research are relatively few, and where clinical trials can be completed more cheaply and more quickly as a result.[31] The largest growth in foreign clinical trials has been in Eastern Europe, Latin America, Russia, India, China, Thailand, and parts of Africa.[32] Drug manufacturers are permitted to use the results of foreign clinical trials to support their applications for authorization to sell new drugs in the United States, the European Union and Japan.[33] From 1990 to 1999, the number of foreign clinical investigators conducting clinical trials in a foreign country under the FDA's investigational new drug authority increased from 271 to 4,458.[34] Likewise, the percentage of new drug applications to the FDA containing at least some data from foreign clinical trials tripled from 1995 to 2000, increasing from about nine percent to about twenty-seven percent.[35]

As manufacturers in the major drug-producing economies outsource clinical trials to foreign countries, they also export financial COIs and the risks those COIs pose to human subject safety. While COIs associated with equity ownership in drug companies and faculty start-ups are unlikely to exist in countries experiencing the largest growth in clinical trials, other kinds of COIs do exist. Many physicians in these countries are eager to receive drug company research grants and human subject recruitment fees, which, in comparison to foreign physicians' often meager salaries, are so substantial that they can double and triple physicians' incomes.[36] Likewise, health care systems in some of these foreign countries are so under-funded that their governments actively pursue privately funded clinical trials as a way of financing health care delivery.[37] All of this creates incentives for those who oversee the clinical trials in foreign countries to serve the interests of visiting drug companies over the interests of science or human subject safety. Consequently, there is evidence that human subjects have been exposed to unnecessary risks.[38] For example, an investigative report published by the *Washington Post* in 2000 reported cases of foreign researchers who were being paid to conduct clinical trials for U.S. drug companies and who deviated from research protocols, failed to report negative findings, failed to inform potential human subjects of the risks of the research or the alternatives, and failed to switch subjects from experimental to standard treatments when their conditions deteriorated in the course of clinical trials.[39]

In the end, policies designed to speed the development of new medicines by encouraging private investment in drug research have created unprecedented financial COIs in clinical trials that threaten the safety of human subjects. Moreover, these COIs and their associated risks exist in relatively poor countries to which drug manufacturers have increasingly turned for fast and cheap clinical trials. The resulting ethical and regulatory challenge is to balance the need for efficient drug development with the need to protect human subjects from unnecessary research risks that result from financial COIs, and to do so both domestically and internationally. In the following two sections, this chapter examines U.S. and international efforts to regulate financial COIs.

The questionable wisdom of institutional self-regulation in the United States

U.S. law relies on research institutions conducting clinical trials to police COIs among investigators, IRB members, and the institutions themselves. Regulations of the U.S. Department of Health and Human Services (HHS) require that investigators with "significant financial interest" in publicly funded research they propose to conduct disclose their interests to the institutions through which the research will be conducted.[40] These regulations also require institutions housing such research to review COI disclosures and "manage, reduce or eliminate" any COIs discovered among their researchers.[41] A "significant financial interest" is defined to encompass some, but not all, of the COIs described above. For example, it does *not* include equity or royalty interests valued under $10,000, payments made by the research institution to its researchers (which would include salary payments underwritten by drug company grants), and payments for service on private advisory panels or for lecturing to private entities.[42] Additionally, FDA regulations require that drug companies seeking approval of a new drug for market disclose to the FDA financial interests and arrangements of investigators who conducted clinical trials from which data were gathered that supports the marketability of the new drug.[43] Those financial interests and arrangements are defined to include equity interests in a trial's sponsor or in any publicly traded company valued at $50,000 or more, ownership interests in the tested material, and payments made by the sponsor to the investigator or research institution in excess of $25,000, but excluding grants designed to cover the cost of conducting the trial.[44] The FDA relies on these disclosures to assess the reliability of the data supporting the drug company's new drug application.[45]

Recently, U.S. regulators reaffirmed their commitment to institutional oversight of financial COIs in human subjects research when the HHS issued a "guidance" in May 2004.[46] The guidance identifies issues that the HHS recommends institutions consider as they track and manage COIs. Most notably, the guidance suggests that institutions more clearly articulate the various steps they will take to manage different kinds of financial COIs, including identifying the kinds of COIs that are prohibited. Additionally, it recommends that each institution monitor and manage financial COIs among their IRB members and COIs of the institutions themselves

While the HHS guidance does not create new regulatory obligations on its face, it is an authoritative interpretation of existing regulations that research institutions cannot afford to ignore. Thus, the guidance will likely cause research institutions to strengthen their internal COI standards. Indeed, this is also the recommendation from the Association of American Medical Colleges (AAMC), a leading professional organization of institutions that conduct clinical trials.

Recent AAMC guidelines, like the HHS guidance, recommend that research institutions continue to regulate their own COIs and those of their researchers. They recommend that institutions prohibit investigators with significant financial interests in particular areas of clinical research from conducting such research unless compelling circumstances justify otherwise.[47] Likewise, they instruct institutions not to house clinical research in which the institution has a significant financial interest absent compelling circumstances.[48] Additionally, the guidelines require disclosure to prospective human subjects of all financial COIs that have not been eliminated.[49]

Thus, the great question is whether institutions can be trusted to adequately police their own financial interests in human subjects research they host and those of their researchers. Certainly, institutions are primarily responsible for overseeing the integrity of clinical trials, and this sets a precedent for deputizing institutions to protect human subjects from the risks associated with financial COIs. Yet, relying on institutions to regulate their own COIs and those of their researchers is like leaving the fox to guard the henhouse.[50] As described above, research institutions have an interest in attracting clinical research grants from drug companies. They also have a stake in the success of their researchers. Additionally, institutions often own an interest in the material being tested and may also have an equity position in the sponsor of a clinical trial. All of this creates a bias among institutions to permit clinical trials despite potential COIs, and institutions bring this bias to the job of protecting human subjects from the risks of those very same COIs.

Of course, there are forces that offset the incentive COIs create for research institutions to regulate COIs in a less than rigorous manner. First, research institutions that want to attract future research grants from drug companies have an incentive to serve the interests of drug company sponsors to gather data that the FDA will consider reliable. If FDA officials reviewing data from a clinical investigation in support of a new drug application believe that the institution conducting the clinical investigation failed to adequately manage financial COIs, then the FDA may ignore those data,[51] which could result in the delay or rejection of the new drug application. Thus, institutions dependent upon private research grants have an incentive to oversee COIs with sufficient diligence to at least assure that data resulting from sponsored clinical trials are reliable in the eyes of the FDA. Second, the risk of tort liability also encourages a minimal degree of rigor from institutions as they police internal COIs. If a COI caused a researcher, IRB member, or other institutional affiliate to act negligently with respect to a clinical trial and injury resulted, then the institution could be held liable for that injury.[52] Accordingly, institutions have an interest to assure that financial incentives associated with a COI are not so strong as to encourage potentially negligent behavior.

As long as COIs associated with a clinical trial are not so egregious, however, as to undermine the reliability of data resulting from the trial or to encourage negligent behavior, research institutions have little incentive to guard against the remaining risks such COIs pose to human subjects; and many such risks could remain. Consider that investigators and institutions make many difficult judgments in the course of conducting a clinical trial, each of which affects the safety of human subjects. They determine how broadly to set the clinical criteria for human subject participation. They identify the risks that need not be disclosed to potential subjects and the wording to be used to inform potential subjects about risks that must be disclosed. Investigators also assess whether and when a subject's condition has become sufficiently poor as to require termination of the subject's participation in a trial and whether the subject's condition must be reported to the institution. For adverse reactions that are reported to an institution, the IRB determines how best to respond, including whether it is necessary to suspend a clinical trial. For each such decision, there is a range of judgments that are "non-negligent." Under current policy, research institutions have little incentive to assure that COIs are not so strong as to become the primary basis for choices made among all non-negligent options. Consequently, it is possible, if not probable, that such judgments are made based on the financial interests of the investigator and institution rather than on the goal of minimizing risks to human subjects.

Thus, there is a need to increase the accountability of research institutions for their management of financial COIs associated with clinical trials they house. One option is for regulators to take greater control by identifying COIs that are absolutely prohibited, those that are permissible but must be monitored closely, and those that are acceptable without further monitoring. Ratcheting up governmental control could backfire, however, if research institutions and researchers feel free under such a regulatory regime to respect only the letter of the law and to exploit all available loopholes.[53] In other words, achieving greater legal accountability through command-and-control regulation could further erode any professional norm among researchers and institutions to preserve the integrity of their research, which, in turn, could undermine public confidence in medical research. While this does not rule out the use of such a regulatory strategy, it means that such a strategy should not be our first choice.

Thus, the challenge is to identify policies that will promote greater accountability among research institutions for their oversight of COIs without undermining existing research norms that promote integrity in science despite commercialism.[54] For example, federal law could require that the details of all clinical trials be registered in a publicly accessible database, including information about financial interests of those involved in each trial.[55] Additionally, regulators could insist that institutional committees overseeing clinical trials or COIs have substantially more members who are unaffiliated with the institution than the one member that is required under current regulations,[56] and they could require that a majority of the unaffiliated members of those committees approve any matters related to a clinical trial in which the institution has a financial interest.[57] Moreover, current tort law could recognize fiduciary causes of action that enable human subjects allegedly injured as a result of a COI to pursue compensation even in the absence of negligence.[58] Each of these proposals, whether taken separately or in combination, promote greater accountability directly to the public and to human research subjects rather than to government regulators.

The mechanism employed by France to approve clinical trials conducted in that country also offers a hybrid approach between self-regulation and government regulation. French law requires that clinical trials receive local ethics committee approval, but the French committees are independent of the research sponsor and institution.[59] They are public institutions created under the French Ministry of Health with specific jurisdictions, and the Ministry also appoints the members of each committee from the research community. Additionally, unlike U.S. rules for the recusal of IRB members, French law establishes that committee members are recused from voting on any project that will be conducted in an institution with which the member is associated.[60] Thus, French committees promote self-regulation by members of the research community by relying only on those members who are unaffiliated with the institution that will house the proposed research. Accordingly, the risk of institutional bias on such committees is minimized.

The need for international cooperation in addressing COIs in foreign clinical trials

While the key domestic issue concerning COIs in clinical trials is whether *self*-regulation will work to address COIs in human subjects research, the key international issue is filling the need for *any* regulation addressing such COIs. As described above, regulators in each of the three major drug-consuming markets – the United States, the European Union, and Japan – permit drug companies to base their applications to market new drugs on data derived from foreign clinical trials. Consequently, drug manufacturers have dramatically increased the number of trials they sponsor in relatively poor countries, attracted by lower costs and the availability of large numbers of individuals with untreated disease who are eager to participate in medical research as a means of securing treatment. Additionally, drug companies benefit from the relative absence of regulation concerning human subjects research and COIs. Yet, anecdotal evidence suggests that COIs are as prevalent in foreign clinical trials as they are domestically, usually taking the form of research grants and human subject recruitment fees.

In the absence of regulation by countries hosting clinical trials, a drug company seeking to use data from foreign clinical trials to support a new drug application in another country need only be concerned with the conditions on the use of foreign data set by the country in which the company hopes to market its new drug. The United States, E.U. countries, and Japan have all established conditions on the use of data from foreign clinical trials, including conditions designed to protect the safety of human subjects.[61] For example, each of these countries permits the use of such data only if they are derived from clinical trials that have been approved by an independent review committee and that have based human subject participation on written informed consent. These conditions are derived from "Good Clinical Practice Guidelines" crafted by the International Conference on Harmonisation of Technical Requirements for Registration of Pharmaceuticals for Human Use, more commonly referred to as the ICH.[62] The ICH is a cooperative initiative among representatives of the pharmaceutical industry and the regulatory authorities of the United States, the European Union, and Japan, with additional participation by Canadian officials and the World Health Organization, among others.[63] Its purpose is to generate uniform standards and procedures for obtaining regulatory authority to market new medicines in the countries that comprise the major drug-consuming markets of the world.

Prior to the ICH guidelines, the leading source for international standards on human subjects research was the Helsinki Declaration, which articulates general principles for conducting clinical trials. The ICH guidelines generally improved upon the Helsinki Declaration by articulating a more detailed set of rules that are consistent with the principles of the Helsinki Declaration, but that are also less susceptible to a wide range of interpretation.[64] Unfortunately, however, the ICH guidelines do not establish standards for managing financial COIs associated with foreign clinical trials.[65] They come no closer than requiring that clinical research be approved by a review committee whose members are independent of the investigator and sponsor of any research protocol under consideration.[66] This requirement, however, does not account for the bias introduced by a committee member's affiliation with the research institution that will house the clinical trial, which institution might have significant financial interests in the outcome of such trials. In fact, the ICH guidelines define the required review committee so broadly as to encompass a U.S.-styled IRB, the membership of which is comprised almost completely of institutional affiliates.[67]

Thus, despite the success of the ICH process in establishing uniform safeguards for data from foreign clinical trials, it has not addressed the need for safeguarding human subjects from the risks of financial COIs associated with foreign clinical trials. The result is an international regulatory regime that mimics U.S. regulation of human subjects research before the HHS and FDA adopted any regulations concerning COIs. Consequently, drug companies intent on both selling a new drug in the major drug-consuming markets and using financial incentives to speed the clinical trials process have an additional reason to conduct their trials in poorer foreign countries. Not only do those countries offer lower costs and a large population of volunteers, but they also permit the use of financial incentives that might not be permitted elsewhere. Moreover, companies do not sacrifice the opportunity to use the data generated from foreign clinical trials involving significant financial COIs to support a new drug application in a major drug-consuming market because the prevailing ICH standards do not address COIs.

Consider U.S. law as an example. Clinical trials conducted in the United States or under the authority of the FDA are subject to the full panoply of federal regulations, including regulations related to COIs as interpreted by the HHS's recent guidance.[68] Data submitted to the FDA from a foreign clinical trial, however, is identified for separate regulation.[69] Although there is substantial overlap among these two sets of regulations, those governing data from foreign clinical trials, having been based on international standards, are silent on the management of COIs.

It is possible to interpret COI regulations that apply to clinical trials conducted in the United States as applicable to any clinical trial generating data used to support a new drug application to the FDA,[70] but it is unlikely. Such an interpretation fails to account for the irreconcilability of current standards applied to U.S.-based clinical trials and foreign clinical trials. For example, current regulations – which are based on the Declaration of Helsinki and refer to ICH guidelines as only a source for additional guidance – permit the FDA to accept data from foreign clinical trials that have not been subject to review by an independent review committee, and acceptance of such data is not conditioned on researchers' obtaining *written* consent of human subjects.[71] Meanwhile, FDA regulations applicable to domestic clinical trials mandate IRB review and written consent by human subjects.[72] Additionally, the FDA has interpreted its rules for data submitted from domestic clinical trials as separate from its rules for data submitted from foreign clinical trials. For example, one rationale the FDA offers for a recent proposal to replace the Declaration of Helsinki with the ICH guidelines is that the ICH guidelines address issues on which the Declaration of Helsinki is silent, such as research monitoring and reporting adverse events.[73] If the FDA believed that monitoring and reporting standards for domestic clinical trials applied to foreign trials as well, then it would not bother with efforts to replace the more vague standards of the Declaration of Helsinki with the more detailed ICH guidelines. Furthermore, the FDA proposal to adopt the ICH guidelines states that data from foreign clinical data are acceptable "if two conditions are met," which it identifies as compliance with ICH guidelines and permitting the FDA to inspect a foreign clinical site.[74] If the FDA also intends for foreign clinical trials to comply with other FDA regulations, including COI regulations, then presumably it would have said so in its list of conditions.

Consequently, there is a gap in the protection of human subjects from the risks associated with clinical trials in which financial COIs are at work, and this gap encourages drug companies to further expand their reliance on foreign clinical trials so as to avoid the need for COI oversight. The FDA must take the lead to close this gap both domestically and internationally. As the agency overseeing new drug development in the United States, the FDA is in the best position to identify and fill the gap in United States regulations concerning COIs in foreign clinical trials. Additionally, as the government agency most experienced in the world with implementing domestic COI rules, the FDA is in the best position to lead an international initiative to develop COI rules that would be adopted in countries that comprise the major drug-consuming markets. Moreover, the FDA is a voting member of the ICH, and thus it has access to a successful mechanism of international standard-setting in drug development. While other avenues exist for international regulation of COIs in human subjects research, the FDA must take advantage of its position in the ICH to improve international human subject safety.

Conclusion

As governments have succeeded in harnessing the profit incentive to improve the efficiency of drug development, they also have increased the risks associated with human subjects research. Scientists and research institutions conducting clinical trials of new drugs on humans have unprecedented financial interests in the outcome of their work. This undermines the objectivity with which those scientists and institutions make professional judgments that affect the safety of human subjects participating in clinical trials. Moreover, as drug companies increasingly conduct trials in foreign countries, COIs in human subjects research are proliferating around the world.

The U.S. law attempts to regulate COIs in clinical trials by mandating that research institutions manage their own COIs and those of their researchers, gambling that institutional self-regulation of COIs will be sufficiently rigorous to protect human subjects. Meanwhile, the leading source for international standards related to clinical trials has yet to address COIs in human subjects research. Consequently, securing adequate protection for human subjects against the risks posed by COIs in clinical trials must be treated as a high priority in law and ethics.

Notes

1 Much of what this chapter presents concerning U.S. drug development policy, conflicts of interest in human subjects research conducted in the United States, and U.S. regulation in the area is derived from an earlier article by the author. *See* Robert Gatter, *Walking the Talk of Trust in Human Subjects Research: The Challenge of Regulating Financial Conflicts of Interest*, 52 Emory L.J. 327 (2003).

2 *See* PhRMA, *Pharmaceutical Companies Receive FDA Approval for 35 New Medicines in 2003; Invest an Estimated $33.2 Billion in R&D*, (Jan. 22, 2004) (press release), http://www.phrma.org/mediaroom/press/releases/22.01.2004.894.cfm (accessed Oct. 15, 2004).

3 *See* IMS, *U.S. Purchase Activity by Channel* (2003), http://www.imshealth.com/ims/portal/front/articleC/0,2777,6599_42720942_44800060,00.html (accessed Oct. 15, 2004).

4 *See* PhRMA, *supra* n. 2.

5 *See* PhRMA, *PhRMA Industry Profile 2003* 63, Fig. 5.5 (2003), http://www.phrma.org/publications/publications/profile02/2003%20CHAPTER%205.pdf (accessed Oct. 15, 2004).

6 *See* Gatter, *supra* n. 1, at 334–40.

7 *See* Bayh-Dole Act, codified at 35 U.S.C.A. §§ 200–12; Stevenson Technology Innovation Act of 1980, codified at 15 U.S.C.A. §§ 3701–14.

8 *See* Gatter, *supra* n. 1, at 335.

9 21 U.S.C.A. § 355(a) (establishing the need for approval by the Food and Drug Administration before a new drug can be marketed in the U.S.); Monica Löfgren & Mia Dreessen, New Drug Approval in the European Union (from Parexel's Worldwide Pharmaceutical Regulation Series) 1–54 (Parexel 2002) (summarizing E.U. drug approval law); Keith B. Russell & W. Michael Bremer, New Drug Approval in Japan (from Parexel's Worldwide Pharmaceutical Regulation Series) 1–15 (Parexel 2002) (summarizing Japanese drug approval law).

10 *See* 21 USCA § 355(d) (U.S. law); Löfgren & Dreessen, *supra* n. 9, at 22 (E.U. law); Russell & Bremer, *supra* n. 9, at 12–13 (Japanese law).

11 *See* AAMC, AAMC Data Book: Statistical Information Related to Medical Schools and Teaching Hospitals 40–41 (The Association 2001), http://www.aamc.org/data/databook/start.htm (accessed Aug. 22, 2005) (In FY 1993–94 academic medical centers received almost $1 billion in operating revenue from private research grants, which represented 22 percent of all research grants and 3.5 percent of total revenue; in FY 1998–99, research grants from sources other than the federal government accounted for 11.3 percent of total revenue). *See also* CenterWatch, *Grant Market to Exceed $4 Billion in 2000*, 7 Centerwatch 1, 6–8 (Nov. 2000) (As many as 50,000 clinical investigators received grant funding for at least one research project involving human subjects in 2000, 76 percent of which came from private firms).

12 *See* Thomas Bodenheimer, *Uneasy Alliance – Clinical Investigators and the Pharmaceutical Industry*, 342 New Eng. J. Med. 1539, 1540 (2000) (Attracted by the faster pace at which CROs could complete clinical trials, drug manufacturers

during the 1990s were just as likely to choose CROs to conduct their clinical trials as they were to choose academic medical centers).

13 *See e.g.* Mark Friedberg, Bernard Saffran, Tammy J. Stinson, Wendy Nelson & Charles L. Bennett, *Evaluation of Conflict of Interest in Economic Analyses of New Drugs Used in Oncology*, 282(15) JAMA 1453, 1453 (1999) (Cancer drug studies sponsored by drug manufacturers arrived at unfavorable conclusions only 5 percent of the time as compared to 38 percent of the time among similar studies that were not funded by drug manufacturers).

14 *See* AUTM, AUTM Licensing Survey: FY 2002: Survey Summary 11–12 (Ashley J. Stevens, ed., AUTM 2003), http://www.autm.net/events/File/Surveys/02_Abridged_Survey.pdf (accessed Aug. 22, 2005) (Over a three-year period from 2000–2002, academic researchers created almost 1,400 faculty start-ups and shared ownership of more than 900, or about 64 percent of those start-ups, with their academic institutions. In fiscal year 2002, AUTM members entered into 4,673 new license agreements and introduced 569 new products. For further reading about faculty start-ups, *see* Peter J. Harrington, *Faculty Conflicts of Interest in an Age of Academic Entrepreneurialism: An Analysis of the Problem, the Law and Selected University Policies*, 27 J.C. & U.L. 775, 780–81 (2001).

15 *See* Elizabeth A. Boyd & Lisa A. Bero, *Assessing Faculty Financial Relationships with Industry: A Case Study*, 284 JAMA 2209 (2000) (reporting the results of a case study monitoring financial conflicts of interest at one research university over a nineteen-year period, which indicate that approximately one percent of all investigators receiving external research funding at the university owned stock or stock options that posed a potential conflict of interest); David Blumenthal, M. Gluck, K.S. Louis, M.A. Stoto & D. Wise, *University–Industry Research Relationships in Biotechnology: Implications for the University*, 232 Sci. 1361, 1364 (1986) (0.5 percent of university researchers surveyed admitted to owning equity in companies while those companies were funding the researchers' work).

16 *See e.g.* Boyd & Bero, *supra* n. 15, at 2211–12 (About 2.5 percent of all investigators receiving extramural research funding in 1999 were paid consulting fees ranging from $1,000 to $120,000 annually with 61 percent reported at $10,000 or less).

17 *See* Henry Thomas Stelfox, Grace Chua, Keith O'Rourke & Allan S. Detsky, *Conflict of Interest in the Debate Over Calcium-Channel Antagonists*, 338(2) New Eng. J. Med. 101, 103–4 (1998) (Among scientists supporting the use of a particular drug, 96 percent had a financial tie to the drug's manufacturer (as compared to 36 percent who opposed the drug), including 21 percent who were either paid consultants or employees).

18 *See* David S. Shimm & Roy G. Spece, *Conflict of Interest and Informed Consent in Industry-Sponsored Clinical Trials*, 12 J. Legal Med. 477, 482 n. 13 (1991) (noting a survey the authors conducted of human research at the University of Arizona College of Medicine and suggesting that every industry-sponsored research project listed at the College involved some version of a human subjects recruitment fee).

19 *See* Sheila Kaplan & Shannon Brownlee, *Dying for a Cure: Why Cancer Patients Often Turn to Risky, Experimental Treatments – And Wind up Paying with Their Lives*, U.S. News & World Rep. 34, 36 (Oct. 11, 1999) (stating that drug companies pay doctors up to $6,000 per subject); David S. Shimm, Roy G. Spece, Jr. & Michelle B. DiGregorio, *Conflicts of Interests in Relationships Between Physicians and the Pharmaceutical Industry*, in Conflicts of Interest in Clinical Practice and Research 321, 323 (Roy G. Spece, Jr. *et al.* eds, Oxford 1996) (asserting that "[t]o obtain a sufficient number of patient-subjects in an acceptable period of time, manufacturers offer clinician-investigators financial inducements to enter patients into studies, typically $2000 to $5000 per patient").

20 *See* 45 C.F.R. part 46 (2001) (Health and Human Services regulations). For an overview of law and policy related to IRBs and the protection of human subjects, *see generally* Leslie Francis, *IRBs and Conflicts of Interest*, in Conflicts of Interest in Clinical Practice and Research 418, 418–22 (Roy G. Spece, Jr. *et al.* eds, Oxford 1996); John A. Robertson, *The Law of Institutional Review Boards*, 26 U.C.L.A. L. Rev. 484 (1979); Office of Human Research Protections, Institutional Review Board (IRB) Guidebook, chs I, II (1993), http://www.hhs.gov/ohrp/irb/irb_guidebook.htm (accessed Nov. 4, 2004).

21 An IRB must have at least five members, only one of whom must be unaffiliated with the institution. 45 C.F.R § 46.107.

22 *See id.* at §§ 46.108(b) and 46.109(a).

23 *See id.* at § 46.111(a).

24 *See id.*

25 *See id.* at § 46.113.

26 The study tested a new genetic mechanism for treating a liver disorder. Mr. Gelsinger, who was eighteen years old at the time of the study, suffered from the disorder. Although the study was highly unlikely to provide any therapeutic benefit to Mr. Gelsinger, he volunteered as a subject to help in the development of a new treatment. He died four days after receiving a high dose of a vector-virus, which caused acute respiratory distress and multiple-organ failure. *See* Sheryl Gay Stolberg, *The Biotech Death of Jesse Gelsinger*, N.Y. Times (Magazine) 137, § 6 (Nov. 18, 1999). For additional accounts of Mr. Gelsinger's death, *see* Nicholas Wade, *Patient Dies While Undergoing Gene Therapy*, N.Y. Times A24 (Sept. 29, 1999); Mary R. Anderlik & Nanette Elster, *Currents in Contemporary Ethics*, 29 J. L. Med. & Ethics 220, 220–21 (2001); *Dateline NBC, "A Family's Quest for Answers"* (NBC Sept. 20, 2002) (TV broadcast). For another example, *See* Duff Wilson & David Heath, *Uninformed Consent*, Seattle Times A1 (Mar. 11, 2001) (describing the deaths of human subjects in the clinical trial of a drug designed to prevent graft-versus-host disease among cancer patients receiving bone marrow transplants and suggesting that those deaths are related to the financial interests of the investigators and the researchers in the commercial success of the test drug).

27 *See* Patricia K. Kuszler, *Curing Conflicts of Interest in Clinical Research: Impossible Dreams and Harsh Realities*, 8 Widener L. Symp. J. 115, 132 (2001); *Gene Therapy Doctors Settle Suit in Death of Teen*, Sunday Patriot-news (Harrisburg) A9 (Nov. 5, 2000); Stolberg, *supra* n. 26.

28 *See* Jesse A. Goldner, *Dealing with Conflicts of Interest in Biomedical Research: IRB Oversight as the Next Best Solution to the Abolitionist Approach*, 28 J.L. Med. & Ethics 379, 379 (2000).

29 *See* Complaint – Civil Action, *Gelsinger v. Trustees of the University of Pennsylvania* (Phila. Cnty. Ct. of C.P. 2000), http://www.sskrplaw.com/links/healthcare2.html (accessed Oct. 15, 2004). The Gelsinger family also claims that the COIs resulted in the inclusion of Mr. Gelsinger as a research subject despite his failing to meet all of the clinical criteria for participation, and that it caused Dr. Wilson's failure to disclose adverse reactions of other subjects in similar studies. *See id. See also* Rick Weiss, *FDA Seeks to Penalize Gene Scientist*, Wash. Post A14 (Dec. 12, 2000) (reporting FDA findings of regulatory violations associated with Mr. Gelsinger's death).

30 *See* Robert Kneller, *University–Industry Cooperation and Technology Transfer in Japan Compared with the United States: Another Reason for Japan's Economic Malaise?*, 24 U. PA. J. Int'l Econ. L. 329, 423–25 (2003).

31 *See* Joanna Slater, *India Emerges as New Drug Proving Ground*, Wall St. J. B1 (Feb. 19, 2004); Janet Rehnquist, Office of the Inspector General (OIG), U.S. Department of Health and Human Services, *The Globalization of Clinical Trials:*

A Growing Challenge in Protecting Human Subjects (OEI-01-00-00190) 6–11 (Sept. 2001), http://oig.hhs.gov/oei/reports/oei-01-00-00190.pdf (accessed Aug. 22, 2005). *See also*, *The Body Hunters* (a six-part series), Wash. Post (Dec. 17–22, 2000).

32 *See id.*

33 *See* 21 C.F.R. part 312 (U.S. FDA Regulations); Russell & Bremer, *supra* n. 9, at 55–56.

34 *See* OIG, *supra* n. 31, at 10.

35 *See* Mary Pat Flaherty, Deborah Nelson & Joe Stephens, *The Body Hunters: Overwhelming the Watchdogs* (second in a six-part series), Wash. Post A1 (Dec. 18, 2000).

36 *See* Flaherty, *supra* n. 35 (citing examples of a Budapest psychiatrist's supplementing his monthly salary of $178 with fees of $1,000 to $2,000 per recruited subject, and a Hungarian cancer specialist who, by signing on for foreign drug company research, "far outpaces his $5000 annual salary"). *See also* Joe Stephens, *The Body Hunters: Exporting Human Experiments* (first in a six-part series), Wash. Post A1 (Dec. 17, 2000) (reporting that one U.S. drug company paid a Nigerian lab technician participating in a clinical trial so well as to "double her pay").

37 *See id.*

38 *See* OIG, *supra* n. 31, at 12–13, 15 (finding that foreign clinical trial investigators often fail to attest in writing that they will uphold international standards for the protection of human research subjects, and citing anecdotal evidence that foreign IRBs are too inadequately organized to protect the interests of human subjects).

39 *See* Flaherty, *supra* n. 35; Stephens, *supra* n. 36.

40 *See* 42 C.F.R. § 50.604.

41 *See* 42 C.F.R. § 50.605.

42 *See* 42 C.F.R. § 50.603.

43 *See* 21 C.F.R. § 54.4.

44 *See* 21 C.F.R. § 54.2.

45 *See* 21 C.F.R. § 54.5.

46 *See* HHS, *Financial Relationships and Interests in Research Involving Human Subjects: Guidance for Human Subjects Protection*, 69 Fed. Reg. 26393-02 (May 12, 2004).

47 *See* AAMC Task Force on Financial Interests in Human Subjects Research, *Protecting Subjects, Preserving Trust, Promoting Progress – Policy and Guidelines for the Oversight of Individual Conflicts of Interest in Human Subjects Research* 7–8 (Biomedical and Health Sciences Research 2001).

48 *See* AAMC Task Force on Financial Interests in Human Subjects Research, *Protecting Subjects, Preserving Trust, Promoting Progress II: Principles and Recommendations for Oversight of an Institution's Financial Interests in Human Subjects Research* 10–11 (Biomedical and Health Sciences Research 2002). The guidelines also recommend that institutions segregate clinical research administration from technology transfer operations. *See id.*

49 *See* AAMC, *Individual COIs*, *supra* n. 47 at 18; AAMC, *Institutional COIs*, *supra* n. 48 at 11.

50 Hamilton Moses, III *et al.*, *Collaborating with Industry – Choices for the Academic Medical Center,* 347 N. Engl. J. Med. 1368, 1371 (2002) (when research institutions are asked to regulate conflicts of interest, the implicit question is "Can the fox guard the chickens?").

51 *See* 21 C.F.R. § 54.5(c)(4).

52 *See* Gatter, *supra* n. 1, at 372–79.

53 *See* Gatter, *supra* n. 1, at 383–99.

54 For those skeptical that *any* professional norm exists among researchers or institutions to preserve the integrity of research, *see* Arti Kaur Rai, *Regulating*

Scientific Research: Intellectual Property Rights and the Norms of Science, 94 NW. U. L. Rev. 77 (1999) (analyzing how some traditional research norms survive policies promoting commercialization).

55 *See* Robert Steinbrook, *Public Registration of Clinical Trials*, 351 N. Engl. J. Med. 315 (2004).

56 *See* 21 C.F.R. § 56.107.

57 *See* Gatter, *supra* n. 1, at 371.

58 *See* Gatter, *supra* n. 1, at 379–83.

59 *See* Ivan Berlin & David A. Gorelick, *The French Law on "Protection of Persons Undergoing Biomedical Research": Implications for the U.S.*, 31 J. L. Med & Eth. 434 (2003).

60 *See id.*

61 The FDA adopted these conditions as an industry guidance in 1997 (*see* 62 Fed. Reg. 25692 (May 9, 1997)) and has recently proposed making them mandatory standards (*see* 69 Fed. Reg. 32467 (June 10, 2004)).

62 *See* ICH, *Guidelines for Good Clinical Practice* (May 1, 1996), http://www.bcgasiapacific.com/docs/ich/ICHE6.pdf (accessed Oct. 15, 2004).

63 *See* ICH, *The Common Technical Document: Putting It All Together – A Decade of Harmonization*, Fifth International Conference on Harmonisation of Technical Requirements for Registration of Pharmaceuticals for Human Use, San Diego, CA (Nov. 2000) (a background paper), http://www.ich.org (accessed Oct. 15, 2004).

64 This is one of the rationales offered by FDA for replacing the Helsinki Declaration with the ICH guidelines as the source for standards applied to data from foreign clinical trials. *See* 69 Fed. Reg. 32467, 32468 (June 10, 2004).

65 Ironically, the Helsinki Declaration has recently been updated to address COIs in human subjects research at the same time that it is being replaced by the ICH guidelines as the leading international source for standards related to clinical trials.

66 *See* ICH, *supra* n. 62, at § 3.2.1.

67 *See* ICH, *supra* n. 62, at §§ 1.27, 1.31, and 3.2.1.

68 *See supra* nn 41 through 47 and the accompanying text.

69 *See* 21 C.F.R. § 312.120.

70 FDA regulations relating to COIs are described as applying to "clinical investigations that support applications for … marketing permits for products regulated by the Food and Drug Administration, including … drugs for human use." 21 C.F.R. § 50.1.

71 *See* 21 C.F.R. § 312.120.

72 *See* 21 C.F.R. §§ 56.103 (requiring IRB approval) and 50.27 (requiring written consent).

73 *See* 69 Fed. Reg. 32467, 32468 (June 10, 2004).

74 *See* 69 Fed. Reg. 32467, 32469 (June 10, 2004).

4 The role and legal status of health care ethics committees in the United States

Diane E. Hoffmann, Anita J. Tarzian

Introduction

Over a quarter of a century has passed since health care ethics committees (HCECs) in the United States received legal recognition as alternatives to the courts in resolving conflicts related to patient end-of-life care. By the mid to late 1980s HCECs had been established in over half of U.S. hospitals and had received a certain legitimacy in the health care system. Given their age and growth one could characterize them developmentally as emerging from adolescence and establishing themselves in young adulthood. As a result, we might expect that they would have resolved the identity crisis characterizing the adolescent years. Yet, HCECs in the United States remain somewhat amorphous. In part, this may be due to their relative lack of legal status. In most U.S. jurisdictions HCECs remain unregulated and lack homogeneity in structure and operation. To the extent that they share common characteristics, these committees are multidisciplinary in membership and exist to address ethical dilemmas that occur within health care institutions. Early on in the evolution of HCECs, judges, in several judicial opinions, encouraged the development of these committees, and two states adopted statutes or regulations that provided them with legal status. Until recently, however, HCECs in most states have been able to develop in a variety of ways and perform a range of functions with limited legal authority or oversight. In the last few years, a handful of states have passed laws giving HCECs legal authority to make certain kinds of decisions. While these states remain in the minority, HCECs in most states serve a role as a mechanism for "alternative" dispute resolution, particularly in cases involving end-of-life care. This chapter reviews both the history of HCECs in the United States and their legal evolution.

History of health care ethics committees in the United States

HCECs in the United States emerged in response to advances in life-sustaining medical technology and landmark legal cases concerning allocation and use of that technology. A forerunner to HECs (hospital ethics committees) was the lay committee established in 1962 at Seattle's Swedish Hospital to decide how to allocate the use of the first community kidney dialysis units. At the time, they were the only dialysis machines available for outpatient treatment in the world. Other life-sustaining technology gaining widespread use in the 1960s and 1970s included cardiopulmonary resuscitation (CPR), long-term mechanical ventilation, and artificial nutrition and hydration ("tube feeding"). Many of the legal cases concerning life and death medical decision making in the 1970s and 1980s involved discontinuing mechanical ventilation or artificial feeding. These cases influenced the formation of HCECs as alternatives to courts in making such decisions. The opinion of the New Jersey Supreme Court in the case of Karen Ann Quinlan was the first to mention the use of ethics committees. In *Quinlan*, Karen Ann's father asked to be given authority to terminate her ventilatory support as she had been in a permanent coma for several years. The Court recommended that each hospital in the state establish an ethics committee composed of physicians, social workers, attorneys, and theologians which would serve to "review the individual circumstances of ethical dilemma[s] and which [would provide] much in the way of assistance and safeguards for patients and their medical caretakers."[1]

Ethics committees were given further endorsement in 1983 when the President's Commission for the Study of Ethical Problems in Medicine wrote its seminal report on withholding and withdrawing life-sustaining treatment. In the report, the Commission encouraged hospitals to "explore and evaluate various administrative arrangements" such as ethics committees "for review and consultation" of cases involving termination of life support for patients who lack decision making capacity in order to protect their interests "and to ensure their well-being and self-determination."[2] In addition, the Baby Doe Regulations, promulgated under the 1985 Amendments to the Federal Child Abuse Prevention and Treatment Act,[3] recommended establishment of Infant Care Review Committees in hospitals caring for newborns and use of the committees when considering withholding or withdrawing life-sustaining treatment from a newborn.

Two states also required hospitals to establish HCECs. In 1987, the Maryland legislature enacted the Patient Care Advisory Committee Act requiring hospitals in the state to establish patient care advisory committees.[4] The law was subsequently amended in 1990 to require that all nursing homes in the state establish or have access to such committees. Also, after the *Quinlan* case, the New Jersey Department of Health mandated that hospitals in that state establish either an ethics committee or prognosis committee as a condition of licensure.[5]

Perhaps the greatest motivation for hospitals to establish ethics committees was the Joint Commission on the Accreditation of Health Care Organizations' requirement in 1992 that, as a condition of accreditation, hospitals have in place a mechanism to resolve ethical dilemmas in patient care.[6]

These recommendations and requirements significantly influenced U.S. hospitals to establish HCECs. The percentage of hospitals responding to surveys conducted by the American Hospital Association indicated an increase in the number of hospitals with ethics committees from twenty-six percent in 1983 to sixty percent in 1985.[7] By 1998, McGee and colleagues reported that over ninety percent of U.S. hospitals had ethics committees.[8]

Membership of HCECs in U.S. hospitals

Hospital ethics committees vary in size and membership. Studies indicate a range of three to thirty members, with the "typical" size between twelve and sixteen.[9] Larger hospitals tend to have larger committees.[10] Virtually all HCECs include physicians, nurses, and social workers. Many include hospital administrators or their designees, hospital board members, and clergy.[11] There are no definitive data on how many include community representatives, bioethicists, or attorneys. In a study of HCECs in Maryland, Virginia, and the District of Columbia, approximately half of the committees included a community representative but less than half had a lawyer or bioethicist.[12]

The prerequisite of multidisciplinary membership and deliberation calls for HCECs to include a variety of health care professionals as well as lay persons from the community and individuals knowledgeable in bioethics. Opinions about the ideal composition of ethics committees are influenced by attitudes about their process of deliberation. Those who view ethics committees as impartial panels that come to consensus on an issue, much like a jury, place importance on diversity of representation, including community members. Dugan writes, "[b]ecause [HCECs'] core interest is to promote patient care that reflects an interest in ethical values of patients, organizations, and healthcare professions, their expertise is the sort that calls more for breadth than depth of specialized knowledge."[13] Those who view ethics committees as providing an expert ethical opinion on an issue may place more emphasis on having members with bioethics expertise. However, definitions of "bioethics expertise" vary.[14] Ethics committees have been criticized for having an over-representation of institutional health care providers and under-representation of community members and members with bioethics expertise. Some critics have argued that committees engage in institutional protectionism and are biased in their membership, which is heavily dominated by health care practitioners. In an article in *The Hastings Center Report*, Cohen argued that "[t]he structure of some committees has been designed to protect institutional interests: a few are chaired by legal counsel for the institution; others are composed almost entirely of members of the board who 'have an interest in ethics.'"[15] In addition, many members have no formal training in bioethics or law and simply sit on the committees out of an interest in the area.[16] Others have also observed how an ethics committee's composition influences its deliberations and how or whether it reaches consensus. In a review of the literature on clinical case consultation, Williams-Jones found that

> when the consultant or chair is a physician, the ethics discussion tends to focus on clinical issues, supporting physicians, and returning the treatment and team to "normal" functioning. By contrast, when the consultant is a non-physician ethicist, the consult is more open, interactive, and open to non-clinical issues; patients and family members are also more likely to be involved in the discussion.[17]

The role of attorneys on HCECs has been controversial, in particular, the appropriateness of the participation of hospital legal counsel. Some writers have argued that their participation may be clouded by conflicts of interest. Others fear that concerns about law will dominate any discussion and chill analysis of the ethical issues involved.[18] In part, the controversy about the role of lawyers on ethics committees may result from confusion about the role of legal standards in HCEC deliberations and whether HCECs should be providing legal advice. A study of hospital ethics committees in three jurisdictions found that health care providers view providing legal advice on issues related to patient care as a primary role of ethics committees, and a majority of respondents in two of the jurisdictions indicated that their committee was influenced a great deal by the legal consequences of its recommendations.[19]

Institutional setting in which HCECs operate

While the large majority of the literature on HCECs focuses on their role and operation in hospitals, HCECs have been adopted by other types of health care institutions including nursing homes, home health agencies, hospices, and managed care organizations (MCOs). A 1997 survey by the American Association of Homes and Services for the Aging (a membership organization of not-for-profit nursing homes) found that sixty-six percent of non-profit nursing homes had established an HCEC.[20] A more recent survey by the New York City Long-Term Care Ethics Network of one hundred and twenty-eight nursing homes indicated that the percentage of these facilities with an ethics committee increased from forty-one percent in 1994 to seventy-one percent in 1999.[21] National statistics on the percentage of hospices or home health agencies that have an ethics committee are not available. Christensen and Tucker, however, see these institutions as poised to confront ethical issues that have, until relatively recently, been the focus of hospital ethics committees. These authors describe several trends influencing the growth of non-hospital HCECs, including declining numbers of hospital inpatients due to technological breakthroughs, incentives to contain costs, and increased acuity in the outpatient setting. Given these trends, they point out the need to address ethical issues in non-hospital settings: "[e]specially as our entire population ages, more and more care is given in long-term care facilities and through [hospice and] home health agencies. The result is a growing need to find ethics structures that transcend organizational boundaries and provide better continuity of services."[22]

A number of MCOs have also established ethics committees. While some MCOs, such as Kaiser Permanente and Harvard Pilgrim Health Care, have active committees and ethics programs, others devote little or no resources to HCECs. For example, in one study, none of the MCOs employing nurses to perform utilization review had an ethics committee to help nurse reviewers in the complex decisions they made regarding medical care utilization.[23] Guzman observed in the late 1990s that the focus of bioethics in managed care had shifted from case consultation to policy development and education and that ethics committees were influencing policy in "a small but growing number of MCOs."[24]

Functions of HCECs

While HCECs vary in their mission and operation, most have three basic functions: education, policy development, and case consultation.[25] In their educational role, HCECs provide information and resources to hospital staff about issues in ethical decision making. Such education is typically accomplished through conferences, seminars, grand rounds, educational materials, resource centers, and so on. Ethics committee networks have been established in a number of states to provide educational resources and programs to assist ethics committees in their educational mission. HCECs may also engage in policy formulation on ethical issues affecting patient care. Examples of policies crafted or revised by HCECs include those addressing Do Not Resuscitate (DNR) Orders, artificial nutrition and hydration, informed consent, surrogate decision making, guardianship, determination of competency, medically ineffective treatment, and advance directives. Case consultation involves the actual discussion of a case by an ethics committee in response to a request from a staff person, patient or their agent, guardian, or surrogate. Case consultation can take two forms: (1) retrospective review, in which those involved in a consult seek feedback on a difficult decision that was already made, or (2) concurrent or prospective review, in which ethics committee members are actively involved in the case as a decision is being made.

A fourth function carried out by some committees is "organizational ethics." This involves looking at ethical issues that arise more broadly within the institution on a system-wide basis. In some institutions, separate committees advise the institution on clinical ethics and organizational ethics; in others, one committee performs both functions. Some argue the two (clinical and organizational ethics) have different, albeit overlapping, goals and functions and thus should be kept separate.[26] Others think that, because most ethical conflicts in a given health care institution have roots at the systems-level, a more efficient approach is to have one committee respond both to individual consult requests as well as to the organizational problems underlying them.[27] Trinity Health, a Catholic health care organization, has developed what it refers to as a "next generation model of clinical ethics." This model involves a shift from a primary focus on education, policy, and case consultation/review to "system change through quality management."[28]

Types of cases that come to HCECs

While there are no comprehensive empirical data on the types of cases or frequency with which cases come to ethics committees, accounts in the literature indicate various common characteristics of cases that are referred to HCECs. Most cases involve the termination or withholding of life-sustaining treatment. In one study of randomly selected internal medicine physicians in the United States, a little over half had requested an ethics consult – most commonly for ethical dilemmas related to end-of-life decision making, patient autonomy issues, and conflicts over patient care.[29] Often, the cases involved patients who lacked decision making capacity. In some of these cases, there was a question about whether the patient was capable of making an informed decision, and health care providers wanted to know if they could rely on the patient's consent or needed to consult a surrogate. This is common when a patient declines a life-saving treatment recommended by the medical staff. In addition, there may be a dispute or question about whether a patient is chronically ill, terminally ill, and/or "imminently dying." While most reports in the literature discuss cases involving elderly adults, cases involving young adults, children, or infants may also come to the committee. In cases involving end-of-life care, types of treatments that may be at issue include ventilatory support, artificial nutrition and hydration, antibiotic therapy, CPR, kidney dialysis, surgery, and chemotherapy. Cases coming to the committees, however, are not limited to termination of life-sustaining treatment. Other issues that may arise include appropriateness of treatment, confidentiality, surrogate decision making, resource allocation, cost containment, and issues related to managed care.[30]

While some cases coming to committees may simply require clarification of issues or facilitation of communication between parties, others involve disputes between patients, families, and providers. Such disputes may occur between an incapacitated patient's family members and the patient's treating physician, or between family members of such patients. Disputes may also arise between health care providers, for example, between physicians, or between nurses and physicians, but these cases seem to surface less frequently.

Common types of disputes

Difference in belief over what the patient wanted or meant by certain statements

Disputes over what an incompetent patient would have wanted may result from undocumented conversations, or different inferences drawn from the patient's statements or behavior. In the case of *Mack v. Mack*,[31] involving a dispute between the wife and father of a patient who had been in a persistent vegetative state for several years, the parties each related stories that they believed conveyed the patient's desires regarding life support in his current state. After visiting his elderly grandmother who was unable to feed herself and required assistance, the patient had stated that if he ever got to the point where he "could not do for himself" he did not want to live. His wife concluded from this statement and others that he would not want to be kept alive via feeding tubes.[32] However, when the patient was a boy his mother died of a stroke. At the time of the stroke, the patient's father was told that there was a small chance that his mother could be kept alive with surgery but that in all likelihood she would be an "80% vegetable." The boy's father chose to have the surgery but his wife died before anything could be done. A few years later the boy thanked his father for considering the surgery. The father believed that this demonstrated his son's desire to be kept alive even with minimal quality of life.[33]

Interpretation of terms

A patient's advance directive may include terms that are not well defined and may be interpreted differently. For example, a patient's living will may state that the patient does not want life-sustaining treatment if terminally ill with no hope of recovery.[34] What constitutes being "terminally ill" with "no hope of recovery" is open to interpretation. Physicians and family members may have differing opinions of a patient's medical prognosis and apply different definitions of "terminal illness." The law in most states does not clearly define terminal illness and leaves room for physician interpretation of the term. Some physicians may decide that someone is terminally ill if they have a life expectancy of six months or less; others may believe that someone is not terminally ill unless they can predict with a good deal of medical certainty that the patient will die within a few weeks. Physicians also have discretion in deciding what is meant by "no hope of recovery." Neither living will forms nor state statutes define the term.[35]

Differing perceptions of the benefits and burdens of a proposed treatment and quality of life

Physicians and patients or their family members may disagree over the benefits and burdens of continued life support and quality of life issues.

Physicians may focus more on the probability of "success" of a certain procedure than on the patient's quality of life after the procedure. Family members, however, may see the burdens associated with life in a persistent vegetative state or with advanced Alzheimer's and not see the benefit of continued treatment. Alternatively, in some cases, family members may believe that life itself is sacred, no matter what its quality, whereas the physician may think that life in certain states is not worth sustaining.[36] Physicians and family members, for example, disagreed over the care of Helga Wanglie, an eighty-eight-year-old woman in a persistent vegetative state. Her physicians wanted to discontinue life support, arguing that it was futile to continue such support under those circumstances, while her husband felt her life was worth continuing.[37]

Lack of clarity as to who has decision making authority

In some states, laws provide that a physician need not follow the instructions of a surrogate if to do so would be contrary to the physician's conscience or inconsistent with "generally accepted standards of patient care."[38] Such provisions, which may allow physicians to usurp decision making authority from family members, can also lead to disputes. The federal Baby Doe Rules,[39] in which decision making authority for the withholding or withdrawal of life support from newborns is given largely to physicians, have also led to disputes in cases where parents believe they should be allowed more input into these decisions.[40] Confusion over who can speak for a patient can also originate from lack of an available surrogate decision-maker or disagreement over who should serve as the surrogate. In the well publicized case of Terri Schiavo, a Florida woman in a persistent vegetative state, family members fought bitterly over who should speak for Terri and whether her feeding should be continued. Michael, her husband, requested that her tube feedings be stopped. Her parents challenged Michael's stewardship as surrogate decision-maker, based on allegations that he had financial and personal conflicts of interest.[41]

Disagreement over when treatment is futile

Different views about futility and the role of spiritual beliefs in effecting a "cure" create disagreements when decisions have to be made about withholding or withdrawing life-prolonging treatments. In the case of a 16-month-old with AIDS who was in constant, agonizing pain, the foster parents thought life support was not futile because God, not man, should make the decision as to when life ends, whereas the health care providers involved viewed the treatments as futile based on the inability to achieve a medical goal.[42] In the oft cited case of Baby K,[43] the hospital sought a declaratory judgment that it had no duty to provide life-sustaining treatment for an anencephalic infant over objections of the mother. The U.S. Court of Appeals for the Fourth Circuit held that under the federal Emergency Medical Treatment and Labor Act (EMTALA)[44] the hospital had a duty to treat Baby K. The Court determined that resuscitating Baby K (who would present in respiratory distress) and putting her back on a ventilator was not medically futile because her admitting diagnosis was respiratory failure, not anencephaly. However, according to a dissenting opinion in the case, there was no obligation to resuscitate Baby K under EMTALA because the relevant condition was anencephaly, not respiratory failure.[45]

Cases arising in non-hospital settings

While most of the literature has focused on cases that come to hospital ethics committees, issues that arise in non-hospital settings may be quite different from those arising in acute care settings. For example, in long-term care facilities, committees may confront questions about the use of chemical or physical restraints, sexual relations between residents, and behavior management (issues that are referred to as matters of "everyday ethics").[46] In home health care, ethical issues addressed by HCECs include maintaining agency solvency without denying care to patients who lack financial resources, practicing health care in situations where patients may be abused or neglected, inadequate care of a patient by the patient or family, termination of home care services (abandonment), and racial intolerance of patients, family members, and/or staff.[47] In mental health and psychiatric treatment settings ethical issues most often involve maintaining patient confidentiality, boundary violations, and special concerns related to resource allocation.[48]

Ethical concerns arising in MCOs often stem from their dual purposes of reducing unnecessary expenditures while maintaining quality. This often creates questions about the need for hospitalization or referrals to specialists and policy issues about coverage of new procedures. Dombeck and Olsan describe several ethical concerns about managed care ranging from conflicts in the fiduciary relationship between physicians and their patients to "making limited health care resources available to some at the expense of others."[49]

How are these cases handled by ethics committees?

Because there are virtually no regulations governing ethics committees, their operations and procedures vary from committee to committee. As regards the process of ethics consultation, committees may adopt different structural and procedural models. In some institutions the full committee may conduct the consult; in others, it may fall on a small team or subcommittee or, in a growing number of institutions, on an individual consultant. The issue of which model is most appropriate or effective is still unresolved in the field. Rubin and Zoloth, who advocate that the full committee engage in consultation, have lamented that "it is a significant problem that there has been no systematic empirical research or sustained philosophical debate to date about the relative effectiveness and desirability of the competing models of doing ethics consultation."[50]

Perhaps more troubling is the lack of consensus regarding deliberative or procedural models for ethics committees addressing the cases that come to them. At least four procedural models are described in the literature: (1) the case conference model, in which the focus is on hearing from all parties and analyzing the advantages and disadvantges of various options without making a specific recommendation; (2) the consultation model, which takes its name from the traditional medical consultation model, in which the committee acts as a consultant or expert and is expected to recommend a specific course of action; (3) the quasi-judicial model in which the emphasis is placed on conflict resolution and due process; and (4) the mediation model in which the committee acts as a facilitator and assists the parties in reaching a consensus on the issue in dispute. In both the consultation and quasi-judicial models the committee makes a recommendation to the parties as to how to proceed.[51]

There remain significant differences among scholars and practitioners as to which of these four models is most appropriate and effective. While the American Society for Bioethics and Humanities (ASBH) has embraced a facilitation model, there are voices that reject the model as inconsistent with the normative role of bioethics. These latter advocates argue that

> [c]linical ethics cannot be agnostic when it comes to making a recommendation. The cases that come for ethics consultation involve real patients and families and real health care professionals, and they involve situations in which a real decision will be made. Advice, not simply a facilitated exchange is what is being sought and what ought to be promised.[52]

When ethics committee members deliberate among themselves and attempt to arrive at a recommendation, relevant legal and ethical norms typically inform the committee's recommendation. Bioethicsts have espoused a number of theories to guide ethical case analysis, such as principle-based ethics, casuistry, consequentialism, deontology, feminist ethics, and narrative ethics. Principle-based case analysis, based on applying and weighing the principles of respect for autonomy, beneficence, non-maleficence, and justice, was the first to gain widespread recognition.[53] However, some have criticized a principled approach as lacking in methodological application and biased toward concerns of individual autonomy.[54] This has led to a continuing conversation in bioethics about how ethical principles and theory should inform deliberation of cases brought before ethics committees.[55]

When considering the cultural diversity within the United States and abroad, some argue that moral issues, which are contextually (e.g., culturally) based, cannot be "resolved" by bioethicists applying cross-cultural moral norms or theories.[56] Yet, universal moral theory is not necessarily incompatible with contextually based case analysis. For example, in the more communitarian cultures, the practices of truth-telling and informed consent are approached differently than in the United States. This, however, does not preclude applying a principles-based approach – rather, the principles will be weighed differently in the context of a communitarian culture, where respecting autonomy might involve allowing an individual to defer decision making to the group, and balancing benefits and harms might entail prioritizing group harmony rather than individual rights.[57] Likewise, use of narrative ethics[58] in case consultation does not preclude application of other ethical theories. Indeed, Macklin argues that many norms are relative to the moralities of individual cultures, while recognizing that basic human rights exist that must be protected across cultures.[59] Beauchamp, claiming that no prevailing ethical theory has been shown to serve any useful purpose in bioethics, calls upon bioethicists to shift the focus toward universal norms (e.g., principles, rights, virtues) that can be applied across practice settings.[60]

While ethical norms play a role in HCEC deliberations, these are also influenced by the characteristics of the U.S. health care system, including growing numbers of uninsured and under-insured persons, technology that shifts the site of treatment from hospitals to outpatient settings, and pressures to cut costs, including an increasing penetration of MCOs.[61] Profit status and religious affiliation may also influence ethics committees' processes and deliberations. Few have studied the influence of an HCEC's profit-status, per se, on ethics committee functioning, although much has been written about the ethical conflicts of interest that may be created by profit seeking. Dugan describes several ways in which religiously based health care organizations (HCOs) differ from non-religious HCOs in their approach to ethical issues. The former, he observes, use a wider "radar screen" by which to capture ethical dilemmas or conflicts in the net of issues for ethical deliberation (e.g., contraceptive sterilization in Catholic hospitals, which must abide by the norms of the U.S. Conference of Catholic Bishops' Ethical and Religious Directives for Catholic Health Care Services); spend greater time researching and reflecting on how interventions that may be grounded in laws and ethical principles are also consistent with the organization's religious mission and core values; and take a different approach to the integration of the organization's mission into clinical decision making (i.e., equipping staff with "the skills and tools to integrate religiously based core values into all aspects of their responsibilities").[62] Heller believes that whether or not an HCO's religious affiliation makes a difference in the nature of the ethical issues it confronts or in the way its ethics committee and consultants work is case specific.[63]

Legal evolution of ethics committees

As stated above, ethics committees have remained largely unregulated in the United States, yet court opinions and statutes in some states have encouraged their establishment, protected their members from liability, mandated basic requirements for membership and due process, and/or given them legal authority for health care decision making. While the majority of courts seem to have embraced the notion of ethics committees, not all have agreed with the wisdom of allowing them to substitute for judicial decision making. Shortly after the *Quinlan* case, the Massachusetts Supreme Judicial Court, in the case of Joseph Saikewicz, a sixty-seven-year-old, never competent, terminally ill cancer patient, challenged the assumptions of the *Quinlan* court regarding the merits of HCECs. The court stated that questions of life and death

> require the process of detached but passionate investigation and decision that forms the ideal on which the judicial branch of government was created. Achieving this ideal is our responsibility and that of the lower courts, and is not to be entrusted to any other group purporting to represent the "morality and conscience of our society," no matter how highly motivated or impressively constituted.[64]

Other courts also expressed skepticism about granting decision making authority to HCECs, especially in the early stages of their development. One court described them as "ill-defined, amorphous bod[ies], which in some hospitals may not even exist."[65]

However, there has been an equally vocal, if not louder, call by a number of courts for the establishment in health care institutions of bodies, such as ethics committees, to deal with the difficult end-of-life care cases that come to them. For example, in *In re Jobes*,[66] in which the husband of a non-elderly woman who was comatose and in a nursing home brought suit seeking termination of her life-sustaining nutrition and hydration, the N.J. Supreme Court stated that

> courts are not the proper place to resolve the agonizing personal problems that underlie these cases. Our legal system cannot replace the more intimate struggle that must be borne by the patient, those caring for the patient, and those who are about the patient. The challenge for the courts will be to evolve innovative and flexible processes by which affected individuals can participate comfortably and confidently to secure the vindication of the interests we all seek to protect.[67]

In a concurring opinion in that case, Justice Pollack more specifically mentioned the need for ethics committees stating that "[a]s an aid to physicians and families, hospitals and other health care facilities, such as nursing homes, should give serious consideration to making available the services of ethicists and institutional ethics committees."[68]

In 1990, the Court of Appeals for the District of Columbia was called upon to determine "who has the right to decide the course of medical treatment for a patient who, although near death, is pregnant with a viable fetus" and "how that decision should be made if the patient cannot make it for herself."[69] The judge, speaking for the court, stated in a footnote

> We observe ... that it would be far better if judges were not called to patients' bedsides and required to make quick decisions on issues of life and death. Because judgment in such a case involves complex medical and ethical issues as well as the application of legal principles, we would urge the establishment – through legislation or otherwise – of another tribunal to make these decisions, with limited opportunity for judicial review.[70]

More recently, in *Quill v. Vacco*, Judge Milner, writing for the Second Circuit, "suggested that a state might 'require the establishment of local ethics committees as resources for physicians' in order to deal with such difficult questions as physician assisted suicide."[71]

State legislatures have also encouraged the establishment of HCECs but have done little to assure their quality. The Maryland law, enacted in 1987, is unique in providing requirements for committee membership and due process. The law, in addition to requiring all hospitals and nursing homes in the state to establish such committees, requires that the committees must have at least four members, including a physician, a nurse, a social worker, and a hospital's chief executive officer or designee.[72] Other members may be added as the hospital chooses, including representatives of the community and ethical advisors or clergy.[73] Each committee must set forth in writing how it shall be convened. It must make a good-faith effort to notify patients and their immediate family members of their rights to petition the committee for assistance. Each committee must also meet with these patients and their immediate family members concerning "options for medical treatment"; it must also provide the patient and immediate family members with an explanation of the "basis of the advisory committee's advice."[74] As part of its deliberations the committee must consult all members of the patient's treatment team, the patient, and the patient's family. The Act further provides that the proceedings of the committee are confidential and that the advice of the committee must become part of the patient's medical record.[75]

A few states have provided protection from liability for ethics committee members. The Maryland statute provides that committee members who give advice in good faith may not be held liable in court for the advice given.[76] In other states, including Arizona, Hawaii, and Montana, statutes grant immunity from civil or criminal liability "to members of ethics committees or healthcare providers who rely on committee advice."[77] As a result, as one author has noted, disputes considered by these committees "are increasingly unlikely to be reviewed substantively by a court."[78] In a number of other states, existing statutes that protect peer review committees and medical staff committee proceedings may also protect members of ethics committees by preventing discovery of their meeting minutes and deliberations.[79]

More recently, states have passed statutes allowing ethics committees to serve as "surrogate" decision-makers in cases where there is a dispute between family members or where no family members are available. In Maryland, if there is a dispute between surrogate decision-makers of equal standing regarding termination of life support for a patient lacking decision making capacity, the institutional ethics committee may make the decision. The patient's physician may then act in accordance with the committee's recommendation without fear of liability for any claim based on lack of consent.[80] In addition, the statute requires that where physicians believe a decision by surrogates or agents is "inconsistent with generally accepted standards of patient care," they bring the case to the ethics committee or to court.[81] Similarly, in Texas, ethics committees may serve as a dispute resolution body. When patients and physicians disagree about life-sustaining treatment, an ethics committee's decision is final unless the patient is transferred.[82]

In several other states ethics committees are given decision making authority when there is no legally authorized surrogate or when one is not available to speak with the patient. For example, the Arizona law regarding surrogate decision making states that if a health care provider cannot locate any of the surrogates designated by the statute in a case involving a patient who lacks decision making capacity, the "patient's attending physician may make health care treatment decisions for the patient after the physician consults with and obtains the recommendations of an institutional ethics committee."[83] The statute, however, further provides that "[i]f this is not possible, the physician may make these decisions after consulting with a second physician who concurs with the physician's decision."[84] The statute defines an "institutional ethics committee" as a "standing committee of a licensed health care institution appointed or elected to render advice concerning ethical issues involving medical treatment."[85]

In Alabama, the statute regarding termination of life support provides that if a patient

> has no relatives known to the attending physician or to an administrator of the facility where the patient is being treated and none can be found after a reasonable inquiry, a committee composed of the patient's primary treating physician and the ethics committee of the facility where the patient is undergoing treatment or receiving care[86]

is authorized to make decisions "regarding the withholding of life-sustaining treatment or artificially provided nutrition and hydration."[87] If there is no ethics committee, a committee consisting of certain specified members and appointed by the chief medical staff or chief executive officer of the facility is authorized to make these decisions.[88] In either of these circumstances, the health care facility involved must notify the Alabama Department of Human Resources to allow the department "to participate in the review of the matter pursuant to its responsibilities under the Adult Protective Services Act."[89]

In Florida, if a patient lacks an advance directive and is unable to make health care decisions for him or herself and the patient does not have a guardian or a family member or close friend who is authorized to make health care decisions for the patient, the bioethics committee of the facility in which the patient is located may select a clinical social worker who is either licensed or a graduate of a court-approved guardianship program to act as a surrogate for the patient.[90] If the social worker asks to withdraw or withhold life support, that decision must be reviewed by the facility's bioethics committee.[91]

In a few states, ethics committees are given the authority to review decisions to withhold or withdraw life-sustaining treatment when the patient is in a specific condition or when a specific type of intervention is going to be withheld. For example, Florida law provides that for patients in a persistent vegetative state, if the patient does not have an advance directive and there is no evidence of whether the patient would have wanted medical treatment in this state, life-sustaining treatment may only be withheld or withdrawn if a court-appointed guardian, in consultation with a medical ethics committee, concludes "that the condition is permanent and that there is no reasonable medical probability for recovery and that withholding or withdrawing life-prolonging procedures is in the best interest of the patient."[92] In Georgia, if there is no legally authorized surrogate, an ethics committee, at the request of a physician with a concurring second opinion, may approve a DNR order for a patient.[93]

In one state, a health care provider may be disciplined for failing to cooperate with an ethics committee. The North Carolina Medicine and Allied Occupations Article provides as grounds for the denial, suspension, or revocation of a license of a psychologist where the psychologist has failed to cooperate with or respond "promptly, completely, and honestly" to a hospital ethics committee.[94]

Self-regulation

While these statutes have given ethics committees significant authority, they have imposed little or no requirements on committee composition, competency, or process. Although academic and certification programs in bioethics exist, there is currently no licensing of ethics consultants. Instead, ethicists rely on self-regulation by way of professional societies (such as the American Society for Bioethics and Humanities (ASBH) and the Canadian

Bioethics Society), or on the norms governing other professions to which they belong, such as nursing, medicine, or social work. The Canadian Bioethics Society convened an ad hoc working group on Employment Standards for Bioethics, which has been worked into a draft Model Code of Ethics for Bioethics.[95] However, the question of professional obligations of bioethics consultants and their scope of practice remains unresolved.

In 1998, the ASBH published its *Core Competencies For Health Care Ethics Consultation*.[96] The publication delineates which skills and sources of knowledge ethics committee members should possess, acknowledging that some members will have more ethical expertise than others, but that all should possess "minimum competencies." These are currently the only "industry wide" standards for ethics committees that have received some consensus in the United States.

Cases where ethics committees have been sued

In jurisdictions where ethics committees have not been granted immunity from liability as institutional committees giving advice to parties about patient treatment issues, they may be subject to lawsuit. While legal action against committees has been rare, it has occurred, most often in cases involving a dispute over whether continuing treatment is futile. Perhaps the earliest suit against an ethics committee was that brought by Elizabeth Bouvia in the mid 1980s.[97] The case involved a dispute between a competent patient and her physician, the hospital, and members of the hospital ethics committee who agreed with the physician's decision to feed the patient against her wishes through a nasogastric tube. By reasoning that the decision was not a medical one nor a "conditional right subject to approval by an ethics committee," a California Appeals court held that the feeding tube should be removed. Subsequently, Bouvia sued the hospital and the physicians for damages, and went so far as to name the ethics committee members in the complaint. Bouvia, however, decided not to pursue the suit against the committee members and subsequently dropped the suit against the hospital and physicians to avoid publicity.[98]

Fletcher has described several other cases brought by patients or their family members against the chair or members of an HCEC after the committee or a committee member determined that life-sustaining treatment would be medically futile and the patient's physician withheld or withdrew such treatment without consulting the patient's family.[99] In *Gilgunn v. Massachusetts General Hospital*,[100] a patient's daughter sued the hospital and the chair of the ethics committee (called the Optimum Care Committee (OCC)) for violations of the daughter's rights as a surrogate. The chairman of the hospital's OCC endorsed a DNR order without consulting the daughter, despite her previous objection. The physician weaned the patient from the respirator and the patient died. At trial, the jury sided with the hospital and physicians.[101] The case was appealed but subsequently dismissed, presumably as a result of settlement. In *Estate of Bland v. Cigna Healthplan of Texas et al.*[102] the patient's family brought suit for intentional infliction of emotional harm due to a decision made by the chair of the ethics committee to remove the patient from a respirator without consulting the family or the patient's original physician. The suit was settled out of court.[103]

Similar cases were filed in Pennsylvania and Virginia. In *Rideout v. Hershey Medical Center*,[104] the parents of a two-year-old comatose patient who suffered from a brainstem tumor sued the hospital because the child had been removed from a ventilator against the parents' wishes. The hospital ethics committee agreed with the physician that a DNR order was appropriate and supported the decision to remove the child from the ventilator. A three-judge panel ruled that the parents could continue with their claims that the hospital committed assault and battery on the child, negligently and intentionally inflicted emotional distress on the parents, and impinged parental rights rooted in the free exercise of religion. However, the case was subsequently settled.[105] The 1996 Virginia case of *Bryan v. Stone. et al.: Bryan v. Rector and Visitors of the University of Virginia, et al.*, involved the family of a patient suffering from multiple disabling medical conditions. The family requested all possible treatment, including resuscitative efforts. Despite the protests of the patient's husband, the attending physician requested assistance from the ethics committee. After an ad hoc advisory committee convened by the ethics committee chair declared CPR to be futile, the physician wrote a DNR order and informed the patient's husband. The patient died eight days later. In their first law suit, the family sued the attending physician and members of the ad hoc group for violation of the patient's religious beliefs and some provisions of the Virginia Healthcare Decisions Act (VHDA).[106] The VHDA stipulates that physicians are not required to prescribe or render treatment that the physician determines to be "medically or ethically inappropriate," and that in such circumstances a good faith effort be made to transfer the patient to the care of another physician.[107] The suit was eventually dismissed.

More recently, suits against ethics consultants have been reported in the press. In response, the ASBH established a committee to make a recommendation on whether ethics consultants and members of ethics committees, not already covered under their institution's malpractice insurance policy, should obtain their own malpractice insurance coverage.[108]

How have courts weighed recommendations by ethics committees in cases that have come to them?

A few courts have also been called upon to address disputes that were previously heard by an ethics committee. While these cases have also been relatively infrequent, in the cases that have been reviewed by the courts, the courts have been inconsistent in how they have regarded them. In a few cases, they have ignored ethics committee recommendations. In others, they have treated the ethics committee recommendation as confirmation of a physician's determination. In at least one case, *In re Torres*,[109] the court noted that the record included the reports of three biomedical ethics committees that reviewed Torres' case, and appeared to regard the committees as authorities on moral issues.[110]

Courts may wish to give different weight to committee recommendations as ethics committees vary significantly in composition, experience, expertise, and procedures. Given the disparity among committees, in reviewing an ethics committee recommendation arguably courts should consider: (1) whether the ethics committee members have had any training in bioethics or law; (2) whether the committee includes community representatives or other individuals who can provide values that may differ from those of health care providers or other staff, for example, patients or family members of patients; and (3) whether the committee followed minimal elements of due process, including providing (i) notice and an opportunity for the relevant parties to be heard, (ii) evidence of diverse committee participation in the deliberative process, and (iii) a rationale for its final recommendation backed by relevant ethical and societal norms.

Conclusion

The role and legal status of ethics committees in the United States remains amorphous. Committees, for the most part, remain unregulated and disagreements exist in the field as to whether regulation is appropriate. Despite the lack of homogeneity in committee function and operation and the inconsistent quality in committee performance, a number of state legislatures have given HCECs legal authority to make health care decisions for patients lacking health care decision making capacity and/or available surrogates. While threats of malpractice may lead to improvements in ethics committee performance, in a number of jurisdictions ethics committees have been protected by statute from liability. In addition, suits have been rare and there are no published judicial opinions that have articulated standards for ethics committee process. As a result, committees continue to operate with minimum oversight and without legal standards.

Notes

1 *In re Quinlan*, 355 A.2d 647, 668 (N.J.) (1976).
2 President's Commission for the Study of Ethical Problems in Medicine and Biomedical and Behavioral Research, Deciding to Forego Life-sustaining Treatment: A Report on the Ethical, Medical, and Legal Issues in Treatment Decisions 5 (U.S. Government Printing Office 1983).
3 42 U.S.C. §§ 5101–5107 (2000); 45 C.F.R. § 1340.15 (2003).
4 MD. Code Ann., Health-Gen. §§ 19-370 to 19-374 (2002).
5 N.J. Admin. Code tit. 8, § 43G-5.1 (1990).

6 Joint Commission on the Accreditation of Healthcare Organizations, Comprehensive Accreditation Manual for Hospitals, Standard R1.1.1.6.1, at 104 (The Joint Commission 1992).
7 *See Ethics Committees Double Since '83: Survey*, 59(21) Hospitals 60, 60 (1985).
8 Glenn McGee, Joshua P. Spanogle, Arthur L. Caplan & David A. Asch, *A National Study of Ethics Committees*, 1(4) Am. J. Bioethics Fall 60, 60–61 (2001).
9 *Id.*; *See also* Diane E. Hoffmann, *Does Legislating Hospital Ethics Committees Make a Difference? A Study of Hospital Ethics Committees in Maryland, the District of Columbia, and Virginia*, 19 Law, Med. & Health Care 105, 107 (1991).
10 *See* Hoffmann, *supra* n. 9, at 107.
11 *Id.* at 108.
12 *Id.* at 108.
13 Dan Dugan, *Ethics Committees in Religious Hospitals: A Different Landscape*, 22 The Park Ridge Center Bulletin 3, 3 (2001).
14 *See* Scott D. Yoder, *Experts in Ethics? The Nature of Ethical Expertise*, 28(6) Hastings Ctr. Rep. 11(1998); Ruth Shalit, *When We Were Philosopher Kings: The Rise of the Medical Ethicist*, 216(17) New Republic 24, 24 (1997).
15 Cynthia B. Cohen, *The Social Transformation of Some American Ethics Committees*, 19(5) Hastings Ctr. Rep. 21, 21 (1989).
16 *See* John C. Fletcher & Diane E. Hoffmann, *Ethics Committees: Time to Experiment with Standards*, 120(4) Annals Internal Med. 335 (1994). *See also* Diane E. Hoffmann, A. Tarzian & J.A. O'Neil, *Are Ethics Committees Competent to Consult?*, 28 J. Law, Med. & Ethics 30 (2000).
17 Bryn Williams-Jones, *A Review of Recent Ethics Literature on Clinical Case Consultations* (Dec. 2000), http://www.ethicscommittee.ca/resources/caseconsult.html (accessed April 5, 2005).
18 *See* Randall B. Bateman, *Attorneys on Bioethics Committees: Unwelcome Menace or Valuable Asset?*, 9 J. L. & Health 247 (1994/95).
19 *See* Diane E. Hoffmann, *The Influence of Law and Lawyers on Patient Care*, 24(2) MD. B.J. 2 (Mar./Apr. 1991).
20 *See* Am. Ass'n of Homes and Services for the Aging, *Ethics Involvement in Long-term Care*, http://www.aahsa.org/member/backgrd8.htm (accessed Aug. 11, 2004).
21 New York City Long-Term Care Ethics Network, *Results of Telephone Survey*, http://www.angelfire.com/on/NYCLTCethicsnetwork/j2000phone.html (accessed Aug. 11, 2004).
22 Kate T. Christensen & Robin Tucker, *Ethics Without Walls: The Transformation of Ethics Committees in the New Healthcare Environment*, 6(3) Cambridge Q. Healthcare Ethics 299, 300 (1997).
23 Sue Ellen Bell, *Ethical Climate in Managed Care Organizations*, 27(2) Nursing Admin. Q. 133 (2003).
24 Susanna E. Guzman, *Managed Care Ethics Committees Make a Difference*, 4(2) Fam. Prac. Mgmt. 50, 50 (1997).
25 *See* David C. Thomasma & John F. Monagle, Health Care Ethics: Critical Issues for the 21st Century, Ch. 43 (Aspen Publishers 1998).
26 Henry J. Silverman, *Organizational Ethics in Healthcare Organizations: Proactively Managing the Ethical Climate to Ensure Organizational Integrity*, 12(3) HEC Forum 202 (2000).
27 Rebecca D. Pentz, *Beyond Case Consultation: An Expanded Model for Organizational Ethics*, 10(1) J. Clinical Ethics 34 (1999).
28 *See* Trinity Health, *Introduction to Next Generation Model of Clinical Ethics*, http://www.trinity-health.org/who/model.shtml (accessed Aug. 16, 2004).

29 Gordon DuVal, Leah Sartorius, Brian Clarridge, Gary Gensler & Marion Danis, *What Triggers Requests for Ethics Consultations?* 27(Supp. 1) J. Med. Ethics i24, i24 (2001).
30 *See* Glenn McGee, Joshua P. Spanogle, Arthur L Caplan, Dina Penny & David A. Asch, *Successes and Failures of Hospital Ethics Committees: A National Survey of Ethics Committee Chairs*, 11(1) Cambridge Q. Healthcare Ethics 87 (2002).
31 618 A.2d 744 (Md. 1993).
32 Brief for Appellant at 10–11, *Mack v. Mack*, 618 A.2d 744 (Md. 1993) (No. 99).
33 Brief for Petitioner at 7-8, *In re Mack*, No. 91T103 (Baltimore Co. Cir. Ct., Mar. 10, 1992).
34 *See* Diane E. Hoffmann, *Mediating Life and Death Decisions*, 36(4) Ariz. L. Rev. 821, 831 (1994).
35 *Id.*
36 *Id.* at 833.
37 *See In re Conservatorship of Wanglie*, No. PX-91-283 (Minn. Dist. Ct., Hennepin Co., July, 1991).
38 *See* Hoffmann, *supra* n. 34, at 834.
39 42 U.S.C. §§ 5101–5107 (2000); 45 C.F.R. § 1340.15 (2003).
40 *See* Hoffmann, *supra* n. 34, at 835.
41 *Schindler v. Schiavo*, 780 So. 2d 176, 178 (Fla. Dist. Ct. App. 2001).
42 Benjamin Weiser, *While Child Suffered, Beliefs Clashed*, Washington Post A1 (July 15, 1991).
43 *In re Baby K.*, 16 F.3d 590 (4th Cir. 1994).
44 42 U.S.C. § 1395dd (2000).
45 *In re Baby K.*, 16 F.3d 590, 599 (4th Cir.) (Sprouse, J. dissenting).
46 *See* Diane E. Hoffmann, Philip Boyle & Steven A. Levenson, Handbook for Nursing Home Ethics Committees 247 (Am. Ass'n of Homes and Services for the Aging 1995).
47 *See* Amy M. Haddad, *Ethical Problems in Home Healthcare*, 22(3) J. Nursing Admin. 46, 46 (1992).
48 *See* Sidney Bloch, Paul Chodoff & Stephen Green eds, Psychiatric Ethics (3d ed., Oxford University Press 1999).
49 Mary T. Dombeck & Thobie H. Olsan, *Ethics and Managed Care*, 16(3) J. Interprof. Care 221, 227 (2002).
50 Susan B. Rubin & Laurie Zoloth, *Clinical Ethics and the Road Less Taken: Mapping the Future by Tracking the Past*, 32(2) J.L. Med. & Ethics 218, 221 (2004).
51 *See* Hoffman *et al.*, *supra* n. 46, at 82–84.
52 Rubin & Zoloth, *supra* n. 50, at 222.
53 Tom L. Beauchamp & James F. Childress, Principles of Biomedical Ethics, (4th ed., Oxford University Press 1994; also 5th ed. 2001). *See also* Tom.L. Beauchamp, *Methods and Principles in Biomedical Ethics*, 29(5) J. Med. Ethics 269 (2003).
54 *See* Robert M. Veatch & Willard Gaylin, *Can the Moral Commons Survive Autonomy?*, 26(6) Hastings Ctr. Rep. 41, 41 (1996).
55 *See* Onora O'Neill, *Practical Principles and Practical Judgment*, 31(4) Hastings Ctr. Rep.15, 15 (2001); Martin Benjamin, *Between Subway and Spaceship: Practical Ethics at the Outset of the Twenty-first Century*, 31(4) Hastings Ctr. Rep. 24, 24 (2001); Margaret Olivia Little, *On Knowing the "Why": Particularism and Moral Theory*, 31(4) Hastings Ctr. Rep. 32, 32 (2001).
56 *See* Leigh Turner, *Zones of Consensus and Zones of Conflict: Questioning the "Common Morality" Presumption in Bioethics*, 13(3) Kennedy Inst. Ethics J. 193 (2003).

57 Valmae Ypinazar & Stephen Margolis, *Western Medical Ethics Taught to Junior Medical Students Can Cross Cultural and Linguistic Boundaries*, BMC Med Ethics, 5:E4 (2004).
58 *See* Rita Charon & Martha Montello, *Framing the Case: Narrative Approaches for Healthcare Ethics Committees*, 11(1) HEC Forum 6 (1999).
59 Ruth Macklin, Against Relativism: Cultural Diversity and the Search for Ethical Universals in Medicine (Oxford University Press 1999).
60 Tom L. Beauchamp, *Does Ethical Theory Have a Future in Bioethics?*, 32(2) J. L. Med. & Ethics 209, 210 (2004).
61 Christensen & Tucker, *supra* n. 22.
62 Dugan, *supra* n. 13, at 4.
63 Jan C. Heller, *Does Religious Affiliation Matter? Religion and Ethics Committees*, 22 The Park Ridge Center Bull. 7 (2001).
64 *Superintendent of Belchertown State Sch. v. Saikewicz*, 370 N.E.2d 417, 435 (Mass. 1977). *See also* Bethany Spielman, *Has Faith in Health Care Ethics Consultants Gone Too Far? Risks of An Unregulated Practice and A Model Act to Contain Them*, 85(1) Marq. L. Rev. 161 (2001) (elaborating on reaction of courts and medical profession to *Quinlan*).
65 *Eichner v. Dillon*, 426 N.Y.S.2d 517 (N.Y. App. Div. 1980). *See also In re Welfare of Colyer*, 660 P.2d 738, 749 (Wash. 1983) (en banc) (stating a preference for a prognosis committee over an ethics committee because of the latter's "amorphous character, for its use of nonmedical personnel to reach a medical decision, and for its bureaucratic intermeddling"); *In re Moorhouse*, 593 A.2d 1256 (N.J. Super. Ct. App. Div. 1991) (steering decision making authority away from an ethics committee to a public advocate in the case of a never-competent ward of the state).
66 529 A.2d 434 (N.J. 1987).
67 *Id.* at 451 (*quoting* Chief Justice Joseph Weintraub, Lecture by Justice Alan B. Handler at Rutgers Law School, March 11, 1987).
68 *In re Jobes*, 529 A.2d at 463.
69 *In re A.C.*, 573 A.2d 1235, 1237 (D.C. 1990).
70 *Id.* at 1237 n. 2.
71 Robin Fretwell Wilson, *Hospital Ethics Committees as the Forum of Last Resort: An Idea Whose Time Has Not Come*, 76(2) N.C. L. Rev. 353, 359 (1998).
72 *See* MD. Code Ann., Health-Gen. § 19-372(a)(1) (2002).
73 *See* MD. Code Ann., Health-Gen. § 19-372(a)(2) (2002).
74 *See* MD. Code Ann., Health-Gen. § 19-374(b)(iii) (2002).
75 *See* MD. Code Ann., Health-Gen. § 19-374(d)(1) (2002).
76 MD. Code Ann., Health-Gen. § 19-374(c) (2002).
77 Wilson, *supra* n. 71, at 363.
78 *Id.*
79 *See* Andrew L. Merritt, *The Tort Liability of Hospital Ethics Committees*, 60(5) S. Cal. L. Rev. 1239, 1252 (1987).
80 MD. Code Ann., Health-Gen. § 5-605(a)(2) (2002).
81 MD. Code Ann., Health-Gen. § 5-612(a) (2002).
82 Tex. Health & Safety Code Ann. § 166.046 (Vernon 2000) (Texas Advance Directives Act).
83 Ariz. Rev. Stat. § 36-3231(B) (2003).
84 *Id.*
85 *Id.*
86 Ala. Code § 22-8A-11(d)(7) (1997).
87 Ala. Code § 22-8A-11(d)(1) (1997).
88 Ala. Code § 22-8A-11(d)(7) (1997).

89 *Id.*
90 Fla. Stat. Ann. § 765.401(1)(h) (West Supp. 2004).
91 *Id.*
92 Fla. Stat. Ann. § 765.404(2) (West Supp. 2004).
93 Ga. Code Ann. § 31-39-2 (2000).
94 N.C. Gen. Stat. § 90-270.15 (2004).
95 Chris Macdonald, *Draft: Model Code of Ethics for Bioethics*, http://www.bioethics.ca/english/workingconditions/ (accessed Aug. 14, 2004).
96 *Core Competencies for Health Care Ethics Consultation.* Report of the Task Force on Standards for Bioethics Consultation, American Society for Bioethics and Humanities (American Society for Bioethics and Humanities 1998).
97 *Bouvia v. Superior Court*, 225 Cal. Rptr. 297 (Cal. Ct. App. 1986).
98 *See* John Fletcher, Introduction to Clinical Ethics, ch. 14 (University Publishing Group, Inc. 1997).
99 *Id.*
100 Civ. Action No. 92-4820 (Mass. Super. Ct., Suffolk County, Apr. 21 1995).
101 *Id.*
102 Case No. 1993-52630-7 (Dist. Ct. Harris County, Tex.).
103 Shalit, *supra* n. 14, at 26.
104 30 Pa. D. & C. 4th 57 (Dauphin County Ct. of Common Pleas 1995).
105 Shalit, *supra* n. 14, at 26.
106 VA. Code Ann. § 54.1-2981 *et seq*. (Michie 2002).
107 VA. Code Ann. § 54.1-2987 (Michie 2002).
108 Gerard Magill, Jill Van Derven, Arthur L. Caplan, Dean Cody, Diane Hoffmann, Sandra Johnson, Jeffrey P. Kahn, Sheila A. M. McLean, Jerry A. Menikoff, Susan B. Rubin & Bethany J. Spielman, *ASBH Task Force Report on Ethics Consultation Liability* (October 2004) (unpublished manuscript), http://www.asbh.org/resources/taskforce/pdf/Ethics%20Consultation%20Liability%20Report.pdf Unpublished manuscript (accessed Sept. 14, 2005).
109 *In re Torres*, 357 N.W.2d 332, 341 n. 4 (Minn. 1984).
110 *See* Susan M. Wolf, *Ethics Committees in the Courts*, 16(3) Hastings Ctr. Rep. 12, 12 (1986).

5 What's wrong with health privacy?[1]

Nicolas P. Terry

Introduction

In 2000, President Clinton introduced the landmark *Standards for Privacy of Individually Identifiable Health Information*[2] (federal standards) with the words "[n]othing is more private than someone's medical or psychiatric records."[3] It is well known that the Health Insurance Portability and Accountability Act of 1996 (HIPAA)[4] committed the federal government to a process of "Administrative Simplification" to reduce healthcare costs, but Congress wanted to limit how far the healthcare industry could externalize attendant privacy risks to patients.[5] Yet, in the aftermath, what should have been a final victory for patient autonomy and informational privacy has turned into another divisive debate about professionalism and health-care regulation. State and federal privacy law may be omnipresent, the pages of medical journals and law reviews may be filled with exhortations of confidentiality, and the media, often disingenuously, may be quick to pounce on system failures, but health information privacy is surprisingly fragile.

Elsewhere, I have argued that the necessity of protecting the privacy of health information is broadly, if not universally, accepted (at least in the ethical and legal domains), yet counter-intuitively dogged by controversy.[6] Rather than an accepted social imperative protected by a powerful triumvirate of ethical constraints, effective laws, and operational necessities, I see a construct that lacks consistent terminology, a convincing rationale, or general principles that can be effectively conveyed to patients and providers.

This chapter seeks to identify some of the reasons why "privacy" remains so contentious. Here I suggest several possible answers ranging from "micro" issues such as what we understand by health privacy to more "macro" and operational issues as we seek to protect health information. First, lawyers have made consistent errors in the terminology applied to the protection of medical privacy; second, both the legal and ethical domains have failed to apply a consistent and robust rationale for health privacy, leaving it prey to consequentialist thought and policy; third, the declining importance of the physician–patient relationship as the touchstone for obligations, particularly confidentiality, has created a "rights" vacuum; fourth, the health information revolution truly is revolutionary in its reach and its concomitant threats to privacy and confidentiality; and, finally, as privacy regulation increasingly lies in the sphere of governmental command-control regulation, it has joined the list of targets in the professionalism-market-regulation conflict over millennial healthcare delivery.

Errors in technology

Upon initial analysis, the legal and ethical domains display a level of synchronization regarding the protection of patient data. As will be discussed below, however, their prevailing rationales either diverge or are used inconsistently.[7] As described in this section, both domains commit errors in their terminology and their operational approaches.

In the ethical domain Beauchamp and Childress describe a patient's right of privacy that is not limited to information about the person but extends to "zones of intimacy, secrecy, anonymity, seclusion, or solitude."[8] Similar observations populate the legal domain. However, unpacking the *legal* notion of privacy yields a picture that is both incoherent and incomplete, suggesting not only terminological flaws but also a considerable disconnect between ethical and legal constructs, a disconnect that seems heightened when we examine the protection of health *information*.

Legal and regulatory systems may potentially utilize three basic models for the protection of personal information: deidentification, collection control, and disclosure control. A deidentification model assumes (more or less correctly) that data that is *deidentified* prior to collection (or, somewhat less successfully, prior to disclosure)[9] reduces or eliminates *personal* risks associated with its use or processing. The second potential protective model is to place limitations on data *collection*. Such a model could, for example, prohibit all collection in certain circumstances (e.g., the harvesting of genetic information by life insurers) or limit collection via a proportionality rule (e.g., information necessary for purposes of treatment). The third protective model, again primarily focusing on informational privacy, is to place limitations on data *disclosure*. (e.g., hospital records may be disclosed to physicians but not drug companies).

Oddly, our legal systems are only dimly cognizant of the deidentification model. For example, while the federal standards are generally inapplicable to deidentified health information,[10] they do not *require* deidentification.[11] Even more surprisingly, the U.S. legal domain recognizes few collection-centric rules. For example, the Restatement's black-letter law of "privacy" provides as follows:

> The right of privacy is invaded by
> (a) unreasonable intrusion upon the seclusion of another … or

(b) appropriation of the other's name or likeness ... or
(c) unreasonable publicity given to the other's private life ... or
(d) publicity that unreasonably places the other in a false light before the public.[12]

This "right of privacy" promises far more than it delivers. On its face the Restatement fails to provide any general or comprehensive "right of privacy." It is no more than a listing of modest protections – nominate and discrete tort actions applicable in a narrow range of circumstances rather than fact-sensitive applications of a general principle or theory of privacy. Further, even a cursory examination of this "right of privacy," as it applies to health providers, suggests that only the protection against "unreasonable intrusion upon the seclusion of another" is in any way applicable.

Overall, this seclusion-based privacy model has seldom been applied to the health domain and its doctrinal elements limit its applicability to outlying cases. A commonly cited example of health privacy protection is *Estate of Berthiaume v. Pratt*,[13] where a physician was held to have intruded into a dying cancer patient's "physical or mental solitude or seclusion" when he took photographs against the patient's wishes. But even where the doctrine is generally applicable to a particular circumstance, the doctrine is quite restrictive. For example, in *Knight v. Penobscot Bay Medical Center*,[14] a nurse's husband arrived at a hospital to pick up his wife. To give him something to do while he waited, the husband was gowned and permitted to observe a stranger's labor and delivery. The plaintiff's cause of action failed because there was no evidence that the husband had *intended* the intrusion into the patient's seclusion. Only in extreme cases will privacy, as understood by the legal system, have an impact on patient health information. For example, in *Swarthout v. Mutual Service Life Insurance*,[15] the court held that the doctrine could apply when a life insurance company altered an applicant's medical information release, used it to obtain information from other sources, and transmitted the information to a medical-records database, which was available to other insurers.

In contrast to deidentification and collection, the third protective model, whereby limitations are placed on data *disclosure*, is well established in U.S. normative circles. For example, in the ethical domain, the American Medical Association (AMA) states that "[t]he physician should not reveal confidential communications or information without the consent of the patient, unless provided for by law or by the need to protect the welfare of the individual or the public interest."[16] Although frequently described in terms of "privacy" and "privacy law," the legal protections applied to patient health information by the common law, state statutes, or the federal standards have very little to do with either. Aside from a few "intrusion upon the seclusion" actions, the modern law of health privacy resides in the far narrower, disclosure-centric doctrine captured in cases, statutes, and regulations dealing with breach of confidence. A patient *exercises* his right of privacy (as recognized by the ethical domain) when he chooses to provide information to his physician (albeit a "right" that is illusory if it is a condition of treatment). Thereafter, dissemination of that information by the physician is limited by ethical *and* legal standards of confidence,[17] hereinafter referred to as confidentiality. Today, when courts and regulators speak of medical "privacy" they are usually in error, mislabeling obligations of "confidentiality."

Long before the promulgation of the federal standards, most states had developed common law[18] and statutory protections applicable to health information.[19] Languidly, the courts articulated a cause of action for breach of confidence. Decisions explained the distinction between defendants in privacy and confidence actions – "Only one who holds information in confidence can be charged with a breach of confidence. If an act qualifies as a tortious invasion of privacy, it theoretically could be committed by anyone."[20] Further decisions have clarified the differences between the types of data at issue in privacy and confidence proceedings: "Not every secret concerns personal or private information; commercial secrets are not personal, and governmental secrets are neither personal nor private. Secrecy involves intentional concealment. 'But privacy need not hide; and secrecy hides far more than what is private.'"[21]

Notwithstanding, the development of the common law of confidentiality has been "distinguished" by quite arcane discussions as to the correct doctrinal basis for protecting patient confidences (including implied contract, breach of a fiduciary relationship, and even "privacy"). Only recently could it be said that "[s]lowly and unevenly, through various gradations of evolution, courts ... moved toward the inevitable realization that an action for breach of confidence should stand in its own right, and increasingly courts have begun to adopt it as an independent tort in their respective jurisdictions."[22]

Generally, state statutory models have been more successful in reflecting the realities of modern healthcare delivery and the particular issues posed by informational privacy. Although still generally limited to a collection-centric approach (and hence frequently mislabeled as going to privacy rather than confidentiality), these statutes have tended to be more comprehensive and coherent than their common law progenitors. Such statutes frequently are more explicit in extending the duty of confidence to the myriad of providers and insurers involved in modern healthcare delivery. This is often accomplished by requiring written authorization for disclosure and making access available to the courts, law enforcement, and public health entities.[23] These state "privacy" statutes, however, have not supplanted the common law action for breach of confidence, primarily because most statutes do not permit a private right of action by patients.[24]

The federal standards apply to a broad range of "covered entities"[25] including, for example, health, but not life, insurers. These providers,[26] such as hospitals, physicians, and health plans, are subject to the regulations if they transmit health information "in electronic form in connection with a [HIPAA–EDI transaction]."[27] (See section Healthcare information: another domain unfolds, subsection Healthcare technologies for a discussion of HIPAA–EDI transactions.) The federal standards place limitations on the disclosure of "protected health information,"[28] including information that "relates to the past, present, or future physical or mental health or condition of an individual"[29] and identifies or could identify the individual.[30] Thereafter, the provider may only disclose private health information (PHI) as permitted by the federal standards.[31]

Unlike the situation at common law, the federal standards do not give patients a private right of action for unauthorized disclosures. Rather, enforcement of the disclosure rules is accomplished with a compliance model, detailing the appointment of a "privacy officer," the incorporation of staff training,[32] and the development and disclosure of "privacy" policies, all, generally, through complex regulatory oversight.[33] For providers, therefore, the federal "privacy" experience owes little to the general principles of confidentiality recognized in the ethical domain and moves closer to other "hated" oversight models such as those applying to patient dumping,[34] reimbursement, or fraud and abuse.[35] This is a theme that I return to below.[36]

An inadequate "privacy-confidence" rationale

In the ethical domain, the most cogent justification for privacy and confidentiality is the principle of autonomy. For example, Beauchamp and Childress argue that claims to privacy "are justified by rights of autonomous choice that are correlative to the obligations expressed in the principle of respect for autonomy"[37] As already noted,[38] in the information domain a patient exercises this autonomy-based right of privacy when he or she shares information with his or her physician and thereafter relies on ethical or legal standards of confidentiality to police subsequent disclosure. It is arguable that today's health confidence laws (particularly the federal standards) do not reference any underlying autonomy model. Rather, they are based on more limited and less satisfying instrumental models[39] and, worse, are increasingly justified on utilitarian constructs (specifically, "rule" Utilitarianism).

Of course, the autonomy rationale for privacy and confidentiality is not universally accepted, and the two principles have had their share of consequentialist and instrumentalist rationales.[40] Even Jay Katz's seminal account of patient autonomy admits that the "right to privacy – the right to keep one's thoughts and feelings to oneself"[41] must "bend to psychological autonomy"[42] so as to further autonomy's central goal of "respectful conversation."[43] Equally, Charles Fried's conception of privacy –

> To respect, love, trust, feel affection for others and to regard ourselves as the objects of love, trust and affection is at the heart of our notion of

> ourselves as persons among persons, and privacy is the necessary atmosphere for these attitudes and actions, as oxygen is for combustion[44]

– on which he bases a robust critique of instrumental (and primarily utilitarian) justifications for privacy is itself somewhat instrumentalist when it argues that "privacy is not just one possible means among others to insure some other value, but that it is necessarily related to ends and relations of the most fundamental sort; respect, love, friendship and trust."[45]

Instrumental justifications for medical privacy and confidentiality are simply stated. Thus, patients provide information to physicians in the belief that it will further their diagnosis and treatment while physicians respect confidences in order to encourage patients to disclose personal and medical information that will make diagnosis and treatment more effective. This justification may not be an entirely flawed way of looking at the physician–patient discourse. However, it is a notion that stumbles outside of the physician–patient paradigm and becomes unstable when applied in, for example, institutional or industrial models of care. In such models, the notion falls prey to modern utilitarian arguments that see the generation, dispersal, and processing of longitudinal patient health information primarily as a necessity to reduce overall healthcare costs and to minimize medical error. As the context changes, therefore, the simple and probably innocuous instrumental approach becomes increasingly utilitarian.

The current tensions in the medical privacy–confidentiality debate are somewhat reminiscent of familiar debates about the nature of informed consent. As described by Beauchamp and Childress, there is a vector between two senses of informed consent. In the first sense, "[a]n informed consent is an *autonomous authorization* by individuals of a medical intervention or of involvement in research.[46] In the second sense, consent is "analyzable in terms of *the social rules of consent* in the institutions that must obtain legally valid consent from patients or subjects before proceeding with therapeutic procedures or research."[47] Consider, for example, Braddock's view that informed consent primarily rotates around social rules, specifically legal notions:

> [T]he well-known mnemonic *PAR* reminds the clinician to disclose the nature of the procedure, alternatives, and risks in any informed consent discussion. The rationale of this approach either satisfies an administrative requirement or protects oneself from liability, rather than viewing the decision making process as a meaningful path toward fostering patient involvement.[48]

Thus, Braddock's observations capture a serious disconnect between the ethical and (common law and statutory) regulatory approaches to informed consent. Beauchamp and Childress argue "from the moral viewpoint, informed consent has less to do with the liability of professionals ... and more to do with the autonomous choices of patients and subjects."[49] Yet, ethical and legal domains continue to grow apart, increasing the vector between the autonomy rationale and social rules informed by legal rules and day-to-day operations. Informed consent law tends to focus on the narrow issue of "consent" rather than the disclosure of information that increases patient choice and participation. Only a few jurisdictions have recognized a broader approach, such as expanding the doctrine's reach to include all treatment risks[50] and other information such as non-medical risks,[51] risks of non-treatment,[52] and physician impairments.[53] Today, courts are far more likely to limit the duty to disclose to cases involving surgical risks.[54] In contrast, ethical observations on disclosure[55] or "choice"[56] are far more nuanced yet far truer to the autonomy rationale.

A similar vector can be detected in the medical confidentiality debate. The common law originally eschewed a rights-based approach, preferring to view breach of confidence as based on fidelity or implicit agreement. In contrast, the movement towards tort-based recovery for breach of confidence, an action recognized by a growing number of jurisdictions,[57] is clearly more rights-based and reminiscent of some of the early autonomy-based informed consent decisions.[58] Consider the frame established in one of the more influential common law confidentiality cases:

> [T]here is widespread public knowledge of the ethical standards of the medical profession and widespread belief that confidences made by a patient to a physician may not be disclosed without the permission of the patient. Patients ... have the right to rely on this common understanding of the ethical requirements which have been placed on the medical profession and to obtain damages against a physician if he violates such confidentiality.[59]

Outside of such private law constructs federal constitutional protections for privacy have been relatively slow to develop.[60] In contrast, a small number of states have specific constitutional protections that use rights-based language in the context of privacy, and some of these constitutional provisions have been applied with rigor in healthcare cases.[61]

Congress adopted what was promulgated as the HIPAA-EDI model of health transactions in order to reduce the "back-end," transactional costs of healthcare delivery. That mandate was accompanied by powers to promulgate protective standards not because of a principled commitment to patient privacy or confidentiality but to minimize objections to and maximize participation in a transactional model desired by industry and promoted by government.

Instrumental fingerprints are all over the federal standards. For example, as originally promulgated, the standards required that patients should consent to disclosure for treatment, payment, or healthcare operations (TPO) purposes.[62] As amended by the Bush administration, this requirement for consent was removed[63] and replaced by the permissive statement that "[a] covered entity may obtain consent of the individual to use or disclose protected health information to carry out treatment, payment, or health care operations."[64] Of course, the original regulation provided little meaningful protection for patients; for example, the required consent could be general and the provider could refuse to treat a patient who refuses consent.[65] However, the value of that initial permission was educational and empowering; it offered a symbolic privacy–confidentiality "moment" that conveyed a "rights" message in much the same way that the requirement of consent to procedures asserts the precedence of autonomy over paternalism.

The adoption of an almost exclusively instrumental approach is further evidenced by the federal government's choice of enforcement models. The federal standards (in common with the majority of state standards on which they are modeled)[66] do not provide an aggrieved patient with enforcement through a private right of action; they are merely a compliance mechanism with regulatory agency oversight and the potential for civil or criminal penalties.[67] The message is that any privacy-confidentiality "rights" belong to the healthcare system and not to patients.

The use of instrumental rationales for patient privacy and confidentiality likely will be increased as systems are introduced to reduce medical error. Process-driven, technologically enabled healthcare delivery seeks to minimize the role of the individual autonomous physician (and the correlate autonomous patient), replacing autonomy and choice with systems that identify while commoditizing patients (e.g., by positively identifying them with bar codes) and reducing discretion in treatment (e.g., by relying on Clinical Practice Guidelines and Clinical Decision Support Systems). Such technologies have a huge, potentially deleterious impact on individuals' privacy and confidentiality. Yet, they are likely to be accompanied by minimalist protections that, as with the federal standards in HIPAA, will be designed so as not to impede the overall error-reducing model, for example, by favoring outcomes research to further the greater good of population-based care.

Just as so many courts have moved informed consent away from autonomy and back towards a type of quasi-paternalism (limiting its applicability by fact-pattern[68] and using professional custom as its standard),[69] so the federal standards have gutted the nascent rights-based approach to privacy and confidentiality, preferring an instrumental rationale that is almost totally focused on institutions and compliance.

Distortions from the physician–patient touchstone

When medicine's professional hegemony was at its most dominant in the legal domain, described by Rand Rosenblatt as a model designed to "support the authority and autonomy of individual physicians engaged in the practice of medicine,"[70] it was supportive of *professional* rather than patient autonomy. In more modern times and even as this core commitment was deconstructed by the courts and ethicists,[71] the physician–patient relationship has continued to play a dominant role in shaping, but ultimately distorting, our privacy-confidentiality model.

As a legal construct, the "physician–patient relationship" was important in the development of confidentiality-based restraints but ultimately corrosive of any broader sense of health privacy. First, the physician–patient relationship paradigm has favored the development of confidentiality rather than privacy models. Second, as the myriad of new relationships and structures that we collectively think of as industrialized medicine took hold (and as market theory began to dominate health regulation),[72] the traditional professional model had been reduced to a primarily operational concept with little or nothing to protect patient information. As a result and as healthcare delivery metamorphosed, industrial providers, who faced few ethical or legal constraints, began to exploit patient information for utilitarian or outright commercial purposes. This negative process can be seen as the product of how the physician–patient relationship developed in overlapping domains and the increasingly fragmented care offered by modern delivery systems.

Overlapping domains and a "race to the bottom"

As an ethical construct the physician–patient relationship is neither monolithic nor singular. Different interpretations or models of the relationship have ranged from those that emphasize paternalism or friendship to the merely technical ("plumber"), amongst several metaphors.[73] Notwithstanding, it is the foundation of competence, respect, and confidence.[74] Thus, the ethical principles provide that, "The patient has the right to confidentiality. The physician should not reveal confidential communications or information without the consent of the patient, unless provided for by law or by the need to protect the welfare of the individual or the public interest."[75]

In the legal domain, the "physician–patient relationship" synopsizes the contractual responsibilities of the parties (such as beginning and end, terms of service and payment), limits the physician's externalization of patient-incurred treatment or informational risks,[76] and defines and delimits various tort or fiduciary-based legal prescriptions ("duties").[77] The transposition of this professional (or ethical) paradigm into legal doctrine did much to preserve medicine's professional hegemony. For example, in the quality domain, it has been used to limit physician duties, impose internal professional standards (as dispositive of quality questions), and demote the importance of institutional responsibility.[78] Compared to the nuanced explication of the ethical domain, the legal domain's use of the physician–patient relationship has been far simpler, essentially contractual in its metaphor, and paternalistic in its policy. Crucially, given the simple delivery model of the physician–patient relationship, confidence arguably sufficed and any broader sense of legal protection of medical privacy was stillborn.

In the operational domain, the physician–patient relationship became synonymous with a simpler model; an ongoing relationship of care and treatment. This concept of "continuity of care" did not denote permanence but was founded on more than, say, the opportunistic prescribing relationship that a patient would have with a physician prescribing drugs on the Internet.[79] It was not a sophisticated state; rather, it identified the parties, denoted access to the patient's history, and highlighted purely operational requirements such as updating records. Instrumental justifications for medical confidence flourished in this operational domain. As already noted, "confidentiality" in this domain has tended to rotate around two co-dependent, practical imperatives: patients disclosing information to physicians to seek protection of their health and physicians respecting confidences in order to encourage patients to disclose needed personal and medical information.

In traditional, pre-industrial medicine, these three domains, ethical, legal, and operational, were essentially synchronized. In context, the parallelism between legal, ethical, and operational domains was not particularly harmful. The physician–patient relationship was not forced to deal with competition or conflict between the domains. But, as a practical matter, patient confidentiality was respected even though the rationale may have been instrumental and the model somewhat paternalistic. Over time, however, I believe that physicians, while cognizant and respectful of the ethical domain (albeit not particularly troubled by nascent legal rules on confidentiality), have primarily viewed confidentiality as a function or property of the operational domain. There was a slide to the lowest common denominator as the practical imperatives of the physician–patient relationship operation overshadowed and ultimately diminished the contributions of the ethical and legal domains. Consider, by way of example, how the AMA's Council on Ethical and Judicial Affairs (CEJA) undercuts its policy on confidentiality – "[t]he information disclosed to a physician during the course of the relationship between physician and patient is confidential to the greatest possible degree" – with the instrumental observation that "[t]he patient should feel free to make a full disclosure of information to the physician in order that the physician may most effectively provide needed services."[80]

By the time that the physician–patient relationship was replaced as the dominant delivery paradigm, little was left but operationally derived instrumental values. Legal conceptions of confidence and privacy were limited or underdeveloped, while the dominant instrumental values were ill prepared for a transition to new models of care.

The ascendancy of fragmented care

The reasons cited to explain the decline of the physician–patient relationship are legion. Twenty years ago James Childress and Mark Siegler explained this phenomenon as follows:

> Numerous causes can be identified: First, the pluralistic nature of our society; second, the decline of close, intimate contact over time among professionals and patients and their families; third, the decline of contact with the "whole person," who is now parceled out to various specialists; fourth, the growth of large, impersonal, bureaucratically structured institutions of care, in which there is discontinuity of care ... [81]

To this catalogue we can add the growth of managed care (not to mention its potential for conflicts of interest and the vertical and horizontal integration it encouraged), an increase in the use of ambulatory care (which is episodic in nature and less stable as to its location), and the insertion of "new" players into the medical industrial complex, such as government rationing care, pharmaceutical companies seeking direct relationships with patients, and web advice sites[82] and online pharmacies[83] ignoring traditional channels. Interestingly, perhaps even ironically, a very similar catalogue (the emergence of managed care, the rise of ambulatory care, and the horizontal and vertical integration of providers into delivery systems) today is used to explain the emergence of technologically mediated care, particularly Electronic Health Records (EHR) systems.[84] These developments bring with them their own problems, as discussed below.[85]

Many of these changes, particularly the emergence of "shared care" (denoting that a patient should share responsibility with his or her provider for care)[86] may be viewed as potentially beneficial and the beginning of a new contracting model of autonomy between rational actors involved in healthcare. In the interim, however, they point to a new healthcare delivery paradigm with primarily negative short-term implications – *fragmented* care delivered in a medico-industrial setting.

Ethicists have long recognized the deterioration of the traditional physician–patient relationship, and its (regrettable) shift from a relationship of intimates to encounters between strangers. As James Childress and Mark Siegler noted:

> Whether medicine is now only a series of encounters between strangers rather than intimates, medicine is increasingly regarded by patients and doctors, and by analysts of the profession – such as philosophers, lawyers, and sociologists – as a practice that is best understood and regulated *as if it were* a practice among strangers rather than among intimates.[87]

A concept of privacy-confidentiality protection that is bound to an outdated conception of the confidence inherent in a single physician–patient relationship was bound to fail when the physician–patient relationship was replaced by fragmented care. Domain synchronization evaporated, and it is unlikely that patients comprehended the extent of their "agreement" to disclose given the institutional settings within which their information was destined to circulate.[88] Equally, patients are unlikely to understand the level of information processing, such as commercial aggregation,[89] that such settings employ or facilitate. At a time of uncertainty (and, specifically, informational asymmetry), it was hopeful that the legal domain would operate as a corrective, by supplying "rights." As already noted, however, the legal domain failed to develop meaningful privacy protections and a rights-based approach to breach of confidence was slow to develop.[90] Breach of confidence was far slower to develop, for example, than informed consent, its autonomy-based fellow traveler. This legal vacuum created the opportunity for the federal standards. Unfortunately, this opportunity came in an atmosphere that by now stressed operational (and hence instrumental) goals rather than the broad principles reflected in ethical or legal rights-based approaches.

Healthcare information: another domain unfolds

It is too early to assess the final impact of the ongoing healthcare technology revolution but, inevitably, aspects of the delivery system will be fundamentally changed. Two key sets of technologies are at issue here. The first can be viewed as disruptive – technologies that replace traditional methods of delivery. These include web-based medical content, online consultations, and Internet-prescribing. The second is more integrative – the leveraging of information technologies (IT) by traditional healthcare providers to improve the quality of care and reduce its cost structure. Both sets bring with them difficult privacy issues. Thus, disruptive technologies, in large part because of their novelty, tend to create issues that our ethical and legal constructs have generally failed to address.[91] For example, non-traditional providers, such as those engaged in Internet advice or prescribing generally are not covered by disclosure-centric confidentiality regulation.[92]

Healthcare technologies

Privacy and confidentiality issues are particularly highlighted by the second cluster of technologies as traditional providers increasingly adopt IT models. In pre-industrial, pre-IT medicine, patient-specific health data was proprietary and non-integrated. Physicians owned their patients' data (both health and billing information)[93] and as a result, data collection models were inconsistent, the data itself was incomplete, and storage was fragmented across the information silos of multiple providers. In contrast, information technologies are built on the premise that processes are improved (both as to outcomes and process efficiencies) by maximizing the collection of information, consolidating or linking information silos (creating longitudinal patient data), and making the information available to multiple users in comparable form and through common and consistent interfaces. U.S. healthcare is in the throes of a fundamental transition to IT-dominated models for healthcare transactions, risk-management, and record keeping.

As already noted, HIPAA's "Administrative Simplification" seeks to improve "the efficiency and effectiveness of the health care system, by encouraging the development of a health information system through the establishment of standards and requirements for the electronic transmission of certain health information." To reduce "back-end" costs associated with billing, reimbursement, eligibility inquiries, insurance claims, and prescription fulfillment,[94] HIPAA adopted the e-commerce model of Electronic Data Interchange (EDI) – the electronic exchange of standardized business documents (or messages) between "trading partners." The HIPAA-EDI requires healthcare-specific data standards:[95] unique identifiers for healthcare providers, health plans, employers, and patients;[96] specific message formats for healthcare transactions such as enrollment, eligibility, payment and remittance advice, claims, health plan premium payments, health claim status, and referral certification and authorization;[97] transaction codes (for example, benefit denial or additional information requested) that are used within the messages; and common formats for healthcare claims attachments (such as excerpts from medical records) and information about diagnoses and treatment.

HIPAA-EDI may have been the first major federal e-health initiative with serious implications for medical information privacy and confidentiality, but it will not be the last. The publication of major national studies of medical error rates[98] has led to broad calls for amelioratory systems or process redesign of healthcare delivery.[99] The resultant, and now rapid, massive infusion of technology into healthcare is a key component in process-based reform.[100] This IT-led system reform is centered on several intersecting technologies. "Tracking" or identifying technologies such as barcodes and Radio Frequency Identification (RFID) positively identify drugs, dosages, and patients.[101] "Entry" technologies consist of computerized physician order entry (CPOE) systems that seek to avoid medication errors caused by illegibility and other recording mistakes.[102] Clinical Decision Support Systems (CDSS)[103] are evolved order entry systems that have lost their passivity and reference drug interaction information, EHR data, or treatment models (such as clinical practice guidelines), and which offer considerable advantages over simple CPOE systems.[104] "Reporting" systems provide for adverse event and medical error disclosure and reporting,[105] and facilitate population-based healthcare models and outcomes research.[106]

On April 26, 2004, President Bush announced his goal of assuring that most Americans will have electronic health records within the next ten years.[107] To this end, the President appointed a National Health Information Technology Coordinator to guide the "nationwide implementation of interoperable health information technology."[108] The EHR is a database record that incorporates a patient's healthcare details from conception to death (i.e., it is longitudinal) and can be distributed over a number of sites or aggregated at a particular source.[109] It is a core technology promoted by the patient-safety movement in large part because it will provide much-needed cohesion for decision-support systems, error reporting, and outcomes research.[110]

Managing privacy in the health information domain

In pre-IT times and consistent with an operational paradigm of fragmented record-keeping, the legal protection of patient data was achieved principally through a physician–patient relationship disclosure-centric rule, expressed as breach of confidence and operationalized through implied contract or torts doctrine. Even given the relative weakness of the disclosure-centric confidentiality model or assuming its occasional breach, patient "privacy" was somewhat protected by the sheer inefficiencies of a system built around unstructured, distributed patient data.

This paradigm has now been overwhelmed by the realities of the modern health information domain. The patient data contained in modern longitudinal systems is comprehensive, portable, and manipulatable. The potential for abuse is immense; there are many parties (pharmaceutical companies and government being the obvious examples) that crave access to this data. As a result, the privacy and confidentiality costs potentially incurred by patients rise exponentially.

The emerging health information domain has several key properties that extend beyond the confidentiality inherent in the physician–patient relationship.[111] In addition to the confidentiality–privacy–anonymity triumvirate that protects (or should protect) the basic input and output of patient data, the contemporary health information domain has (or should possess) several additional properties (or qualities). These protective rules give rise to "process" controls such as "security" (a confidentiality correlate that restricts access to data to those authorized to receive it) and "integrity" (data "checksum" validation and protection against unauthorized modification). As data is aggregated, additional properties such as "unity," "quality," and "accountability" become paramount because information domains lose their value proposition when they are incomplete or their data is otherwise flawed. "Unity" refers to health information that is "longitudinal," consisting of records from various providers that are consolidated or interlinked to provide a comprehensive view of a patient's healthcare encounters. A longitudinal approach provides the data necessary to interface with other technologies (such as CDSS) that analyze diagnoses and treatments and support shared care from multiple providers. "Quality" denotes that the data must be current or timely and subject to quality auditing from extrinsic sources such as clinical practice guidelines. Finally, the "accountability" property denotes not only substantive responsibility by providers for the accuracy of the data they enter but also procedural identification of providers responsible for specific data.

The modern health information domain must also take into account and integrate the increasing demands for access to the data it contains. Thus, the "access" property describes the various recognized claims to view and, in some cases, modify patient information. Justice and public health systems make the most persistent claims. However, most mature health information domains also recognize patients' rights of access and correction of their own data. Outcomes assessment and error-reporting mandates will substantially increase demands for access to individual and population-based health records from accreditation bodies and government regulators.

What the discussions of privacy and confidentiality in the context of transaction standards, error reduction, and electronic health records have in common is a heavily instrumental approach to health information. This is because the IT revolution that has brought about the health information domain has less to do with improving or increasing patient access to services and more with business imperatives. Such imperatives include reducing healthcare transaction costs (the expenses associated with medical errors), the inefficiencies associated with multiple providers, and changing roles of physicians in a managed care environment.[112] As a result, individual autonomy tends to be viewed as subordinate to broader goals (e.g., lower costs and a reduction in medical errors) that may or may not directly benefit the individual involved.

When it came time (during the HIPAA debate) to force providers to internalize some of the privacy risks associated with new technologies, it was perhaps inevitable that federal architects would eschew traditional "rights" approaches and strike a new direction. After all, and as already discussed,[113] the physician–patient relationship model of privacy-confidentiality protection had become operational rather than principled, and the common law models were unsophisticated and underdeveloped. There is every indication that any new privacy protections that are clustered around the emerging EHR model will adopt a similar style and correspondingly lower the level of protection. It does not have to be this way. For example, the ongoing Australian EHR experiment, known as Health*Connect*,[114] eschews utilitarianism for models clearly based on a "contracting" autonomy model. Health*Connect* is a "push" system, selectively sending data to a centralized record, and the patient controls which elements of the centralized record may be used for what purposes or displayed in which "views."[115] The Australian model does not create a comprehensive longitudinal record. Rather, patients, with their providers, choose which elements may be extracted from an existing health record and transferred to their separate but centralized Health*Connect* record.

In contrast, what is striking about the administrative standards and compliance mechanisms of the U.S. federal standards is the relatively low level of patient protection they contain; the complex regulations read more like a catalogue of exceptions than of rights.

Professional hegemony, compliance, and distrust

In the last few decades, healthcare's legal domain has experienced its most fundamental revolution; a change from profession-dominated medical boards and *ex post facto* torts regulation (based on professional standards) to regulatory systems that not only are frequently federal rather than state but also use a "command-control" approach. This regulation began as a way of pushing the health system during what Rand Rosenblatt has labeled the "egalitarian social contract" model of health law[116] and, thereafter, as a method of reducing market distortions in the same author's "market competition" model.[117] It represents a fundamental shift from hegemony to compliance-based legal regulation. Once confidentiality, courtesy of the federal standards, joined the regulatory matrix, it became a target for those who criticize the level and style of governmental regulation of healthcare.

Unsupportive regulation

Mark Hall has provided one modern theoretical context for this battle over privacy and confidentiality. In an influential article, Hall has argued that "trust" can be an organizing principle (or at least a dominant theme) for health law.[118] He premises this "centrality" of trust on both instrumental ("Trust is the core, defining characteristic of the doctor–patient relationship – the 'glue' that holds the relationship together and makes it possible")[119] and therapeutic (both empirical and jurisprudential) grounds.[120]

Hall regards "trust" in healthcare as the Mary Tyler Moore Show viewed love in Minneapolis. Thus, "[trust] is all around, no need to waste it"[121] is the foundation for his contractarian attack on healthcare regulation.[122] Hall categorizes health law principles as predicated on, supportive of, or skeptical of trust.[123] In this matrix, Hall views confidentiality laws as attempts to support trust and argues they are unnecessary because of the existence of trust or because they frustrate the role of trust in promoting market approaches to securing the appropriate level of confidentiality and privacy.[124] Further, he views both the traditional common law of confidence and the federal standards as "explicitly premised on the therapeutic need to reassure patients that they can trust their physicians with sensitive, embarrassing, or even incriminating information, rather than on inherent rights arising from the mere expectation of privacy."[125]

As follows from the discussion above, Hall's description of modern health privacy-confidentiality law is partially correct; it *is* based on instrumental values rather than, say, autonomy.[126] However, that does not amount to an approval of such a theoretical basis. Further, the instrumental values displayed by the federal standards are not, as Hall states, "therapeutic" but far more utilitarian in character.[127] Greg Bloche meets Hall's approach head-on:

> A large body of scholarship and caselaw treats privacy as a right, important for personal dignity and psychological welfare. The law's protection for medical privacy follows from this more general right. Yet Hall disregards both the existence of this right and its grounding in the law's concern for citizens' dignity and mental well-being. . . . [A]ll that matters for Hall in evaluating the need for these (and other)

> legal protections for medical privacy is whether these safeguards do in fact promote trust. The actual protection these safeguards provide for citizens' privacy interests does not count within Hall's evaluative framework, since these interests, in themselves, are not part of his framework.[128]

Bloche's painting of Hall as a cardboard contractarian is tempting because of the latter's "over-selling" of "trust"; his trust hypothesis is just that, and he fails to provide convincing evidence or arguments that "trust" is more important, illuminating, or unifying than traditional ethical and legal underpinnings such as autonomy, rights-analysis, or social contract theories. Yet, "trust" *is* appealing. It is common to most of the positive metaphors that are used to explicate the physician–patient relationship (such as friendship and negotiation) and so is worthy of Hall's "glue" appellation. It is also a comforting aspiration, something that combines therapeutic soundness with the potential to rehabilitate some of the more corrosive states of the healthcare delivery system.

"Trust," however, is not a current state, and Hall's empirical evidence[129] may be premature because there is good reason to suspect growing patient *distrust* of healthcare providers. For example, a 2004 poll found that the reputations of pharmaceutical and health insurance companies continue to slide precipitously.[130] When asked specifically about the extent of their trust for healthcare providers, fifty-nine percent of Americans replied that they distrusted health insurers and forty-one percent distrusted pharmaceutical companies. While physicians and nurses fared better, some forty percent of those polled did not trust them "a lot."[131] Furthermore, patient concerns about the security and privacy of their health information continue to be significant in surveys measuring patient satisfaction in technologically mediated care.[132] Finally, his approach is fundamentally flawed in treating contemporary issues of health information privacy today as essentially similar to those in pre-IT healthcare. To the contrary, and as noted by architects of the United Kingdom's new health information system,

> [T]rust relating to the use of data needs to be earned. In practice this means health professionals need to understand current anxieties about the ways in which health information is handled; they need to learn the rules and apply them and accept that unfettered access to personal health information is a thing of the past and that, among the many tools they need for modern clinical practice are those of skilled information management.[133]

Patients, physicians, and regulators alike are nervous and skeptical about the new demands placed on health information. Unfortunate and debilitating of the therapeutic relationship it may be, but today, it is distrust that is all around.

Limitations and gaps

Hall classifies the federal standards within his matrix as attempts to be "supportive" of trust. More extreme anti-regulatory contractarians might view those same standards as attracting Hall's more damning categorization of a type of health law, as "skeptical of trust."[134] Market proponents should be able to argue that such information regulation imposes immense costs whose benefits have not been bargained for and distort healthcare markets by impeding provider–provider arrangements. Indeed, twenty years ago Richard Posner criticized "economically perverse legislative responses to privacy issues,"[135] arguing against a "trend toward elevating personal and downgrading organizational privacy."[136]

The transition to HIPAA-EDI and the federal standards has not been easy. Implementation woes continue, as a result of missing or delayed claims, non-standardized transactions, multiple party processing, and unsuccessful massaging by clearinghouses.[137] The AMA has even set up an online system to facilitate complaints.[138] Regarding privacy, there are frequent reports that the federal standards are impeding the delivery of healthcare,[139] and the Centers for Medicare & Medicaid Services (CMS) is continually updating its web site to answer detailed questions about the applicability of the privacy standards.[140] Even avid supporters of the federal standards would find it difficult to disagree with the scathing comments of Senator Larry Craig that "as is often the case with federal rulemaking, a kernel of congressional intent has grown into a towering tree of regulatory complexity. But even by federal bureaucratic standards, HIPAA is extraordinary."[141] Not surprisingly, some healthcare providers, although avowing support for patient confidentiality, have challenged the validity of the federal standards[142] with no more success than the medical privacy advocates who challenged the Bush administration amendments.[143]

In fact, there are some very real criticisms that should be aimed at the federal standards – not criticisms of regulatory inappropriateness but, rather, under-regulation and a level of complexity that diminish the educative value of the standards. The catalogue of HIPAA privacy blunders is large and that which follows is not an exhaustive list. First, the privacy architecture seems backwards; it concentrates almost exclusively on the *process* of patient consent to disclosure. A privacy regime should be more *substantively* concerned with limiting the collection and dissemination of personal health information. Only at the margins should questions of patient consent to disclosure need to be addressed. Further, as already detailed, the Bush administration removed an already weak consent-to-disclosure provision, thus, denying a privacy-autonomy "moment" at the commencement of the provider–patient relationship.[144] Second, although HIPAA confidentiality is premised on national standards, limitations in the enabling legislation prevented the inclusion of patient protective features extant in some state laws. Unwilling to detract from existing privacy protections, the drafters constructed a confusing and operationally obstructive "more stringent" partial preemption rule.[145] The result is that simply establishing the applicable standard of health privacy protection in a particular state requires complex (and ongoing) analysis. Third, and true to their instrumental rationale, the federal standards apply broad exceptions (public health, judicial, and regulatory) where patient consent to data processing is not required.[146] Fourth, the privacy standards are still too lax regarding secondary uses of patient information. There are still many unrestricted uses of patient information outside of treatment and billing; in too many situations patient consent for secondary uses is not required[147] and in other situations, consideration should have been given to prohibiting some consented-to secondary uses (e.g., the sale of patient data for pharmaceutical marketing).

Above all, the standards lack transparency and clarity. They may be labeled as promotional of "privacy" (in fact mislabeled because they deal only in confidentiality) but their sheer weight and obliqueness detracts from any educative or principled "message." With all the amendments, the combined privacy and security standards now consist of fifty-five pages of dense regulatory language.[148] By way of contrast, the Australian Health Privacy Principles, which provide far more protection of health information using both collection-centric and disclosure-centric models, take up a mere nine pages of text.[149] What was required of the federal standards was a more generalized statement of principle based clearly on an autonomy-focused rationale; a legal guarantee that patients have control of their health information. Exceptions should have been far more narrowly constructed and tightly controlled by concepts of proportionality and relevance to medical and billing services.

The health insurance crises of the last three decades likely fueled the decision to omit a private right of action for breach of the federal standards. But, clearly stated rights and duties have an important educational value that is not captured by *pro forma* privacy notices, and caps on recovery (or other limitations) would have been a better tool of litigation-management. A far better model would have been to appoint an independent, statutorily authorized patient privacy advocate, such as the Australian Federal Privacy Commissioner,[150] Ontario's Information & Privacy Commissioner,[151] or the United Kingdom's Information Commissioner,[152] who could investigate consumer complaints, attempt to mediate disputes, and where necessary apply sanctions.

Conclusion

Of course there are more problems with health privacy than detailed in this chapter. As I have argued elsewhere, aggressive plaintiffs' lawyers likely will now add common law or per se styled breach of privacy allegations in medical error cases, just as duty to warn counts now routinely turn up in products liability actions and as informed consent counts are used to buttress lackluster surgical or medication error cases. Also, it is likely that plaintiffs will use any knowledge they have of provider non-compliance with the federal regulations – along with all of the penalty ramifications that brings – as leverage to negotiate a settlement in tangentially related malpractice cases.[153]

Admittedly, my litany of complaints about the state of health privacy and healthcare delivery is not entirely consistent. For example, I bemoan the decline of the physician–patient relationship because of its negative impact on the development of privacy, yet I welcome the breakdown of professional hegemony. While this chapter may paint a dire picture of technologically mediated care impacting patient information, here and elsewhere I have been an advocate for technological models.

The goal here, however, is modest. To combine the normative and descriptive aspects of this chapter's ambiguous title, if there's nothing wrong with health privacy why isn't it what it seems, why aren't its foundation stronger, why is it likely to get worse before it gets better, and why can't we explain the goals and basic principles of modern health privacy law to patients and providers in just a few sentences? The answers to those questions suggest to me that health privacy lies in a fragile state.

Notes

1 Copyright © 2004, Nicolas Paul Terry. All Rights Reserved. I thank Kathy Cerminara, Tim Greaney, and Trevor Wear for their helpful comments on an earlier draft, and Brian Bohnenkamp for his research assistance.
2 45 C.F.R. §§ 160, 164 (2003).
3 *Remarks by the President on Medical Privacy*, Press Release, Office of the Press Secretary (Dec. 20, 2000), http://www.hhs.gov/ocr/whpress.html (accessed Sept. 20, 2004).
4 Health Insurance Portability and Accountability Act of 1996, Pub. L No. 104–91, 110 Stat. 1988 (codified as amended in scattered sections of 29 U.S.C., 42 U.S.C. and 18 U.S.C.).
5 42 U.S.C.S. § 1320d-2(d)(2) (1996).
6 Nicolas P. Terry, *Privacy and the Health Information Domain: Properties, Models and Unintended Results*, 10 Eur. J. Health L. 223, 223 (2003) [hereinafter *Health Information Domain*].
7 Tom L. Beauchamp & James F. Childress, Principles of Biomedical Ethics 410 (4th ed., OUP 1994) [hereinafter Beauchamp & Childress].
8 Beauchamp & Childress, *supra* n. 7, at 408. This is reflected in *Privacy in the Context of Health Care*, AMA CEJA E-5.059, http://www.ama-assn.org/apps/pf_new/pf_online?f_n=browse&doc=policyfiles/HnE/E-5.059.HTM&&s_t=&st_p=&nth=1&prev_pol=policyfiles/HnE/E-4.07.HTM&nxt_pol=policyfiles/HnE/E-5.01.htm& (accessed Sept. 23, 2004).

> ... Physicians must seek to protect patient privacy in all of its forms, including (1) physical, which focuses on individuals and their personal spaces, (2) informational, which involves specific personal data, (3) decisional, which focuses on personal choices, and (4) associational, which refers to

family or other intimate relations. Such respect for patient privacy is a fundamental expression of patient autonomy and is a prerequisite to building the trust that is at the core of the patient–physician relationship.

9 Primarily because of questions as to the level of identifier-stripping necessary to create deidentified data. For example, "anonymized" data is not deidentified.
10 45 C.F.R § 164.514(a) ("Health information that does not identify an individual and with respect to which there is no reasonable basis to believe that the information can be used to identify an individual is not individually identifiable health information.").
11 In contrast, for example, European law requires that cell phone customers be allowed to request non-itemized billing and requires providers to anonymize data that it collects regarding a user's location.
Directive 2002/58/EC of the European Parliament and of the Council of July 12, 2002, Official Journal of the European Communities, L 201, 31/07/2002 P. 0037 – 0047, http://europa.eu.int/eur-lex/pri/en/oj/dat/2002/l_201/l_20120020731 en00370047.pdf (accessed Sept. 20, 2004) (concerning the processing of personal data and the protection of privacy in the electronic communications sector (Directive on privacy and electronic communications)).
12 Restatement (Second) of Torts § 652A(2) (1965).
13 365 A.2d 792 (Me. 1976).
14 420 A.2d 915 (Me. 1980).
15 632 N.W.2d 741 (Minn. Ct. App. 2001).
16 American Medical Association, *E-10.01 Fundamental Elements of the Patient–Physician Relationship*, Report of the Council on Ethical and Judicial Affairs of the American Medical Association. Principle #4, http://www.ama-assn.org/ama/pub/category/8313.html (originally adopted June 1990; updated 1993) (accessed Aug. 18, 2004) [hereinafter *Fundamental Elements*].
17 Beauchamp & Childress, *supra* n. 7, at 410. It may also be limited by express agreement between the parties.
18 *See e.g. Humphers v. First Interstate Bank of Oregon*, 298 Or. 706, 696 P.2d 527 (Or. 1985); *Biddle v. Warren Gen. Hosp.*, 86 Ohio St.3d 395, 715 N.E.2d 518 (Ohio 1999); *Givens v. Mullikin ex rel. Estate of McElwaney*, 75 S.W.3d 383, 2002 WL 451822 (Tenn. 2002); *Alberts v. Devine*, 479 N.E.2d 113 (Mass. 1985); *Hurvitz v. Hoefflin*, 101 Cal. Rptr. 2d 558 (Cal. Ct. App. 2001); *Tadlock & Keeney*, 101 Cal. Rptr. 2d 916 (Cal. Ct. App. 2000); *Anonymous v. CVS Corp.*, 728 N.Y.S.2d 333 (N.Y. Sup. Ct. 2001); *McCormick v. England*, 494 S.E.2d 431 (S.C. Ct. App. 1997); *Berger v. Sonneland*, 26 P.3d 257 (Wash. 2001).
19 *See e.g.* Cal. Civ. Code §§ 56–56.37 (West 2001); Haw. Rev. Stat. Ann. § 323(c) (Michie 2001); Mont. Code Ann. §§ 50-16-501 to 16-553 (2003); Wash. Rev. Code Ann. §§ 70.02.005 to .02.904 (West 2003); Wis. Stat. § 146.83 (2001).
20 *Humphers v. First Interstate Bank of Oregon*, 298 Or. 706, 696 P.2d 527 (Or. 1985).
21 *Id.* at 529.
22 *Biddle v. Warren Gen. Hosp.*, 86 Ohio St.3d 395, 715 N.E.2d 518, 523 (Ohio 1999).
23 *See e.g.* Cal. Civ. Code § 56.10.
24 A small number of state statutes do allow such an action. *See e.g.* Wis. Stat. § 146.84(c) (2001) ("An individual may bring an action to enjoin any violation of § 146.82 or 146.83 or to compel compliance with § 146.82 or 146.83 and may, in the same action on, seek damages as provided in this subsection."). *See also* Cal. Civ. Code § 56.35 (West 2001); Haw. Rev. Stat. Ann. § 323(c) (Michie 2001).
25 45 C.F.R. § 164.502(1).

26 Defined in 45 C.F.R. § 160.103.
27 45 C.F.R. § 160.102.
28 45 C.F.R. § 164.501.
29 45 C.F.R. § 160.103.
30 45 C.F.R. § 164.501.
31 45 C.F.R. § 164.502(a).
32 45 C.F.R. § 164.530.
33 45 C.F.R. §§ 160.300 to .312.
34 *See e.g.* Emergency Medical Treatment and Active Labor Act, 42 U.S.C.A. § 1395dd.
35 *See e.g.* Medicare & Medicaid Anti-Kickback Statute, 42 U.S.C. §1320a-7b(b); Ethics in Patient Referrals Act (STARK), 42 U.S.C. §1395nn.
36 *See infra* text accompanying n. 116, *et seq.*
37 Beauchamp & Childress, *supra* n. 7, at 410.
38 *Supra*, text accompanying n. 17.
39 *Id.* at 409–10.
40 Beauchamp & Childress, *supra* n. 7, at 409–24.
41 Jay Katz, The Silent World of Doctor and Patient, 127 (The Free Press 1984).
42 *Id.* at 128.
43 *Id.* at 141–42.
44 Charles Fried, *Privacy [A Moral Analysis]*, 77 Yale L. J. 475 (1968); *reprinted in* Philosophical Dimensions of Privacy: An Anthology 203, 205 (Ferdinand D. Schoeman, Ed., Cambridge University Press 1984).
45 *Id.*
46 Beauchamp & Childress, *supra* n. 7, at 143.
47 *Id.* at 144.
48 Clarence H. Braddock, III, Kelly A. Edwards, Nicole M. Hasenberg, Tracy L. Laidley & Wendy Levinson, *Informed Decision Making in Outpatient Practice: Time to Get Back to Basics*, 282 J.A.M.A. 2313, 2313–14 (1999).
49 Beauchamp & Childress, *supra* n. 7, at 146.
50 *See e.g. Matthies v. Mastromonaco*, 733 A.2d 456, 464 (N.J. 1999):

> It is not dispositive that the alternative that the physician recommends is more or less invasive than other alternatives. . . . The critical consideration is not the invasiveness of the procedure, but the patient's need for information to make a reasonable decision about the appropriate course of medical treatment, whether invasive or noninvasive.

51 *See e.g. Arato v. Avedon*, 858 P.2d 598, 599–600 (Cal. 1993) (declining to require mandatory disclosure of life expectancy in case where physician allegedly failed to discuss the low life expectancy of a patient suffering from pancreatic cancer).
52 *See e.g. Truman v. Thomas*, 611 P.2d 902, 907 (Cal. 1980) (holding that physician had a duty to provide the decedent with all information material to her decision whether or not to undergo pap smear diagnostic test). *Cf. Vandi v. Permanente Med. Group, Inc.*, 9 Cal. Rptr. 2d 463, 467 (Cal. Ct. App. 1992) (holding that the duty of disclosure is predicated upon a recommended treatment or diagnostic procedure and the failure to recommend a procedure must be addressed under ordinary medical negligence standards).
53 *See e.g. Johnson by Adler v. Kokemoor*, 545 N.W.2d 495, 498 (Wis. 1996).
54 *See e.g. Morgan v. MacPhail*, 704 A.2d 617, 618 (Pa. 1997) (holding that informed consent was not required in cases involving non-surgical procedures). *See also Duttry v. Patterson*, 771 A.2d 1255, 1259 (Pa. 2001) ("[T]he doctrine of informed consent is not the legal panacea for all damages arising out of any type of malfeasance by a physician.").

55 Beauchamp & Childress, *supra* n. 7, at 145–50.

56 Robert M. Veatch, *Abandoning Informed Consent*, 25(2) Hastings Ctr. Rep., 5, 5 (Mar./Apr. 1995) ("Consent may be what can be called a transition concept, one that appears on the scene as an apparently progressive innovation, but after a period of experience turns out to be only useful as a transition to a more thoroughly revisionary conceptual framework.").

57 *See e.g. Hurvitz v. Hoefflin*, 101 Cal. Rptr. 2d 558 (Cal. Ct. App. 2001); *Jeffrey H. v. Imai, Tadlock & Keeney*, 101 Cal. Rptr. 2d 916 (Cal. Ct. App. 2000); *Anonymous v. CVS Corp.*, 728 N.Y.S.2d 333 (N.Y. Sup. Ct. 2001); *Biddle v. Warren Gen. Hosp.*, 715 N.E.2d 518 (Ohio 1999); *McCormick v. England*, 494 S.E.2d 431 (S.C. Ct. App. 1997); *Berger v. Sonneland*, 26 P.3d 257 (Wash. 2001).

58 *See e.g. Canterbury v. Spence*, 464 F.2d 772 (DC Cir. 1972); *Cobbs v. Grant*, 8 Cal. 3d 229, 104 Cal. Rptr. 505, 502 P.2d 1 (1972).

59 *Humphers v. First Interstate Bank of Oregon*, 684 P.2d 581, 587 (Or. Ct. App. 1984), aff'd in part, rev'd in part, 298 Or. 706, 696 P.2d 527 (Or. 1985). *See also Duquette v. Superior Court In and For County of Maricopa*, 778 P.2d 634, 640 (Ariz. Ct. App. 1989) ("[T]he public has a widespread belief that information given to a physician in confidence will not be disclosed to third parties absent legal compulsion, and we further believe that the public has a right to have this expectation realized.").

60 There are exceptions. *See e.g. Norman-Bloodsaw v. Lawrence Berkeley Lab.*, 135 F.3d 1260, 1269 (9th Cir. 1998) (holding that research institution violated federal privacy rights of clerical and administrative workers who were tested for intimate medical conditions without their knowledge as part of an employee health examination). *See also United States v. Westinghouse Elec. Corp.*, 638 F.2d 570, 580 (3d Cir. 1980) (holding that employee medical records fall within protected zone of privacy); *United States v. Sutherland*, 143 F. Supp. 2d 609, 610 (W.D. Va. 2001) (holding that government can not disclose prescription records without giving patients a chance to object).

61 *See e.g. In re Guardianship of Browning*, 568 So. 2d 4 (Fla. 1990) (discussing Fla. Const. art. I, para. 23); *King v. State*, 535 S.E.2d 492, 494 (Ga. 2000) (discussing Ga. Const. art. I, § 1, para. 1). *But see Rollins v. Ulmer*, 15 P.3d 749, 750 (Alaska 2001) (finding that the registration requirements of Alaska's medical marijuana law were constitutional).

62 The original 45 C.F.R. § 164.506 (2001).

63 45 C.F.R. § 164.506(a).

64 45 C.F.R. § 164.506(b)(1).

65 The original 45 C.F.R. § 164.506(b) (2001).

66 *See supra* text accompanying n. 24.

67 Of course, some courts will "patch" this omission by backfilling a tort remedy modeled on statutory breach or informed by breach of the federal standards. *See e.g. United States v. Sutherland*, 143 F. Supp. 2d 609, 612 (W.D. Va. 2001); *Doe v. Community Health Plan-Kaiser Corp.*, 709 N.Y.S.2d 215, 216 (N.Y. App. Div. 2000).

68 *See supra* n. 54.

69 *See e.g. Campbell v. Palmer*, 568 A.2d 1064, 1067 (Conn. App. Ct. 1990). This "professional standards" or custom-based approach represents judicial backsliding from the patient expectations, autonomy-based approach of seminal cases such as *Canterbury v. Spence*, 464 F.2d 772 (D.C.Cir.1972). *See generally Ketchup v. Howard*, 543 S.E.2d 371 (Ga. Ct. App. 2000) (appendix providing a summary of different jurisdictions' approaches to the standard of disclosure).

70 Rand E. Rosenblatt, *The Four Ages of Health Law*, 14(1) Health Matrix Clevel.155, 162–66 (2004) [hereinafter Rosenblatt].

71 *Id.* at 168–69.
72 *Id.* at 175–90.
73 James F. Childress & Mark Siegler, *Metaphors and Models of Doctor–Patient Relationships: Their Implications for Autonomy*, 5 Theoretical Med. 17 (1984) [hereinafter Childress & Siegler].
74 *See e.g.* American Medical Association, *Principles of Medical Ethics* (June 2001), http://www.ama-assn.org/ama/pub/category/2512.html (accessed Sept. 20, 2004).
75 *Fundamental Elements*, *supra* n. 16, at Principle #4.
76 *See e.g. Gray v. Grunnagle*, 223 A.2d 663 (Pa. 1966).
77 *See e.g. Sterling v. Johns Hopkins Hosp.*, 802 A.2d 440 (Md. Ct. Spec. App. 2002); *Kruger v. Jennings*, 2002 WL 652098 (Mich. Ct. App. Apr. 19, 2002).
78 *See generally* Nicolas P. Terry, *Through an E-Health Lens, Darkly: Observations on Law, Industry, and Innovation in Medicine and Industry*, *in* Changing Paradigms in Health Law, Policy and Ethics (George F. Tomossy, David N. Weistraub & Tom Campbell, eds) (Forthcoming 2005); Nicolas P. Terry, *The Law-Medicine Center 50th Anniversary Symposium: The Field of Health Law: Its Past and Future: A Medical Ghost in the E-Health Machine*, 14(1) Health Matrix Clevel. 225 (2004).
79 Nicolas P. Terry, *Prescriptions sans Frontières (or How I Stopped Worrying about Viagra on the Web but Grew Concerned about the Future of Healthcare Delivery)*, 4 Yale J. Health Pol'y, L., & Ethics 183, 188, 251 (2004) [hereinafter *Prescriptions sans Frontières*].
80 *Id.*
81 Childress & Siegler, *supra* n. 73, at 22.
82 *See generally* Nicolas P. Terry, *Cyber-Malpractice: Legal Exposure for Cybermedicine*, 25 Am. J. L. & Med. 327 (1999).
83 *See generally Prescriptions sans Frontières*, *supra* n. 79.
84 Paul C. Tang & W. Ed Hammond, *A Progress Report on Computer-based Patient Records in the United States*, *in* The Computer-based Patient Record: An Essential Technology for Health Care 2–3 (D.E. Detmer *et al.*, eds., rev. ed., IOM, USA, 1997).
85 *See infra* text accompanying n. 93, *et seq.*
86 *See e.g.* Peter Briss *et al.*, *Promoting Informed Decisions About Cancer Screening in Communities and Healthcare Systems*, 26(1) Am. J. Preventive Med. 67 (2004).
87 Childress & Siegler, *supra* n. 73, at 22.
88 Beauchamp & Childress, *supra* n. 7, at 419–20.
89 *See e.g. R. v. Department of Health; Ex parte Source Informatics Ltd* [2000] 2 WLR 940 (UK CA) (information aggregator seeking to collect information about physician prescribing habits and sell data to pharmaceutical companies challenged U.K. policy prohibiting same); *In re Pharmatrak, Inc* Privacy Litigation, 292 F. Supp. 2d 263 (D. Mass. 2003) (class action against information aggregator and pharmaceutical companies, alleging that they intercepted and accessed Plaintiffs' personal information through the use of computer "cookies" and other devices, in violation of state and federal law).
90 *See supra* n. 20, *et seq.*
91 *See generally Prescriptions sans Frontières*, *supra* n. 79.
92 *See generally Prescriptions sans Frontières*, *supra* n. 79, at 247–48.
93 *See e.g. Breen v. Williams*, 186 CLR 71 (Austl 1996) ("Documents prepared by a professional person to assist the professional to perform his or her professional duties are not the property of the lay client; they remain the property of the professional." At ¶ 11).
94 Health Insurance Portability and Accountability Act of 1996, Pub. L No. 104–91, § 261, 110 Stat. 1988 (1996). *See South Carolina Med. Ass'n v. Thompson*, 327 F.3d 346, 348 (4th Cir. 2003).

> HIPAA's Administrative Simplification provisions ... were designed to improve the efficiency and effectiveness of the health care system by facilitating the exchange of information with respect to financial and administrative transactions carried out by health plans, health care clearinghouses, and health care providers who transmit information in connection with such transactions.

95 *See generally* Office of the Assistant Secretary for Planning and Evaluation, *Administrative Simplification in the Health Care Industry*, U.S. Dep. of Health and Human Services, http://aspe.hhs.gov/admnsimp/index.shtml (accessed Sept. 20, 2004).

96 *HIPAA Administrative Simplification – Identifiers*, Centers for Medicare and Medicaid Services, http://www.cms.hhs.gov/hipaa/hipaa2/regulations/identifiers/default.asp (accessed Sept. 20, 2004).

97 *See Transaction Standards*, Centers for Medicare and Medicaid Services, http://www.cms.hhs.gov/hipaa/hipaa2/regulations/transactions/nprm/tx05.asp (accessed Sept. 20, 2004).

98 Janet Corrigan *et al.*, eds, Comm. on Quality of Health Care in Am., Iom, To Err is Human: Building a Safer Health System (Nat'l Academy Press 1999); Chunliu Zhan & Marlene R. Miller, *Excess Length of Stay, Charges, and Mortality Attributable to Medical Injuries during Hospitalization*, 290 JAMA 1868 (2003).

99 *See generally* Lucian L. Leape, *Preventing Medical Accidents: Is "Systems Analysis" the Answer?*, 27 Am. J. L. & Med. 145, 147 (2001); James Reason, *Human Error: Models and Management*, 320 Brit. Med. J. 768 (2000).

100 Comm. on Quality of Health Care in Am., Iom, Crossing the Quality Chasm: A New Health System for the 21st Century 15 (Nat'l Academy Press 2001).

101 *See generally* Bar Code Label Requirement for Human Drug Products and Biological Products, 69 FR 9120 (Feb. 26, 2004).

102 *See generally* Cal. Health Care Found., E-prescribing (2001), http://www.chcf.org/documents/hospitals/EPrescribing.pdf (accessed Sept. 20, 2004).

103 *See generally* Rainu Kaushal & David W. Bates, *Computerized Physician Order Entry (CPOE) with Clinical Decision Support Systems (CDSSs)*, *in* Making Health Care Safer: A Critical Analysis of Patient Safety Practices, Prepared for: Agency for Healthcare Research and Quality, Evidence Report/Technology Assessment, No. 43, July 2001, Chapter 6, http://www.ahrq.gov/clinic/ptsafety/pdf/ptsafety.pdf (accessed Sept. 20, 2001).

104 *See e.g.* Anne Bobb, Kristine Gleason, Marla Husch, Joe Feinglass, Paul R. Yarnold & Gary A. Noskin, *The Epidemiology of Prescribing Errors: The Potential Impact of Computerized Prescriber Order Entry*, 164 Arch Intern Med. 785 (2004) (noting the desirability of matching CPOE systems to decision support and pharmacy systems to reduce medication errors). *See* Bernard Fernando *et al.*, *Prescribing Safety Features of General Practice Computer Systems: Evaluation Using Simulated Test Cases*, 328 Brit. Med. J. 1171 (2004).

105 *See e.g.* Australian Council for Safety and Quality in Health Care, *Open Disclosure: A National Standard for Open Communication in Public and Private Hospitals Following an Adverse Event in Health Care* (July 2003), http://www.safetyandquality.org/articles/publications/OpenDisclosure_web.pdf (accessed Sept. 20, 2004).

106 *See generally* Agency for Healthcare Research and Quality, *Outcomes & Effectiveness*, http://www.ahrq.gov/clinic/outcomix.htm (accessed Sept. 20, 2004).

107 *Transforming Health Care: The President's Health Information Technology Plan*, http://www.whitehouse.gov/infocus/technology/economic_policy200404/chap3.html (accessed Sept. 20, 2004).

108 *Incentives for the Use of Health Information Technology and Establishing the Position of the National Health Information Technology Coordinator*, Executive Order 13335 of April 27, 2004, 69 FR 24059, Sect. 3 (Apr. 30, 2004), http://a257.g.akamaitech.net/7/257/2422/14mar20010800/edocket.access.gpo.gov/2004/pdf/04–10024.pdf (accessed Sept. 20, 2004).
109 Nicolas P. Terry, *Electronic Health Records: International, Structural, and Legal Perspectives*, 12 J. L. & Med. (AU) 26 (2004) [hereinafter *Structural and Legal Perspectives*].
110 *Id.*
111 *See generally Health Information Domain, supra* n. 6.
112 *See generally* Nicolas P. Terry, *The Law-Medicine Center 50th Anniversary Symposium: The Field of Health Law: Its Past and Future: A Medical Ghost in the E-Health Machine*, 14(1) Health Matrix Clevel. 225 (2004).
113 *See supra* n. 73, *et seq.*
114 Health*Connect*, http://www.healthconnect.gov.au (accessed Sept. 20, 2004).
115 *See generally Structural and Legal Perspectives*, *supra* n. 109, at 32.
116 Rosenblatt, *supra* n. 70, at 166–75.
117 Rosenblatt, *supra* n. 70, at 175–90.
118 Mark A. Hall, *Law, Medicine, and Trust*, 55 Stan. L. Rev. 463, 464–66 (2002) [hereinafter Hall].
119 Hall, *supra* n. 118, at 471.
120 Hall, *supra* n. 118, at 479–82.
121 The MTM show's theme "Love is All Around" was written by Paul Williams.
122 *See generally* M. Gregg Bloche, *Trust and Betrayal in the Medical Marketplace*, 55 Stan. L. Rev. 919, 922–26 (2002) [hereinafter Bloche].
123 Hall, *supra* n. 118, at 486.
124 Hall, *supra* n. 118, at 504–6.
125 Hall, *supra* n. 118, at 499.
126 *See supra* n. 40.
127 *See supra* n. 44, *et seq.*
128 Bloche, *supra* n. 122, at 940.
129 Hall, *supra* n. 118, at 473.
130 Harris Interactive, *Reputations of Pharmaceutical and Health Insurance Companies Continue Their Downward Slide*, 4(11) Healthcare News (June 22, 2004), http://www.harrisinteractive.com/news/newsletters/healthnews/HI_HealthCare News2004Vol4_Iss11.pdf (accessed August 16, 2005). The same poll found the reputation of hospitals also declining but that they are generally well regarded, albeit ranked behind, for example, software companies and airlines.
131 Harris Interactive, *Health-Care Professionals, Pharmacies, Hospitals Gain the Public's Top Trust*, 3(2) The Wall Street Journal Online/Harris Interactive Health-Care Poll (Jan. 28, 2004), http://www.harrisinteractive.com/news/newsletters/wsjhealthnews/WSJOnline_HI_Health-CarePoll2004vol3_iss02.pdf (accessed Aug. 15, 2004).
132 *See e.g.* Christopher N. Sciamanna, Joseph Diaz & Puja Myne C.N. Sciamanna, *Patient Attitudes toward Using Computers to Improve Health Services Delivery*, 2(1) BMC Health Serv Res.19 (Sept. 11, 2002); Andrea Hassol, James M. Walker, David Kidder, Kim Rokita, David Young, Steven Pierdon, Deborah Deitz, Sarah Kuck & Eduardo Ortiz, *Patient Experiences and Attitudes about Access to a Patient Electronic Healthcare Record and Linked Web Messaging*, 11(6) J. Am. Med. Inform. Assoc. 503–13 (Aug. 6, 2004).
133 Jim Chalmers & Rod Muir, *Patient Privacy and Confidentiality*, 326 Brit. Med. J. 725 (2003) (discussing NHS Information Authority initiatives).
134 Hall, *supra* n. 118, at 512–24.

135 Richard A. Posner, *An Economic Theory of Privacy*, *in* Philosophical Dimensions of Privacy: An Anthology 333, 344 (Ferdinand D. Schoeman, ed., Cambridge University Press 1984).

136 *Id.* at 343.

137 Joel B. Finkelstein, *HIPAA's Promise Undermined by Claims-Processing Tangle*, AMNews, (Sept. 13, 2004) http://www.ama-assn.org/amednews/2004/09/13/gvsa0913.htm (accessed Sept. 20, 2004).

138 *HIPAA Complaint Form*, http://www.ama-assn.org/ama/pub/category/11132.html (accessed Sept. 20, 2004).

139 *See e.g.* Ondria C. Gleason & William R. Yates, *Suicide Attempt Due to a Misunderstood HIPAA Notice*, 161 Am. J. Psychiatry 374 (2004) (noting the misinterpretation of a privacy notice from an insurer as a notice of non-coverage, possibly contributing to a suicide attempt).

140 CMS-OCR, FAQ, http://answers.hhs.gov/cgi-bin/hhs.cfg/php/enduser/std_alp.php?p_sid=xPmDQ6Gg&p_lva=&p_li=&p_page=1&p_cat_lvl1=7&p_cat_lvl2=%7Eany%7E&p_search_text=&p_new_search=1 (accessed Sept. 20, 2004).

141 Statement of Senator Larry Craig, Senate Special Committee on Aging, *HIPAA Medical Privacy and Transactions Rules: Overkill or Overdue?* (Sept. 23, 2003), http://aging.senate.gov/hearings/hr111lc.pdf (accessed Sept. 20, 2004).

142 *See e.g. S.C. Med. Ass'n v. Thompson*, 327 F.3d 346 (4th Cir. 2003), *cert. denied*, 157 L. Ed. 2d 371 (2003) (physicians and medical association challenged federal privacy rule for vagueness and impermissible delegation). *See also Ass'n of Am. Physicians & Surgs., Inc. v. United States Dep't of Health and Human Serv.*, 224 F. Supp. 2d 1115 (S.D. Tex. 2002).

143 *Citizens for Health v. Thompson*, 2004 U.S. Dist. LEXIS 5745 (E.D. Pa. Apr. 2, 2004) (court denied challenge to Bush administration amendment to the privacy rule, holding that the Secretary had examined the evidence and provided a reasoned analysis).

144 *See supra* n. 62, *et seq.*

145 45 C.F.R. § 160.202.

146 45 C.F.R. § 164.512.

147 *See generally* 45 C.F.R. §§ 164.505, 164.508, 164.510.

148 U.S. Department of Health and Human Services Office for Civil Rights, *Complete Privacy, Security, and Enforcement (Procedural) Regulation Text* (45 CFR Parts 160 and 164), Dec. 28, 2000 as amended May 31, 2002, Aug. 14, 2002, Feb. 2003, and Apr. 17, 2003 – "Unofficial" Version, Aug. 2003.

149 National Privacy Principles (Extracted from the Privacy Amendment (Private Sector) Act 2000), http://www.privacy.gov.au/publications/npps01.pdf (accessed Sept. 20, 2004).

150 Office of the Federal Privacy Commissioner, Privacy Complaints, http://www.privacy.gov.au/privacy_rights/complaints/index.html (accessed Sept. 20, 2004).

151 Information and Privacy Commissioner of Ontario, http://www.ipc.on.ca/ (accessed Sept. 20, 2004).

152 Information Commissioner's Office, http://www.informationcommissioner.gov.uk/ (accessed Sept. 20, 2004).

153 Nicolas P. Terry, *An eHealth Diptych: The Impact of Privacy Regulation on Medical Error and Malpractice Litigation*, 27 Am. J. L. & Med. 361, 385 (2001).

6 Health care and the human genome

Regulatory challenge and response

Roberta M. Berry

Introduction and overview

The explosive growth in genetic knowledge and technologies at the turn of the twenty-first century – propelled by the Human Genome Project (HGP) and a wealth of related research programs – continues to test the coping capacity of the American legal system. This chapter examines current law and its rationale and looks to the horizon for the shape of legal controversies yet to come in two areas of regulatory law: (1) regulation of access to and use of genetic information by health insurance companies, and (2) regulation of gene transfer research, genetic engineering, and reproductive cloning.

The American legal system has already undergone significant change stimulated by new genetic science and technologies. New regulatory regimes have been fashioned to meet early concerns about genetic testing and the use of genetic information; additional change is likely as the social implications come into clearer focus and the policy debate – on issues from privacy rights to promoting research to appropriate underwriting practices in insurance – proceeds. The leading edge of genetic technology has already tested the regulatory framework for gene transfer research, stimulated debate regarding the promise and perils of genetic engineering, and prompted proposals for the prohibition of human reproductive cloning. The issues at stake, ranging from the safety of human subjects in clinical trials to the redesign and replication of the human genome, pose daunting challenges. U.S. law addressing health care and the human genome is nearly as fast moving as the science and technology that press against it, challenging its capacity to comprehend and address the issues arising at the interface between genetic science and technology and health care in a diverse society.

Regulating access to and use of genetic information by health insurers

The impetus to regulation of genetic information

Overview of concerns

Individuals who contemplate undergoing genetic testing are concerned about whether the results will be released to third parties, notably health insurance companies, and whether these companies might use the information in their underwriting process to justify increases in premiums, limitations on or exclusions from coverage, or refusals to offer any coverage. Insurance companies warn of the negative consequences, not only for themselves but for most of their insureds and the larger society, if they are prohibited from obtaining and using the information in their underwriting process. Assessing these competing concerns and determining what policy measures strike the proper balance in addressing them have become the twin tasks of the U.S. Congress and state legislatures.

Rapid legislative response

Governmentally sanctioned – and even mandated – abuse of biological information led to the involuntary eugenic sterilization of tens of thousands of Americans deemed "unfit" from the 1920s into the 1950s. In addition, misguided and scientifically misinformed efforts to help at-risk populations deprived African-Americans who were carriers of sickle cell disease of insurance coverage and employment opportunities from the late 1960s to the early 1980s. These practices eventually attracted attention, condemnation, and correction, but only after great harm had been done to many Americans.[1]

Other uses of biological and genetic information, however, have been commonplace for generations and have attracted relatively little attention or concern. Genetically caused or influenced diseases have long been listed on insurance application forms and noted in pre-employment physicals. But the advent of widespread predictive genetic testing in the 1990s – testing that reveals the increased risk or, in some cases, the virtual certainty of suffering future disease – has aroused widespread concern about the potential use of genetic information by insurance companies, employers, and, potentially, other social institutions to the detriment of future generations of Americans.[2] The concern has been sufficiently intense to drive the first significant legislative agenda to arise out of the sea of policy issues generated by the HGP and related research programs.

The reasons for the rapid emergence of this legislative agenda surrounding private health insurance include: (1) as health care has become increasingly effective, the threat of exclusion from coverage has grown in significance; (2) predictive genetic testing threatens to shift many Americans from the category of healthy to the category of asymptomatic but at increased risk of or destined to suffer from disease, so the class of those potentially excluded has grown much larger; and (3) the concerns of health care providers, genetic researchers, and the genetic testing industry in curing, researching, and expanding genetic testing have been aligned with the concerns of the individuals who are their patients, potential research subjects, and potential customers.[3] These factors have generated a powerful initial impetus to legislative reform measures and evoked a forceful response from insurance companies.

Health insurance: coping with new knowledge

Framing the debate

Health insurance enables individuals in the United States to manage the financial risks associated with ill health by (1) reducing their financial losses in the event of illness, and (2) reducing uncertainties in connection with these financial losses by substituting the certainties of fixed monthly premiums for the uncertainties of health care expenses – whether, when, and how much. In the latter half of the twentieth century, as health care became both more effective and more expensive, the motivation and means to manage these risks increased and insurance evolved into a centrally important social institution.[4]

With the emerging importance of insurance came increasing criticism of some of its features – in particular, the use of personal health information in insurance underwriting to (1) determine premium rates, (2) impose coverage limitations or exclusions, or (3) refuse coverage altogether.[5] The ongoing controversy surrounding these practices serves as the backdrop to the more particular debate surrounding insurance company use of personal genetic information – a debate touched off by the advent of predictive genetic testing near the end of the twentieth century.

Insurance companies defend the use of personal health information, in general, as an indispensable feature of a functioning insurance system. To stay in business, insurance companies must take in enough money, in the form of premiums plus income earned on investments, to cover claims payments, administrative expenses, and profits. While predicting administrative expenses and hoped-for profits is a relatively straightforward undertaking, predicting claims payments, projected out typically for a year or longer, is difficult. Insurance companies assert that they sometimes need access to personal health information because of its statistical correlation with future ill health and, hence, potential claims for payment under an insurance policy.

Most health insurance is underwritten on a group basis – usually for an employment group – and insurance companies generally do not use personal health information when underwriting group policies. Instead, group insurance is "experience rated" – insurance companies gather information about past claims payments for the group and project this past experience into the future, making adjustments for increases in health care costs and other factors, and then determine premium amounts, limitations, and exclusions on the basis of this information. While insurance companies generally do not use personal health information in group underwriting, they sometimes make limited use of this information – if not prohibited by law. For example, they may use this information to exclude coverage for a specified period of time for individuals' "pre-existing conditions" – health care conditions in existence before the individuals joined the group. The rationale for this exclusion is that these pre-existing conditions introduce an additional and unpredictable risk of future claims that is not reflected in the group's prior claims experience.

In underwriting individual health insurance policies, insurance companies gather and use substantial personal health information, including age, health care history, and family health care history. They then consult statistical data correlating this information with ill health to predict whether the applicants will make claims and the amounts of the claims. Insurance companies then establish premium amounts and other policy terms, such as limitations and exclusions of coverage, based on these predictions. If insurance companies determine that the risk posed is too great or too unpredictable, they may refuse coverage altogether.[6]

Insurance companies claim that using personal information to determine risk and establish terms – or deny coverage – accordingly is fair to all. Each pays according to the risk each poses, large risks are limited or excluded from coverage, and excessively high-risk individuals are denied coverage altogether. This keeps the premiums charged to the vast majority of insureds reasonable in relation to the risk they pose and ensures that large or unpredicted risks will not drive insurance companies into insolvency.

If, instead, insurance companies made no use of personal information and charged all of their insureds the same premium and offered them the same coverage terms, those insureds who posed the lowest risk would quickly desert the insurance companies. They would instead purchase coverage on better terms from other companies that did use personal information to tailor price and other terms. The highest-risk insureds, on the other hand, would remain behind to take advantage of the uniform premium and coverage terms. The insurance companies would be forced to ratchet up their uniform premium again and again to cover the increasing costs of claims of these high-risk insureds. Increasing numbers of relatively low-risk insureds would be motivated to take their business elsewhere, and the insurance companies would begin to stagger under the weight of the claims owed to their ever more high-risk insureds. Eventually, the insurance companies would collapse into insolvency at the conclusion of this "adverse selection" death spiral.[7]

Finally, if all insurance companies were required by law to charge their insureds the same premium so that the lowest-risk insureds could not purchase insurance at lower premiums from competitors, then, at some premium price point, these low-risk insureds would drop their coverage because it no longer seemed worth it in light of their anticipated health care expenses. The result would be an increase in the population of uninsured Americans and a threat to the viability of the insurance industry.[8]

These arguments for why insurance companies sometimes must use personal health information are countered by critics in several ways. Some critics argue that the fears of adverse selection, increasing the uninsured population, and undermining the viability of the insurance industry are simply overblown and can be dealt with by carefully tailored regulation.

Other critics accept the arguments of insurance companies as valid on at least some points – and as good evidence of the need to institute a system of mandatory, universal, government-sponsored health insurance that would eliminate the need for underwriting. Critics also assert that the use of personal health information to the detriment of high-risk individuals violates conceptions of social justice, solidarity, or basic fairness: those who suffer misfortune through no fault of their own should be compensated for their misfortune, not made to bear it themselves. Insurance, whether provided through a regulated private insurance system or by a government-sponsored system, ought to provide coverage for all in time of need.[9]

The debate about genetic information

The particular debate on insurance company use of genetic information recapitulates the points of this larger framing debate.[10] The points of the debate are sharpened by the nature of predictive genetic testing, which offers asymptomatic individuals a glimpse, however murky, into their health future. Eventually, our new genetic knowledge and techniques – predictive and diagnostic genetic testing, improved understanding of disease processes, the development of gene transfer therapies, the tailoring of conventional and gene-based therapies to particular genotypes – will significantly improve the efficacy of modern health care. But, for most Americans living in the early twenty-first century, these benefits are distant. Our capacity to glimpse the future far exceeds our power to alter it. And this gap is likely to persist for the foreseeable future as increasing numbers of predictive tests are developed and increasing numbers of currently asymptomatic Americans learn that they are at risk.[11]

From the perspective of individuals at risk, it seems at least paradoxical, if not cruel, that a genetic test that triggers one's deepest concerns about a future disease – learning, for example, of one's genetic predisposition to breast cancer at a time when prevention and cure are far from guaranteed – might make one uninsurable for health expenses associated with the disease. This fuels the argument that any problems insurance companies might face if denied the use of genetic information could be managed by carefully tailored regulation, as well as the argument that a government-sponsored health insurance program must be the right answer if private insurance companies truly cannot cope with these problems. It also makes vivid critics' arguments about the requirements of social justice, solidarity, and fairness. Finally, it introduces a concern distinctive to the use of genetic information – a concern that the genetically unfortunate may not only lose their insurance coverage, but be relegated to a genetic underclass, subject to social stigmatization and prejudice.[12]

These concerns give rise to the further worry that realization of the promise of the HGP and related research programs might be delayed because of individuals' concerns about insurance companies' use of genetic information to their detriment. Health care providers may want to recommend that their patients undergo genetic testing in light of limited but real benefits; researchers may want individuals to serve as test subjects for experiments that could advance the frontiers of genetic testing and of prevention and cure; the genetic testing industry may be eager for customers so that they can continue to develop and market more and better tests. Yet, for individuals weighing the often limited benefits of testing against the potential risk – restriction or loss of insurance coverage so vital to modern life – it may not seem worth it.[13]

There is disagreement, however, about whether or to what extent insurance companies actually use genetic test information or wish to use it. And there is disagreement about whether individuals, correctly or incorrectly, believe that insurance companies use this information. But there is at least some degree of shared concern among health care providers, genetic researchers, and the genetic testing industry that the individuals who are or might be their patients, test subjects, and customers are forgoing genetic testing for fear that insurance companies may obtain and use this information to their detriment. Hence, the call by a broad coalition of advocates for legal prohibitions on the use of some or all genetic information by insurance companies.[14]

Insurance companies, on the other hand, fear that if increasing numbers of individuals avail themselves of genetic testing and insurance companies are not permitted access to their test results when writing individual policies of insurance, then individuals with forward-looking knowledge of their level of risk might purchase insurance at bargain premiums, setting off an adverse-selection spiral that concludes in the insurance companies' insolvency. Yet, if insurance companies attempt to defend against this by requiring individuals to undergo genetic testing, more and more individuals will be found uninsurable, also reducing the number of insurance customers – not to mention provoking intense opposition from critics and calls for wholesale reform of the private insurance market.

Insurance companies find themselves in this awkward position in consequence of the same two factors that have sharpened the debate surrounding the use of genetic information: predictive genetic testing introduces a new source of forward-looking knowledge about the risk of future ill health, and, for the near term, there is relatively little that can be done to forestall or cure disease foretold by these tests. Under these circumstances, individuals with forward-looking knowledge will have every incentive to protect themselves and their families by purchasing health insurance coverage under terms that reflect their current rather than anticipated future health status.

Those insurance companies that have chosen to enter the debate have arrived at two policy positions designed to protect their core concerns in light of these factors: (1) they do not wish to require insurance applicants to undergo genetic testing because, if both sides to the insurance contract remain ignorant of predictive genetic information, individuals will have no incentive to buy insurance coverage at bargain rates and insurance companies will have no reason to fear an adverse selection spiral into insolvency; but (2) if applicants for individual insurance coverage have undergone genetic testing of their own volition, insurance companies insist that they should be entitled to obtain and use the test results in their underwriting to guard against adverse selection.[15]

Thus, individuals, health care providers, researchers, the genetic testing industry, and insurance companies are locked in a policy struggle that none has sought and all would like to resolve. The terms of that resolution cannot help but be controversial, however, given the background debate about the practice of underwriting in private insurance and the particulars of the debate surrounding the use of genetic information. Both state and federal policymakers have responded with a first round of regulations addressing the use of genetic information by health insurance companies.

Law regulating the use of genetic information by insurance companies

State law

Primary authority for regulating the business of insurance resides in the states, pursuant to the federal McCarran-Ferguson Act.[16] In the 1970s and 1980s, before the new wave of predictive genetic testing following on the HGP and related research programs, several states enacted legislation that generally prohibits insurance companies from using information indicating that an individual is a carrier of a genetic disease, as opposed to information that an individual is afflicted by the disease.[17]

With the rapid expansion of genetic testing in the 1990s, states began to enact laws that were much broader in scope. These laws vary in significant particulars, including whether they: (1) apply to all genetic information, including information that might appear, for example, in a family history, or only genetic testing information; (2) prohibit all uses of this information or only those uses that are not "actuarially justified," that is, that are not correlated to increased risk of claims; and (3) regulate individual, group, or both kinds of health insurance. As of June 2002, forty-seven states had enacted some sort of legislation regulating health insurance company use of genetic information.[18]

Critics of insurance company use of genetic information generally favor state legislative enactments that sweep broadly, prohibiting use of any genetic information, regardless of whether or not the information is actuarially justified. In their view, this approach is needed to ensure that individuals will be willing to undergo genetic testing and participate in research and to ensure that no one with a genetic condition will suffer loss of insurance coverage and potential stigmatization. Insurance companies, on the other hand, are particularly concerned about broad definitions of genetic information that may prohibit the use of patient health care information that has long been used in underwriting, such as information contained in family histories, and information that is actuarially justified. These issues continue to be contested at the state legislative level.[19]

Federal law

There have been ongoing efforts since the 1990s to enact federal legislation to supplement these state enactments for two main reasons. First, proponents of federal regulation point to the variability and inadequacy of state laws. Many of these laws apply only to genetic testing information rather than all genetic information or apply only to the use of genetic information that is not actuarially justified. And a few states have failed to act at all. A second reason turns on the effect of "ERISA preemption:" under the federal Employee Retirement Income Security Act (ERISA),[20] group health plans that are self-funded by employers – a significant portion of the market – are exempt from state insurance laws. Thus, federal legislation is necessary if there is to be any regulation of the practices of these ERISA-exempt plans.[21]

In 1996, the U.S. Congress enacted the Health Insurance Portability and Accountability Act (HIPAA),[22] which includes provisions prohibiting the use of genetic information – including but not limited to genetic test information – in several contexts. HIPAA prohibits refusing or canceling coverage, limiting or excluding coverage, or increasing premiums for individuals under group health plans – including ERISA-exempt plans – on the basis of information about health status, including genetic information.[23] HIPAA also prohibits group health plans from treating predictive genetic information as a pre-existing condition – and thereby excluding coverage for a specified period of time – in the absence of a diagnosis of disease.[24]

Proponents of additional federal legislation cite several shortcomings in HIPAA: (1) failure to regulate individual health insurance to the same extent as group health plans, (2) failure to prohibit increases in premiums for all members of group health plans due to genetic information about some members, and (3) failure to enact privacy restrictions prohibiting insurance companies from collecting and disclosing genetic information to third parties.[25] Opponents of additional federal legislation object on all points: (1) individual insurance is the setting in which individuals with forward-looking knowledge would be able to purchase insurance at bargain premiums, potentially leading to adverse selection problems; (2) prohibiting across-the-board premium increases in group health plans in light of the increased risk of plan members would constitute the imposition of price controls, an approach to business regulation that has proved to be non-viable; and (3) (a) other privacy laws now protect genetic as well as other health care information; (b) privacy interests should be balanced against the need to share patient information to ensure quality of care; and (c) insurance companies presently have a good record of maintaining patient privacy.[26]

A number of proposals addressing the concerns of proponents of additional regulation have been introduced since enactment of HIPAA. In February 2005, the U.S. Senate passed, by a vote of 98–0, the Genetic Information Nondiscrimination Act of 2005 (S. 306). If enacted, the measure would prohibit group plans, including ERISA-exempt plans, individual health plans, and issuers of Medicare supplement policies from: (1) refusing coverage on the basis of the receipt of or request for genetic testing by an individual or his or her family member; (2) increasing premiums on the basis of an individual's or family member's genetic test or genetic disease – including the premiums of a group that includes the individual; and (3) requiring genetic testing. An identical bill was introduced in the U.S House of Representatives (HR 1227) in March 2005. President George W. Bush has indicated his support for the measure. A similar bill passed the Senate in 2003, but no action was taken in the House of Representatives. The weighing and balancing of the interests at stake may yield a definitive answer – at least for the near term – with enactment of this measure.[27]

Regulating gene transfer research, genetic engineering, and cloning

Health care and reproductive applications of genetic knowledge and technology

Sustained public and private support for the HGP and related research programs through the 1990s and early twenty-first century reflects the conviction of scientists, health care professionals, policymakers, and private industry that new genetic knowledge and technologies might unlock the door to a host of benefits – from predictive and diagnostic genetic testing, to new gene transfer therapies, to therapies tailored to the genomes of particular individuals. The early products of these research programs yielded at least as many concerns as benefits, however. Concerns about the potential uses of genetic information by insurance companies drove the first wave of regulatory reform. New concerns emerged in the mid-1990s as early attempts to develop gene transfer therapies proved disappointing and, in one case, fatal. The path to realizing benefits through gene transfer research appeared longer, riskier, and more difficult than had been hoped. There have been growing concerns of a different kind as well – not about how to overcome difficulties on the path to benefits, but about how to determine what should count as a benefit. The emerging controversies surrounding genetic engineering and reproductive cloning challenge us to articulate our conception of beneficial applications of genetic knowledge and technology – and to explain why the law should defend our conception rather than someone else's.

B. Gene transfer research and regulation: failed promise, regulatory reform, renewed effort

Development of gene transfer research

Gene transfer entails transferring genetic material to target cells in the body of a living human being to achieve a therapeutic purpose by, for example, repairing a mutated gene or supplying a copy of a normal gene to supplement its functioning. The focus of gene transfer research shifted in the early years of the twenty-first century; while experimentation to find cures for genetic disorders continues, most clinical research aims to use gene transfer techniques to develop new treatments for cancer. There are several delivery vehicles, or "vectors," that may be used to deliver the genetic material. The most common are viruses that have been altered so that they no longer cause disease. The concept of gene transfer, or "gene therapy," was contemplated by researchers beginning in the 1970s and was first attempted in an officially approved experiment in 1990. In the course of the 1990s, approximately 400 clinical trials were undertaken involving over 4,000 human patients.[28]

Early clinical trials were undertaken with very high hopes, but yielded very little clinical benefit. A 1995 report to the U.S. National Institutes of Health (NIH) concluded that no clinical trial to date had demonstrated clinical benefit to patients and recommended that gene transfer investigators refocus their efforts on basic research in the field. By the end of the 1990s there was encouraging news, however, including success in a French trial involving patients with X-Linked Severe Combined Immunodeficiency Disease (SCID). And encouraging results were achieved in other trials, including in patients with hemophilia and cancer of the head and neck. But there were setbacks as well: two of the children cured of SCID later developed a leukemia-like condition, apparently due to the gene transfer.[29]

Regulation of gene transfer research

From its inception, gene transfer experimentation has been subject to a complex regulatory regime, including pre-existing U.S. Food and Drug Administration (FDA) authority over investigational new drugs (IND) and Recombinant DNA Advisory Committee (RAC) authority over genetic technologies, as well as review at the local institutional level. This regime underwent close scrutiny and reconfiguration at the turn of the twenty-first century, prompted by the first death caused by a gene transfer experiment.

REGULATORY FRAMEWORK IN THE 1990s

In 1986, FDA asserted regulatory jurisdiction over INDs consisting of gene transfer products and, over the course of the 1990s, elaborated the regulatory procedure for industry sponsors of gene transfer clinical trials. All sponsors were required to submit IND applications to FDA, which could approve, disapprove, or require modifications. FDA also required sponsors to report adverse events experienced in the course of ongoing clinical trials and could respond to this information in a variety of ways, ranging from requiring changes to informed consent forms for trial participants to placing clinical trials on hold. FDA's regulatory interactions with sponsors, generally, were conducted confidentially, although FDA could report adverse events to other sponsors – if there was a risk to the health and safety of participants in other clinical trials – and could disclose some safety issues to the public.[30]

At the initiation of gene transfer research in 1990, the RAC also held regulatory approval authority over the great majority of gene transfer clinical trials – those trials conducted by investigators who received NIH funding for the research or that were conducted at or sponsored by institutions that received NIH funding. Principal investigators were required to submit research protocols and to report adverse events in ongoing trials and the RAC was responsible for review and approval or disapproval of each proposed clinical trial and for analysis and review of data on adverse events.

The RAC had been established in 1974 in response to a proposed recombinant DNA (rDNA) experiment involving the insertion of a DNA sequence from a cancer-causing virus into a bacterium. From a dialogue among a group of scientists about the appropriate regulatory framework for this new kind of research, the first RAC emerged. The RAC drafted safety standards for rDNA research that were adopted as the *NIH Guidelines for Research Involving Recombinant DNA Molecules* (*NIH Guidelines*) in 1976. Beginning in 1978, non-scientists were included in the membership of RAC and, in 1984, the RAC was charged with addressing ethical as well as scientific issues raised by proposals. Thereafter, a working group of the RAC drafted a set of ethical and scientific considerations that were approved in 1985 and, in 1990, were incorporated as *Appendix M* to the *NIH Guidelines*.[31]

The first gene transfer protocol was approved in 1990 by FDA and by a RAC subcommittee charged with reviewing the ethical and scientific merits of the protocol together with the full RAC. As increasing numbers of protocols were filed over the course of the 1990s, the RAC's regulatory authority was scaled back; in 1992, RAC subcommittee review was eliminated and, beginning in 1995, full RAC approval was required only for those protocols that posed novel risks or significant ethical or safety questions. The need for any RAC review was debated and, in a 1997 compromise, RAC membership was reduced from twenty-five to fifteen members and its role in the approval process was reduced to advisory only. From its inception and continuing throughout the evolution of its responsibilities, RAC procedures – in contrast to FDA procedures – were conducted publicly.[32]

Also under the aegis of NIH, gene transfer investigators, generally, have been subject to additional reporting and approval requirements at the institutional level. These processes are conducted by Institutional Review Boards (IRBs) and Institutional Biosafety Committees (IBCs).[33]

A TRAGIC DEATH AND ITS CONSEQUENCES

While early hopes for significant benefits were disappointed in the 1990s, early fears had not been realized: gene transfer research seemed neither as promising as hoped nor as risky as feared. In 1999, early concerns were reignited and refocused on vector toxicity, however, with the death of Jesse Gelsinger, a volunteer in an experiment at the University of Pennsylvania's Institute for Human Gene Therapy ("Institute").[34]

Mr. Gelsinger suffered from ornithine transcarbamylase deficiency ("OTC deficiency") – a liver disorder that prevents the production of enzymes that remove ammonia from the body. Although Mr. Gelsinger's disease was controlled by medication, the outlook is very bleak for most individuals with OTC deficiency: only half live past the age of five and, of those who do survive, most have severe disabilities. Mr. Gelsinger volunteered to participate in a gene transfer experiment conducted at the Institute in 1999, hoping his participation would contribute to the eventual development of a cure for OTC deficiency. Mr. Gelsinger died four days after undergoing the experimental gene transfer, apparently due to a massive immune reaction to the viral vector used in the therapy. He was eighteen years old at the time of his death.[35]

Mr. Gelsinger's death triggered a cascade of events. An FDA order suspended all clinical trials at the Institute after an FDA investigation found several regulatory violations. A study by an external review board commissioned by the University of Pennsylvania questioned the adequacy of the Institute's training of young scientists for clinical trials and the propriety of the principal investigator's financial interest in the company that sponsored the experiment – a company that he had founded and that held exclusive rights to the discoveries of the Institute. In May of 2000, after receipt of the study, the University announced that the Institute would no longer engage in clinical trials and that the University would revamp its oversight of clinical trials conducted across the University and would review its conflict-of-interest policies.[36]

REGULATORY RECONFIGURATION

The impact of Jesse Gelsinger's death extended well beyond the immediate consequences for the researchers involved and the University of Pennsylvania and its Institute. Concerns centered both on the rights and welfare of participants in other experiments and on the social consequences of failure to ensure their protection, including undermining the willingness of individuals to volunteer as participants – and of the public to fund research.[37] Regulators responded to these concerns with reforms focused on two areas: (1) avoiding the appearance or reality of conflicts of interest between investigators and participants in clinical trials; (2) improving the monitoring of clinical trials, accomplishing systemic analysis of clinical trials data for safety implications, and making information on clinical trials widely available while maintaining the confidentiality of sponsors' commercial secrets and the privacy of participants.

Regarding conflicts of interest, at the time of Mr. Gelsinger's death, NIH-funded research and FDA-regulated research were subject to regulations aimed at reducing bias in the design, execution, or reporting of research due to investigators' financial conflicts of interest. HHS and FDA regulations also required IRBs to review NIH-funded and FDA-regulated research to ensure, among other things, that risks to human subjects were reasonable and minimal in proportion to benefits, that informed consent had been sought, and that coercion and undue influence had been minimized.[38]

Ongoing concerns about the adequacy of this conflicts-of-interest regulatory framework were reinforced when the financial interests of those involved in the experiment resulting in Mr. Gelsinger's death came to light. The concerns centered on whether financial interests might influence the judgment of investigators, leading them, for example, to underestimate the risks or overestimate the benefits of an experiment when applying for approval or funding, or to withhold or color information in the informed consent process, or to submit incomplete or biased reporting of adverse events or of experimental results.[39] Re-examination and some regulatory reconfiguration followed on the death of Mr. Gelsinger.

In June 2000, NIH issued a document directed at investigators and institutional review boards summarizing the requirements of the applicable regulations on reducing bias and protecting human subjects and announcing that "[b]ecause of the complexity of the issues and the potential threats to the integrity of research posed by ... conflicts of interest, the NIH is issuing these points to consider and announcing a pubic consultation to be held on this issue in the Summer of 2000."[40] Following this public consultation held in August of 2000, in May 2004, HHS released an extensive guidance, applicable to both NIH-funded and FDA-regulated gene transfer research, addressing IRB review of human subjects research. The guidance document lists points for IRBs to consider in determining whether the financial interests of investigators and institutions may impinge on the rights and welfare of participants, including: who funds, designs, receives compensation or incentives, or holds proprietary interests or equity interests in the research. The document also specifies actions that might be undertaken to safeguard participants, including: separating institutional responsibility for research from institutional management of financial interests; providing training to investigators regarding institutional financial interest requirements; and establishing policies regarding the financial relationships that may be held by investigators. In March 2001, FDA also issued a guidance document, directed at industry, providing detailed instruction regarding the interpretation and application of FDA regulations aimed at reducing bias due to conflicts of interest.[41]

Some commentators question whether the response to concerns about conflicts of interest has been adequate given the scope and nature of the concerns and the extent to which the fortunes of institutions are tied to the success of their researchers and to their associations with private industry partners. While disclosure and management of financial interests are required, and IRBs are charged with safeguarding participants against threats that might be posed by conflicts of interest, it is left to institutions to devise and enforce the particulars of their compliance policies and practices. In addition, financial interests may not be the only, or even the most important, source of conflicting interests; the quest for tenure, promotion, publicity, recognition, and honors may be more worrisome sources of conflict.[42] Governmental and non-governmental oversight of financial conflicts of interest is certain to receive continuing attention and critique.

Disagreement also persists about the second set of concerns – monitoring clinical trials, systemic data analysis, and providing access to information while protecting commercial confidentiality and participant privacy. Most of the controversy has centered on the reporting of adverse events. Following the death of Mr. Gelsinger, investigations revealed widespread failures to report adverse events to NIH, confusion about the nature of the reporting requirements, and shortcomings in the sharing and analysis of adverse event information between FDA and NIH. While all involved in the debate – sponsors, representatives of patient groups, regulators, commentators – agree that reporting is essential to ensuring the safety of participants, concerns about preserving commercial secrets and participant privacy have generated disagreement about what information should be held confidential and who should determine this, and how.

Regulatory efforts to clarify and enforce reporting and monitoring requirements were undertaken in the immediate aftermath of Mr. Gelsinger's death. In November 1999, FDA issued a letter to sponsors and investigators calling attention to requirements for reporting of adverse events both to FDA's Center for Biologics Evaluation and Research (CBER) and to NIH's Office of Recombinant DNA Activities (ORDA). In a subsequent letter in March 2000, FDA required sponsors to submit detailed information beginning three months thereafter on their monitoring plans for ensuring, among other things, compliance with regulatory requirements and with their approved research protocol. In June 2000, NIH also notified investigators of its policy, effective October 2000, requiring submission of data and safety monitoring plans – including the procedure for reporting adverse events to NIH, FDA, and the local IRB – prior to initiation of clinical trials.[43]

In an effort to enhance and harmonize the protection of participants, in October 2000, further amendments to NIH Guidelines require that all levels of regulatory review involving human subjects protection – both any required RAC review plus local IRB and IBC review – are completed before a participant is enrolled in a clinical trial. The amendments also permit protocols to be submitted for RAC review prior to IRB approval – allowing the IRB review process to benefit from the results of RAC review. If RAC review yields recommendations, these are sent by the RAC not only to the investigator but also to the local IRB and IBC. In December 2001, additional amendments allowed for expanded RAC membership beyond the minimum of fifteen. These amendments were aimed at enabling the RAC to cope with the demands of reviewing diverse proposals by including additional expertise. Also, the amendments include expertise in laboratory safety and protection of human subjects among the areas of expertise appropriate for additional members.[44]

Amendments to the NIH Guidelines announced in November 2001 established a more refined and harmonized system of reporting, provided for systemic analysis of adverse-event data by a newly created committee, and struck a still-controversial balance between confidentiality of commercial information and ensuring public access to information. The amendments require expedited reporting of serious and unexpected adverse events associated with a gene transfer product and permit summaries of other adverse events to be included in annual reports. The amendments also establish a RAC working group, the NIH Gene Transfer Safety Assessment Board (GTSAB), including members drawn from the RAC and FDA. GTSAB is charged with ongoing systemic review of adverse-event data to determine whether any trends with safety implications emerge from the data. The amendments also specify that NIH will determine whether reports of adverse events contain confidential commercial information and, with respect to any information that is determined to be confidential, NIH will seek agreement from the submitting party to disclose the information if public disclosure would advance understanding of key safety or scientific issues. To preserve the privacy of participants, the amendments specify that reports on adverse events should omit any personally identifiable information.[45]

While improved analysis of data is universally welcomed, the authority of NIH to determine whether commercial information is entitled to confidentiality remains controversial. Because of the intense competition to develop and market gene therapy products – and the importance of confidential information to winning the competition – industry representatives claim that regulatory recognition of the confidentiality of commercial information is essential to the development of safe and effective gene transfer products.[46]

Finally, in a joint effort to improve harmonization, regulatory oversight, and access to information, NIH and FDA announced in March 2004 the establishment of a joint gene transfer research data system, "Genetic Modification

Clinical Research Information System" (GeMCRIS). The GeMCRIS web site provides for secure reporting of adverse events and allows for regulatory monitoring and analysis of the data submitted. GeMCRIS also coordinates the reporting requirements and procedures of NIH and FDA, facilitating submission of adverse event reports to both agencies with minimal additional effort.[47]

The sum of these regulatory reforms in the five years following on the 1999 death of a participant in a gene transfer experiment is a significantly more comprehensive and integrated system of review and oversight than that in place throughout the first decade of gene transfer clinical research in the 1990s. With this framework in place, renewed effort to realize the promise of gene transfer research continues at an accelerating pace.

Renewed effort

Gene therapy clinical trials in the twenty-first century address a far wider array of potential clinical conditions than in the 1990s, including "cancer, inborn errors of metabolism, cardiovascular diseases, autoimmune disorders, and neurologic disease," and employ a wide array of viral vectors "including vaccinia, fowl pox, canary pox, herpes simplex, virus, adeno-associated virus, adenovirus, and retroviruses."[48] The development of a leukemia-like condition in two children in France in clinical trials aimed at SCID led FDA to halt similar experiments in the United States in January 2003. But, after continuing review of adverse events and consideration of the circumstances under which trials might be resumed, FDA has permitted one trial to go forward on older patients as a last resort.[49] FDA also published a draft guidance in August 2005 addressing concerns surrounding delayed adverse effects and establishing a regulatory mechanism to address these concerns.[50]

While the promise of gene transfer research is far from realized, substantial investment in its prospects continues. The regulatory response to the rapid cycle of early promise followed by disappointment and then the death of a participant has centered on improving reporting and other communication between the regulated community and regulators, heightened and more time-sensitive regulatory oversight, and increased coordination among regulatory agencies. As renewed and expanded experimentation proceeds and increasing numbers of participants are enrolled in trials, the adequacy of these efforts will be tested.

Genetic engineering of humans: novel issues and regulatory challenges

Introduction and overview

Human genetic engineering, or inheritable genetic modification, refers to the anticipated, but not yet feasible, modification of the human genetic constitution. Modifications might include elimination of genetic predispositions to disease, creation of disease resistance, or "enhancement" of physical features, abilities, or behavioral predispositions. Genetic engineering might be accomplished by a variety of approaches: (1) genetic modification of a human egg or sperm; (2) genetic modification of a zygote (the early product of the union of the human egg and sperm); or (3) modification of a donor nucleus, which is then transferred into an enucleated human egg to create a genetically engineered clone. Genetic engineering of non-human animals to create "transgenic" animals is commonplace; these transgenic animals serve as models for the study of human disease, as with the Harvard "oncomouse"; "factories" for the production of products, such as human insulin; and devices to serve human purposes, such as the clean-up of oil spills. The techniques used to create transgenic animals, however, frequently yield non-viable or unhealthy animals, thus rendering them unsuitable for use in human genetic engineering. Nonetheless, the prospect of human genetic engineering is sufficiently real and imminent to merit consideration of the appropriate regulatory response.[51]

Devising an apt regulatory framework for human genetic engineering will be challenging, given the range of issues raised and the intensity and diversity of beliefs about them. The technology would aim to redesign future children at the biological level, with potentially important implications for their well-being. Parents would make design choices for their children, with implications for procreative liberty and for the parent–child relationship. And, if widely practiced, genetic engineering could carry significant implications for society and the relations among the engineered and the non-engineered.

Regulating genetic engineering: novel ethical and policy issues

At the turn of the twenty-first century, the U.S. regulatory framework does not specifically address the biologics or the techniques that might be employed in human genetic engineering. However, the FDA's existing regulatory regime governing biologics, including those used for gene transfer, arguably would apply to genetic engineering as well. Also, genetic engineering likely would be accomplished in conjunction with in vitro fertilization (IVF) procedures performed at assisted reproduction clinics. While IVF clinics are largely unregulated, the health care professionals who provide services within them are subject to governmental licensure and disciplinary regulation as well as the regulatory effects of private medical malpractice and other tort law.[52]

If attempts to perform genetic engineering come to light, or if the prospect appears imminent, it is quite likely that new regulatory measures would be proposed given the novel ethical and policy issues that would be raised.[53] These issues fall into three main categories: (1) risks and benefits for children; (2) the exercise of parental "rights" or "control"; and (3) the consequences for society. A survey of these issues, with arguments and counterarguments drawn from a range of sources, reveals the likely scope of coverage, if not the particular contents, of future regulatory measures.[54]

With respect to the concern about risks and benefits to children, the ordinary risk–benefit calculus that factors into health care decision making will be complicated by questions about the social-psychological risks and benefits for engineered children and their parents in the social-cultural context of procreation and parenting. While we expect children to feel cared for and grateful when their parents obtain medical treatment for them or provide them with opportunities for education and cultivation of their talents, we do not know whether genetically engineered children would feel cared for and grateful or controlled and resentful, or whether this would depend on the nature of the genetic engineering – whether to cure disease or enhance a feature, for example. Also, in current health care decision making for children, our risk–benefit assessments are anchored in the current status and prognosis of a living child. In the case of genetic engineering, the risk–benefit calculus would have to be performed in the absence of an existing child whose well-being or best interests might be assessed. Finally, health care decisions ordinarily need only take into account the individuals directly affected; in the case of genetic engineering, the implications for genetic descendents would have to be considered as well if the modifications were heritable. These considerations would be especially complex with respect to decision making about genetic enhancement – akin to making choices about cosmetic surgery or cognitive enhancers not only for one's child but for that child's descendants as well.

Proponents argue that these concerns are overblown. We should embrace the possibility of future generations who might be engineered to be disease-free, long-lived, intelligent, strong, agile, and free of hyper-aggressiveness. While genetic engineering might be a novel technique, they argue, the motivations and results are no different from those of parents who inoculate their children against disease or undertake other health care or educational initiatives to increase their children's longevity, enrich their intellect, build their physical fitness, and civilize their destructive impulses and behaviors.

The second set of issues focuses on the moral rightness of exercises of parental choice quite aside from any risks or benefits to children. Current controversies about the exercise of parental choice – such as whether it is always, never, or sometimes right or wrong to select a child of a desired sex through an IVF procedure or by selective abortion – will multiply if the options increase via genetic engineering. Opponents argue that the choice to engineer, if not other reproductive choices, crosses a line between acceptable and unacceptable exercises of control over others – at least if the choice is motivated by the desire to "design" the child's features as opposed to prevent the child from suffering from a genetically influenced disease. Proponents argue that parents should have the right to choose whether to engineer their children – assuming that their choices, on balance, benefit their children rather than harm them – and that this right belongs among other reproductive rights to which individuals are entitled, including the right to procreate or not to procreate.

There is also disagreement about the social implications of genetic engineering. If access to genetic engineering is available only to some because others are unable to afford it, we might evolve into a two-tier society consisting of a genetic "nobility" and a genetic "underclass," undermining our conceptions of social, political, and economic equality and the goals and practices of a democratic civil society. On the other hand, if we subsidize genetic engineering to render it accessible to all – on the model of the universal availability of public education – the social imprimatur and resulting social pressure might be troublesome: we might question whether human well-being would be advanced by the drive to keep pace with the genetic engineering practices of our neighbors.

Proponents of genetic engineering argue, to the contrary, that free choice coupled with modest regulation to prevent harmful engineering practices will not yield a two-tier society or force parents into defensive engineering choices to keep up with the competition. Instead, society will likely look much as it does now, with differing engineering choices by parents reflecting their differing values. The vast majority of parental choices will be motivated then as now by a desire to do what it best for their children. And, if the results prove beneficial to children, more resources, private and public, likely will be devoted to genetic engineering just as more resources have been devoted to beneficial health care and educational interventions.

The diversity of views on these issues, and the foundations of these diverse views in deeply held ethical beliefs, raises a separate set of issues about what the role of the law should – or could – be. Some argue that, regardless of our personal views on these issues, we must tolerate diverse choices rather than attempting to dictate by law what all must or must not do. Others argue that the political community must arrive at some basic points of moral agreement on some fundamentally important issues – genetic engineering among them – if it is to survive as a political community worthy of the respect and allegiance of its members.

Human cloning: reproduction reconceived

Introduction and overview

Reproductive cloning of mammals was first accomplished by the transfer of nuclear DNA from a sheep's mammary gland cell into an enucleated egg; the fused product of this transfer was then developed into a blastocyst, transferred to the womb of a sheep, and brought to term. This method of cloning yielded the live birth of a lamb named Dolly in 1996. There were very high losses in the procedure, however: only 29 of 277 attempted fusions succeeded, and of the 29 blastocysts transferred to wombs, only Dolly was born alive. Since this breakthrough, several other mammals have been cloned, including cattle, mice, pigs, and cats. While success rates remain low, some of these cloned animals have been born healthy, thrived, and reproduced. These limited but genuine successes have opened the door to two additional applications, both highly controversial in their ethical and policy implications: (1) cloning of human embryos as sources of stem cells to be used in research aimed at finding cures for diseases including Parkinson's and Alzheimer's ("research cloning"); and (2) reproductive cloning of human beings, the focus of this discussion.[55]

As with human genetic engineering, there are diverse and strongly held beliefs about the implications of human reproductive cloning for the well-being of cloned children and for the parent–child relationship. The particulars of the ethical and policy debate diverge from the debate surrounding genetic engineering, however, in that the motivations for reproductive cloning are centered primarily on the desire to have biologically related children under circumstances in which other means of doing so are problematic for one or more reasons and in that cloning would introduce the novel prospect of asexual human reproduction – the genetic contributions of a male and female would not be required. The debate also is distinctive in that reproductive and research cloning are linked by common techniques, so advance in one domain influences the prospects for advance in the other domain and carries other implications as well. If research cloning proceeds, will it be ethically desirable and practically feasible to insist on the destruction of cloned human research embryos to prevent reproductive cloning? Concern that technological breakthroughs that began with the cloning of Dolly may render human reproductive cloning feasible at any time has added a final distinctive note of urgency to the ethical and policy debate.

Regulating cloning: searching for an appropriate framework

RAPID FIRST RESPONSE AND EVOLVING RATIONALES

In response to the February 1997 announcement of the cloning of Dolly, President Clinton asked the National Bioethics Advisory Commission (NBAC) to prepare a report and recommendations on human cloning and imposed an immediate moratorium on federal funding for any attempt at human cloning – and called upon private researchers to refrain from such attempts as well. In June 1997, NBAC concluded that cloning was unsafe for human reproduction and recommended, accordingly, extension of the moratorium – suggesting imposition of a three to five year federal legislative ban. NBAC was not able to arrive at a consensus regarding the ethical issues other than safety and urged further study of these issues followed by a congressional determination whether to extend the moratorium. A number of federal legislative proposals were introduced soon thereafter, but none was enacted.[56]

The President's Council on Bioethics (PCB), appointed by President Bush in 2001, pursued the ethical issues associated with human cloning in a report published in July 2002 and concluded with majority and minority policy recommendations. Both recommendations called for a ban on reproductive cloning; the majority recommendation, in addition, called for a four-year moratorium on research cloning. The rationale for the recommended ban on reproductive cloning included safety concerns: the clinical trials required to establish safety might themselves be unethical due to the anticipated high morbidity and mortality rates. In addition, PCB cited consensus ethical concerns, including (1) identity problems because the cloned child would look like a person already living; (2) perceiving children as designed manufactures rather than "gifts" to be accepted as they are; (3) the pursuit of eugenic perfection; (4) troubled family relationships because of cross-generational genetic twinning; and (5) fostering social acceptance of the exercise of non-therapeutic control over subsequent generations. PCB acknowledged that there were reasons to favor reproductive cloning as well, including (1) procreative liberty, (2) the value of the existence of the cloned individuals, and (3) the well-being of parents and cloned children. Uses of cloning that might advance these goods would include (1) procreation by infertile couples or parents who wished to avoid transmitting a genetic disease, (2) creating a suitable donor for organs needed to rescue another person, (3) preserving a tie to a dying or dead relative, and (4) capturing the genetic component of talented individuals who were cloned. But PCB did not believe these outweighed the safety and ethical concerns that argued against the practice of reproductive cloning.[57]

INTERIM REGULATORY RESPONSE

In the absence of congressional action following the NBAC report in 1997, FDA, in 1998, asserted its jurisdiction to regulate cloning and its intention to prohibit reproductive cloning due to unresolved safety issues.[58] In 2001, the U.S. House of Representatives held a series of hearings culminating in passage of a bill backed by President George W. Bush banning both reproductive and research cloning – rejecting an alternative bill that would have banned only reproductive human cloning. The measure was never taken up by the Senate, however. In 2005, several cloning bills were introduced, including bills that would ban both reproductive and research cloning and competing bills that would ban only reproductive cloning. None of these bills was expected to be taken up by Congress, however.[59] Several states have enacted legislative prohibitions on human cloning; most of these state statutes expressly exempt research cloning from their prohibitions.[60]

Attempts since 1997 to formulate a national regulatory framework for reproductive cloning appear to reflect widely shared views that safety issues as well as concerns about effects on the well-being of children, the parent–child relationship, and the nature of human reproduction outweigh any reproductive liberty interests of parents in having access to reproductive cloning technology. Disagreement about research cloning, however, runs wide and deep and the linkage between reproductive and research cloning likely will continue to stymie efforts to formulate a national regulatory framework for either for the foreseeable future. In the meantime, the underlying ethical and policy debate about reproductive cloning continues; the apparent consensus among federal policymakers is not universally shared and the eventual resolution of these issues is not certain.

The future of cloning regulation: coping with diversity and disagreement

The ethical and policy issues that NBAC was unable to resolve in its 1997 report and that PCB addressed in its 2002 report continue to provoke debate and defy ready resolution. Although there is general agreement that human reproductive cloning currently is unacceptable because it is unsafe, there is a wide diversity of beliefs about its ultimate ethical acceptability and about the appropriate role of governmental regulation of procreational activities, including reproductive cloning. The ongoing debate suggests that a proposed federal ban on reproductive cloning for some or all purposes may encounter significant opposition, if not in the legislative process, then in courtroom challenges to the constitutionality of the measure after enactment – or in the decisions of some parents to obtain cloning services from providers in countries that do not ban the practice or do not enforce their bans.[61]

For some opponents, cloning would introduce a harmful emphasis on perfectionism in selecting the complete preferred genome of a future child, undermining the bedrock commitment of parents to accepting their children as they are and of society to accepting a diversity of human types. In addition, children would not enjoy the sense of freedom and distinctiveness that comes from having unique genomes. For proponents, the opportunity to engage in biological reproduction would serve both the procreational interests of parents and the interests of cloned children in their own existence. Furthermore, in some cases, the use of cloning technology would be motivated by a desire to avoid passing along a heritable genetic condition to future children, a motivation akin to that of parents who obtain health care for their existing children. Finally, proponents point to the experiences of identical twins who share nearly identical genomes but do not appear to suffer for it.

In the view of some opponents, the prospect of cloning that yields an identical genetic twin of one parent would introduce confusions of identity that would threaten the well-being of the cloned child, the parent–child relationship, and the relationship between parents. In the view of proponents, this concern is overblown given that the child would look very different from the grown parent who shares the child's genome and would be a wholly different person despite sharing the parent's genome. For those who find rich religious or secular ethical significance in reproduction that involves the genetic contributions of men and women, cloning – whether or not "safe" – would be destructive of a core human relationship. Those who instead see expanded options for human reproduction as contributing to the richness of the human reproductive experience conclude the opposite.

Finally, as in the case of genetic engineering, there is disagreement about the role of law in mediating among these conflicting beliefs. Those who oppose reproductive cloning generally argue that the law should advance the appropriate moral stance of the political community on these core issues involving the well-being of children and the preservation of the family. Those who argue for the liberty of individuals to engage in reproductive cloning – assuming its safety is assured – generally argue that the political community should refrain from enforcing anyone's moral stance in the realm of reproductive decision making. In addition, they point to constitutional case law recognizing liberty interests in procreation, including constitutional law protecting the right to abortion, as potentially rendering bans on reproductive cloning unconstitutional.[62]

These differing ethical and religious beliefs about the significance of human reproduction, the relationship between parent and child, and, in the case of research cloning, the status of the human embryo may permit consensus from time to time – as with respect to banning human reproductive cloning for as long as it is unsafe. But the leading edge of science and technology will repeatedly challenge the capacity of the political community to cope with reproductive and research cloning given the fact of ethical and religious pluralism in the United States.

Conclusion: law at the leading edge of health care and the human genome

The ambition of the HGP and related research programs is vast – to generate the bioscientific and biotechnological foundations for a reworking of our relationships to nature and to one another that would be at least as profound as the changes realized with the advent of highly effective individual health care and public health measures in the twentieth-century developed world. Changes in consequence of these efforts are already underway, but future implications for us as biological and social beings – if we can obtain comprehensive knowledge of our genomes, conquer currently devastating diseases, and redesign or replicate our genomes – will be considerably more far reaching.

Law is one way in which we strive collectively to comprehend and guide the implications of bioscientific and biotechnological change. In the twenty-first century, new knowledge and technique, repeatedly, and at an accelerating pace, will test our capacity to respond appropriately through regulatory action or inaction. The challenges will be substantial, given that bioscientific and biotechnological change in the realm of genetics touches on deeply held – and diverse – beliefs about the ethical significance of, among other things, human biological diversity, procreation and parenting, nature and nurture, and religion and science.

Law and the law-making process are, however, well suited to coping with ethically fraught challenges. Law is a kind of social science and social technology that enables us to consider the significance of problems presented to us in concrete and contextualized ways, and to pursue a peaceful process of collective, incremental response – always subject to reconsideration and revision after additional experience, study, argument, and reflection. We see in the early regulatory response to new genetic science and technology evidence of this process underway.

Notes

1 *See* Daniel J. Kevles, In the Name of Eugenics 104–12, 164–69, 278–79, 300 (Alfred A. Knopf 1985). *See also* Roberta M. Berry, *From Involuntary Sterilization to Genetic Enhancement: The Unsettled Legacy of Buck v. Bell*, 12 Notre Dame J.L. Ethics & Pub. Pol'y 401 (1998) at 420; Mark H. Haller, Eugenics: Hereditarian Attitudes in American Thought 139 (Rutgers University Press 1963); Kenneth M. Ludmerer, Genetics and American Society: A Historical Approach 95 (Johns Hopkins University Press 1972); Donald K. Pickens, Eugenics and the Progressives 91 (Vanderbilt University Press 1968); and Philip Reilly, The Surgical Solution: A History of Involuntary Sterilization in the United States 141 (John Hopkins University Press 1991).

2 *See e.g.* Kathy L. Hudson, Karen H. Rothenberg, Lori B. Andrews, Mary Jo Ellen Kahn & Francis S. Collins, *Genetic Discrimination and Health Insurance: An Urgent Need for Reform*, 270(52535) Science 391 (1995) (an article by a group associated with the National Human Genome Research Institute of the National Institutes of Health that urges prohibition of the use of genetic information by health insurance companies). *See also* Ronald M. Green & A. Mathew Thomas, *DNA: Five Distinguishing Features for Policy Analysis*, 11 Harv. J.L. & Tech. 571, 575–76 (1998) (discussing historical use and more intense concern in connection with new genetic tests).

3 *See* Roberta M. Berry, *The Human Genome Project and the End of Insurance*, 7 U. Fla. J.L. & Pub. Pol'y 205, 206–31 (1996) (discussing the history and social function of health insurance); Roberta M. Berry, *Genetic Information and Research: Emerging Legal Issues*, 15 Healthcare Ethics Forum 70, 70–82 (2003) (discussing the expansion of those vulnerable to exclusion and the alignment of concerns among health care providers, researchers, genetic testing companies, and individuals).

4 *See* Berry, *supra* n. 3, at 210–21 (1996) (discussing the history of these lines of insurance, alternative risk management devices, and the distinctive advantages of insurance as a risk management device).

5 *See e.g.* Donald W. Light, *The Practice and Ethics of Risk-Related Health Insurance*, 267 JAMA 2503 (1992); Deborah Stone, *The Struggle for the Soul of Health Insurance*, 18 J. Health Pol., Pol'y & L. 287 *et seq.* (1993).

6 For discussions of underwriting, *see* Kenneth Abraham, Distributing Risk: Insurance, Legal Theory and Public Policy 64–100 (Yale University Press 1986); and Mark A. Hall, Reforming Private Health Insurance 11 (American Enterprise Institute 1994).

7 For discussions of the use of risk classification to avoid adverse selection, *see* Abraham, *supra* n. 6, at 15, 68, 123–24; and Hall, *supra* n. 6, at 10–12.

8 *See* Hall, *supra* n. 6 (discussing the consequences of "community rating" – imposing uniform or near uniform premium rates across communities); *see also* House Committee on Energy and Commerce, Subcommittee on Commerce, Trade, and Consumer Protection, *The Potential for Discrimination in Health Insurance Based on Predictive Genetic Tests*, *at* Testimony of Dr. Donald A. Young (Jul. 11, 2001), http://energycommerce.house.gov/107/hearings/07112001 Hearing322/Young519.htm (accessed Oct. 1, 2005).

9 *See e.g.* Stone, *supra* n. 5, at 287 (arguing that insurance companies can achieve their objectives without separating individuals by risk categories and encouraging selfishness). *See generally* Berry, *supra* n. 3, at 207 *et seq.* (1996) (discussing the various arguments).

10 *See* Robert J. Pokorski, *Use of Genetic Information by Private Insurers*, in Justice and the Human Genome Project 91 *et seq.* (Timothy F. Murphy & Marc A. Lappé, eds, University of California Press 1994); House Committee on Energy and Commerce, Subcommittee on Commerce, Trade, and Consumer Protection, *supra* n. 8, *at* Testimony of Dr. Donald A. Young (Jul. 11, 2001), http://energy commerce.house.gov/107/hearings/07112001Hearing322/Young519.htm (accessed Oct. 1, 2005); Norman Daniels, *The Genome Project, Individual Differences, and Just Health Care*, in Justice And The Human Genome Project (Timothy F. Murphy & Marc A. Lappé, eds, University of California Press 1994); Jon Beckwith & Joseph S. Alper, *Reconsidering Genetic Antidiscrimination Legislation*, 26 J. L., Med. & Ethics 205 (1998); Susan M. Wolf, *Beyond "Genetic Discrimination": Toward the Broader Harm of Geneticism*, 23 J. L. Medicine & Eth. 345, 345–53 (1995); Berry, *supra* n. 3 (1996).

11 *See* Roberta M. Berry, *The Genetic Revolution and the Physician's Duty of Confidentiality*, 18 J. Legal Med. 401, 402–3 (1997); Berry, *supra* n. 3, at 207–8 (1996); C. Thomas Caskey, *Molecular Medicine; A Spin-Off from the Helix*, 269 JAMA 1986, 1989–90 (1993); Charles Cantor, *The Challenges to Technology and Informatics*, in The Code of Codes: Scientific and Social Issues in the Human Genome Project 98, 105 (Daniel J. Kevles & Leroy Hood, eds, Harvard University Press 1993); Evelyn Fox Keller, *Nature, Nurture, and the Human Genome Project*, *in* The Code of Codes 281, 295–96; Leroy Hood, *Biology and Medicine in the Twenty-First Century*, in The Code of Codes 136, 159, 163; Nancy Wexler, *Clairvoyance and Caution: Repercussions from the Human Genome Project*, in The Code of Codes 211, 224.

12 *See* discussions in Norman Daniels, *The Genome Project, Individual Differences, and Just Health Care*, *supra* n. 10, at 110 *et seq.* (locating his critique of risk classification within the broader conception of justice outlined by John Rawls); Beckwith & Alper, *supra* n. 10 (arguing in favor of a single-payer universal health care system); Wolf, *supra* n. 10, at 345–53.

13 *See* Kathy L. Hudson *et al.*, *supra* n. 2 (regarding the negative effects on genetic research of insurance companies' use of genetic information). *See also* Berry, *supra* n. 3, at 76–79 (2003).

14 *See e.g.* House Committee on Energy and Commerce, Subcommittee on Commerce, Trade, and Consumer Protection, *supra* n. 8, *at* Testimony of Mary Davidson (Jul. 11, 2001), http://energycommerce.house.gov/107/hearings/07112001 Hearing322/Davidson518.htm (accessed Oct. 1, 2005); NIH-DOE Working Group on Ethical, Legal, and Social Implications of Human Genome Research, *Genetic Information and Health Insurance: Report of the Task Force on Genetic Information and Insurance*, (NIH, No. 93-3686, May 10, 1993), http://www.genome.gov/ 10001750 (accessed Dec. 9, 2005); Beckwith & Alper, *supra* n. 10, at 206. *Compare* House Committee on Energy and Commerce, Subcommittee on Commerce, Trade, and Consumer Protection, *supra* n. 8, at Testimony of Dr. Donald A. Young (Jul. 11, 2001), http://energycommerce.house.gov/107/hearings/07112001

Hearing322/Young519.htm (accessed Oct. 1, 2005); Pokorski, *supra* n. 10, at 91 *et seq. See also* Mark A. Hall & Stephen S. Rich, *Laws Restricting Health Insurers' Use of Genetic Information: Impact on Genetic Discrimination*, 66 The American Journal of Human Genetics 293 (2000) (a study showing almost no evidence of insurance company use of genetic test information in states with and without laws restricting such use).

15 *See* House Committee on Energy and Commerce, Subcommittee on Commerce, Trade, and Consumer Protection, *supra* n. 8, at Testimony of Dr. Donald A. Young (Jul. 11, 2001), http://energycommerce.house.gov/107/hearings/07112001 Hearing322/Young519.htm (accessed Oct. 1, 2005); and Pokorski, *supra* n. 10, at 91 *et seq. See also* Berry, *supra* n. 3, at 207 *et seq.* (1996).

16 15 U.S.C. § 1011 *et seq.* (1945).

17 *See* House Committee on Energy and Commerce, Subcommittee on Commerce, Trade, and Consumer Protection, *supra* n. 8, at Testimony of Karen H. Rothenberg (Jul. 11, 2001), http://energycommerce.house.gov/107/hearings/07112001Hearing 322/Rothenberg521.htm (accessed Oct. 1, 2005) (discussing the nature and status of state regulation). *See also* Wolf, *supra* n. 10, at 346.

18 For state-by-state summary listings of health, life, and disability insurance laws regulating the use of genetic information, *see* National Conference of State Legislatures, Genetic Technologies Project, *State Genetics Laws*, http:// www.ncsl.org/programs/health/genetics/charts.htm (accessed Oct. 1, 2005). *See also* the searchable listings maintained by the National Cancer Institute, current through June 2005, http://www.scld-nci.net/DB_Search/Help/HLPIntro.htm (accessed Oct. 1, 2005).

19 For state-by-state listings of current legislative activity regarding use of genetic information in health, life, and disability insurance, *see* National Conference of State Legislatures, *supra* n. 18, at *Legislative Activity*, http://www.ncsl.org/programs/ health/genetics/charts.htm (accessed Oct. 1, 2005). For assessments of the implications of various approaches to regulation, *see* Berry, *supra* n. 3, at 207 *et seq.* (1996); Richard A. Epstein, *The Legal Regulation of Genetic Discrimination: Old Responses to New Technology*, 74 B. U. L. Rev. 1 (1994); *Genetic Information and Health Insurance: Report of the Task Force on Genetic Information and Insurance*, *supra* n. 14; Pokorski, *supra* n. 10, at 91 *et seq.*; and Wolf, *supra* n. 10, at 345–53.

20 29 U.S.C. § 1001 *et seq.* (1974).

21 *See* House Committee on Energy and Commerce, Subcommittee on Commerce, Trade, and Consumer Protection, *supra* n. 8, at Testimony of Karen H. Rothenberg (Jul. 11, 2001), http://energycommerce.house.gov/107/hearings/07112001Hearing 322/Rothenberg521.htm (accessed Oct. 1, 2005).

22 Public Law 104–91, August 21, 1996.

23 29 U.S.C. § 1182 (a) (1).

24 29 U.S.C. § 1181 (a) and (b); 42 U.S.C. § 300 gg (a) and (b).

25 *See* House Committee on Energy and Commerce, Subcommittee on Commerce, Trade, and Consumer Protection, *supra* n. 8, at Testimony of Karen H. Rothenberg (Jul. 11, 2001), http://energycommerce.house.gov/107/hearings/07112001Hearing 322/Rothenberg521.htm (accessed Oct. 1, 2005); and House Committee on Energy and Commerce, Subcommittee on Commerce, Trade, and Consumer Protection, *supra* n. 8, at Testimony of Mary Davidson (Jul. 11, 2001), http://energycommerce. house.gov/107/hearings/07112001Hearing322/Davidson518.htm (accessed Oct. 1, 2005).

26 *See* House Committee on Energy and Commerce, Subcommittee on Commerce, Trade, and Consumer Protection, *supra* n. 8, at Testimony of Dr. Donald A. Young (Jul. 11, 2001), http://energycommerce.house.gov/107/hearings/07112001 Hearing322/Young519.htm (accessed Oct. 1, 2005).

27 Regarding the 2005 proposal, *see* discussion and linked documents at National Human Genome Research Institute, *Genetic Discrimination in Health Insurance or Employment* http://www.genome.gov/11510227 (accessed Oct. 5, 2005). Regarding failure of enactment of a 2003 proposal, *see* discussion in Henry T. Greely, *Banning Genetic Discrimination*, 353 The New England Journal of Medicine 865 (2005), http://content.nejm.org/cgi/content/full/353/9/865 (accessed Dec. 19, 2005).

28 *See* Leroy Walters & Julie Cage Palmer, The Ethics of Human Gene Therapy, 17–59 (Oxford University Press 1997) (regarding early clinical trials); National Institutes of Health, Advisory Committee to the Director, Working Group on NIH Oversight of Clinical Gene Transfer Research, *Enhancing the Protection of Human Subjects in Gene Transfer Research at the National Institutes of Health* (Jul. 12, 2000), http://www.nih.gov/about/director/07122000.htm (accessed Oct. 1, 2005) (regarding clinical trials in the 1990s); Nancy M. P. King, *RAC Oversight of Gene Transfer Research: A Model Worth Extending?* 30 Journal of Law, Medicine & Ethics 381 (2002) at 382–83 (regarding shift to research on cancer in the early twenty-first century and regarding "gene transfer research" as more accurate terminology than "gene therapy").

29 *See* National Institutes of Health, *Report and Recommendations of the Panel to Assess the NIH Investment in Research on Gene Therapy*, Stuart H. Orkin, M.D. & Arno G. Motulsky, M.D., Co-chairs (Dec. 7, 1995), http://www.nih.gov/news/panelrep.html (accessed Dec. 19, 2005) (regarding failure to realize clinical benefits by late 1995); Nathan Seppa, *"Bubble" Babies Thrive on Gene Therapy*, 157 Science News 277 (2000) (reporting success in gene therapy experiment with SCID patients); Nathan Seppa, *Genetically Altered Cells Ease Hemophilia*, 159 Science News 357 (2001) (reporting encouraging results in treatment of hemophilia); King, *supra* n. 28, at 382 and sources cited in n. 19 (referring to mixed successes). *See* Office of Biotechnology Activities, National Institutes of Health, Fact Sheet, *Serious Adverse Event in a Study of Gene Transfer in X-Linked Severe Combined Immunodeficiency* (Jan. 14, 2003) http://www4.od.nih.gov/OBA/RAC/Fact_Sheet.pdf (accessed Oct. 15, 2005) (referring to development of condition in SCID experiment); and Utpal P. Davé, Nancy A. Jenkins & Neal G. Copeland, *Gene Therapy Insertional Mutagenesis Insights*, 303 Science 333 (Jan. 26, 2004) (referring to cause of development of condition in SCID experiment).

30 *See* Food and Drug Administration, Center for Biologics Evaluation and Research, *Cellular & Gene Therapy*, http://www.fda.gov/cber/gene.htm (accessed Dec. 19, 2005); and Food and Drug Administration, Center for Biologics Evaluation and Research, *Cellular & Gene Therapy Publications*, http://www.fda.gov/cber/genetherapy/gtpubs.htm (accessed Dec. 19, 2005).

31 *See* National Institutes of Health, *Guidelines for Research Involving Recombinant DNA Molecules ("NIH Guidelines")*, http://www4.od.nih.gov/oba/rac/guidelines/guidelines.html (accessed Dec. 19. 2005). Regarding the creation and evolution of RAC, *see* Joseph M. Rainsbury, *Biotechnology on the RAC–FDA/NIH Regulation of Human Gene Therapy*, 55 Food Drug L. J. 575 at 575–81; National Institutes of Health, Advisory Committee to the Director, Working Group on NIH Oversight of Clinical Gene Transfer Research, *supra* n. 28, at Appendix B, http://www.nih.gov/about/director/07122000.htm#appendb.

32 *See* Rainsbury, *supra* n. 31, at 581–92.

33 *See NIH Guidelines*, *supra* n. 31, at Section III, http://www4.od.nih.gov/oba/rac/guidelines_02/NIH_Guidelines_Apr_02.htm#_Toc7261559; and King, *supra* n. 28, at 381.

34 *See* Rainsbury, *supra* n. 31, at 592; and King, *supra* n. 28, at 382–83.

35 *See* Rainsbury, *supra* n. 31, at 592–93; and Susan Jenks, *Gene Therapy Death – "Everyone Has to Share in the Guilt,"* 92 Journal of the National Cancer Institute 98 (2000).

36 *See* Mike Pezzella, *In Wake of Patient Death, U Penn Gene Therapy Program Closes*, Biotechnology Newswatch, 5 (Jun. 2000); and Sheryl Gay Stolberg, *Institute Restricted After Gene Therapy Death*, N.Y. Times, 20 (May 25, 2000). *See also* University of Pennsylvania President Judith Rodin's *Letter to U.S. Senate on Gene Therapy* (Jan. 31, 2000), http://www.upenn.edu/almanac/v46/n20/benchmarks.html (accessed Oct. 1, 2005).

37 Regarding the array of concerns raised, *see* Robert Gatter, *Human Subjects Research and Conflicts of Interest: Walking the Talk of Trust in Human Subjects Research: The Challenge of Regulating Financial Conflicts of Interest*, 52 Emory L. J. 327, at 355ff. (2003). For a comprehensive report on gene transfer experimentation and the safety of human subjects, *see* National Institutes of Health, Advisory Committee to the Director, Working Group on NIH Oversight of Clinical Gene Transfer Research, *supra* n. 28. For a discussion of reports pertaining to IRBs, *see* Robert Finn, *Reports Bring Several Changes to IRBs*, 92 Journal of the National Cancer Institute 1287 (2000). For an account of the new guidelines adopted by the American Society of Gene Therapy, *see* Sheryl Gay Stolberg, *Despite Ferment, Gene Therapy Progresses*, N.Y. Times, F1, (Jun. 6, 2000). For an account of the administrative initiatives undertaken by the Office of the Secretary of HHS, *see* Donna Shalala, *Protecting Research Subjects – What Must Be Done*, 343 New Eng. J. Med. 808 (2000).

38 For NIH-funded gene transfer research, *see* 42 CFR part 50, subpart F, and 45 CFR part 94. For FDA-regulated gene transfer research, *see* 21 CFR part 54. For HHS-funded research and IRB requirements, *see* 45 CFR Part 46 for HHS. For FDA-regulated research and IRB requirements, *see* 21 CFR Parts 50 and 56.

39 *See* Gatter, *supra* n. 37, at 329–30, 351 (regarding the financial interests of those involved and claims of Mr. Gelsinger's family regarding nondisclosure of these interests prior to the experiment); and Patricia C. Kuszler, *Curing Conflicts of Interest in Clinical Research: Impossible Dreams and Harsh Realities*, 8 Wid. L. Symp. J. 115 (2001) at 131–32 (regarding concerns about the effects of financial conflicts of interest).

40 National Institutes of Health, *Financial Conflicts of Interest and Research Objectivity: Issues for Investigators and Institutional Review Boards* (Jun. 5, 2000), http://grants.nih.gov/grants/guide/notice-files/NOT-OD-00-040.html (accessed Dec. 15, 2005).

41 *See* Office of Public Health and Science, *Financial Relationships and Interests in Research Involving Human Subjects: Guidance for Human Subject Protection*, 69 *Fed. Reg.* 26393–97 (May 12, 2004), http://a257.g.akamaitech.net/7/257/2422/14mar20010800/edocket.access.gpo.gov/2004/04–10849.htm (accessed Dec. 22, 2005) (guidance for IRB review); Food and Drug Administration, Center for Drug Evaluation and Research, Center for Biologics Evaluation and Research, Center for Devices and Radiological Health, *Guidance, Financial Disclosure by Clinical Investigators* (Mar. 20, 2001), http://www.fda.gov/oc/guidance/financialdis.html (accessed Dec. 15, 2005) (guidance regarding conflicts of interest and bias). For a report on the public consultation in August 2000, *see* Steve Benowitz, *Lines Disintegrating Between Industry, Academic Research*, 92 Journal of the National Cancer Institute 1377 (2000). *See also* American Society of Gene Therapy, *Policy of The American Society of Gene Therapy, Financial Conflict of Interest in Clinical Research* (Apr. 5, 2000), http://www.asgt.org/position_statements/conflict_of_interest.html (accessed Nov. 20, 2005) (a policy adopted by an association of gene therapy researchers for its membership directing that no investigator involved in patient selection, the informed consent process, or management of a clinical trial could hold a financial interest in the companies sponsoring the trial).

42 *See* Gatter, *supra* n. 37, at 348–50, 373–74; Kuszler, *supra* n. 39, at 130–43, 148ff.; Greg Koski, *Research, Regulations, and Responsibility: Confronting the*

Compliance Myth – A Reaction to Professor Gatter, 52 Emory L J. 403, 408–10 (2003).

43 *See* Food and Drug Administration, Center for Biologics Evaluation and Research, *Dear Gene Therapy IND Sponsor/Principal Investigator Letter* (Nov. 5, 1999), http://www.fda.gov/cber/ltr/gt110599.htm (accessed Nov. 30, 2005); Food and Drug Administration, *New Initiatives to Protect Participants in Gene Therapy Trials*, March 7, 2000, http://www.fda.gov/bbs/topics/NEWS/NEW00717.html (accessed Dec. 1, 2005); Food and Drug Administration, *Dear Gene Therapy IND or Master File Sponsor Letter*, March 6, 2000, http://www.fda.gov/cber/ltr/gt030600.htm (accessed Dec. 1, 2005); National Institutes of Health, *Further Guidance on Data and Safety Monitoring for Phase I and Phase II Trials*, June 5, 2000, http://grants2.nih.gov/grants/guide/notice-files/NOT-OD-00-038.html (accessed Dec. 23, 2005). *See also* discussion in King, *supra* n. 28, at 385–86.

44 *See* National Institutes of Health, Office of Biotechnology Activities, *Recombinant DNA Research: Action Under the Guidelines; Notice*, 65 *Fed. Reg.* 60327-60332 (Oct. 10, 2000), http://www4.od.nih.gov/oba/rac/frnotices/10-10-00act.htm (accessed Dec. 23, 2005) (regarding timing of review by RAC, IRB, and IBC); National Institutes of Health, Office of Biotechnology Activities, *Recombinant DNA Research: Proposed Actions Under the NIH Guidelines*, 66 *Fed. Reg.* 64052–54 (Dec. 11, 2001), http://www4.od.nih.gov/oba/rac/frnotices/FR12-11-01-rac.htm (accessed Dec. 23, 2005) (regarding membership of RAC). *See also* National Institutes of Health, Advisory Committee to the Director, Working Group on NIH Oversight of Clinical Gene Transfer Research, *supra* n. 28; and King, *supra* n. 28, at 385.

45 *See* National Institutes of Health, Office of Biotechnology Activities, *Recombinant DNA Research: Actions Under the NIH Guidelines*, 66 *Fed. Reg.* 57970–77 (Nov. 19, 2001), http://www4.od.nih.gov/oba/rac/frnotices/11-19-01act.htm (accessed Dec. 23, 2005).

46 American Society of Gene Therapy, *Letter to Office of Information and Regulatory Affairs, Office of Management and Budget* (Dec. 18, 2001), http://www.asgt.org/regulatory_issues/nih_recombinantdna_response.html (accessed Dec. 1, 2005). *See also* discussion of confidentiality issues in King, *supra* n. 28, at 385–86.

47 *See* announcement of launch of database, National Institutes of Health, *NIH and FDA Launch New Human Gene Transfer Research Data System* (Mar. 26, 2004), http://www.nih.gov/news/pr/mar2004/od-26.htm (accessed Dec. 23, 2005). For links to public information web site, public data on human gene transfer trials, and adverse event reporting, begin at: http://www4.od.nih.gov/oba/RAC/GeMCRIS/GeMCRIS.htm (accessed Dec. 2, 2005). *See also* discussion in King, *supra* n. 28, at 385–86.

48 National Institutes of Health, Office of Biotechnology Activities, *Recombinant DNA Research: Proposed Actions Under the NIH Guidelines*, *supra* n. 44.

49 *See* Food and Drug Administration, FDA Talk Paper, *FDA Places Temporary Halt on Gene Therapy Trials Using Retroviral Vectors in Blood Stem Cells* (Jan.14, 2003), http://www.fda.gov/bbs/topics/ANSWERS/2003/ANS01190.html (accessed Dec. 3, 2005); Food and Drug Administration, FDA Talk Paper, *FDA Advisory Committee Discusses Steps for Potentially Continuing Certain Gene Therapy Trials That Were Recently Placed on Hold* (Feb. 28, 2003), http://www.fda.gov/bbs/topics/ANSWERS/2003/ANS01202.html (accessed Dec. 3, 2005); Andy Coghlan, *Gene Therapy to Resume on "Bubble Boys,"* New Scientist 12 (Jan. 8, 2005).

50 *See* Food and Drug Administration, Center for Biologics Evaluation and Research, *Guidance for Industry, Gene Therapy Clinical Trials – Observing*

Participants for Delayed Adverse Effects (Aug. 2005), http://www.fda.gov/cber/gdlns/gtclin.htm (accessed Dec. 3, 2005). *See also* discussion of workshop of regulators, investigators, and industry representatives to discuss these issues prior to issuance of the FDA Guidance, Kara Nyberg, Barrie J. Carter, Theresa Chen, Cynthia Dunbar, Terrence Flotte, Stephen Rose, Daniel Rosenblum, Stephanie Simek & Carolyn Wilson, *Workshop on Long-term Follow-up of Participants in Human Gene Transfer Research*, 10 Molecular Therapy 976 (Dec. 2004).

51 *See* Francis. S. Collins, *The President's Council on Bioethics (Transcripts), Genetic Enhancements: Current and Future Prospects* (Dec. 13, 2002), http://www.bioethics.gov/transcripts/dec02/session5.html (accessed Dec. 24, 2005) (discussing past and prospective techniques, including the development of artificial chromosomes); American Association for the Advancement of Science, *Human Inheritable Genetic Modifications: Findings and Recommendations*, 15–26 (Sept. 2000), http://www.aaas.org/spp/sfrl/projects/germline/main.htm (accessed Dec. 24, 2005) (discussing range of techniques and their shortcomings); and Gregory Stock, Redesigning Humans: Our Inevitable Genetic Future 65 (Houghton Mifflin 2002) (discussing the potential use of artificial chromosomes).

52 *See* Emily Marden & Dorothy Nelkin, *Displaced Agendas: Current Regulatory Strategies for Germline Gene Therapy*, 45 Mcgill L J. 461, 473–76 (2000) (discussing FDA's regulatory authority, including whether it would apply to genetic engineering for enhancement of human features rather than for curing, treating, or preventing disease); The President's Council on Bioethics, Reproduction and Responsibility: The Regulation of New Biotechnologies 46–71 (Washington, D.C. 2004), http://www.bioethics.gov/reports/reproductionandresponsibility/index.html (accessed Dec. 24, 2005) (discussing limited regulation of assisted reproductive technologies, including IVF).

53 For a discussion of a framework for regulation, *see* American Association for the Advancement of Science, *Human Inheritable Genetic Modifications: Findings and Recommendations*, *supra* n. 51.

54 For a variety of arguments and points of view on these issues, *see* George J. Annas, *The Man on the Moon, Immortality, and Other Millennial Myths: The Prospects and Perils of Human Genetic Engineering*, 49 Emory L. J. 753 (2000); Ronald Bailey, Liberation Biology: The Scientific and Moral Case for the Biotech Revolution 149–81 (Prometheus Books 2005); Roberta M. Berry, *Eugenics after the Holocaust: The Limits of Reproductive Rights*, in Humanity at the Limit: The Impact of the Holocaust Experience on Jews and Christians (Michael A. Signer, ed., Indiana University Press 2000); Roberta M. Berry, *Genetic Enhancement in the Twenty-first Century: Three Problems in Legal Imagining,* 34 Wake Forest L. Rev. 715 (1999); Berry, *supra* n. 1, at 401; Allen Buchanan, Dan W. Brock, Norman Daniels & Daniel Wikler, From Chance to Choice: Genetics and Justice (Cambridge University Press 2000); Engineering the Human Germline: An Exploration of the Science and Ethics of Altering the Genes We Pass to our Children (Gregory Stock & John Campbell, eds, Oxford University Press 2000); Enhancing Human Traits: Ethical And Social Implications (Erik Parens, ed., Georgetown University Press 1998); John Harris, Clones, Genes, and Immortality: Ethics and the Genetic Revolution (Oxford University Press 1998); Leon R. Kass, *Triumph or Tragedy? The Moral Meaning of Genetic Technology*, 45 Am. J. Juris. 1 (2000); Glenn McGee, The Perfect Baby: Parenthood in the New World of Cloning and Genetics (2d ed., Rowman & Littlefield 2000); Maxwell J. Mehlman, Wondergenes: Genetic Enhancement and the Future of Society (Indiana University Press 2003); The President's Council on Bioethics, Beyond Therapy: Biotechnology and the Pursuit of Happiness 27–57 (2003), http://www.bioethics.gov/reports/beyondtherapy/index.html (accessed Dec. 25, 2005); John A. Robertson, *Genetic Selection of Offspring Characteristics*, 76 B. U. L. Rev. 421 (1996); and

Lee M. Silver, Remaking Eden: How Genetic Engineering and Cloning Will Transform The American Family (Avon 1998).

55 *See* The President's Council on Bioethics, Human Cloning and Human Dignity: An Ethical Inquiry 57–73 (2002), http://www.bioethics.gov/reports/cloningreport/index.html (accessed Dec. 24, 2005) (discussing techniques and applications in humans and nonhuman animals and for research).

56 *See* Katharine Q. Seelye, *Clinton Bans Federal Money for Efforts to Clone Humans*, New York Times, 13 (Mar. 5, 1997) (regarding immediate moratorium on federal funding for attempts at human cloning); National Bioethics Advisory Commission, Cloning Human Beings 107–10 (1997), http://www.bioethics.gov/reports/past_commissions/nbac_cloning.pdf (accessed Dec. 24, 2005) (regarding recommendations for extending the moratorium by federal legislation); and The President's Council on Bioethics, Human Cloning and Human Dignity: An Ethical Inquiry, *supra* n. 55, at 28–32 (regarding failed Congressional efforts to enact a ban).

57 The President's Council on Bioethics, Human Cloning and Human Dignity: An Ethical Inquiry, *supra* n. 55, at 199–227.

58 For a discussion of asserted FDA jurisdiction in House Committee on Energy and Commerce, *see* Subcommittee on Health, *Legislative Hearing on H.R. 1644, Human Cloning Prohibition Act of 2001, and H.R. 2172, Cloning Prohibition Act of 2001*, Testimony of Claude Allen (June 20, 2001), http://energycommerce.house.gov/107/hearings/06202001Hearing291/Allen449.htm (accessed Oct. 1, 2005). *See also* Gregory J. Rokosz, *Human Cloning: Is the Reach of FDA Authority Too Far a Stretch?* 30 Seton Hall L. Rev. 464 (2000) (analyzing FDA's jurisdictional claim).

59 H.R. 1644, Human Cloning Prohibition Act of 2001. *See* CNN, *House Votes to Ban Human Cloning* (Aug.1, 2001), http://www.cnn.com/2001/ALLPOLITICS/07/31/cloning.bush (accessed Oct. 1, 2005). *See also* Association of American Medical Colleges, *Somatic Cell Nuclear Transfer (Therapeutic Cloning)* (2005), http://www.aamc.org/advocacy/library/research/res0003.htm (accessed Dec. 4, 2005).

60 For listings of current state cloning laws, *see* National Conference of State Legislatures, Genetic Technologies Project, *State Genetics Laws: Human Cloning*, http://www.ncsl.org/programs/health/genetics/charts.htm (accessed Oct. 1, 2005). For listings of current state legislative activity on human cloning, *see* National Conference of State Legislatures, Genetic Technologies Project, *Legislative Activity: Human Cloning*, http://www.ncsl.org/programs/health/genetics/geneticsDB.cfm (accessed Oct. 1, 2005).

61 For a variety of views on these issues, *see* Lori B. Andrews, The Clone Age: Adventures in the New World of Reproductive Technology (Henry Holt 1999); Bailey, *supra* n. 54, at 135–48; Dena S. Davis, Genetic Dilemmas: Reproductive Technology, Parental Choices, and Children's Futures (Routledge 2001); Harris, *supra* n. 54; Leon R. Kass & James Q. Wilson, The Ethics of Human Cloning (American Enterprise Institute 1998); Leon R. Kass, *A Debate on Human Cloning: Why We Should Ban the Cloning of Human Beings*, 4 Tex. Rev. Law & Pol. 39 (1999); Gina Kolata, Clone: The Road to Dolly and the Path Ahead (Quill 1999); National Bioethics Advisory Commission, Cloning Human Beings, *supra* n. 56; Gregory E. Pence, Who's Afraid of Human Cloning? (Rowman & Littlefield 1998); The President's Council on Bioethics, Human Cloning and Human Dignity: An Ethical Inquiry, *supra* n. 55; Radhika Rao, *The Legal Debate Surrounding Human Cloning: What's So Strange About Human Cloning?* 53 Hastings L. J. 1007 (2002); and John A. Robertson, *Liberty, Identity, and Human Cloning*, 76 Tex. L. Rev. 1371 (1998).

62 *See* Robertson, *supra* n. 61, at 1387–403 (presenting an argument for constitutional protection of reproductive cloning for infertile parents).

7 Bioethics issues surrounding the beginning of life

Legal aspects in the United States

Robyn S. Shapiro

Dramatic advances in our ability to assist human reproduction and to assess and improve the health status of a fetus in utero, along with intensified debate about preventing and terminating pregnancy, have raised challenging legal questions and resulted in important legislative and judicial developments. This chapter will provide an overview of key legal issues that surround medical and bioethical aspects of life's beginning.

Birth control

In a number of cases, the United States Supreme Court has held that both married and unmarried adults have a constitutional right of privacy, which encompasses the right to learn about and use contraceptives. In one landmark case, the Court said: "If the right of privacy means anything, it is the right of the individual, married or single, to be free from unwarranted governmental intrusion into matters so fundamentally affecting a person as the decision whether to bear or beget a child."[1] Accordingly, the right of a single or married adult to make decisions about birth control may not be infringed upon by state action unless the state's action furthers a compelling state interest in the least restrictive manner possible.[2]

The issue of contraception for minors is more complicated. In a landmark case decided in 1977, the United States Supreme Court held that a state statute forbidding the sale of contraceptives to minors unconstitutionally infringed upon their privacy rights.[3] However, a majority of the Court did not agree that minors have the same fully protected right of privacy in procreative decisions as do adults. Some states have adopted laws requiring parental consent for minors' access to contraceptives. The United States Supreme Court has not considered the issue of parental notification regarding minors' access to contraceptives. However, the Sixth Circuit Court of Appeals has held that a publicly operated clinic's provision of contraceptives to minors without notice to their parents did not violate parents' constitutional right to participate in important decisions concerning their children.[4]

With respect to liability issues in contraception, as is true in other areas of medical care, the health care provider must adhere to accepted standards of care in order to avoid negligence liability exposure. Accordingly, the provider must take an adequate patient history before prescribing or administering birth control, advise the patient about risks of and alternatives to the prescribed birth control, and monitor for adverse side effects.

In some cases, health care providers have been held liable for wrongful pregnancy due to negligence in prescribing or administering birth control. For example, in one case, an appellate court held that plaintiff could state a claim against a physician for failure to reinsert an IUD after a patient's pelvic examination.[5] In such cases, while courts may allow recovery for the mother's pregnancy and childbearing expenses, plaintiffs most often do not recover damages for the full cost of rearing an unwanted but healthy child.

Sterilization

When competent individuals seek sterilization – that is, the termination of their ability to procreate – relevant law provides that patients must be fully informed about the nature and consequences of the procedure and that they must be acting voluntarily.[6] When sterilization is to be performed on an incompetent person, legal issues are more complex.

Some states have specific statutes governing the sterilization of incompetents. Under some of these statutes, specific procedures must be followed to confirm that the patient is incompetent and to assure that the sterilization is in the patient's best interests.[7] In some states, even if a patient is found to be incompetent and the sterilization is found to be in his or her best interests, the patient nonetheless may refuse the procedure if he or she understands the consequences of a refusal.[8] Other states have statutes that permit sterilization of incompetent persons if the purpose is to avoid the procreation of children who would have an inherited predisposition to a mental disease or who likely would be neglected because of their parents' mental inability to care for them.[9]

In some states that do not have a sterilization statute, courts have held that in the absence of legislation expressly authorizing sterilization of incompetents, the procedure may not be done.[10] On the other hand, in other states with no sterilization statutes, courts have held that an incompetent may be sterilized as long as there are adequate procedural safeguards in the treatment decision making process.[11]

Abortion

For decades, abortion has spurred intense debates not only in the medical profession but in American society at large. Prior to the United States Supreme Court's 1973 *Roe v. Wade* decision,[12] each state regulated abortion as it wished. In Texas, for example, the performance of abortion in most circumstances was a criminal offense, while in New York the law was much more liberal.

Roe v. Wade, along with a companion U.S. Supreme Court case, *Doe v. Bolton*,[13] established that a woman's constitutional right to privacy encompasses her decisions about whether or not to terminate her pregnancy, and that a law or other state action that unduly burdens that right is unconstitutional unless it is necessary to further a compelling state interest in the least restrictive manner possible. The Court reasoned that the state could invade the pregnant woman's privacy to a limited extent when its interest in protecting the health of the mother or the life of the fetus became sufficiently strong, and it imposed these limitations:

1. Prior to the end of the first trimester, the decision to abort is between the woman and her physician;
2. Beginning in the second trimester but before the fetus becomes viable, the state may impose regulations reasonably related to the woman's health;
3. During the period of fetal viability, the state may pass laws for the purpose of preserving fetal life, including legislation that regulates or prohibits abortion, except where abortion is medically necessary for "the life or health of the mother."[14]

Since 1973, states have passed various laws to govern or restrict the availability of the procedure, such as requirements that the woman receive certain information to assure her informed consent, laws governing abortion methods, and laws limiting funding for abortions. Many of these laws have been challenged as illegal restrictions, and this has led the U.S. Supreme Court to revisit the *Roe* decision on a number of occasions.

For example, in *Colautti v. Franklin*,[15] the Supreme Court considered a statute that required physicians to use an abortion technique most suited to fetal survival unless a different method was necessary in order to preserve the mother-to-be's life or health. The Court held that the statute unconstitutionally infringed upon the pregnant woman's rights by requiring use of the technique that would be safe for her only if it were "necessary." The Court also found the statute to be unconstitutionally vague because it was not clear whether physicians could consider their duty to the woman to be paramount to their duty to the fetus or whether it required physicians to "make a 'trade-off' between the woman's health and additional percentage points of fetal survival."[16]

In *Akron v. Akron Center for Reproductive Health*,[17] later overruled in *Planned Parenthood v. Casey*,[18] the Court struck down a requirement that all second trimester abortions be performed in a hospital, as well as statutory provisions that required physicians to disclose to women seeking abortions certain information about the fetus' ability to feel pain and "a 'parade of horribles' intended to suggest that abortion is a particularly dangerous procedure."[19] The Court said that in the absence of evidence that routine hospitalization for second trimester abortions was medically necessary, the regulations would unconstitutionally decrease the availability of abortions by substantially increasing the cost; and that the disclosure provisions unreasonably restrained the physician from tailoring information to the particular woman's need.[20] Three years later in *Thornburgh v. American College of Obstetricians & Gynecologists*,[21] the Court again struck down informed consent provisions in a Pennsylvania statute that appeared to be designed to "intimidate women into continuing pregnancies,"[22] as well as provisions that required detailed and extensive reporting about the physicians and facilities involved; the woman's residence, age, race, marital status, prior pregnancies, and last menstrual period; the basis for any judgment that a medical emergency existed and/or for any determination of fetal nonviability; and payment sources for the abortion. These reporting requirements, the Court said, went beyond health-related interests and would discourage women from undergoing an abortion out of fear about their identity becoming publicly known.[23]

In the 1989 Supreme Court's *Webster v. Reproductive Health Services* decision,[24] the Court, while not overturning *Roe*, indicated its willingness to uphold more restrictive abortion legislation;[25] and since 1989 the Court has upheld a number of federal government regulations and state laws that restrict abortion. In 1991, for example, the Supreme Court decided *Rust v. Sullivan*,[26] which upheld regulations promulgated by the Department of Health and Human Services that prohibit recipients of funds under Title X of the Public Health Services Act from engaging in any abortion-related activities.[27]

In *Planned Parenthood of Southeastern Pennsylvania v. Casey*,[28] decided in 1992, the Supreme Court analyzed and upheld all but one of the challenged provisions of Pennsylvania's statute – including requirements that a physician inform the woman of the fetus' gestational age, the nature and risks of the abortion procedure, and the risks of childbirth; and that a physician or qualified non-physician inform the woman of the availability of state-issued printed materials describing the fetus as well as alternatives to abortion, and that the woman sign a form confirming that she was informed about these materials and was provided them upon her request; and that the abortion be delayed following the informed consent interchange for a twenty-four-hour waiting period except in medical emergencies;[29] and that the facility performing the abortion file specified and detailed reports.[30] The Court held unconstitutional only the portion of the statute that required spousal notification.[31] A five to four majority concluded that the essential holding of *Roe v. Wade* should be retained, but that the *Roe* approach undervalued the interest in potential life and that the state's interest in protecting the life of the fetus is legitimate from the outset of the pregnancy. The *Casey* majority did not provide specific guidance for determining what standard should apply in analyzing abortion regulations, but a joint opinion by Justices O'Connor, Kennedy, and Souter suggested that the criterion should be whether the regulation presents an "undue burden" on the woman's abortion decision – that is, whether its purpose or effect places "a substantial obstacle in the path of a woman seeking an abortion of a nonviable fetus."[32] Using this analysis, the three Justices found that a state may regulate abortion to assure that a woman's abortion choice is thoughtful and informed, and it may express a preference for "childbirth over abortion, even if [the statutory] measures at [issue] do not further a health interest."[33]

In the wake of *Webster* and *Casey*, while the constitutional right to choose abortion remains intact, its exact reach is less clear. The "undue burden" standard adopted in *Casey's* joint opinion opened new opportunities for evaluating the constitutionality of abortion restrictions. In 1992, however, the Supreme Court denied certiorari in *Ada v. Guam Society of Obstetricians and Gynecologists*[34] – in which the Ninth Circuit held as unconstitutional Guam's statute prohibiting all abortions except for medical emergencies;[35] and in *Stenberg v. Carhart*,[36] the Supreme Court held that a Nebraska statute banning "partial-birth" abortion procedures was unconstitutional. The statute, the Court said, imposed an undue burden on a woman's constitutional right to obtain a previability abortion because: (1) the statute lacked any exception to preserve a woman's health, and (2) the statutory definition of "partial-birth" applied to the most frequently used second trimester abortion method as well as to an infrequently used variation of that procedure. Yet, a similar federal statute did not meet the same fate. In *Carhart v. Gonzales*,[37] the U.S. Court of Appeals struck down the 2003 federal Partial-Birth Abortion Ban Act,[38] because it forbids doctors from using the disputed dilation and extraction procedure even if medical experts say this is the safer method of performing second-term abortions. However, in *Gonzales v. Carhart*,[39] in a 5-4 vote, the Supreme Court ruled that the Act does not violate a woman's right to have an abortion under the *Roe v. Wade* ruling. This ruling marks a departure from the Supreme Court's past practice of requiring a "health exception" in laws limiting abortion, and it is the first time the Supreme Court has upheld a ban on a specific procedure.

Assisted reproductive technologies

In the past several decades, a variety of medical techniques have been developed that allow individuals who otherwise would not be able to reproduce to have biologically related children. These techniques, commonly referred to as "assisted reproductive technologies" (ARTs), include many which attempt to accomplish pregnancy by means other than sexual intercourse. While a number of legal issues surround ARTs, the practice of assisted reproduction is subject to only limited governmental oversight in this country. The remainder of this section will address legal aspects of specific ART procedures.

In vitro *fertilization*

In vitro fertilization (IVF), which may be used to create a child if a woman has blocked or absent fallopian tubes or her partner has a low sperm count, involves withdrawal of sperm from a man and an ovum from a woman, joining the sperm and ovum outside the woman's body, and implantation of the fertilized ovum in the woman's womb. If the couple has produced more embryos than the number that are reimplanted, they often have the options of freezing the extra embryos for subsequent IVF attempts, donating the extra embryos to other couples or for research, or discarding them. As discussed below, IVF poses a number of legal issues, with bioethical implications, regarding patient selection, informed consent, and control over cryopreserved embryos.

Patient selection

Commonly, IVF clinics impose medical indications in their patient selection and accept only those patients who have not been able to conceive despite trying other fertility treatments. Some clinics also assess whether potential patients would be fit parents; at least one state has passed a statute that requires nonmedical evaluation of couples seeking in vitro fertilization.[40] In addition, while no state laws explicitly limit IVF to married couples, many clinics do; and a Maryland statute that requires insurers to cover IVF if they cover other pregnancy-related services applies only to IVF for married couples in which the wife's eggs are fertilized with her husband's sperm.[41] The assumption about parental unfitness that appears to underlie clinics' refusals to offer IVF to unmarried individuals is contradicted by empirical evidence[42] and disputed by number of professional organizations.

Informed consent

In order to provide prospective IVF patients with sufficient information to allow them to make a knowledgeable choice about whether to proceed, health care professionals should provide them with data about the nature and risks of IVF (including the risk of infection, spontaneous abortion, stillbirth, and psychological risks), the potential success of the proposed procedure, and alternative means of treatment. In addition, patients should receive information about the clinic's policy with respect to embryo cryopreservation and disposition of spare embryos.

Control over cryopreserved embryos

There are over 400,000 frozen embryos stored in the United States, with those numbers increasing annually,[43] and with the fate of significant numbers of them subject to dispute.[44] To date, the resolution of most disagreements between progenitors and IVF clinics over the fate of frozen embryos have favored the decision making authority of the couple.[45] When the disagreement is between the progenitors themselves, resolution is often more difficult. In an attempt to ward off these difficulties, several courts and legislatures have urged couples to execute an agreement indicating their preferred disposition of frozen embryos prior to undergoing the IVF procedure. For example, in *Davis v. Davis*, the Tennessee Supreme Court stated:

> We believe, as a starting point, that an agreement regarding disposition of any untransferred preembryos in the event of contingencies (such as the death of one or more of the parties, divorce, financial reversals, or abandonment of the program) should be presumed valid and should be enforced as between the progenitors.[46]

In *Kass v. Kass*, the New York Court of Appeals explained the importance of prior agreements, stating that they "minimize misunderstandings and maximize procreative liberty by reserving to the progenitors the authority to make what is in the first instance a quintessentially personal, private decision," and that "knowing that advance agreements will be enforced underscores the seriousness and integrity of the consent process."[47] In that case, the court concluded that several documents signed by Maureen and Steven Kass at the request of their IVF provider clearly indicated the parties' mutual intention to donate any disputed embryos to the IVF program for research purposes. Maureen disputed this intent and requested the court to allow her to implant the embryos, but the court insisted on adherence to the contract.[48]

On the other hand, some courts have refused to recognize as binding couples' prior agreements regarding the desired disposition of their frozen embryos. For instance, in *A.Z. v. B.Z.*,[49] the Supreme Judicial Court of Massachusetts refused to enforce a consent form that indicated a couple's desired disposition of their frozen embryos, since circumstances had changed significantly since the time that they had entered into the agreement and it was "dubious at best" that the form expressed the husband's and wife's intent "in the case of a dispute between them."[50] Moreover, the court said that even if the agreement clearly applied under the circumstances, as a matter of public policy it "would not enforce an agreement that would compel one donor to become a parent against his or her will."[51]

Davis v. Davis involved a dispute regarding frozen embryos between a divorcing couple that had not executed a prior agreement.[52] After Mary Sue Davis' five tubal pregnancies, she and her husband, Junior Lewis, underwent seven rounds of IVF. Following the seventh attempt, extra embryos were cryopreserved but the couple did not execute an agreement regarding disposition in the event of their divorce. In the Davis' divorce proceedings, the primary issue of dispute was the disposition of their frozen embryos. Mrs. Davis wanted to use them to try to become pregnant; Mr. Davis wanted to leave the embryos in storage "until he decided whether or not he wanted to become a parent outside the bounds of marriage."[53] In the course of the litigation, though, both parties remarried and both changed their minds about the frozen embryos. By the time the case reached the Tennessee Supreme Court, Mrs. Davis wanted to donate the frozen embryos to an infertile couple, and Mr. Davis wanted to discard them.

The Court addressed the situation as follows:

> [W]e hold that disputes involving the disposition of preembryos produced by in vitro fertilization should be resolved, first, by looking to the preferences of the progenitors. If their wishes cannot be ascertained, or if there is dispute, then their prior agreement concerning disposition should be carried out. If no prior agreement exists, then the relative interests of the parties in using or not using the preembryos must be weighed.[54]

In weighing the relative interests of the parties, the court said that "[o]rdinarily the party wishing to avoid procreation should prevail, assuming that the other party has a reasonable possibility of achieving parenthood by means other than use of the preembryos in question."[55] The Court also noted that if the party seeking control of the embryo intends merely to donate them to another couple, "the objecting party obviously has the greater interest and should prevail."[56] Along similar lines, in a New Jersey case, *J.B. v. M.B.*,[57] a divorcing husband wished to exercise control over stored embryos over his ex-wife's objection, in a situation where there was no clear written directive to guide disposition of the embryos. The court held that the general rule would be to "enforce agreements entered into at the time in vitro fertilization is begun subject to the right of either party to change his or her mind about disposition up to the point of use or destruction of any stored preembryos," and that in the absence of such an agreement, public policy would dictate that the party choosing not to become a biological parent would prevail.[58]

Artificial insemination by donor (AID)

When a man is infertile or has a genetic condition that he does not want to pass on to his offspring, or when a single woman wishes to have a child, the man's partner or the single woman can conceive with sperm from a donor. Two legal issues that arise with this technique concern: (1) paternity, and (2) confidentiality.

Paternity

In every state, the legislature has passed a statute that establishes that the husband of a woman who conceives during marriage or within a certain number of days thereafter is presumed to be the father of the child and has legal child-rearing responsibilities.[59] Some of these statutes provide roadblocks to utilization of new reproductive technologies. For example, some state laws provide an exception to the presumption of paternity if the husband is sterile – which would create problems for a sterile husband who wishes to be considered the legal father of a child born to his wife through the use of AID. In response to this problem, some states have passed laws that establish that a child resulting from AID is the legal offspring of the sperm recipient and her consenting partner.[60]

Even in the absence of an AID statute, courts have held that a consenting husband of a woman who gives birth following AID is the legal father of the resulting child. In *People v. Sorenson*,[61] for example, the court held that an infertile man who actively participated in and consented to his wife's AID could not disclaim his parental responsibility after the child was born. In *K.S. v. G.S.*,[62] a woman's husband consented to AID but claimed that he later revoked his consent and therefore could avoid child support responsibilities. Evidence in the case established that the husband continued, after the alleged revocation, to accompany his wife to the doctor's office for the insemination procedure, and the court held that a consent continues to be effective "unless the husband establishes by clear and convincing evidence that such consent has been revoked or rescinded."[63]

Confidentiality

Generally, the identity of the sperm donor is kept confidential. Increasingly, however, as is true of adopted children, AID children have interest in learning the identity of their donor-biological fathers. In these circumstances, the donor, as well as the mother of the AID child and her husband, may have an equally strong interest in keeping the donor's identity confidential. To date, no jurisdiction has enacted legislation requiring the disclosure of AID donors' identities under such circumstances. The Uniform Parentage Act, and some state laws, provide that records pertaining to AID are subject to inspection "upon an order of the court for good cause shown."[64] No court has yet had occasion to consider what constitutes "good cause" for such inspection. However, by way of analogy, adopted children have been able to convince several courts that there was "good cause" for giving them access to information about the identity of the biological parents to promote their emotional, physical, or financial well-being.[65] These decisions could serve as precedents for recognizing similar rights for AID children. In addition, in *Johnson v. Superior Court*,[66] the California Court of Appeal determined that a provision of a contract limiting the discovery of the identity of a sperm donor was against public policy and therefore unenforceable. The court explained that California "has a compelling interest in the health and welfare of children, including those conceived by artificial insemination," and that there may be times when disclosing the identity of a donor is necessary for medical reasons.[67]

Egg donation

In some situations where a woman cannot produce eggs or is a carrier of a genetic condition that she does not wish to pass on to her offspring, she may wish to conceive using a donated egg. Two legal issues that arise with this process concern: (1) payment to donors, and (2) legal parenthood.

Payment

While some institutions pay egg donors, others do not on account of concern that payment could unduly pressure women into becoming donors. A statute in Louisiana expressly prohibits payment to egg donors,[68] and laws in several other states governing organ transplantation could be used to prohibit payment to egg donors.[69]

Legal parenthood

Since the law generally recognizes the birth mother as the legal mother, the woman who gestates an embryo created with a donated egg often will be presumed to be the mother. Several states have laws that specifically address legal parenthood when egg donation is involved.[70]

Surrogate parenthood

In some circumstances where a couple can provide genetic material for reproduction but (1) the woman cannot provide the gestational component (e.g., she has no uterus or a condition that makes pregnancy dangerous or that is threatening to a fetus), (2) she wishes not to be pregnant, or (3) where the woman cannot provide the genetic component of reproduction, the couple may utilize a surrogate mother. In these arrangements, the couple wanting to become parents enter into a contractual relationship with the surrogate mother, who agrees to have the couple's or donor's embryos transferred to her womb, or to be artificially inseminated with the man's sperm, to bear a child, and to relinquish her rights to the child in exchange for a fee and payment of expenses. Such a contractual arrangement raises legal questions concerning: (1) payment to the surrogate mother, and (2) legal parenthood.

Payment

In some states, statutes ban payment to a mother for giving her child up for adoption. If the surrogate gestational mother is considered to be the legal mother, and if the couple must adopt the child (see discussion below), these statutes may ban payment by the couple to the surrogate mother. Some states, however, have laws that explicitly exempt surrogacy arrangements from the ban on receiving money for giving a child up for adoption,[71] and other states have laws that specify that payment other than expenses may not be made to surrogate mothers.[72] Moreover, at least ten states have laws that prohibit compensation of "brokers" who bring couples together with prospective surrogate mothers.[73]

Legal parenthood

Since the birth mother is generally considered to be the legal mother,[74] it appears that when a surrogate is used, adoption by the intended parents would be required. However, in early surrogate gestational motherhood cases in Michigan and California, the genetic parents, who brought actions to establish maternity and paternity during pregnancy, were held to be the legal parents without having to adopt the child.

Johnson v. Calvert involved a case where a gestational surrogate mother, to whom the intended parents' embryos were transferred, changed her mind and tried to assert parental rights to the child.[75] The California Supreme Court found that under the Uniform Parentage Act (UPA), both the genetic mother and the gestational mother had statutory claims to being the child's legal mother because the UPA allows a woman to establish legal parenthood both through evidence of having given birth to the child and through blood testing.[76] Nevertheless, the court said, since California law recognizes only one legal mother for a child, the intent of the parties as manifested in the surrogacy agreement should determine legal parentage.[77] This result, the court reasoned, would not violate the surrogate's right of privacy because the choice to gestate and then hand over a baby to the genetic parents pursuant to a surrogacy agreement is not the constitutional equivalent of a decision to bear a child of one's own.[78] The court said:

> A woman who enters into a gestational surrogacy arrangement is not exercising her own right to make procreative choices; she is agreeing to provide a necessary and profoundly important service without (by definition) any expectation that she will raise the resulting child as her own.[79]

In contrast to the result in *Calvert*, some states have enacted statutes that give the surrogate gestational mother a right to change her mind;[80] while in others, the surrogate and her husband are presumed to be the legal parents of the child.[81] Other states, though, have passed laws that make surrogate motherhood contracts unenforceable.[82]

A 1998 case demonstrates how difficult the issue of legal parenthood can be in gestational surrogacy cases. *In re Buzzanca*[83] involved a surrogacy agreement between a husband and wife and the surrogate and her husband, pursuant to which the surrogate was implanted with an embryo that resulted from a donated egg and donated sperm. Before the birth of the child (who had no biological link, either genetic or gestational, to either member of the couple), the intended parents separated, and several months later the wife sued the intended father for child support. The intended father claimed that the surrogate mother was the legal mother because she had given birth to the child. The trial court held that the child had no legal parents. The Court of Appeals reversed, holding that the intended parents were the legal parents, given their "initiating role" in the child's conception and birth, and that therefore the intended mother could be awarded custody of the child and the intended father could be held financially responsible for the child's care.[84]

Mandating health care services for pregnant women to benefit the fetus

In some circumstances, pregnant women refuse medical procedures that are recommended for the benefit of the fetus. Resolving these conflicts involves balancing the rights of the pregnant woman with those of her fetus. As discussed below, court cases that have addressed such conflicts have reached different results.

Some courts have maintained that a pregnant woman has a duty to her unborn child, who has a right to be born with a sound mind and sound body, and that if she breaches this duty, she may be criminally liable. In *Hoener v. Bertinato*,[85] for instance, the defendant parents were charged with "endangering the life of the unborn child and neglecting to provide it with proper protection" on account of the failure to consent to a blood transfusion needed to save their unborn child's life.[86] The court held that "the law recognizes that rights which [an unborn child] will enjoy when born can be violated before his birth," and that the parents' failure or refusal to take necessary steps to protect their unborn child's life was "obviously neglect of the child."[87]

Other courts, however, have refused to impose criminal liability for a pregnant woman's alleged breach of duties to her fetus. In *Reinesto v. Superior Court of Arizona*,[88] the Arizona Court of Appeals held that a woman cannot be held criminally liable for drug use during pregnancy even if later her child is born addicted.[89] The Court noted that "[a]llowing the state to define the crime of child abuse according to the health or condition of the newborn child would subject many mothers to criminal liability for engaging in all sorts of legal or illegal activities during pregnancy."[90]

Frequently, motions for court orders to compel certain actions or decisions during a woman's pregnancy implicate the woman's autonomy, right to privacy, and right to refuse medical treatment. In *In re AC*,[91] for example, during her twenty-sixth week of pregnancy, a woman was admitted to the hospital with terminal lung cancer. The patient, her family and the medical team decided on passive treatment because of slim chances for her or her fetus to survive. The hospital administrator, however, sought a declaratory court order for a Cesarean Section (C-Section) in an effort to enhance the fetus' chance for survival. When the patient refused to consent to the C-Section, the matter went to a hearing, after which the trial court granted, and the appellate court affirmed, the hospital's motion to proceed with the C-Section. The court found that the fetus had a better chance of surviving with the C-Section and that, therefore, the state's interest in protecting an innocent third party was strong enough to overcome the woman's right to bodily integrity. The fetus was surgically delivered and died shortly thereafter, and the woman died two days after that. The case was later reheard *en banc* by the D.C. Court of Appeals,[92] which vacated the trial court order for the C-Section, stating:

> A court must determine the patient's wishes by any means available and must abide by those wishes unless there are truly extraordinary or compelling reasons to override them. When a patient is incompetent, or when the court is unable to determine competency, the substituted judgment procedure must be followed.[93]

In contrast to the rehearing decision in *In re AC*, in *Pemberton v. Tallahassee Mem. Regional Medical Center, Inc.*,[94] the court upheld a court-order C-Section despite the woman's constitutional claims. The court held that the state's interests in preserving fetal life outweighed the woman's right to refuse treatment, in part because the fetus was full term.[95]

Posthumous reproduction

In recent years, courts and legislatures have addressed issues that have arisen due to the ability to create children with sperm from a man who has died. In *Hecht v. Superior Court*,[96] for example, a man contemplating suicide had his sperm frozen, and made specific arrangements in his will and with the sperm bank for his girlfriend to be inseminated with it after his death. After the man committed suicide, however, his two children from a previous marriage contested his will, arguing for destruction of the sperm even though his girlfriend had signed a release disclaiming any inheritance rights on behalf of children resulting from insemination with the frozen sperm. The trial court ruled in favor of the man's children, on grounds that any resulting children would not know their father, and that subsequent births would disrupt the existing family and would violate the institutions of family and marriage. The appellate court reversed, finding that the sperm was property under the California Probate Code, and that the deceased had decision making authority with respect to his property. On remand, the trial court awarded the girlfriend twenty percent of the sperm as her representative share of her deceased boyfriend's estate.

In some situations, health care providers are asked to collect sperm from dead men. Currently, there are no federal or state statutes that govern this situation, but a bill introduced in New York on two occasions would have made it illegal for physicians to retrieve sperm after a man's death unless explicit written consent had been given by the man prior to his death.[97]

Cloning

Cloning refers to the replication of an existing DNA sequence, cell, or individual. Somatic cell nuclear transfer was the technique used to clone Dolly the sheep; and some believe that it could be used to clone humans. In somatic nuclear transfer, nucleic DNA is extracted from an adult cell (in

Dolly's case, an adult mammary tissue cell) and transferred to an enucleated egg cell, and the resulting embryo is then transferred to a female's uterus for gestation and then birth of the clone. A clone created by somatic cell nuclear transfer does not share the exact same DNA as the nucleic DNA donor, because a small amount of the clone's DNA is inherited from the cytoplasm located in the enucleated egg donor's cell.

Legal issues surrounding cloning include regulation of the procedure, as well as legal parenthood.

Regulation

Following Dolly's birth, then-President Clinton issued an executive order banning the use of federal funds for human cloning; and several months later the National Bioethics Advisory Commission recommended that Congress enact federal legislation to ban the creation of a child through cloning for three to five years, regardless of the source of funds. To date, there is no federal law banning cloning, but a number of states have passed legislation that prohibits human cloning. For example, a California statute makes it a violation of the Medical Practices Act for any corporation, firm, clinic, hospital, laboratory, or research facility to clone a human being, with civil penalties up to $1,000,000;[98] and in Michigan, an individual who violates the cloning prohibition may be guilty of a felony punishable by imprisonment for up to ten years and/or a fine of up to $10,000,000, in addition to a $10,000,000 civil fine.[99]

To the extent that cloning bans apply not only to reproductive cloning, but also to therapeutic cloning research, they may be subject to constitutional challenge. Some have argued that government action that bans all forms of cloning violates constitutionally protected freedom of scientific inquiry.[100]

Parenthood.

Under current law, it is difficult to determine who would be considered the parents of a human clone. As noted by Lori Andrews, even if an individual cloned him or herself, he or she might not be recognized as the legal parent because traditional paternity testing would indicate that the parents of the person cloned are the parents of the clone.[101] Nanette Elster has noted that a clone might have received genetic material from as many as four individuals (the nucleic DNA donor, the nucleic DNA donor's biological parents, and the enucleated egg donor), and if carried by a married surrogate mother, might have as many as thirteen different parental configurations.[102]

Conclusion

Issues discussed in this chapter present significant legal and ethical challenges to health care providers, patients, and society. Comprehensive bioethical and legal analyses will be critical as scientific and technological advances continue to enhance reproductive treatment capabilities.

Notes

1 *Eisenstadt v. Baird*, 405 U.S. 438, 453 (1972).
2 *See e.g. Carey v. Population Services Int'l*, 431 U.S. 678, 685–86 (1977).
3 *Carey v. Population Services Int'l, supra* n. 2.
4 *Doe v. Irwin*, 615 F.2d 1162, 1168–69 (6th Cir.), *cert denied* 449 U.S. 829 (1980).
5 *Jackson v. Bumgardner*, 71 N.C. App. 107, 321 S.E.2d 541 (1984).
6 Some facilities do not provide sterilization, and federal law states that individuals and facilities will not be denied federal funds for refusing to perform sterilizations or for refusing to make their facilities available for the performance of sterilizations due to religious or moral convictions. 42 U.S.C. § 300a-7(b) (1999).
7 *See e.g.* Conn. Gen. Stat. §§ 45a-691, 45a-697, and 45a-699.
8 *See e.g.* Colo. Rev. Stat. § 27–10.5–128.
9 *See e.g.* Miss. Code Ann. § 41-45-1.
10 *See e.g. Guardianship of Kemp*, 43 Cal. App. 3d 758, 118. Cal. Rptr. 64 (Cal.Ct. App.1974).
11 *See e.g. In re Grady*, 85 N.J. 235, 426 A.2d 467 (N.J.1981).
12 410 U.S. 113 (1973). *Roe v. Wade* involved a challenge to a Texas statute that made it a crime to attempt, actively procure, or perform an abortion except for the purpose of saving the woman's life.
13 410 U.S. 179 (1973). *Doe v. Bolton* involved a law requiring that abortions be performed only in Joint Commission on Accreditation of Healthcare Organizations (JCAHO) accredited hospitals.
14 *Roe*, 410 U.S. at 163–65.
15 439 U.S. 379 (1979).
16 *Id.* at 397–401.
17 462 U.S. 416 (1983).
18 505 U.S. 833 (1992).
19 *Akron, supra* n. 17, at 445.
20 *Id.* at 433–34.
21 476 U.S. 747 (1986).
22 *Id.* at 759.
23 *Id.* at 767.
24 492 U.S. 490 (1989).
25 The *Webster* decision addressed four aspects of a Missouri statute that restricted access to abortions: (1) the preamble, which required that state laws be interpreted to provide fetuses with legal rights from the time of conception; (2) a requirement that physicians make a determination of viability before performing an abortion at twenty weeks; (3) a prohibition against the use of public funds, employees, and facilities to perform abortions not necessary to save a woman's life; and (4) a prohibition against spending public funds to encourage or counsel a woman to have an abortion.
26 500 U.S. 173 (1991).
27 In January 1993, as one of his first official acts, President Clinton rescinded these federal regulations.
28 505 U.S. 833 (1992).
29 In *Akron v. Akron Center for Reproductive Health*, 462 U.S. 416 (1983), the Supreme Court had held that a twenty-four-hour waiting period between the informed consent discussion and the abortion itself was unconstitutional because it increased the cost of obtaining an abortion and it presented the

possibility that the procedure would be delayed more than twenty-four hours and would therefore be more hazardous.

30 *See* 505 U.S. at 844.

31 *Id.* at 888.

32 505 U.S. at 877.

33 *Id.* at 886.

34 506 U.S. 1011 (1992).

35 962 F.2d 1366 (9th Cir. 1992).

36 U.S. 530 914 (2000).

37 413 F.3d 791 (8th Cir. 2005).

38 18 U.S.C. § 1531.

39 550 U.S. ___ (2007). [2007 U.S. Lexis 4338 (2007)]

40 N.H. Rev. Stat. Ann. § 168 B:13 requires a woman and her husband, if she is married, to undergo counseling by a psychiatrist, psychologist, pastoral counselor, or a social worker and to provide a written certification that the counseling has been performed.

41 Md. Code. Ann. Ins. § 15–810.

42 *See* Maureen McGuire & Nancy J. Alexander, *Artificial Insemination of Single Women*, 43(2) Fertility & Sterility 182 (1985).

43 David I. Hoffman, Gail L. Zellman, C. Christine Fair, Jacob F. Mayer, Joyce G. Zeitz, William E. Gibbons & Thomas G. Turner, Jr., *Cryopreserved Embryos in the United States and Their Availability for Research*, 79 Fertility and Sterility 1063–69 (May 2003).

44 Lori B. Andrews, *Embryonic Confusion. When You Think Conception, You Don't Think Product Liability. Think Again*, Washington Post B01 (May 2, 1999).

45 *See e.g. Kass v. Kass*, 91 N.Y. 2d 554, 673 N.Y. S.2d 350, 696 N.E.2d 174 (N.Y. 1998); *Davis v. Davis*, 842 S.W.2d 588 (Tenn. 1992).

46 *Davis*, 842 S.W.2d at 597.

47 *Kass*, 696 N.E.2d at 180.

48 *Id.* at 182.

49 431 Mass. 150, 725 N.E.2d 1051 (2000).

50 *Id.*, 725 N.E. 2d at 1056.

51 *Id.*, 725 N.E. 2d at 1057.

52 *Davis*, 842 S.W.2d 588.

53 *Id.* at 589.

54 *Id.* at 604.

55 *Id.*

56 *Id.*

57 170 N.J. 9, 783 A. 2d 707 (2001).

58 *Id.*, 783 A.2d at 719.

59 *See e.g.* Ala. Code § 26-17-5 (a)(1)(2003).

60 *See e.g.* Wis. Stats. § 767–47(9); Ga. Code Ann. § 19-7-21; Nev. Rev. Stat. § 126.051.

61 68 Cal.2d 280, 437 P.2d 495, 499, 66 Cal. Rptr. 7 (1968).

62 182 N.J. Super. 102, 440 A. 2d 64 (N.J. Super. Ct. Ch. Div. 1981).

63 *Id.*, 440 A.2d at 68.

64 *See* 9B U.L.A., Master E. § 5; Cal. Fam. Code § 7613(a); Colo. Rev. Stat. § 19-4-06(i); Minn. Stat. § 257.56; Conn. Gen. Stat. § 45a-773; Kan. Stat. § 23–130; Wis. Stat. § 891.40(i).

65 *See e.g. Mills v. Atlantic City Dept. of Vital Statistics*, 148 N.J. Super. 302, 372 A. 2d 646 (N.J. Super. Ct. Ch. Div. 1977); *In re Adoption of Spinks*, 32 N.C. App. 422, 232 S.E. 2d 479 (N.C. Ct. App. 1977).

66 80 Cal. App. 4th 1095, 95 Cal. Rptr. 2d 864 (Ct. App.), *rev. denied*, 2000 Cal LEXIS 6741.

67 *Id.*, 95 Cal. Rptr. 2d at 875.
68 La. Rev. Stat. Ann. § 9:122 (West Supp. 2004).
69 *See e.g.* D.C. Code Ann § 7–1501.02 (2004); 6–2601 (1999); Tex. Penal Code Ann § 48.02 (Vernon 1999).
70 Fla. Stat. Ann § 742.14; N.D. Cent. Code § 14-18-04; Okla Stat. Ann. tit 10 § 554; Tex. Fam. Code § 160.754; Va. Code Ann. § 20–15; Rev. Code Wash. 26.26.735.
71 *See* Nev. Rev. Stat. Ann. § 127.287.
72 *See e.g.* Fla. Stat. Ann § 63.212(1)(h); Mich. Comp. Laws Ann. §§ 722.853(a); Nev. Rev. Stat. Ann. § 126.045(3); N.Y. Dom. Rel. Law § 123; Va. Code Ann. §§ 20–156, 160(B)(4); Wash. Rev. Code Ann. § 26.26.210(1).
73 *See e.g.* N.H. Rev. Stat. Ann. § 168-B:16(IV); Utah Code Ann. § 76-7-204(1)(b); Ariz. Rev. Stat. Ann. § 25–218(A); D.C. Code Ann. § 16–402(b); Ky. Rev. Stat. Ann. § 199.590(4).
74 *See e.g.* Ala. Code 922–29A-7; Ark. Stat. Ann. 920-18-40(2).
75 5 Cal. 4th 84, 19 Cal. Rptr. 494, 851 P.2d 776 (1993), *cert. denied*, 510 U.S. 874, 114 S.Ct. 206, and *cert. dismissed, Baby Boy J. v. Johnson*, 510 U.S. 938, 114 S. Ct. 374 (1993).
76 *Id.*, 851 P.2d at 780.
77 *Id.*, 851 P.2d at 782.
78 *Id.*, 851 P.2d at 787.
79 *Id.*
80 Fla. Stat. Ann. § 63.213(2)(a),(6)(h); N.H. Rev. Stat. Ann. § 168-B:25(IV); Va. Code Ann. §§ 20-158(D), 20-161(B).
81 Ariz. Rev. Stat. Ann. § 25-218; N.D. Cent. Code § 14-18-05; Utah Code Ann. § 76-7-204.
82 *See e.g.* Fla. Stat. Ann. § 63.212(l)(h); Ky. Rev. Stat. Ann § 199.590(4); Mich. Comp Laws § 722.851 to .86B 9(2004).
83 72 Cal. Rptr. 2d 280 (Cal. Ct. App 1998).
84 *Id.* at 293.
85 171 A.2d 140 (N.J. Juv. and Dem. Rel. Ct. 1961).
86 *Id.* at 141.
87 *Id.* at 143–45.
88 182 Ariz. 190, 894 P.2d 733 (Ariz. Ct. App. 1995).
89 *Id.*, 894 P.2d at 735.
90 *Id.*, 894 P.2d at 737.
91 533 A.2d 611 (D.C. 1987), *vacated and rehearing granted*, 573 A.2d 1235 (D.C. 1990).
92 573 A.2d 1235 (D.C. 1990) (*en banc*).
93 *Id.* at 1247.
94 66 F. Supp. 2d 1247 (N.D. Fla. 1999).
95 *Id.* at 1251–52.
96 16 Cal. App. 4th 836, 20 Cal Rptr. 2d 275 (Cal. Ct. App. 1993).
97 NYS Bill 8043, 222nd Ann Legsl. Sess (1999).
98 California Health and Safety Code § 24285 (West 1999).
99 Mich. Comp. Laws Ann., Chap. 633, Sect. 333.16274. *See also* Gen. Laws of R.I. Ann., title 23, Sect. 23–16.4–2; VA Code Ann., Sect. 32.1–162.22.
100 Robyn Shapiro, *Legislative Research Bans on Human Cloning*, 12 Cambridge Q. Healthcare Ethics, 393 (2003).
101 Lori B. Andrews, The Clone Age: Adventures in the New World of Reproductive Technology (Henry Holt 1999).
102 Nanette Elster, *Who is the Parent in Cloning*? 27 Hofstra L. Rev. 533, 536 (1999).

8 Acquiring and allocating human organs for transplant

U.S. law

Bethany J. Spielman

Introduction

A half century of human organ transplantation has presented law with numerous challenges: how to help solve a persistent shortage of organs, how to keep up with constantly changing technology, and how to transmit and reinforce important social values. Law's most fundamental tasks in this arena, however, have been to help answer two basic questions: How should organs be obtained for transplant? And how should they be allocated? This chapter will summarize features of federal and state law that govern answers to these two questions. The first part is divided into two major questions: How does law reduce the likelihood of killing or exploiting patients to obtain organs? And by what legal authority can organs be obtained from one human being for transplant into another? The second part of the chapter examines how organ allocation law incorporates factors such as the ability to pay, medical factors, geography, and donor directives.

How are organs acquired for transplant?

How does law reduce the likelihood of killing or exploiting human beings for their organs?

One of the most important roles that law has played in transplantation is reducing the risk that organ harvesting will become, or be perceived as, legalized killing. Laws that establish what counts legally as death, that prohibit certain conflicts of interest that could hasten or cause death, that punish killing, and that prohibit organ sales, are intended to reduce these risks.

Clarifying the definition of death and prohibiting killing

In order to ensure that organ harvesting does not cause the death of organ sources, it can be performed only after pronouncement of death by legal standards. The usefulness of this "dead donor rule" depends on the soundness and clarity of the definition of death. Like the medical standards for determining death to which it defers, the legal definition of death has evolved during the last decades but still suffers from a great deal of ambiguity.

Under the common law, death occurs upon the "cessation of life; the permanent cessation of all vital signs."[1] The first court to face the limits of this definition in the context of transplantation was a Virginia court deciding *Tucker v. Lower*,[2] an early 1970s wrongful death suit. The plaintiff's brother had suffered serious head injuries in a fall. From a neurological standpoint, he was dead. But for the most part he maintained normal body temperature, pulse, blood pressure, and respiration. The respirator was discontinued. Mr. Tucker was pronounced dead, and his organs were removed for transplantation.

The suit against the Virginia transplant surgeon alleged that the patient had been prematurely declared dead. At the time, Kansas and Maryland had adopted a cessation of brain function standard of death, but the Commonwealth of Virginia had not yet done so. The trial judge therefore declined to dismiss the case against the surgeon, stating that death should be determined under the common law's "cessation of bodily functions" standard. A brain death standard, the judge stated, could be adopted only by the legislature.[3]

At the end of the trial, however, the judge instructed the jury that:

> In determining the time of death ... under the facts and circumstances of this case, you may consider the following elements, none of which should necessarily be considered controlling, although you may feel, under the evidence, that one or more of these conditions are controlling: The time of the total stoppage of the circulation of the blood; the time of the total cessation of the other vital functions consequent thereto, such as respiration and pulsation; the time of complete and irreversible loss of all function of the brain; and whether or not the aforesaid functions were spontaneous or were being maintained artificially or mechanically.[4]

Although the surgeon was not found liable, the *Tucker* dispute contributed to the adoption of a state statute that recognized cessation of brain function as one basis for declaring death.

As artificially maintaining patients' hearts and lungs and transplanting organs became more common, a broader legal definition of death along the lines suggested by the Tucker court appealed to state legislatures across the country. In order to help promote legal uniformity among the states in determining death, the Uniform Determination of Death Act (UDDA) was promulgated in 1980.[5] It set the general legal standard for determining death, but not the medical criteria for doing so. The UDDA provided that death occurs when an individual sustains "either (1) irreversible cessation of circulatory and respiratory functions, or (2) irreversible cessation of all functions of the entire brain, including the brain stem ... and that a determination of death must be made in accordance with accepted medical standards."[6] Most states have modeled their definitions of death on this Act.

A dual definition of death such as that in the UDDA creates the potential for two legal categories of cadaver organ sources. When a patient's physician certifies death using traditional cardiac criteria (death upon the cessation of heartbeat), the individual may become one category of donor, a non-heart-beating cadaver donor (NHBCD).[7] When a physician determines that a patient's whole brain is dead, however, as did Mr. Tucker's physician, the patient may become another category of donor.

Since some states' adoptions of the dual legal definition of death, courts and legislatures have rejected efforts to further expand the definition by creating a third category that would consist of "live but brain absent" sources. Interest in the use of anencephalic infants as organ sources grew quickly after a successful heart transplant in 1987 from an anencephalic Canadian infant to a child in the United States. Five years later, in *T.A.C.P.*, a Florida court faced the question whether anencephaly could be legally equated with death so that such an infant could be the source of organs for transplant.[8] Florida's version of the UDDA used the whole brain definition of death in situations where a person's cardiopulmonary function was maintained artificially. It used the common law cardiopulmonary definition of death whenever the brain death definition was inapplicable, that is if cardiopulmonary function was not maintained artificially. Neither definition fit the situation of *T.A.C.P.* Finding no precedent, persuasive analogy, public necessity, fundamental rights, or consensus about the ethical and legal issues that would lead them to equate anencephaly with death, the Florida Supreme Court declined to do so.[9]

Questions occasionally arise about whether the demise of certain individuals who have been used as sources of organs falls within the constraints of the dead donor rule. An example of this questioning for each of the two categories of deaths follows: Protocols for NHBD (non-heart-beating donor) are used where a potential donor is breathing on a ventilator, and is not expected either to recover or to meet the standards for brain death. Within minutes after ventilator support is withdrawn, breathing and heartbeat stop, death is pronounced using the cardiorespiratory definition of death, and the organs are harvested. The speed of this process has created uncertainty about how long physicians must wait before declaring the patient dead, and about the possibility that drugs used to improve chances of transplant success may blur the line between life and death. In 1997, an Ohio prosecutor believed one of the drugs involved in a NHBD protocol could make it appear that live donors were dead. He thought the ambiguity of the potential donor's condition might contribute to hastening the death of the donor. Convinced that the protocol violated state law on death and homicide, the prosecutor threatened to seek a court order to block the procedure. The protocol was not implemented.[10]

In 2004, the difficulty of ascertaining when whole brain death criteria have been met was highlighted when a county coroner in Colorado ruled that a man who had attempted suicide was not properly tested for brain death and died from the removal of his organs after withdrawal of ventilator support. Although the coroner listed the cause of death as homicide, the district attorney disagreed and did not prosecute.[11]

In addition to publicly defining and enforcing boundaries of "the dead donor rule," law helps protect potential organ sources in two others ways: by prohibiting conflicts of interest that might cause distortion of physician judgment in declaring death, and by prohibiting sales of organs.

Prohibiting conflicts of interest

The Uniform Anatomical Gift Act of 1968 (UAGA) was drafted by the National Conference of Commissioners on Uniform State Laws, adopted within a few years by all of the states, revised in 1987, and adopted in the revised version by twenty-two states.[12] The main purpose of UAGA was to facilitate removal of organs from cadavers. But lawmakers recognized that physicians who declare deaths, might be susceptible to distortions of judgment in this task if they also had direct responsibilities for transplantation. Both versions of UAGA require, therefore, that the time of an organ source's death may not be determined by a physician or surgeon who participates in procedures for removing or transplanting a body part unless the individual had previously designated a particular physician or surgeon to do so. This provision helps prevent physicians from declaring patients' deaths prematurely in order to obtain organs that will be more viable for transplant (UAGA does not, however, prevent the donor's attending physician from communicating with the transplant team or others to transfer important knowledge about the organ source).

Prohibiting organ sales

In addition to prohibiting certain conflicts of interest, federal law protects against harm to potential organ sources by criminalizing organ sales. It became clear, relatively early in the history of transplantation, that an unregulated market in organs could develop, jeopardizing the well-being of organ sources. In 1983, a Virginia physician established a business to broker kidney sales, including sales by inhabitants of the Third World.[13] Congress responded by passing the National Organ Transplant Act (NOTA) the next year.[14] NOTA criminalized interstate commercial transactions in organs, making it unlawful for any person to knowingly acquire, receive, or otherwise transfer any human organ for valuable consideration for use in human transplantation if the transfer affects interstate commerce.[15] The 1987 UAGA also prohibits some sales and purchases of body parts for transplantation, though its prohibition does not cover sales by living donors if removal of the organs is intended to occur before death.[16]

Limitations on the sales and purchases of organs do not prevent all procurement and transplant-related market transactions. Health care providers have always sold their services. Further, organ seekers can purchase organs on the global market. And finally, no U.S. laws prevent advertising for live organ donations; families and individuals have paid for media, billboards, and internet businesses, exercising their First Amendment rights as they plead for donors.

By what legal authority can organs be obtained from one human being for transplant into another?

Organs cannot be taken from one individual for transplant into another without authorization. In 1947, the California legislature became the first to address this issue when it adopted laws regulating the bequeathal of organs. The California law authorized donation of organs through a written instrument and provided that heirs and executors of the estate abide by the donor's intent.[17] Today, four kinds of legal authorization are used: explicit consent of competent adults; document of gift or next of kin consent for cadavers; judicial determination for minors and incompetent adults; and presumed consent for some cadaver organs.

Explicit consent of competent adult

In general, U.S. law has been too individualistic to explicitly require that persons give organs to others. This general principle is illustrated in *McFall v. Shimp*.[18] In 1978, Robert McFall, who suffered from a fatal bone marrow disease, asked a court to compel his cousin to undergo the bone marrow harvest. Mr. Shimp had undergone compatibility testing, which showed he was a match for his cousin, but he had declined to donate. The Pennsylvania court warned, "for a society which respects the rights of *one* individual, to sink its teeth into the jugular vein ... of one of its members and suck from it sustenance for another member, is revolting to our hard-wrought concepts of jurisprudence."[19] The court concluded that under the law, a competent adult could not be forced to submit to a medical procedure for the benefit of a third party.

Instead, voluntary, informed consent to donate an organ is the general rule when the organ source is a competent adult. This principle is illustrated in *Lawse v. University of Iowa Hospitals*.[20] Thirteen years after Mr. Lawse had donated a kidney to his brother, the donor's remaining kidney failed. In a suit for wrongful removal of the kidney, the donor claimed that his consent had been coerced, and that the physician and hospital had misinformed him. Specifically, he complained that despite the fact that his brother had been doing well on dialysis, he had been told that his brother would die without the kidney; that there was very little risk to him; that information about his tissue typing had been shared with other family members before he had learned of the results; and that information about another brother's refusal to donate was kept from the donor.[21] Though the statute of limitations had run out, the court's discussion of the problem of coercion reflects its commitment to the principle of voluntary informed consent.

Many organ sources are not competent adults at the time of the organ removal, however. Some are cadavers, and some are living minors or incompetent adults. Obtaining organs from each of these sources requires modifying the principle of voluntary informed consent.

Document of gift or explicit next of kin consent for cadavers

Contrary to the common law tradition that families possess quasi-property rights in cadavers, both versions of UAGA treat organs of a living person age eighteen or over as his or her own assets, which can be distributed upon death. State versions of the UAGA establish flexible consent procedures for individuals to express their intent to donate their cadavers at death. Individuals may express their intent through a will, signed donor card, driver's license, telegraphic, recorded telephonic, or other recorded message, or other form of signed communication.[22]

The 1968 UAGA established a priority list of persons authorized to consent if decedents had not indicated, before death, their wish to donate.[23] In the case of individuals who had expressed their wishes, those wishes were to be respected. But the notion that families could not override individuals' wishes was undercut by organ procurement organizations (OPOs), which continued to give families veto power over individuals' documents of gift. In addition, the Omnibus Reconciliation Act of 1986 required Medicare/Medicaid hospitals to discuss with next of kin the right to donate organs of the deceased.[24] Many states copied this "required request" statute. Some individuals interpreted required request legislation to mandate that the discussion with families proceed as if a family's right to donate or refuse were unqualified by the organ sources' expressed intent. The 1987 version of UAGA stated even more clearly than did the 1968 version that an individual's donative intent could not be revoked by another, including those persons on the prioritized list of decision makers, after the organ source's death. It also emphasized that donation did not require the consent or concurrence of any person other than the individual from whom the organs would be removed.[25] The state of Minnesota has since enacted a statute for a similar purpose: to clarify that an individual's intent to donate is legally binding.[26]

Donor registries record a donor's intent, indicated on a driver's license, in a central repository. Registries are intended to improve OPOs' ability to identify donor wishes and to convince next of kin of that intent, but are operated in fewer than half the states.

Judicial determination of psychological best interest for minors and incompetent adults

When a potential organ source is an incompetent adult or a minor, informed voluntary donor consent is not possible. In the absence of this consent, however, if health care providers or legal guardians ask for a judicial authorization to take the organs, the organ harvest will sometimes be approved, especially if the relationship between the incompetent adult or minor source and the potential recipient has been close.

In *Strunk v. Strunk*, for example, the Kentucky Court of Appeals held that a kidney could be removed from Jerry Strunk, an incompetent adult, and transplanted into his adult brother, who was suffering from kidney disease.[27] Jerry, who had been institutionalized, had an IQ equivalent to that of a six-year-old child. Jerry's mother petitioned the court to allow the organ donation because it would be beneficial to Tommy but also to Jerry, who was psychologically dependent upon Tommy. The court agreed after expert testimony that keeping Tommy alive, and therefore also harvesting Jerry's kidney, was in Jerry's best interests. Likewise in *Little v. Little*, a Texas Court of Civil Appeals authorized removal of a kidney from a fourteen-year-old girl with Down syndrome, reasoning that she would benefit psychologically from donating to her brother.[28]

Some courts, however, have declined to authorize organ removal from incompetent sources. In *Guardianship of Pescinski*, the sister and guardian of an incompetent Wisconsin man who was institutionalized for catatonic schizophrenia petitioned the court for permission to remove a kidney from him.[29] The state supreme court reasoned that it had no statutory authority to order the organ harvest and could not find that it served the man's interests. Louisiana courts faced the same issue in *In re Richardson*.[30] The parents' petition to remove a kidney from their seventeen-year-old, who suffered from Down syndrome, in order to transplant it to his sister, was denied. A state appellate court concluded that the surgical intrusion and loss of a kidney would not be in his best interests. And in *Curran v. Bosze*, the Supreme Court of Illinois refused to approve testing of two minors for a bone marrow transplant when the relationship between them and their half brother, who was the potential recipient, had not been close.[31]

Exception: presumed consent for some cadaver organs

Under certain circumstances, neither the consent of the organ source nor that of the family is required to remove organs for transplant. The 1987 UAGA authorizes coroners, medical examiners, and public health officials to remove body parts for transplantation if several conditions are met.[32] Separate presumed consent laws for corneas and pituitary glands have been passed in numerous states.[33] Some states use a limited system of presumed consent in which coroners may remove corneas from cadavers if there is no objection by the family or if there has been a reasonable inquiry to determine if there is an objection.

Occasionally, events draw attention to the role of race and socioeconomic status in the use and misuse of such laws. For example, in 1993, the media highlighted the likely impact on the District of Colombia's disadvantaged population of a new presumed consent law. The District law was among the first in the nation specifically to authorize harvest of heart valves with only presumed consent. And in 1997, corneas were harvested from a young black man's body in Los Angeles before the family had registered its objection. An investigative journalist subsequently published a racial and economic analysis of the city coroner's harvesting and profitable reselling of corneas under California's presumed consent law.[34]

Presumed consent laws have been challenged in court, with mixed results. For example, in *Georgia Lions Eye Bank, Inc. v. Lavant*, parents of a deceased Georgia child had no notice before the removal of his corneas.[35] The Georgia Supreme Court found the presumed consent statute authorizing removal of the cornea of a decedent for transplant purposes to be constitutional. By contrast, the 6th Circuit found in *Brotherton v. Cleveland* that a widow had a legitimate claim on her husband's corneas under the Due Process Clause of the U.S. Constitution.[36] The 9th Circuit found in *Newman v. Sathyavaglswaran* that parents had a legitimate claim on their children's corneas under the same Constitutional clause, and that they had properly complained of unconstitutional deprivation of property under color of state law.[37]

Finally, the District of Columbia, Florida, and Virginia have enacted a type of presumed consent law to facilitate non-heart-beating donation from trauma victims. Rapid Organ Procurement Programs (ROPP) permit *in situ* preservation, but not actual harvest, of the organs without consent.[38]

How does law encourage consent to donate?

The problem of generating an adequate supply of organs while remaining within the constraints of a system based in large part on voluntary consent is one with which the transplant field has struggled since its inception. Law has gradually shifted from relying on individuals and families to initiate a donation to encouraging individuals and families to donate. It facilitates education efforts, requests for donations, reduction of financial barriers, prioritization of kidney donors in organ allocation, and provision of modest incentives, including offering small but controversial financial incentives to permit organ harvest.

Educating

A plethora of state and federal laws facilitate organ donation awareness and education. These laws enable state agencies and departments to receive contributions when citizens make voluntary contributions through driver's license renewals, vehicle registrations, or state income tax returns, and to allocate funds for grants to develop awareness programs. The programs include organ donation awareness and education efforts for secondary schools, state employees, and the general public.

Under the 1984 NOTA, a public–private partnership was created under which the United Network for Organ Sharing (UNOS), a private OPO located in Richmond, Virginia, was selected by DHHS to be the nation's Organ Procurement and Transplantation Network (OPTN). UNOS must educate physicians about organ donation. It must also conduct studies concerning organ donation and transplants

Requesting and referring to other requestors

As mentioned above, state and federal laws that were passed in the 1980s required that families be asked to donate their next of kin's organs upon death. The 1987 UAGA also requires that on or before admission to a hospital, a person designated by the hospital ask all adult patients whether they are organ or tissue donors.[39]

Under the National Organ and Tissue Donation Initiative (NOTDI), Health and Human Services issued regulations in 1998 that direct every hospital to enter into an agreement with an OPO specifying that the hospital will notify the OPO of all brain dead and recently deceased patients in a timely manner (routine referral). In addition, participating hospitals must also maintain potential cadaveric organ sources while tests are conducted to determine medical suitability for transplantation.

Minimizing financial barriers

Despite massive efforts to educate and encourage cadaveric donation, the organ shortage persists into the twenty-first century, prompting the transplant community to reconsider its previous reluctance to encourage live donation between strangers. The Organ Donation and Recovery Improvement Act of 2004 reduces financial barriers to live donation by authorizing the federal government to reimburse live donors for travel, subsistence, and incidental non-medical expenses.[40]

Wisconsin has begun to give living organ sources a tax deduction of up to $10,000 for medical costs, travel, and lost salary.[41] Georgia and South Carolina have passed similar laws. And Minnesota requires employers to provide paid leaves-of-absence for employees who undergo medical procedures to give an organ for transplant.

Providing incentives

The drafters of UAGA understood that the opportunity to provide an organ for someone to whom one is emotionally attached would be a powerful incentive to give. UAGA therefore permits directed donation.[42]

Pennsylvania also offers a financial incentive to families for providing organs of their deceased relatives.[43] A funeral benefit incentive law states that the Pennsylvania Department of Health may disperse funds for reasonable medical expenses, paid to the funeral home or hospital.

How are organs allocated?

Both federal and state law addresses a second key transplant question: how should organs be allocated? Several factors in addition to organ availability determine which individuals receive organ transplants in the United States. Under UAGA, a hospital, physician, surgeon, or procurement organization can receive organs for transplant, or a designated individual can receive organs for transplantation or therapy needed by that individual.[44] But ultimately, it is individuals who receive organs for transplant. Access to transplantation, like access to most other health care in the United States, is dependent on ability to pay. Because the costs of transplantation and post-transplantation care are so large, insurance is, for most recipients, the only way that payment can be made.

Ability to pay

Medicare's End Stage Renal Disease Program, which pays for kidney transplants for even the non-elderly, pays for most kidney transplants in the United States.[45] Medicare, Medicaid, and private insurers now cover many other transplants, although access to Medicaid coverage for transplants varies from state to state, and access to private health insurance is increasingly difficult to obtain. In 1987, the death of an Oregon boy who was not covered under Medicaid for a bone marrow transplant prompted Medicaid reform in that state, thus initially increasing access to some transplants for Medicaid recipients. Since then, some Medicaid programs, including Oregon's, have become financially unable to fund post-transplant care. Medicaid recipients have, as a result, again become ineligible for transplants.

Several federal circuit courts of appeal have held that states are not required to fund organ transplants under Medicaid even if a transplant offers the patient's only chance for survival.[46] Other circuits, construing the federal Medicaid Act differently, have held that states must fund medically necessary transplants if they are not experimental.[47]

The states also vary in willingness to fund organ transplants for their prison populations. In *Estelle v. Gamble* the United States Supreme Court based violations of the Eighth Amendment's ban on cruel and unusual punishment on deliberate indifference to serious medical needs.[48] In *Fernandez v. United States*, the Eleventh Circuit held that that Eighth Amendment ban had been violated when a prisoner was refused a medical furlough, a reduction in sentence, a parole, or a pardon for the purpose of seeking a life-saving heart transplant, because he had not met a Federal Bureau of Prisons requirement that he establish his ability to pay for an organ transplant and the willingness of a transplant program to consider accepting him.[49]

Private health insurance plans do not always cover transplants, especially if the transplant is considered by the plan to be experimental.[50] Tens of millions in the United States who have no insurance, or insurance that does not cover transplants, are therefore financially ineligible for transplants other than kidney transplants covered by Medicare's End Stage Renal Disease Program.

When an individual has insurance that will pay for a transplant and is accepted by a transplant center, several other factors will also play a role in determining whether that individual receives an organ. One of the purposes of the 1984 NOTA was to ensure equitable allocation of transplantable organs, in part, by developing a list of patients needing organs and a national system for matching providers and recipients. In order to facilitate a national approach to organ sharing, NOTA also established regional OPOs and required them to participate in the OPTN.

Among the factors that UNOS, the national OPTN, has addressed in its policies are: clinical factors, geography, time on the waiting list, donor directives, and a history of kidney donation.

Clinical factors

Clinical factors play a central role in determining who receives organ transplants. UNOS is charged with the responsibility of determining how those factors affect allocation for each type of organ. UNOS policies have emphasized clinical factors that affect the urgency of the patient's condition and the likelihood that the transplant will be effective.

Recently, a rule issued by the DHHS pursuant to NOTA has required UNOS "to develop standardized criteria for listing patients and defining their medical urgency status." It mandates that organs be provided first to those patients with the greatest need, within the constraints of ischemic time and medical considerations, such as recognizing that some patients are too ill to benefit from a transplant. The rule also establishes an independent scientific review board to help the DHHS Secretary to evaluate, oversee, and enforce the organ allocation policies under the rule and as formulated by UNOS.[51]

Surgeons occasionally "fudge" the system for categorizing potential recipients' medical needs. Misrepresenting the medical needs of patients awaiting organs is a matter of health care fraud under the jurisdiction of state attorneys general and the federal Justice Department.[52] The U.S. Attorney's Office recently settled a lawsuit with Chicago hospitals alleged to have committed fraud in their liver transplant programs by significantly overstating the seriousness of their patients' conditions.

One clinical factor has recently been directly incorporated into state law, increasing the probability that HIV-positive patients will receive organs. Illinois provides legal immunity to professionals who transplant HIV-positive organs into HIV-positive patients.[53] HIV-positive organs would otherwise not be transplanted.

Geography

While NOTA originally allowed for the allocation of organs on a local basis, Congress has twice amended the statute to reflect its interest in national distribution. Some states have reacted against a NOTA regulation that shifted allocation from a local-first basis to a nationwide system. Several states, including Louisiana, South Carolina, Wisconsin, Oklahoma, Texas, Arizona, and Florida, have placed restrictions on transfers of organs out of state except when no suitable in-state recipient could be found, or there is a reciprocal organ-sharing agreement. These laws are the first foray of the states into the law of organ allocation, and raise questions about federalism.[54]

Waiting time

Waiting list rules vary by organ.[55] The average waiting time for an organ in the United States recently has been at least a year, but the waiting time for any particular individual is impossible to predict.[56] UNOS warns that waiting for an organ is not like waiting for your number to be called at a deli counter. What is called "the waiting list" really is many lists, each of which is formed as a particular donor organ, with unique characteristics, becomes available.

Donor directives

Under UAGA, organs may be directed to a named individual if that individual has a medical need for them. Some individuals and groups have sought to use the directed donation provisions to donate organs preferentially or solely to members of a particular class or group. UNOS has opposed the idea of directing donations either toward or away from classes of individuals, but is open to providing some special considerations for donors as individuals.[57] In 1994, after the parents of a deceased Ku Klux Clan sympathizer offered his organs to any person who was "white," the U.S. Office of Civil Rights determined that the practice of allocating organs to a specific race violates the Federal Civil Rights Act of 1964 forbidding discrimination based on race, color, or national origin. In 2002, when the LifeSharers Club was organized to offer organs first to those who have joined and agreed to donate their organs at death, UNOS sought legal advice from DHHS attorneys to determine if that kind of class donation violated federal law.[58]

History of donating

UNOS policy also gives preferred status to individuals who have been kidney donors and later develop a need for a kidney transplant.

Concluding comments

As the brief summary above demonstrates, the law of organ acquisition and allocation in the United States has evolved incrementally during the last fifty years. Some scholars have, in the past, been highly critical of U.S. law governing transplantation, describing it as "almost wholly at odds with the decentralized and market-based legal principles that are emerging in the larger health policy context."[59] Three recent developments noted above bring the currency of this characterization into question: a longstanding prohibition on compensating providers of organs seems to be giving way to permitting modest financial incentives (or at least removing financial disincentives) to donate; the states have for the first time entered the arena of organ allocation law, which had previously been the province of federal law and UNOS; and internet brokering of live donation poses new challenges to governing the allocation of organs for transplant. If market elements and decentralization are indeed mainstream principles in U.S. health policy, organ procurement and transplantation law seem, for better or for worse, to be moving into that mainstream.

Finally, in light of changes in federal law and related developments in the field of organ donation, the National Conference on Commissioners of Uniform State Laws will soon revisit UAGA. The Drafting Committee on Amending the Uniform Anatomical Gift Act is currently preparing amendments and revisions. The law governing how organs are obtained and allocated for transplant will thus continue to evolve as we begin the second half-century of human organ transplantation.

Notes

1 Black's Law Dictionary: Definitions of the Terms and Phrases of American and English Jurisprudence, Ancient and Modern, 360 (5th ed., Joseph R. Nolan & Michael J. Connolly, eds, West Publishing Co. 1979).
2 2831 (Richmond, Va., Law & Eq. Ct. May 23, 1972).
3 *Id.*
4 *Id.* at 8–10.
5 Uniform Determination of Death Act § 1–3 (1980), http://www.law.upenn.edu/bll/ulc/fnact99/1980s/udda80.pdf. (accessed Oct. 14, 2004).
6 UDDA § 1, 12 U.L.A. 340 (supp. 1991).
7 Sometimes the process of non-heart-beating donation is called "donation after cardiac death" or "DCD."
8 *In re T.A.C.P.*, 609 So.2d 588, 591 (Fla. 1992).
9 *Id.* at 595.
10 Ted Wendling, Joan Mazzolini, John Funk & Dave Davis, *Clinic Will Modify Contested Organ-Procurement Procedure*, Plain Dealer (Cleveland, Ohio) 1A (April 5, 1997).

11 Karen Auge, *Review of Organ-Harvesting Case Due Today; Montrose County's District Attorney Will Reveal Findings on the Coroner's Ruling of a Homicide in the Death Declaration for an Organ Donor*, The Denver Post B-02 (Oct.12 2004).
12 Uniform Anatomical Gift Act (1968)(superceded 1987) 8A U.L.A.
13 Margaret Engel, *Va. Doctor Plans Company to Arrange Sale of Human Kidneys*, Washington Post A9 (Sept. 19, 1983).
14 National Organ Transplant Act, Pub. L. No. 98–507, 98 Stat. 2339 (1984) (codified at 42 U.S.C. 273–74 (1994)).
15 *Id.*
16 U.A.G.A. § 10 (1987).
17 Lloyd R. Cohen, *Organ Transplant Market Would Save Lives*, Natl. L. J. A19 (Jan. 29, 1996).
18 *McFall v. Shimp*, 10 Pa. D. & C.3d 90 (Allegheny County Ct.,1978).
19 *Id.* at 92.
20 *Lawse v. University of Iowa Hospitals*, 434 N.W.2d 895 (Iowa App. 1988).
21 *Id.*
22 U.A.G.A. § 3(c) (1968).
23 U.A.G.A. § 2(b) (1968).
24 Omnibus Budget Reconciliation Act of 1986, Pub. L. 99–509, 100 Stat. 1874, 2009–10 (codified in scattered sections of 42 U.S.C.). 42 U.S.C. 1320b-8 requires that families be informed of their option to donate or decline.
25 U.A.G.A. § 2(h) (1987).
26 Minn. Stat. 171.07 (2003).
27 445 S.W.2d 145 (Ky. 1969).
28 576 S.W. 2d 493 (Tex. Civ. App. 1979).
29 226 N.W.2d 180 (Wis. 1975).
30 284 So. 2d 185 (La. Ct. App. 1973).
31 566 N.E.2d 1319 (Ill. 1990).
32 U.A.G.A. § 4 (1968).
33 755 ILCS 55/1 *et. seq.* (2003); Conn. Gen Stat. 19a-281 (2003).
34 Michele Goodwin, *Deconstructing Legislative Consent Law: Organ Taking, Racial Profiling & Distributive Justice*, 6 VA. J.L. & Tech. 2–45 (2001); Ralph Frammolino, *Harvest of Corneas at Morgue Questioned: Corneas Taken Without Survivors' Permission Are Resold at Huge Markup by Eye Bank, Which Pays Coroner's Office a Fee; The Practice is Legal, but Critics Cite Ethical Lapses*, Los Angeles Times 1A (Nov. 2, 1997).
35 255 Ga. 60, 335 S.E.2d 127, 129 (1985).
36 923 F.2d 477, 482 (6th Cir. 1991).
37 287 F.3d 786 (9th Cir., 2002); 42 U.S.C.S. sec. 1983.
38 D.C. Code Ann. § 2–1509.1 (1998).
39 U.A.G.A. § 5(a) (1987).
40 Organ Donation Recovery Improvement Act, 42 U.S.C. 274f-1 *et seq.* (2004).
41 2003 Wis. ALS 119; 2003 Wis. Act 119; 2003 Wis. Laws 119; 2003 Wis. AB 477.
42 U.A.G.A. § 3(d) (1987).
43 20 Pa. Cons. Stat. 8622 (1999).
44 UAGA § 3 (1968).
45 42 U.S.C. 426–1.
46 *Ellis v. Patterson*, 859 F.2d 52 (8th Cir. 1988); *Todd v. Sorrell*, 841 F.2d 87 (4th Cir. 1998).
47 *Pereira v. Kozlowski*, 996 F.2d 723 (4th Cir. 1993).
48 429 U.S. 97, 50 L. Ed. 2d 251, 97 S. Ct. 285 (1976).
49 941 F.2d 1488 (11th Cir. 1991).
50 *DiDomenico v. Employers Coop. Indus. Trust*, 676 F. Supp. 903 (N.D. Ind. 1987).

51 *Third Chicago Hospital Pays to Settle Transplant Fraud Allegations*, 42(12) Report On Medicare Compliance 5 (Nov. 20, 2003).
52 64 Fed. Reg. 71,626 (1999).
53 2003 ILL. ALS 737,5.
54 Ariz. Rev. Stat. Ann. 36–846 (West 1999); La. Rev. Stat. Ann. 17:2353 (West 1999); Okla. Stat. Ann. tit. 63, 2204 (West 1999); S.C. Code Ann. 44-43-420 (Law. Co-op. 1998); Wis. Stat. Ann. 157.06(9) (West 1998); Act of June 18, 1999, ch. 615, sec. 4, 692.0145, 1999 Tex. Sess. Law Serv. (Vernon); Fla. Stat. Ann. 732.922(6) (West 1999).
55 Jeff Testerman, *Should Donors Say Who Gets Organs?* St Petersburg Times (Florida) 1A (Jan. 9 1994); Landers, *supra* n. 56.
56 Fred H. Cate, *Human Organ Transplantation: The Role of Law*, 20 Iowa J. Corp. L. 69, 81 (1994).
57 Organ Procurement and Transportation Network, *Policies*, http://www.optn.org/policiesAndBylaws/policies.asp (accessed Nov. 21, 2006).
58 Organ Procurement and Transportation Network, *Data*, http://www.organtransplants.org/understanding/unos/ (accessed April 26, 2007).
59 Susan J. Landers, *LifeSharers Offers One Way to Increase Organ Donations*, American Medical News (July 14, 2003), https://www.lifesharers.com/presscoverage/amnews.htm (accessed Sept. 7, 2005).

9 End-of-life legal issues in the United States

John Robinson

For all those centuries during which there was little that medicine could do for all the ills to which flesh is heir, the end of life was, as a legal matter, relatively unproblematic. Neonatal, perinatal, and puerperal deaths were common, as were childhood and adolescent deaths from accident and disease. For those few who survived to old age, death usually occurred at home with minimal medical intervention. With respect to each of these forms of death, the law was distinctly a background figure, lightly policing the scene for evidence of foul play, and loosely presiding over the distribution of whatever assets the decedent had left behind.

The emergence of modern medicine has changed radically how life ends for a large number of people and thereby has changed the role that law plays in deaths of all sorts. Modern medicine has changed how life ends in several different ways. First, and most dramatically, it has effected a massive reduction in early deaths: a child born in the industrial world today is much more likely to survive to old age than was a child born anywhere at anytime before the modern era. Second, for the vast majority of us who will die in old age, our deathbeds have been moved from our home to a hospital or nursing home. Where once our families presided over our deaths, now health care providers do. Third, while death retains its wonted inevitability, that a particular dying person should die now as opposed to a day, a month, or a year from now is often far from inevitable. As a result, choice plays a role in death that it formerly did not. Where there is choice, there can be conflict, and where there is conflict, law sometimes steps in as a conflict resolution device. This is what has happened to death in the modern world.

With respect to choice, the crucial question is always "Who gets to make the choice?" The traditional answer to that question was that doctors, morally bound to act in their patients' best interest, should make all crucial health care decisions for those patients.[1] During the course of the twentieth century, however, medical paternalism gave way to patient autonomy as the centerpiece of medical ethics.[2] In theory, at least, dying patients, and not their doctors, make the crucial decisions about the medical care that they will receive during the course of their demise. I say "in theory" because the realities of morbidity and mortality often make a mockery of our legal and ethical commitment to patient autonomy. Weakened by illness, confused by medical science, impoverished by the cost of treatment, troubled by the prospect of death, a dying person may well have lost most of his or her functional autonomy. Despite this, however, it remains true for modern American law that each of us, for so long as we are competent to decide, ought to have the last word with respect to the decisions that are made concerning our medical care, especially when that word is "NO" and when it is said in response to a medical intervention that, in our doctor's judgment, would be in our best interest.

The qualification that was required to make the preceding sentence true ("for so long as we are competent to decide") raises an important subquestion: namely, who makes choices for those who are incompetent to make choices for themselves? For decades now, the law has striven mightily to have the answer to that question be that those of us who at some point in our lives are competent should decide in advance what will be done to and for us if it ever should happen that we are incompetent and in need of medical care. The mechanisms for these proleptic decisions are known generally as advance directives, and they come in two basic varieties. The first sort of advance directive is a document known as a living will. By means of a document of that sort, in almost every American state, currently competent adults are legally empowered to specify in writing and in detail just what sort of medical care they want or do not want to be administered to them if they should become incompetent and in dire physical straits.

Of living wills, it must be said that they do not work very well at all. Most competent adults, even those who should have an easy time envisioning their own imminent incompetence, simply refuse to execute the requisite document. Among those who become incompetent and do have living wills, when they are rushed to a hospital and their treating physician has access to their living will and looks to it for guidance, the physician hardly ever gets much guidance from it. Most health care providers tend to ignore living wills even in the relatively rare cases in which the document is attached to the appropriate chart. That is true both because of the enormity of the gulf between the language spoken by the medical laity and the language spoken by medical professionals and because of the difficulty all of us have anticipating either the ills from which we will suffer at some indeterminate time in the future or the array of interventions that will be available to the medical profession at that time.[3]

One response to the failure of living wills as embodiments of patient preferences is to make them less likely to fail. Much work was done towards the end of the twentieth century to achieve that result. To increase the probability that competent individuals would execute living wills, the federal government in 1990 enacted the Patient Self-Determination Act,[4] requiring health care facilities that receive Medicare or Medicaid funds to alert patients of their advance directive rights as those patients are being admitted to the facility. If at that point in their lives, it was hoped, Americans are reminded of their right to have advance directives in effect, many of them would overcome their tendency to deny their own mortality and execute a living will right there on the spot. If, furthermore, hospitals and nursing homes are crucially involved in the process by which living wills are elicited, those institutions and the doctors who work in them, it was hoped, would become more aware of a particular patient's possession of an advance directive and be more respectful of it. To make it more likely that physicians who genuinely want to be guided in their delivery of health care to a currently incompetent patient by that patient's living will actually get some guidance from the document that the patient has executed, living will forms were made significantly more detailed, and efforts were made to find living will language that was simple enough for lay comprehensibility yet technical enough for professional utility. None of these initiatives was very successful. As a result, attention has focused in recent years on perfecting another kind of advance directive – the durable power of attorney for health care decisions, or some similar proxy device.[5]

Powers of attorney are not new to the law. They have been used for some time to facilitate one person's handling of another person's ordinary business transactions while the other person is, for example, out of town on an extended vacation. Power of attorney of that sort is subject to two constraints. First of all, it is limited to business affairs; second, it retains its validity only so long as the vacationer, in my example, is competent to engage in business transactions for himself or herself. Once the creator of the power loses competence, the holder of the power loses authority to act for its creator. In order to make power of attorney useful as an advance directive, it had first to be made "durable" (so that it survives its creator's loss of competence), then to be extended to cover health care decisions. This has now been accomplished in almost every state in the Union.

A validly executed durable power of attorney for health care decisions (or health care representative designation) addresses many of the problems that permanent decisional incompetency poses to the patient-autonomy paradigm; it does this by designating a surrogate who, under terms specified by the patient, steps into the patient's shoes and exercises the patient's autonomous decisional power on the patient's behalf. When executed in conjunction with a living will, which educates the holder of the power as to the patient's frame of mind with respect to the end-of-life decisions, a durable power of attorney is potentially an effective device for dealing with one of the great defects of the living will taken by itself. With a durable power vested in a person who, on the one hand, knows and loves the patient, and, on the other hand, is apprized of the patient's current condition and of the treatment options available to address it, serious inroads can be made into the ignorance that, as we saw earlier, is usually incident to the execution of a living will.

It remains true, however, that durable powers share with living wills the immense practical weakness that very few people bother to execute them.[6]

They also possess a weakness that does not afflict living wills in that it is always possible that the holder of the power of attorney may predecease its creator, precede the creator in loss of decisional capacity, or grow distant from or hostile to its creator in the years that may elapse between the time at which the power is created and the time at which a surrogate decision must be made. This defect can be addressed to some extent by the creator's naming alternate holders of the power, in case the primary holder should die or become incompetent, and by the creator's revisiting his or her power of attorney document at regular intervals. But it is not easy to get people to do either of these things.

When we turn from the few people who, while competent, plan for the medical care that they think they would want to receive if ever they should become permanently incompetent to the many who either make no plans of that sort at all or fail to embody their plan in a written document that doctors, lawyers, and judges will treat as binding, things become much more complicated. The first step towards uncomplicating things in this regard is to break this latter class into two subclasses. The first of these consists of once competent adults who never executed an advance directive. The second consists of all those people who, due to their youth or mental disability, were never able to execute a valid advance directive. I will discuss the law affecting the first of these subclasses in some detail here, and the law affecting the second of them more cursorily.

The first of the two subclasses just described contains far and away the largest number of permanently incompetent individuals about whom medical decisions are being made today. We might usefully think of their permanent incompetence as having created a gap between them and their own power of choice, and we might think of the law as doing what it can to bridge that gap. In the standard case, both the relevant case law and the relevant statutes use the incompetent individual's family as the bridge, hoping that family members will know and love the incompetent person well enough to be able to offer a reliable estimate as to how that person would want to be treated. Getting to this seemingly obvious solution to the problem of the advance-directive-less incompetent person took years of hard judicial and legislative work, and it is to a highly selective sketch of that work that I now turn.

By common consent, the case of Karen Ann Quinlan[7] is treated as the first, and most famous, right to die case of the modern era.[8] In that case, Karen Quinlan, then age nineteen and in apparent good health, suffered a loss of oxygen to her brain one night in April of 1975. That anoxic event lasted long enough to cause massive and permanent injury to her brain, leaving her eventually in a persistent vegetative state. She was not brain dead, but she appeared to be wholly lacking in cognitive ability and extremely unlikely ever to recover that ability. Her father sought the removal of the respirator on which she was thought to be dependent, and her physician refused. At that point, litigation ensued. When the case reached the Supreme Court of New

Jersey, the court said that Karen possessed a constitutional privacy right to have her respirator disconnected, a right that she was, of course, in no position to exercise. The court went on to say that her father, acting as her guardian, could assert her right to have her respirator disconnected if (as turned out to be the case) that was what he thought she would have preferred if, *per impossibile*, she could have enjoyed a single moment of lucidity at any point after she entered into her persistent vegetative state.

Quinlan accomplished three things. First, it made it clear that sick and injured adults have the right to refuse medical treatment even when the treatment in question is necessary to their survival. Second, it made it equally clear that when illness or injury has rendered once competent persons incompetent to exercise this right of refusal for themselves, someone else – usually a family member – should be allowed to exercise that right for them. Third, it treated the right to decisional privacy, which earlier cases had found in the federal Constitution, as the legal warrant for its assertion of a right to refuse medical treatment. The first of these accomplishments does little more than reassert the primacy of patient autonomy in modern American health care, but the second and third of these accomplishments both required further elaboration by the New Jersey Supreme Court, and both require a word of comment here.

Once the court had committed itself to letting one person exercise another person's right to refuse for him or her, it had to provide more guidance than *Quinlan* did with regard to the criteria that should drive the surrogate's decision-making processes. *Quinlan*'s suggestion that the father be guided by what his daughter would have wanted if she could have a moment's cognitive reprieve from her vegetative state made it clear that ideally, at least, the surrogate is to be guided by a subjective standard – namely, what *this particular patient* would have chosen – in making treatment decisions for that person. Beyond that, *Quinlan* was silent.

In *Matter of Conroy*,[9] the New Jersey Supreme Court sought to take up where *Quinlan* left off. In particular, the *Conroy* court attempted to determine what should guide a surrogate's decision when the now incompetent person left few or no indicia of the sort of decisions he or she would make in his or her current circumstances. To answer this question, the court came up with two tests. One was a peculiar hybrid of subjective and objective considerations, and it applied only where there is some, but not much, trustworthy evidence with regard to what this particular patient would want now if he or she now had any decisional capacity. The second test was a pure objective test, applicable where there was no trustworthy evidence with regard to what this patient would want done now. Both of these tests allow the surrogate to order the discontinuation of treatment once it becomes clear that the burdens incident to the treatment outweigh the benefits that it conveys to the person being treated.

This objectification of the standard by which surrogates were to be guided in making decisions for once competent persons who left no reliable indicia of how they would want to be treated if ever they should become incompetent made it possible for other courts in other cases to develop usable standards for surrogates who were making treatment decisions for handicapped infants and for profoundly retarded individuals who never were in a position to express their preferences with respect to treatment options. In these cases, however, the courts have been especially conscious of how hard it is to devise mechanisms that seek to respect the autonomy of patients who, as a practical matter, lack it without endorsing, even obliquely, the termination of lives that seem to others to be devoid of social utility or otherwise unworthy of being lived.

Quinlan's final accomplishment is also its most dubious one. Recall that in *Quinlan* the legal warrant for the court's claim that Karen had a right to have her respirator disconnected came from the federal Constitution, at least as the modern Supreme Court has read that document. In *Matter of Conroy*, the New Jersey Supreme Court backed away from that warrant, substituting for it a cluster of common law doctrines relating to battery and informed consent. This may appear to be a distinction without a difference, but nothing could be further from the truth. As common law rights go, the right to refuse unwanted medical care, even when that care is essential to a person's survival, is well established in the law of every state, at least with respect to competent individuals who are exercising that right on their own behalf. Its strengths are its pedigree, its non-controversiality, and its incontestable limitation to refusing treatment. Like the common law itself, the right to refuse resists easy abstraction and capacious generalization. Only slowly and after careful case-based consideration could it be transformed into a more general right to die, if, in fact, it was possible to do that even then. As a practical matter, furthermore, a court's delineation of the contours of a common law right does not prevent the relevant legislature from enacting statutes that refine or alter those contours. Common law adjudication does not foreclose legislation; it is an invitation to it.

As one moves from the common law to constitutional law there is the potential to remove authority from the states in an anti-democratic and anti-federalist fashion. Insofar as constitutional rights are recognized, states' authority to regulate end-of-life (or other) practices is diminished. This substantive due process initiative requires judges to add the procedural guarantees that the phrase "due process of law" suggests an open-ended list of fundamental rights that are protected against legislative diminution except in serious circumstances. This can inhibit legislative efforts at the state level, an effect which is anti-democratic. Two other features of a constitutional warrant for the right to refuse medical treatment must be mentioned here. The first is that, unlike the common law right to refuse, as a constitutional warrant it invites abstraction and generalization, so that it could be transformed into a generalized right to die, perhaps even into a right to receive medical assistance in the active termination of one's own life. (The U.S. Supreme Court to this point has rejected a claim for a constitutional right to physician-assisted suicide and has accepted only a very vague and limited constitutional right protecting refusal of medical treatment on behalf of incompetent patients.) The second noteworthy feature of a constitutional warrant for the right to refuse is that, unlike the common law right to die, it takes control over the scope of the right out of the hands of the several state judiciaries and vests it exclusively in the hands of the United States Supreme Court anytime it decides to review an end-of-life issue. (It is for this reason that substantive due process adjudication is described as anti-federalist.) For all of these reasons, we must at this point attend to the Supreme Court's treatment of the two major end-of-life cases that it has considered in recent years to see how it has resolved the tension between a common law and a constitutional warrant for the end-of-life rights that it acknowledges.

The first end-of-life case to come before the Supreme Court in recent years was *Cruzan v. Director, Missouri Department of Health.*[10] Nancy Cruzan, the nominal plaintiff in the case was, in some ways, much like Karen Quinlan – a perfectly healthy young woman who by virtue of a tragic mishap, suffered prolonged anoxia that eventually plunged her into a persistent vegetative state. A crucial difference between Karen's condition and Nancy's was that Karen could not breathe, it was thought, without the help of a respirator, while Nancy could not swallow food or water and had to be fed through a gastrostomy tube. This difference is crucial because in Karen's case there was always a chance that she would breathe on her own once her respirator was disconnected – indeed, that is exactly what she did for the next nine years – but in Nancy's case it was virtually certain that she would die within two weeks after the removal of her gastrostomy tube. The progress of Karen's legal case was different from Nancy's too. In Karen's case, the state supreme court endorsed the disconnection of her respirator, but in Nancy's case the state supreme court refused to endorse the removal of her gastrostomy tube. The Missouri Supreme Court in Nancy's case, like the New York Court of Appeals in a similar case, required clear and convincing evidence that the person whose life hinged on the decision had, while competent, expressed a desire not to be kept alive by medical means if ever she should be in a state of permanent incompetence, and it found that the evidence of Nancy's pre-accident mind set that had been presented to the trial court had not measured up to that demanding standard.

The only real question that the United States Supreme Court had to answer in its review of the *Cruzan* case was whether or not the federal Constitution permitted Missouri to require clear and convincing evidence in Cruzan-like circumstances, and its answer was that it did. In reaching that result, the Court surveyed the right-to-refuse cases that had undergone appellate review in the state courts since *Quinlan*, noting both their highly convergent results – the right to refuse extends to medical treatment that is necessary to continued existence, and the right to refuse can be exercised for the incompetent by persons recognized as acting with their best interest at heart – and the disparate legal warrants arrayed in support of those results. Some courts, the Supreme Court noted, relied on common law warrants, some on federal constitutional warrants, some on state constitutional warrants, and some on an amalgam of the three.

The Court then announced, "The principle that a competent person has a constitutionally protected liberty interest in refusing unwanted treatment may be inferred from our prior decisions."[11] The deprivation of a constitutionally protected liberty interest is constitutionally permissible, the Court intimated, whenever the state interests that motivate the deprivation outweigh the liberty interest in question; otherwise, it is impermissible. So, famously, a state's interest in preventing disease justifies the deprivation of an individual's liberty interest in refusing to be vaccinated against smallpox. But were the Court to be confronted with a competent person who was dependent on a feeding tube for survival and who was attempting to ward off state-mandated continuation of that form of treatment, it would, the Court speculated, find that the individual's liberty interest outweighed the state's countervailing interests and decide the case in favor of the competent person.

Nancy's circumstances were, of course, of a different order entirely: she was permanently and profoundly incompetent, and Missouri was demanding more evidence of her pre-accident preferences with regard to her current circumstances than courts usually require in non-criminal cases. Where an incompetent person's life hangs in the balance, the Court said, states are constitutionally entitled to set a high evidentiary standard both because of a general interest in the preservation of life and because of a particular interest in protecting the incompetent from self-interested surrogates. (In later proceedings in state court, Nancy's family produced more evidence than it had initially. Basing its decision on this better evidence, the court found there to be clear and convincing evidence that Nancy had, while competent, expressed a desire not to be kept alive by artificial means if ever she should become permanently incompetent. Her gastrostomy tube was removed, and a short while later she died.)

For reasons best known to itself, the Supreme Court built a strategic imbalance into its *Cruzan* decision. On the one hand, all it *did* in the decision was to affirm the right of a state to demand convincing evidence of a particular person's pre-accident state of mind before it would authorize the pulling of the plug. What it *said*, however, went far beyond the issue before it. It said, or it seemed to say, that competent persons have a constitutional right to refuse unwanted medical treatment, and it seemed to suggest that they also have a constitutional right to have that right exercised for them by someone they have appointed if at the time of decision they are no longer competent. By thus constitutionalizing the interests at stake in end-of-life matters, the Court, wittingly or not, invited lower courts to analogize end-of-life issues to the abortion cases that, since *Roe v. Wade* was decided in 1973, [12] have divided the Court almost as much as they have divided the nation.

The first court to accept the Supreme Court's invitation was a state court in Michigan, which, in December of 1993, held that the right of decisional privacy on which the abortion cases are predicated, included a right to commit suicide just so long as the person asserting the right was terminally ill and facing a painful death-process.[13] Richard Kaufman, the judge who wrote that decision, felt entitled to read the decisional privacy right as expansively as he did in large part because the Supreme Court had recently done the same thing, saying that "the right to define one's own concept of existence, of meaning, of the universe, and of the mystery of human life" lay at the heart of the liberty that current constitutional law protects against intrusive governmental regulation.[14] According to this logic, once a court is convinced that a particular kind of decision – for example, the decision to end one's life – involves the decision-maker's "concept of existence" and so on, that court is, in principle, free to strike down laws that interfere with the exercise of that right. That is just what a federal court in the state of Washington did in May of 1994, thereby setting the stage for what, for now, is the final act of the great constitutional drama into which *Cruzan* so rashly thrust the assisted suicide debate.[15]

In the Washington case, Judge Barbara Rothstein, like Judge Kaufman, found in the Fourteenth Amendment's Due Process Clause a constitutional right that entitles "adults who are mentally competent, terminally ill, and acting under no undue influence ... to voluntarily hasten their death by taking a lethal dose of physician-prescribed drugs."[16] Like Judge Kaufman's decision in the Michigan case, Judge Rothstein's, which had invalidated Washington's law against aiding a suicide, was promptly reversed on appeal. The key difference between Judge Rothstein and the federal appellate panel that reversed her decision is that she took her cue as to how to apply the Due Process Clause, read substantively, to assisted suicide questions from the Supreme Court's abortion decisions, and the panel did not. The appellate panel feared that applying the abortion precedents to suicide questions would make "the right to suicide and the right to assistance in suicide ... the prerogatives of at least every sane adult,"[17] a result that the panel viewed as a *reductio ad absurdum* of Judge Rothstein's approach. When the panel's decision was itself reviewed by a federal appellate banc (a group of judges larger than a panel and composed of appellate judges from the same circuit as the panel), the banc rejected the panel's reversal of Judge Rothstein's decision, relying, as Judge Rothstein had, on the Supreme Court's abortion decisions as a guide to determining "the essence of the substantive component of the Due Process Clause."[18]

When a federal appellate court in New York reached the same result as the appellate banc in the West had (albeit on Equal Protection grounds),[19] the Supreme Court decided to step in.[20] In doing so, the Court did three things. First, it upheld the constitutionality of laws prohibiting assisting a suicide against both Due Process and Equal Protection challenges. Second, it imposed severe restraints on substantive due process adjudication outside of the abortion area. Third, it invited the legislatures of the several states to adopt legislation regarding assisted suicide, and it suggested that, in principal at least, bans on it or permission of it could be equally valid insofar as federal constitutional law is concerned. There is no doubt that these decisions put American constitutional law in deep conflict with itself – capacious substantive due process doctrine with regards to abortion, constricted substantive due process doctrine with regards to assisted suicide – but there is equally no doubt that they also settled the constitutional status of laws against assisting in a suicide for the time being.

Since the conclusion of the constitutional drama just sketched, two substantial non-constitutional dramas have opened at opposite ends of the nation – the first in Oregon, the second in Florida. The Oregon drama involves a ballot measure first approved by the people of Oregon in November of 1994, then approved by them again in November of 1997. That measure, know as The Oregon Death with Dignity Act,[21] allows certain terminally ill Oregonians to obtain from their physicians prescription for medication that is intended to cause the death of the person who takes it, if, in fact, the person does so. The Oregonians in question must be adults who are capable of making health care decisions for themselves. The Act contains provisions designed to discourage impulsive or uninformed requests for lethal prescriptions and to minimize the chance that the request is the product of psychological illness. A doctor who prescribes a lethal dose of medication to a terminally ill Oregonian and who complies with all of the procedural requirements of the Act can do so without fear of criminal prosecution under Oregon law.

Between 1998 and 2006, 455 prescriptions for lethal doses of medication were written pursuant to this law and 292 Oregonians died after taking a lethal dose of the prescribed medication.[22] These deaths amounted to slightly more than 0.1 percent of all Oregonian deaths over the course of those eight years. Experts debate the significance of these, and related, data, but the real drama in this instance comes from the United States Department of Justice, where, in November of 2001, Attorney General John Ashcroft determined that any doctor in Oregon who prescribed a lethal dose of medication with the intention of assisting a patient to commit suicide would be violating a federal statute known as the Controlled Substances Act, and that the doctor in question could lose his or her ability to prescribe a wide array of medications in the future. That determination led to litigation that, in January of 2006, resulted in a decision from the United States Supreme Court to the effect that the so-called "Ashcroft Directive" was unlawful.[23]

The Florida drama could have been played out in Michigan in the early 1990s or in California later in that decade if the supreme courts of those states had not ruled that the evidence presented in those cases did not warrant the cessation of life-support for the patients in question. Both of those states were the sites of bitter and protracted disputes among family members of once healthy men who had suffered debilitating injuries in vehicular accidents.[24] When their wives sought to have their tube-feeding discontinued, other close family members opposed that course of action, and litigation ensued. In the Michigan case, the state supreme court eventually held that the wife, who was seeking to discontinue her husband's tube-feeding, had failed to provide the trial court with clear and convincing evidence of his pre-injury preference regarding the discontinuation of tube-feeding if he should ever fall into the condition that precipitated the litigation. As a result of that evidentiary shortfall, the wife's petition for authorization to terminate her husband's tube-feeding was denied. The California case proceeded similarly, except that the patient whose tube-feeding was at issue died before the state supreme court issued its ruling in the case.

Neither the Michigan case nor the California case concluded with a court-authorized removal of a feeding tube. Not so in the Florida case. There, in February of 1990, a young woman named Terri Schiavo suffered cardiac arrest due to a potassium imbalance caused by unhealthy dietary practices. The arrest caused extensive damage to Terri's brain. Terri was hospitalized, intubated, ventilated, and given a tracheotomy. Eventually, doctors performed a gastrostomy on Terri, inserting a feeding tube that was accessible from outside of her abdomen. For a short time Terri was comatose, but later she was diagnosed as being in a persistent vegetative state. For the first two years after Terri's cardiac arrest, her husband, Michael, and her parents, Robert and Mary Schindler, worked together in the hope of her regaining some level of cognitive function. During the third year, however, the relationship between Michael and the Schindlers collapsed. The struggle between them over who should speak for Terri with regard to the continuation of her tube-feeding dragged on for years, seeming to come to an end in January of 2001, when an intermediate appellate court upheld a trial judge's ruling that authorized Michael to discontinue Terri's life support. In April of that year Terri's feeding tube was removed for a short time. The litigation continued, however, and Terri's tube-feeding was resumed as mediation was attempted and as the trial court heard more evidence on Terri's physical condition.[25]

When in October of 2003, Terri's feeding tube was again removed on order of the trial court, the Florida legislature passed a law entitling Florida's governor to order its reinsertion, which he did. That law led to satellite litigation that in September of 2004 produced a ruling from the Florida Supreme Court to the effect that the law in question was unconstitutional because it violated the separation of powers provision of the Florida Constitution.[26] In January of 2005, the United States Supreme Court declined to review that decision, setting the scene for the final chapter of the Schiavo saga. On March 18, 2005, Terri's feeding tube was again removed on order of the trial court, and Terri's death seemed to be both inevitable and imminent. At that point, however, the United States Congress passed legislation empowering the federal court for the middle district of Florida, where Terri and her family were located, to decide if any of Terri's federal rights had been denied her during the years her fate was being litigated in the state courts of Florida.[27] President Bush signed that bill into law three days after Terri's feeding tube had been removed. When the Schindlers sought to have the federal court issue a temporary restraining order that would have resulted in Terri's feeding tube being reinserted (lest she die while the litigation progressed), the federal court refused, asserting that the Schindlers had not shown that they were likely to succeed in their attempts to prove that Terri's federal rights had been violated. The Schindlers appealed that decision to the Eleventh Circuit Court of Appeals, where the district court's ruling was upheld.[28] A few days later, thirteen days after her feeding tube had been removed, Terri died.

The Schiavo case revealed several troublesome features of the end-of-life legal regime that the states, with some help from the federal government, had cobbled together in the thirty years between Karen Quinlan's anoxic event and Terri Schiavo's death. The first of those features is that the designation of the family as the default surrogate for incompetent individuals is productive of smooth decision-making only when the family in question is in agreement among themselves as to the preferred course of treatment. Even when the relevant state law sets out in detail just which family member has priority over other family members with regard to the making of health care decisions for incompetent individuals, ugly and protracted litigation can issue from disagreement between, say, a spouse and the parents of the incompetent individual when they disagree about something as important as the decision to terminate tube-feeding for someone who depends upon it for his or her life.

Mention of tube-feeding calls to mind the second troublesome feature of American end-of-life legal regimes that the Schiavo case highlights. Since *Cruzan*, in which the Supreme Court appeared to assimilate the cessation of tube-feeding to the removal of a ventilator and to describe both abstractly as forms of medical "treatment," several state courts and several state legislatures have decided that tube-feeding ought to be regarded as just another medical procedure and have said that incompetent individuals have the legal right – to be exercised by their proxies – to refuse tube-feeding or to require its cessation, just as they have the right to refuse other medical procedures. This may make good medical sense and even good legal sense, but many people are deeply troubled by the knowledge that a persistently vegetative person is slowly dying in part, at least, because of the decision of someone else to terminate the nutrition and hydration that, if provided, could have kept him or her alive indefinitely. There is something about feeding, even when it is through a PEG tube, that strikes us as natural and normative, and something about its deliberate cessation that looks so much like the severing of the fragile bonds that connect us with the persistently vegetative that we balk at their assimilation to other procedures.

Mention of the prolonged death process in Schiavo-like cases calls to mind the third troublesome feature of American end-of-life legal regimes.

We can bring that feature into focus by asking ourselves seriously, and not rhetorically, why our end-of-life legal regimes tolerate the subjection of persistently vegetative persons to death by a process that lasts for weeks and could conceivably cause pain to the persons in question, even as those regimes prohibit their quick and painless death by the injection of some lethal substance into their veins. Surely history is of some help here, as no American assistance-in-dying advocate wants to resemble the Nazis in their zeal to terminate all lives judged not worthy of life. Current events also play a role, as every American end-of-life legal regime worries, at least a little, about what is going on in the Netherlands, where voluntary euthanasia is recognized as legal so long as certain conditions are met, and where involuntary euthanasia appears to have become a not uncommon practice.[29] But to think that we can keep ourselves from sliding down the slippery slope at the bottom of which lies wide-scale euthanasia just because we didn't use a needle and syringe to bring about the death of a Terri Schiavo is to engage in a form of thought that will not stand up to analysis. As the proponents of the right of the terminally ill regularly argue, the line between the pulled plug and the lethal injection is not nearly as bright as we might like it to be.[30] The emergent practice of terminal sedation, in which patients who are near death and who are experiencing intractable pain are put into deep sleep by means of carefully titrated intravenous sedatives, with the expectation that the patient will die without ever waking up, raises hard questions about the possibility of policing the distinction between palliative care, which the law encourages, and euthanasia, which it forbids.[31] Where the heavy sedation is combined with the discontinuation of nutrition and hydration, it is reasonable to suspect that the line between honoring a patient's rejection of unwanted medical care and assisting the patient in a suicide – or putting the patient to death without his or her consent – may have been fatally blurred.[32]

The final troublesome feature of our current end-of-life regimes that the Schiavo case brings to the fore stems from our own ineluctable fallibility. We would like to have been more sure than we were that Terri's doctors were correct in saying that her cerebral cortex had been irreversibly destroyed in the early years of her ordeal, that her husband really did speak for her when he sought the termination of her tube-feeding even though he was at that time involved in a quasi-marital relationship with another woman, and that the trial judge who presided over the case, and the appellate panel who reviewed it, were not over-invested in the correctness of their earlier decisions as they ruled on the Schindlers' several efforts to have those decisions reassessed. Those concerns could have been allayed if Terri's brain had undergone an fMRI or PET scan sometime in the last few years of her life so that expert claims about the state of her cerebral cortex would have had more credibility, if the trial judge had made better use of a guardian ad litem during those years so that the public could see that someone other than Michael Schiavo was speaking for Terri, and if the Florida Supreme Court, like the supreme courts of Michigan and California in the pre-Schiavo cases, had played a more active role in the appellate review of the trial judge in Terri's case. If one or more of those steps had been taken, the Schiavo case may never have become the cause célèbre that it became.

In response to the troublesomeness of the Schiavo case, bills have been introduced in state legislatures that create a presumption in favor of continued tube-feeding for persistently vegetative persons, a presumption that could be rebutted only by a written document signed by the currently vegetative person at a time when he or she was competent. Other bills would police more closely than Florida law currently does the conditions under which one person can become, or remain, the guardian of an incompetent person. Neither sort of law would seriously undermine the end-of-life legal regime described earlier in this entry, although the first sort might motivate many people in the affected states to put into writing their preferences regarding the medical care they would like if ever they become permanently incompetent.

As troublesome as particular end-of-life cases can be, it is hard to imagine any of the states making a radical change in the legal regime that governs those cases. Much of the troublesomeness of the Schiavo case was rooted in concerns with how well the key players in the case played the roles that the law assigned them. Concern about Florida's end-of-life legal regime, considered in abstraction from the contested particulars of the Schiavo case, never played a significant role in the whole imbroglio. So deeply rooted has the notion of patient autonomy become in our social and legal culture that it is unlikely in the extreme that it will lose its current position at the center of end-of-life medical care decision-making, even when that autonomy must be exercised by someone who we can only hope to be acting on behalf of a person whose functional autonomy has come to an end. It is, on the other hand, politically conceivable that tube-feeding will be disaggregated from the set of practices now thought to constitute "life support" and be designated as a form of comfort care that can be discontinued only when it has been shown to cause pain to its recipient or to worsen his or her physical condition – as can happen, for example, with individuals who are in the advanced stages of Alzheimer's disease. Such a shift might remove tube-feeding from the anticipatory or vicarious control that currently competent persons have over the continuation of life-support in the event they become incompetent and dependent upon it, and it might diminish our concerns about the apparent similarity between the removal of a feeding tube and the different forms of euthanasia at which we currently recoil.

If we could put the Schiavo imbroglio of 2005 to one side, we could say with confidence that the trend in both case law and legislative action with respect to the end-of-life legal regimes that the several states have created in recent decades has been overwhelmingly in the direction of classifying tube-feeding as a form of medical care, and, as such, subject to the instructions embodied in a living will or to the decisional control of an attorney-in-fact or of a duly designated health care representative.[33] It is quite unlikely that the legal upshot of the Schiavo affair will be the reversal of that trend. It is more likely that the states will continue on the trajectory defined by *Quinlan* and *Cruzan*, hoping that their citizens execute advance directives before they become permanently incompetent, trusting families to agree on the sort of care that one of their loved ones would have wanted in cases in which no advance directive is available, and struggling with the challenges that the next development in medicine will pose to the unstable end-of-life legal paradigm under which we now live – and die.

Notes

1 Tom L. Beauchamp & James F. Childress, Principles of Biomedical Ethics, 176–81 (5th ed., Oxford University Press 2001).
2 Jessica W. Berg, Paul S. Appelbaum, Charles W. Lidz & Lisa S. Parker, Informed Consent: Legal Theory and Clinical Practice, 20 (2d ed., Oxford University Press 2001).
3 The secondary literature in this area is vast. On advance directives, *see* the following text and its later supplements: Alan D. Lieberson, Advance Medical Directives (West 1992). On the ineffectiveness of advance directives, *see* the SUPPORT Study: *The SUPPORT Principal Investigator, A Controlled Trial to Improve Care for Seriously Ill Hospitalized Patients. The Study to Understand Prognoses and Preferences for Outcomes and Risks of Treatments* (SUPPORT), 274(20) JAMA 1591 (1995). *See also* Mark Garwin, *The Duty to Care – The Right to Refuse*, 19 J. Leg. Med. 99 (1998). For a vigorous argument against the entire policy of urging individuals to execute living wills (but not durable powers of attorney), *see* Angela Fagerlin & Carl Schneider, *Enough: The Failure of the Living Will*, 34 Hastings Ctr. Rep. 30 (2004).
4 The Patient Self-Determination Act may be found in the Omnibus Budget Reconciliation Act of 1990, Pub. L. No. 101–508, §§4206 and 4751, 104 Stat. 1388, 1388-115 to 1388-117 and 1388-204 to 1388-206. It has been codified at 42 U.S.C. § 1395 cc (1194 and Supp. 1999).
5 *See* Fagerlin & Schneider, *supra* n. 3.
6 Fagerlin & Schneider, *supra* n. 3, at 32.
7 *In re Quinlan*, 355 A.2d 647 (N.J. 1976).
8 On the right to die debate, many of the relevant documents may be found in Marjorie B. Zucker (ed.), The Right to Die Debate: A Documentary History (Greenwood 1999).
9 *In re Conroy*, 486 A.2d 1209 (N.J. 1985).
10 *Cruzan v. Director, Missouri Dept. of Health*, 497 U.S. 261 (1990).
11 *Id.* At 278.
12 410 U.S. 113 (1973).
13 *People v. Kevorkian*, 1993 WL 603212 (Mich. Cir. Ct. 1993), rev'd sub nom. *Hobbins v. Attorney General*, 518 N.W.2d 487 (Mich. Ct. App. 1994), aff'd in part and rev'd in part sub nom. *People v. Kevorkian*, 527 N.W.2d 714 (Mich. 1994). I discuss this case and the other physician-assisted suicide cases in *Physician Assisted Suicide: A Constitutional Crisis Resolved*, 12 Notre Dame Journal of Law, Ethics and Public Policy 369 (1998).
14 *Planned Parenthood of Southeastern Pennsylvania v. Casey*, 505 U.S. 833, 851 (1992).
15 For the moral and legal debate over assisted suicide, *see* John Keown, Euthanasia Ethics And Public Policy: An Argument Against Legalisation (Cambridge

University Press 2002); and Ronald Dworkin, Life's Dominion: An Argument About Abortion, Euthanasia, and Personal Freedom (Vintage 1994). For two good anthologies of articles on physician-assisted suicide, one *pro* and one *contra*, *see* Timothy Quill & Margaret Battin (eds), Physician-assisted Dying: The Case for Palliative Care & Patient Choice (John Hopkins University Press 2004), and Kathleen Foley & Herbert Hendin (eds), The Case Against Assisted Suicide: for the Right to End-of-life Care (John Hopkins University Press 2002). Both of these anthologies contain essays on assisted suicide in Oregon and the Netherlands.

16 *Compassion in Dying v. Washington*, 850 F. Supp. 1454, 1456 (W.D. Wash. 1994), rev'd 49 F.3d 586 (9th Cir. 1995), aff'd *en banc* 79 F.3d 790 (9th Cir. 1996), rev'd sub nom. *Washington v. Glucksberg*, 521 U.S. 702 (1997).

17 *Compassion in Dying*, 49 F.3d 591.

18 *Compassion in Dying* 79 F.3d 812.

19 *Quill v. Vacco*, 80 F.3d 716 (2d Cir. 1996), rev'd sub nom. *Vacco v. Quill*, 521 U.S. 793 (1997).

20 *See Washington v. Glucksberg*, 521 U.S. 702 (1997), and *Vacco v. Quill*, 521 U.S. 793 (1997).

21 Oregon's Death With Dignity Act may be found at §§ 127.800–127.897 of Oregon Revised Statutes.

22 For data on the number of Oregonians who receive prescriptions for lethal doses of medication annually (and on related matters), *see* the Annual Report on Oregon's Death with Dignity Act, published each year by the state of Oregon, Department of Human Services, *Physician-Assisted Suicide*, http://oregon.gov/DHS/ph/pas/or-index.shtml; select Annual Reports (accessed April 24, 2007).

23 *Gonzales v. Oregon* 546 U.S. 243 (2006).

24 The major pre-*Schiavo* cases addressing disputes between the spouse of an incapacitated person and other close family members regarding end-of-life treatment options are *Martin v. Martin*, 538 N.W. 2d 399 (Mich. 1995), and *Conservatorship of Wendland*, 28 P.3d 151 (Cal. 2001).

25 The major published decisions of the Florida courts on Michael Schiavo's decision to have his wife's life support terminated may be found at 780 So.2d 176 (Fla. App. 2 Dist. 2001) (Schiavo I); 792 So.2d 551 (Fla. App. 2 Dist. 2001) (Schiavo II); 800 So.2d 640 (Fla. App. 2 Dist. 2001) (Schiavo III); 851 So.2d 182 (Fla. App. 2 Dist. 2003) (Schiavo IV) and 916 So.2d 814 (Fla. App. 2 Dist. 2005) (Schiavo V).

26 *Bush v. Schiavo*, 885 So.2d 321 (Fla. 2004).

27 Act for the Relief of Parents of Theresa Marie Schiavo, Pub. L. No. 109–3, 119 Stat. 15 (2005).

28 For the key opinion of the Federal Court of Appeals for the Eleventh Circuit in that case, *see* 403 F.3d 1223 (11th Cir. 2005).

29 For a discussion of euthanasia policies and practices in the Netherlands, *see* Joseph B. Vander Veer, *Euthanasia in the Netherlands*, 188(5) J. Am. College Surgeons 532 (1999); and Charles T. Canady, *Physician-Assisted Suicide and Euthanasia in the Netherlands: A Report to The House Judiciary Subcommittee on The Constitution*, 14(3) Issues In L. & Med. 301 (1998).

30 For further discussion of the view that there may be no significant difference between "pulling the plug" and lethal injection, *see* Ernlé W.D. Young, *Physician-Assisted Suicide: Where to Draw The Line?* 9(3) Cambridge Q. Healthcare Ethics 407 (2000); and Helga Kuhse, *Critical Notice: Why Killing is Not Always Worse – And Is Sometimes Better – Than Letting Die*, 7(4) Cambridge Q. Healthcare Ethics 371 (1998). For the argument that there is a sharp distinction between "pulling the plug" and lethal injection, *see* Daniel P. Sulmasy, *Killing and Allowing to Die: Another Look*, 26 J. L. Med. & Ethics 55 (1998).

31 For essays on the moral status of terminal sedation, *see* Torbjörn Tännsjö (ed.), Terminal Sedation: Euthanasia In Disguise? (Kluwer 2004). For discussion of the legal status of terminal sedation in the wake of the *Glucksberg* decision, *see* David Orentlicher, *The Supreme Court and Physician-Assisted Suicide: Rejecting Assisted Suicide but Embracing Euthanasia (Sounding Board)*, 337(17) New Eng. J. Med. 1233 (1997); and Norman Cantor, *Glucksberg, the Putative Right to Adequate Pain Relief, and Death with Dignity*, 34(3) J. Health L. 301 (2001).

32 For further support of this view, *see* Howard Brody, *Causing, Intending, and Assisting Death*, 4(2) J. Clinical Ethics 112 (1993). For discussion by those who hold that terminal sedation combined with the discontinuation of nutrition and hydration is morally different from physician-assistant suicide or euthanasia, *see* Lynn A. Jansen & Daniel P. Sulmasy, *Sedation, Alimentation, Hydration, and Equivocation: Careful Conversation about Care at The End of Life*, 136(11) Annals Of Internal Med. 845 (2002); Timothy Quill, Bernard Lo & Dan Brock, *Palliative Options of Last Resort: A Comparison of Voluntarily Stopping Eating and Drinking, Terminal Sedation, Physician-Assisted Suicide, and Voluntary Active Euthanasia*, JAMA 278(23): 2099 (1997).

33 A number of professional medical organizations also have stipulated that artificial nutrition and hydration are both forms of medical treatment that may be withheld or withdrawn by competent patients or their legal surrogates. These include: American Medical Association, *E-2.20 Withholding or Withdrawing Life-Sustaining Medical Treatment*, http://www.ama-assn.org/ama/pub/category/8457.html (accessed April 23, 2007); American Academy of Neurology, *Certain Aspects of The Care and Management of The Persistent Vegetative State Patient: Report of The Ethics and Humanities Subcommittee*, 39 Neurology 125 (1989); American Nurses Association, *Ethics and Human Rights Position Statements: Foregoing Nutrition and Hydration (Summary) (1992)*, http://www.nursingworld.org/readroom/position/ethics/etnutr.htm (pending review and update 2005) (accessed April 23, 2007); American Geriatrics Society, *Position Statement: Physician Assisted Suicide and Voluntary Active Euthanasia* (2002), http://www.americangeriatrics.org/products/positionpapers/vae94.shtml (accessed April 23, 2007).

10 Pediatrics, the law, and bioethics

Susan E. Zinner

With the goal of protecting children from making unwise decisions, the medico-legal model used in the United States traditionally has allowed parents to make all health care decisions for their minor children. Children are presumed to be incompetent to make their own decisions in all arenas, including health care, due to cognitive limitations and immaturity. While this legal presumption has been relaxed in recent decades as common law and statute have created exceptions, the courts originally were quite strict in their refusal to grant any rights, including constitutional rights, to children. This chapter addresses medical decision making in the pediatric population with attention to important legal cases concerning the role of parents, children, and the state in making treatment decisions. Historically, children were considered chattel and states were reluctant to intervene in the parent–child relationship. In an 1874 case, a young girl was discovered chained to a bed, having been fed only bread and water by her parents. The American Society for the Prevention of Cruelty to Animals succeeded in removing her from her parents' home "on the ground that she was a member of the animal kingdom and that therefore her case could be included under the laws against animal cruelty."[1] The law had to resort to animal protection laws as no child protection laws existed at the time.

Children's constitutional rights have been recognized only in the last several decades. It was not until 1967, for instance, in *Application of Gault*,[2] that the Supreme Court acknowledged that minors had the same rights as adults to counsel, to notice of judicial proceedings, to confront accusers, and to cross-examine witnesses. The Supreme Court, in reversing the Arizona Superior Court and the Arizona Supreme Court, found that "neither the Fourteenth Amendment nor the Bill of Rights is for adults alone."[3] While the Court explored valid reasons for treating children and adults differently in certain circumstances, the majority found that there is no reason to withhold these rights in juvenile court proceedings. Child advocates were heartened by this Supreme Court decision explicitly granting constitutional rights to granted children.

Two years later, in *Tinker v. Des Moines Independent Community School District*,[4] the Supreme Court for the first time recognized children as persons under the law. Status as persons allows children to be accorded constitutional rights. This case acknowledged the right of students to wear black armbands to protest the Vietnam War. The Supreme Court found that, since children are persons they are entitled to First Amendment protections just as adults are and were therefore exercising their constitutional rights in protesting the war. As the court noted,

> In our system, state-operated schools may not be enclaves of totalitarianism. School officials do not possess absolute authority over their students. Students in school as well as out of school are "persons" under our Constitution. They are possessed of fundamental rights which the State must respect, just as they themselves must respect their obligations to the State. In our system, students may not be regarded as closed-circuit recipients of only that which the State chooses to communicate. They may not be confined to the expression of those sentiments that are officially approved.[5]

While these two cases do not explicitly concern health care and medicine, they are nonetheless significant in that they acknowledge that children possess specific constitutional rights. These rights will become more apparent as the reader examines the continuum of medical care provided to children in the United States from infancy through early adulthood.

Decision making standards for children

Parents (or legally appointed surrogates) are required to make health care decisions on behalf of children using the best interests standard.[6] A child's best interest typically is determined by a child's parents in consultation with health care professionals. "Best" is not understood strictly in terms of medical best interest but rather best overall interest, taking into account factors such as family values and religion, as well as the reality of resource limitations. This understanding of "best" has been recognized in the courts. For example, a Delaware case relied on utilization of the "best interests" standard in allowing parents to refuse to grant permission to a pediatric oncologist to provide chemotherapy to their very ill child.[7] The parents, both Christian Scientists, were allowed to treat the child by spiritual means consistent with their religion. While this may strike the reader as a surprising legal result, the court noted that the child was unlikely to survive for more than several months even with the chemotherapy and deference to parental control was appropriate in this case.

A second decision making standard employed by surrogates making treatment decisions for patients who cannot make decisions is the substituted judgment standard. On this standard, surrogates make decisions that they believe the patient would make were the patient competent. This standard typically is used only when the patient previously was competent and when something is known about the patient's general values and preferences. Only with knowledge of what the patient valued when competent is it possible to judge what the patient would choose were the patient still competent. Because children are not considered competent, this decision making standard generally is not applicable in the pediatric setting.[8]

Decision making authority and capacity

The law generally presumes that minors are incompetent to give informed consent for medical treatment. To provide informed consent, a person must be able to understand and appreciate information about a diagnosis, treatment options, as well as risks and benefits. It generally is assumed that a child cannot adequately understand and appreciate such information and that the parents (or other legally appointed surrogate) have decision making authority. There are some important exceptions to this legal requirement. First, no consent is necessary in the event of an emergency situation.[9] Our legal system assumes that parents would have consented to emergency medical treatment for their child had they been present and providers are protected from liability if they provide emergency treatment without parental consent. Second, "mature minors" may make health care decisions without parental involvement. "Mature minors" are children "[j]udicially recognized as possessing sufficient understanding and appreciation of the nature and consequences of treatment despite their chronological age."[10]

> [I]t appears that a minor must demonstrate maturity of understanding and intelligence along with chronological age. The degrees of risk and complexity associated with a particular procedure also seem to be factors considered by the courts. The more routine the procedure and the more minimal the risk of harm, the more likely that a minor will fall within the exception.[11]

Providers are responsible for ascertaining the minor's level of maturity to make his or her own medical decisions. Determinations are made on a case-by-case basis, raising the inevitable specter of subjectivity by providers. That is, one provider may feel a particular sixteen-year-old is sufficiently mature to make her own decisions while another physician may disagree. Rozovsky suggests that this is perhaps why states have enacted statutory ages of consent in many cases.[12]

A third exception to the general requirement that parental consent is mandatory before a child receives medical treatment is that of emancipated minors. These are minors engaged in traditionally adult activities and who are therefore treated as adults capable of making their own decision. While the specific requirements vary by state, typical examples include minors living on their own, minors who are self-supporting, minors in the armed forces, or minors who have a court order granting them emancipation.[13]

Fourth, some states allow minors to receive specific types of health care without parental consent. Some states have enacted laws allowing minors as young as twelve to consent to their own outpatient mental health treatment, sexually transmitted disease treatment, and substance abuse treatment. States adopting this approach appear to think that treatment of the minor is more crucial than parental involvement in medical decision making.

In addition to the legally recognized exceptions, some have argued that there is an ethical obligation to include children in health care decision making as they mature, even when they are not legally authorized to provide consent. Several writers have proposed a sliding scale of competency to assist providers in determining when a minor should have a role in the process. In the field of psychiatry, for instance, different standards have been established. Minimal proposed requirements range from awareness and assent (explicit or implied) to understanding and choice to appreciation and rational decisions.[14] Similarly, the American Academy of Pediatrics[15] and the Midwest Bioethics Center Task Force on Health Care Rights for Minors[16] have argued that as children mature, they should play an increasing role in making their own medical decisions. Others have argued against granting too much latitude to children/adolescents and removing too much decision making authority from parents.[17]

Many of those who believe that as children age and mature they should play a greater role in health care decision making refer to evidence from developmental psychologists. Such evidence suggests that children may be able to understand and appreciate the information necessary to make at least some health care decisions before they reach the age of eighteen. These studies are generally premised on cognitive development theories created by Jean Piaget. He created a scheme designed to explain the four phases of cognitive development in normal children. They include the sensorimotor period (birth to one-and-a-half to two years), the preoperational period (one-and-a-half to two years to six to seven years), the concrete operational period (six to seven years to eleven to twelve years) and the formal operational period (eleven to twelve years through adulthood).[18]

Piaget's concepts are relevant to a discussion of a child's participation in medical decision making because his theories about immature and mature cognitive development signal when minors may possess the competence to consent. As noted earlier, an individual must be competent to consent to treatment and, relying on Piagetian notions of reasoning abilities of minors, children at the formal operations stage (ages eleven to twelve) may possess the requisite maturity.

In an attempt to measure children's abilities to make medical decisions, Lois Weithorn, in a classic study, divided subjects into four age groups (nine, fourteen, eighteen and twenty-one) and offered each group the same hypothetical scenarios to determine if the subjects would consent to research participation. The scenarios presented included a range of facts, complexity, and treatment options.[19] The author found that nine-year-olds chose the same options as the three older groups of subjects in three of the four scenarios.[20] The key difference in the fourth scenario was that the younger children preferred hospitalization to outpatient treatment, which Weithorn attributes to the notion that "more treatment is necessarily better treatment."[21] Further, Weithorn notes that

> although the differences among the groups were statistically significant, the findings suggest that the nine-year-olds were able to demonstrate an impressive level of understanding about the information provided to them. Further, as demonstrated by their performance on the scale examining [the] reasoning process, the nine-year-olds tended to focus upon relatively important and sensible factors.[22]

In a similar study, Weithorn and Scherer found that preschoolers, first graders and third graders took more time to make decisions they were told were irreversible compared to decisions they were told were reversible.[23] The researchers conclude that their findings

> support the anecdotal observations of many clinicians and researchers that children who might appear to make hasty, foolish or oppositional decisions about some things (such as how to wear their hair) are capable of making thoughtful and careful decisions about those things they view as important to their health and well-being (such as treatment or research participation).[24]

Billick, in recognition of the developing cognitive abilities of children, has suggested that the respective roles played by the child and parent shift as the child matures. He thinks that the parents should be responsible from birth to age six for all medical treatment decisions. For children ages seven and eight, the parents should make decisions while the child participates. For children nine to eleven, the parents and child should jointly make decisions. Children twelve to fourteen should make decisions and parents are expected to ratify the chosen course of treatment. Finally, children fourteen and older may make their own decisions.[25]

Efforts to increase the role and decision making authority of children as they age necessarily depend on decreasing or limiting the role of the parents. The tension between a child's emerging autonomy and parents' rights to make decisions they believe are in a child's best interest raises complex ethical and legal issues. In *Pierce v. Society of Sisters*,[26] the Supreme Court acknowledged that parents and guardians of children had a collective liberty interest in making specific choices in raising their children. While this specific case addressed a parent's right to choose the most appropriate school for their child, it is not too great a leap in logic to presume that states will also generally defer to parental wishes in health care decisions. Similarly, in *Prince v. Massachusetts*,[27] the Supreme Court, relying upon the earlier *Pierce v. Society of Sisters* decision, wrote that "these decisions have respected the private realm of family life which the state cannot enter."[28]

While deference to parental control is still a respected legal principle in this country, this principle may conflict with decisions that may not be in the best interests of the child. Courts often decline to challenge parental refusals to consent to treatment where the risk to the child appears greater than the benefit,[29] as indicated in the *Newmark v. Williams* case previously. The state also has the right to deny parents from making decisions which the court thinks could harm the minor. This is nowhere more apparent than in organ donation scenarios. In both *In re. Richardson*[30] and *In re. Pescinski*,[31] the fact that the incompetent individual lived in an institutional setting away from the family appears to have been instrumental in the court's decision to refuse to allow organs to be harvested from an incompetent person to benefit a family member, despite permission from the parents.[32]

Minors often wish to make their own decisions whether they possess the requisite maturity or not. If the minor is a mature or emancipated minor who refuses to allow parental involvement, the provider can treat the minor unless "(1) there is likelihood of harm to the minor or to others that requires parental involvement to avoid or (2) institutional policy requires parental involvement."[33] For the physician caring for a child who does not fall into the emancipated or mature minor legal exceptions, the legal challenge can prove quite difficult if the minor refuses to consent to parental involvement.

> Realistically, how is the minor to enforce his refusal to undergo care? Unless a child protection agency is involved, no successful way may be available for the child to prevail. However, the physician whom the parents have asked to treat the minor may be in a position to bring the matter into perspective. Perhaps the parents simply do not appreciate the feelings of their child. A third person not as intimately involved may be able to help them understand the situation. When the parents remain adamant, the doctor has the option of refusing to accommodate them. She is treating the minor, *not* the parents, and a reasonable refusal on the minor's part should be heeded. Still, situations will arise when the minor's refusal [of] care is unreasonable. In those circumstances, the physician should consult with the patient and explain why the medical or surgical intervention is necessary, as well as provide information about the expected benefits.[34]

One proposed model lists relevant factors to be used by the provider in determining the minor's maturity such as age, cognitive abilities, moral development, life experiences, strengths and vulnerabilities, and current functioning.[35] The model goes on to suggest that the following factors receive a routine level of scrutiny: well-accepted treatments, low risk/high benefit, trivial or reversible procedures, and the consequences of treatment or non-treatment.[36] However, the following factors mandate a heightened level of scrutiny: controversial treatments, high risk/low or ambiguous benefit, and short- or long-term negative consequences of treatment or non-treatment.[37]

There are a number of special areas of health care or types of health care decisions in which there have been significant disputes and concerns regarding parents' rights to determine what is in their child's best interest and children's authority to make decisions. These include treatment decisions in neonates, medical treatment for adolescents (especially requests for contraception, abortion, or mental health care), participation in medical research, and refusals for treatment by minors. These issues are considered in the remainder of this chapter.

Health care decisions for infants

In the case of infants, questions about a child's decision making capacity are moot. Here parents generally have decision making authority, though a number of important cases involving infants born with various impairments or disabilities have raised serious questions about how much latitude parents have in determining what is in their child's best interest and in making treatment decisions for infants.

One key case, *In re. T.A.C.P.*,[38] addresses the status of anencephalic infants as potential organ donors. This Florida case involved a couple who learned in the eighth month of pregnancy that their child would be born with anencephaly, missing major portions of her brain and skull. Due to the significant disability anencephaly poses, infants born with the condition often live only a few days. The parents agreed to continue the pregnancy in the hope that their infant's organs could be donated to other children. Their providers and hospital, however, refused to comply with the parents' request. The Florida Supreme Court found that the cardiopulmonary standard used to determine life and death in Florida mandated that this child be considered alive for organ donation purposes. Therefore, the infant could not be considered a potential donor, since organ donors must be dead prior to donation.

Another case concerning an anencephalic infant which generated considerable controversy is that of *In the Matter of Baby "K."*[39] The Fourth Circuit addressed the issue of a hospital's obligation to provide emergency treatment to this severely impaired child. The mother of the infant preferred a more aggressive medical approach than the father and the hospital felt to be medically appropriate. The child had lived in a nursing home since her birth in 1992 for limited periods of time until she required periodic respiratory support to prevent damage to her bodily functions.[40] During those periods, the child relied upon the hospital for mechanical ventilation and a pediatric intensive care.[41]

Perhaps the major issue in this case was whether the Emergency Medical Treatment and Active Labor Act (EMTALA), which mandates the provision of emergency services to all patients in unstable condition or to women in active labor, was applicable to this patient. The court found that EMTALA did not include any exceptions for those who are not likely to live for any extended period. Specifically, the court wrote that "it is bradypnea or apnea [abnormally slow breathing or failure to breathe], not anencephaly, that is the emergency medical condition that brings Baby K to the Hospital for treatment."[42]

A third case generating controversy concerned an infant born with Down syndrome and an esophageal anomaly in Bloomington, Indiana in 1982 (unreported case). His parents refused to consent to surgery necessary to correct his defect and ordered that his intravenous feeding be stopped.[43] The parents' decision was affirmed by the Indiana Supreme Court and the child soon died.

One writer has noted that "[s]ome commentators argue that it is the presence of Down's syndrome, or some other form of mental incapacity, that results in the decision not to treat in these cases, and that therefore the decision is a disguised quality of life call that possibly ought not be made in this manner."[44] This decision, which many in the medical and disability rights community found disturbing, affirms the role of parents in decision making even, it appears, if that decision ultimately results in the death of the child. Traditionally, however, courts have ordered providers to treat these infants.[45]

In the wake of cases in which parents and physicians had chosen not to treat an infant and allow the infant to die because of his or her disability, federal regulations were designed to guide physicians and others in determining when treatment was not medically indicated. The so-called Baby Doe Regulations were controversial, and various versions of the regulations were struck down in the courts. Nevertheless, Congress incorporated the basic principles into the Child Abuse Prevention and Treatment Act through the 1984 Child Abuse Amendment. The Child Abuse Amendment holds that to withhold medically indicated treatment from disabled infants constitutes medical neglect. This does not mean that physicians always must pursue all measures to save such an infant's life.[46] Under these guidelines, physicians are not mandated to provide treatment to impaired infants if:

1. the infant is chronically and irreversibly comatose,
2. treatment would merely prolong dying,
3. treatment would not be effective in correcting all of the life-threatening conditions,
4. treatment would be futile in terms of physical survival,
5. treatment would be virtually futile and inhumane.[47]

Although the 1984 Child Abuse Amendment guidelines do not have to be followed, states receiving federal funds through the Child Abuse Prevention and Treatment Act must incorporate the guidelines into state law. Hence, the guidelines have been incorporated into law in many states.[48]

Health care for adolescents

The Society for Adolescent Medicine has recognized the need to protect the confidentiality of older minors in health care in general and offers the following guidelines, among others:

> Confidentiality protection is an essential component of health care for adolescents because it is consistent with their development of maturity and autonomy and without it, some adolescents will forgo care.
>
> Health care professionals should educate adolescent patients and their families about the meaning and importance of confidentiality, the scope of confidentiality protection, and the limits to confidentiality.
>
> Health care professionals and delivery systems should review and, if necessary, revise their procedures (including scheduling, billing, and recordkeeping) to ensure that adolescents' privacy and the confidentiality of their health information are protected to the extent possible.
>
> Laws that allow minors to give their own consent for all or some types of health care and that protect the confidentiality of adolescents' health care information are fundamentally necessary to allow health care professionals to provide appropriate health care to adolescents and should be maintained.[49]

In ethics and in the law, special attention has been given to confidentiality and decision making authority for adolescents regarding access to contraception and abortion as well as mental health treatment.

Contraception and abortion

Traditionally, the law has recognized two potential sorts of involvement when an adolescent requests these services: parental notification and parental consent.

In *Planned Parenthood of Central Missouri v. Danforth*,[50] the Supreme Court found that a Missouri law mandating parental consent prior to abortion was unconstitutional. This 1976 case specifically noted that the medical relationship between the adolescent and her physician should not be subject to challenge by the girl's parents. In a similar decision three years later, the Supreme Court again overturned a Massachusetts law requiring that both the adolescent and both parents consent to the abortion. The case, referred to as *Bellotti II*,[51] creates an option for an adolescent reluctant to obtain parental permission prior to abortion. This established the "judicial bypass" concept, which allows a minor to appear before a judge and attempt to convince him or her that she possesses the requisite maturity to be treated as a *de facto* adult, rendering parental consent unnecessary.

> First, bypass procedures must be expeditious and confidential. In addition, they must allow a minor to show that she is "mature enough and well enough informed to make her abortion decision, in consultation with her physician, independently of her parents' wishes." This requirement has come to be known as the "mature minor standard." Finally, the Court stated, if the minor cannot show that she is "mature," she must be allowed to argue that, "even if she is not able to make this decision independently, the desired abortion is in her best interests." This requirement is called the "best interests" test.[52]

Therefore, a minor considered to be a mature minor may consent to an abortion following a judicial determination of maturity. Should the minor fail to meet that test, however, the judge may still allow an abortion if it appears to be in the minor's best interests.

A Massachusetts court clarified these standards. Factors to be considered by the judge in ascertaining maturity include

> the minor's tone of voice, expressions, and overall demeanor; the extent to which the minor's responses were articulate and informed; the minor's analysis of her ability to raise a child and her family's ability and willingness to help; the minor's understanding of childrearing; the minor's consideration of the potential consequences of childrearing on her education; and in that the minor had considered and ruled out the alternative of adoption; and the degree to which the minor possessed, evaluated, and made deliberate decisions based on relevant information.[53]

In explaining relevant factors in the determination of whether an abortion was in the best interests of the adolescent, the court recommended that judges consider the girl's "'lack of significant life experiences, her lack of understanding of the responsibilities of motherhood,' and the shallowness of her analysis of the situation."[54]

According to the Alan Guttmacher Institute, as of August 2005, nineteen states require parental consent before a minor may obtain an abortion (Alabama, Arizona, Arkansas, Indiana, Kentucky, Louisiana, Massachusetts, Michigan, Mississippi, Missouri, North Carolina, North Dakota, Pennsylvania, Rhode Island, South Carolina, Tennessee, Virginia, Wisconsin, and Wyoming).[55] North Dakota and Mississippi mandate the involvement of both parents.[56] In five states, parental consent requirements are legally enjoined (Alaska, California, Idaho, Ohio, and New Mexico).[57]

Fifteen states require parental notification prior to a minor's abortion (Colorado, Delaware, Florida, Georgia, Iowa, Kansas, Maryland, Minnesota, Nebraska, Ohio, Oklahoma, South Dakota, Texas, Utah, and West Virginia); Arkansas and Minnesota require involvement of both parents as of August 2005.[58] Five states enjoin parental notification laws (Illinois, Montana, Nevada, New Hampshire, and New Jersey).[59]

Similarly, in an attempt to avoid unintended teen pregnancies, contraceptive laws vary from state to state concerning the role of parents in this process. As of August 2000, twenty-five states and the District of Columbia have laws allowing the minor to consent to contraceptive services.[60] The role of the minor's parent in these decisions is much smaller. "Some states justify the differential treatment of abortion and other reproductive health services on the ground that the decision to terminate a pregnancy is less a medical choice than a major life decision."[61]

One key case addressing this issue is *Carey v. Population Serv. Intl.*,[62] where the Supreme Court struck down a New York law forbidding the sale of contraceptives to anyone under sixteen years old. The court noted that, like adults, minors are entitled to a "zone of privacy" in certain areas of their lives.

While laws addressing the privacy rights of adults are held to the "compelling" standard (i.e., states may only intrude in private areas of an adult's life when they have a compelling need to do so), laws addressing the privacy rights of minors use the lower "significant" state interest standard (i.e., states may only intrude in private areas of a minor's life when they have a have a significant reason for doing so). In using this standard in *Carey v. Population Serv. Intl.*, the Supreme Court acknowledged that states do not have a significant reason to interfere with the rights of minors in buying non-prescription contraceptives.

The challenge for providers in providing contraceptive and abortion services to adolescents and, indeed, which exists in all aspects of the adolescent–provider relationship, is determining the proper role, if any, of the parent. Given the varying cognitive abilities of minors, providers must determine, on a case-by-case basis, whether the child falls into any of the exceptions allowing minors to make their own decisions. If a minor is able to make his or her own decisions, then the provider will generally be obligated to protect confidential patient information.

Minors may be understandably reluctant to confide information to their provider, especially information they may feel is shameful, such as a suspected STD, without the certainty that this information will remain confidential. Many states opt to keep the information confidential and withhold it from the parents, while others allow the provider the discretion to determine if the minor's spouse, parent or guardian should be informed.[63] Rozovsky further notes that the better position for the provider caring for the adolescent is to disclose this information only with the patient's permission.[64] Exceptions to this general guideline include public reporting requirements.[65]

Mental health care

To encourage minors to receive mental health care and treatment for substance abuse as needed, many states allow minors to receive such care without parental permission. According to a study by the Alan Guttmacher Institute, as of 2000, forty-four states and the District of Columbia have laws or policies authorizing minors with substance abuse problems to consent to counseling and medical care without parental permission or notification. Twenty states and the District of Columbia have laws giving minors the authority to consent to outpatient mental health services.[66] There is, however, concern that a child's mental illness will render the child unable to participate in the decision at all because the mental illness could impair the reasoning process.[67]

In 1979, the Supreme Court ruled that Georgia could allow parents to commit their minor children for involuntary mental treatment without a hearing before commitment. In *Parham v. J.R.*,[68] the Supreme Court determined that none of the child's constitutional rights, specifically his or her due process rights, were violated in the event of involuntary mental institution commitment. In making this determination, the Supreme Court examined a three-prong due process test. The three factors courts will consider in making this determination are: (1) the privacy interest affected by the commitment; (2) the governmental interest; and (3) the risk of erroneous deprivation of privacy during the process.[69]

In making this determination, the Supreme Court acknowledged that the due process rights of children are less significant than are the due process rights of adults. The court was in the difficult position of determining whether deference to parental authority was more important than the possibility of an inappropriate commitment of a minor. The court chose to defer to parental control and found that state law did not mandate any sort of judicial inquiry prior to involuntary commitment. "Rather, a determination could be made by a staff physician, provided she were given the latitude to evaluate the mental and emotional state of the child and the need for care. Furthermore, the Court indicated that the hearing need not be formal – or even quasi-formal."[70]

Child advocates were alarmed that constitutional protections were being denied to children. Justice Brennan, in a strongly worded dissent, wrote:

> [I]t may well be argued that children are entitled to more protection than are adults. The consequences of an erroneous commitment decision are more tragic when children are involved. Children are, on the average, confined for longer periods than are adults. Moreover, childhood is a particularly vulnerable time of life and children erroneously institutionalized during their formative years may bear the scars for the rest of their lives.[71]

The primary concern of child advocates was that children would be forced into treatment which was not in their best interest or perhaps not even medically necessary.

Research

The research context may provide some valuable insights to the vexing problem of the appropriate role of parents when making medical decisions for their minor child. The HHS regulations mandate both parental permission and the assent of the child.[72] Assent is comparable to informed consent but is a lower standard for the child not legally capable of providing an effective consent. The assent requirement allows the child to participate in the decision to the extent of his or her cognitive abilities. As one writer has noted, "[t]he assent regulation as written seems to reflect a presumption that the capability to assent is an all-or-none phenomenon: the child is either capable or incapable of assent. This presumption is incorrect and, I believe, unintended by the regulation writers."[73]

A key document governing the use of human subjects in research is the Nuremberg Code, which was created during the Nuremberg Trial of Nazi war criminals following World War II. In an attempt to prevent egregious experiments from ever occurring again, the Allies established ten fundamental principles governing research projects. The first, and arguably most significant, principle states that "[t]he voluntary consent of the human subject is absolutely essential."[74] As children are legally incapable of providing consent in many situations, the Nuremberg Code would, on its face, exclude children from ever participating in research.[75] The World Medical Association's Declaration of Helsinki specifically addresses the use of children in research. Principles twenty-four and twenty-five note that

> [f]or a research subject who is legally incompetent, physically or mentally incapable of giving consent or is a legally incompetent minor, the investigator must obtain informed consent from the legally authorized representative in accordance with applicable law. These groups should not be included in research unless the research is necessary to promote the health of the population represented and this research cannot instead be performed on legally competent persons. When a subject deemed legally incompetent, such as a minor child, is able to give assent to decisions about participation in research, the investigator must obtain that assent in addition to the consent of the legally authorized representative.[76]

Finally, the HHS regulations put much of the burden of determining if research using minors as subjects is permissible on the institutional review committee (IRB) of the hospital sponsoring the research or researchers.[77] Further, the regulations divide research projects into four categories: those "not involving greater than minimal risk," those "involving greater than minimal risk but presenting the prospect of direct benefit to the individual subjects," those "involving greater than minimal risk and no prospect of direct benefit to individual subjects, but likely to yield generalizable knowledge about the subject's disorder or condition," and those "not otherwise approvable which presents an opportunity to understand, prevent, or alleviate a serious problem affecting the health or welfare of children."[78]

Research not involving greater than minimal risk is permissible when the IRB ensures that provisions exist to obtain both the assent of the child and the permission of the parents.[79] The regulations define "assent" as "a child's affirmative agreement to participate in research. Mere failure to object should not, absent affirmative agreement, be construed as assent."[80]

Research involving greater than minimal risk but likely to directly benefit the minor research subject is acceptable if the IRB thinks that:

(a) the risk is justified by the anticipated benefit to the subjects;
(b) the relation of the anticipated benefit to the risk is at least as favorable to the subjects as that presented by available alternative approaches; and
(c) adequate provisions are made for soliciting the assent of the children and permission of their parents or guardians.[81]

Similarly, research involving greater than minimal risk and likely to yield generalizable results about the condition being studied is acceptable if the IRB finds:

(a) the risk represents a minor increase over minimal risk;
(b) the intervention or procedure presents experiences to subjects that are reasonably commensurate with those inherent in their actual or expected medical, dental, psychological, social, or educational situations;
(c) the intervention or procedure is likely to yield generalizable knowledge about the subjects' disorder or condition which is of vital importance for the understanding or amelioration of the subjects' disorder or condition; and
(d) adequate provisions are made for soliciting assent of the children and permission of their parents or guardians.[82]

In *Grimes v. Kennedy Kriger Institute, Inc.*,[83] the Maryland Court of Appeals addressed the federal definition of risk. This issue remains unresolved as some writers advocate an objective notion of risk (i.e., the risk posed to the ordinary child), while others advocate a subjective concept of risk (i.e., the risk posed to each individual child in a study). Children growing up in an unsafe environment would presumably be subject to greater risk if a subjective definition were adopted.

Finally, research not falling into any of the previous three categories but which presents an opportunity to more fully understand a particular condition or disease affecting children will be acceptable only if:

(a) the IRB finds that the research presents a reasonable opportunity to further the understanding, prevention, or alleviation of a serious problem affecting the health or welfare of children; and

(b) the Secretary, after consultation with a panel of experts in pertinent disciplines (for example: science, medicine, education, ethics, law) and following opportunity for public review and comment, has determined either:
   (1) that the research in fact satisfies the conditions of 46.404, 46.405 or 46.406, as applicable, or
   (2) the following:
      (i) the research presents a reasonable opportunity to further the understanding, prevention, or alleviation of a serious problem affecting the health or welfare of children;
      (ii) the research will be conducted in accordance with sound ethical principles;
      (iii) adequate provisions are made for soliciting the assent of children and the permission of their parents or guardians.[84]

It should be apparent that the federal regulations require increasingly higher levels of scrutiny by the IRB as the corresponding risks rise and the prospect of direct benefit decreases. The IRB is also responsible for determining when the researcher is obligated to obtain the assent of children.[85]

A case which studied whether a minor can be forced to participate in a research study was that of *T.D. et al. v. New York State Office of Mental Health*.[86] This case challenged regulations created by the New York State Office of Mental Health (OMH) governing the participation of adults and children living in OMH facilities and unable to provide informed consent to participate in non-censensual, non-therapeutic research involving more than minimal risk. The research was designed to ascertain the side effects of specific psychiatric medications. The court noted that

> [w]e are not dealing here with parental choice among reasonable treatment alternatives, but with a decision to subject the child to non-therapeutic treatments and procedures that may cause permanent or fatal side effects. It follows therefore that a parent or guardian, let alone another adult who may be a member of the child's family, may not consent to have the child submit to painful and/or potentially life-threatening research procedures that hold no prospect of benefit for the child and that may have the same result as a denial of necessary medical treatment.[87]

The court is clearly concerned that the researchers protect the rights of all unwilling participants, including minors. While trying to balance the potentially valuable information to be obtained from research with the very real possibility of harm to the subjects, the New York court acknowledged the vulnerable position of children in this context. The New York Court of Appeals dismissed an appeal by the New York OMH in 1997.[88]

Treatment refusals

Of all the challenges facing the provider treating for minors, perhaps the most difficult is caring for the minor who refuses treatment. Competent adults are generally able to refuse all medical treatment, even those simple procedures which could save their lives. Children, however, have limited rights in this arena. If parents refuse to consent to life-saving treatment of their child, their wishes will be ignored; this situation is not uncommon when parents are Jehovah's Witnesses.[89] However, when the child refuses to consent, different legal issues are raised. These include issues such as whether the adolescent's wishes may ever be ignored and the potential liability for the provider who complies with the adolescent's wishes or who ignores the patient's wishes, contrary to the wishes of the parents.

One category of patients facing this issue are minors who are not terminally ill. For instance, parents may ask their adolescent daughter's provider to insert an IUD or prescribe birth control pills[90] if they believe their daughter is sexually active. The provider should consider whether the minor falls into the state's definition of an emancipated or mature minor[91] to determine if she may be treated as an adult patient might.

Blustein and colleagues have proposed a model to address situations where minors refuse treatment in both emergency and non-emergency situations.[92] In non-emergency scenarios, the provider should address "possible misunderstandings, [the minor's] emotional state, consequences of nontreatment delay, alternative treatments, risk of alienating [the] adolescent from care and [the] duration of treatment, pain [and] side effects." Only after this discussion, should a decision be made. The authors note that

> [s]ome refusals may reflect the adolescent's failure to understand the facts, concern about body image, excessive concern about peer judgments, hopelessness, fear of pain, poor ability to think in terms of future consequences, or panic. In other cases the adolescent may simply be asking for more time, or more attention, before consenting. Adolescents alone may need more patience and support than other adolescents because of their prior history and lack of trust.[93]

When providing care to minors in emergency situations, Blustein and colleagues suggest a two-pronged model. The first prong, appropriate for unanticipated life- or health-threatening emergencies, mandates providers treat minors.[94] The second prong, to be used when a minor is facing chronic or terminal illness, requires the use of advance planning or a formal directive to make health decisions.[95] Rozovsky notes that "[c]hildren aged 12 or 13 who are veterans of prolonged therapy regimens and who sense or know that further treatment would be futile should have their wishes to withhold additional intervention respected."[96]

Perhaps the most significant factor in these cases is the prognosis of the patient. Children, especially those nearing the end of a terminal illness, recognize the risks and benefits of chemotherapy and similar treatments to a much greater extent than their non-terminally ill counterparts. That is,

> should a child have a life-threatening disease that is curable and should there be no reasonable alternative to the treatment offered by physicians, the court would more likely than not come down in favor of treatment. … A different result would likely occur if the child's condition were terminal or if the benefits of medical treatment were largely uncertain.[97]

For instance, in *Custody of a Minor*,[98] the Supreme Court of Massachusetts, citing *Pierce v. Society of Sisters* and *Prince v. Massachusetts*, used the "best interests" standard to require parents of a young child to resume chemotherapy to treat his leukemia. The court found that "[t]he expert testimony established that, in the child's case, chemotherapy was more than a brief means of prolonging life in that it offered the child a substantial hope for cure."[99]

In the context of mental health treatment, a survey of judges and hospitals found that most judges felt minors, especially older minors, should be consulted about treatment; hospitals, however, did not routinely seek consultation.[100] According to this survey, the U.S. legal system appears to be more willing to ascribe specific rights to minors than does the U.S. medical system.

Conclusion

The rights we accord to minors reveal a great deal about the values of our society. Blustein and colleagues have established several principles for treating providers treating adolescents:

1. Health care providers have a moral obligation to respect each adolescent as a unique person and to support his or her developing autonomy.
2. Health care providers have a moral obligation to promote the well-being of their patients and to minimize harm.
3. Because of the need for beneficent guidance, health care providers should work with adolescents to identify a supportive and responsible adult who will assist them in decision making.
4. Health care providers have a moral obligation to treat adolescents fairly – that is, to avoid discrimination, on the basis of economic, social, or familial circumstances, sexual orientation, race or ethnicity, or other personal characteristics.[101]

Recognition that adolescents, as they move from childhood into adulthood, have correspondingly larger roles in the medical decision making arena, is one crucial step for providers. Younger children may also be able to participate, albeit in a more limited way, in this process.

The law faces the challenge of recognizing the ability of children to make more and more decisions as they mature, while still acknowledging the special role of parents in their lives. Recent case law has evolved from recognition of the fundamental rights of children in the 1960s (e.g., *In re. Gault*) [102] to a more conservative and paternalistic orientation.[103]

The law can be both a friend and a foe to children facing the often complex medical system. Working with both providers and parents, children should be encouraged to develop their newly acquired cognitive reasoning skills to participate in this process. This ability can only serve to enhance the decision making aspects of all areas of their lives. While deference to a child's wishes is not always appropriate, at the very least, providers and parents need to take these wishes into consideration. Respect for our children's values and the ethical value of patient autonomy mandate that we involve them in decision making.

Notes

1 Tom Christoffel, Health and the Law: A Handbook for Health Professionals 415 (The Free Press 1982) (citing D.P. Wilcox, *Child Abuse Laws: Past, Present, and Future*, 21 J. Forensic Sci. 71, 72 (1976)) (citing R. E. Helfer & C. H. Kempe, eds, The Battered Child (University of Chicago Press 1968)).
2 387 U.S. 1.
3 387 U.S. 13.
4 393 U.S. 503.
5 393 U.S. 511.
6 Loretta M. Kopelman, *Children and Bioethics: Uses and Abuses of the Best-Interests Standard*, 22(3) J. Med & Phil. 213 (1997).
7 *Newmark v. Williams*, 588 A.2d 1108 [1991].
8 Albert. R. Jonsen, Mark. Siegler & William. J. Winslade, Clinical Ethics 87–90 (4th ed., McGraw-Hill 1998).
9 Fay. A. Rozovsky, Consent to Treatment: A Practical Guide 259 (2d ed., Little, Brown and Company 1990).
10 *See Id.* at 260.
11 *See Id.* at 265–66.
12 *See Id.* at 265.
13 *See Id.* at 266.
14 James F. Drane, *The Many Faces of Competency*, in Ethics of Psychiatry: Insanity, Rational Autonomy, and Mental Health Care 206, 211 (R. B. Edwards, ED., Prometheus Books 1997).
15 American Academy of Pediatrics Committee on Bioethics, *Informed Consent, Parental Permission, and Assent in Pediatric Practice*, 95:2 Pediatrics 314–17 (1995).
16 Midwest Bioethics Center, Task Force on Health Care Rights for Minors, *Health Care Treatment Decision-Making Guidelines for Minors*, 11(4) Bioethics Forum A1–16 (1995).
17 Lanie Friedman Ross, *Health Care Decisionmaking by Children. Is it in Their Best Interest?*, 27(6) Hastings Ctr. Rep. 41–45 (1997).
18 Ruth L. Ault, Children's Cognitive Development: Piaget's Theory and the Process Approach 22 (Oxford University Press 1977).

19 Lois. A. Weithorn, *Children's Capacities to Decide about Participation in Research*, 5(2) IRB: A Review of Human Subjects Research 1, 3 (1983).
20 *Id.*
21 *Id.*
22 *Id.*
23 Lois. A. Weithorn, & David. G. Scherer, *Children's Involvement in Research Participation Decisions: Psychological Considerations*, in Children as Research Subjects: Science, Ethics & Law 133, 152 (M. A. Grodin & L. H. Glantz, eds, Oxford University Press 1994).
24 *Id.* at 153.
25 Nancy. E. Walker, Catherine. M. Brooks & Lawrence. S. Wrightsman, Children's Rights in the United States: In Search of a National Policy 151 (Sage Publications 1999) (citing S. B. Billick, *Developmental Competency*, 14 Bulletin of the American Academy of Psychiatry and Law 301–8 (1986)).
26 268 U.S. 510 [1925].
27 321 U.S. 158 [1944].
28 321 U.S. 166.
29 Robert D. Miller, Problems in Health Care Law 419 (Aspen Publishers 1996).
30 284 So.2d 185 [La.App.] [1973].
31 226 N.W.2d 180 [1975].
32 Leonard. H. Glantz, *The Law of Human Experimentation with Children*, in Children as Research Subjects: Science, Ethics & Law 103, 109–10 (M. A. Grodin & L. H. Glantz, eds, Oxford University Press 1994).
33 Miller, *supra* n. 29, at 418.
34 Rozovsky, *supra* n. 9, at 358–59.
35 Jeffrey Blustein, Carol Levine & Nancy N. Dubler, *Ethics Guidelines for Health Care Providers*, in The Adolescent Alone: Decision Making in Health Care in the United States 251, 258 (J. Blustein, C. Levine & N. N. Dubler, eds, Cambridge University Press 1999).
36 *Id.*
37 *Id.*
38 609 So.2d 588 (1992).
39 16 F.3d 590 (1994).
40 16 F.3d 596.
41 16 F.3d 595.
42 16 F.3d 596.
43 C. Richard Cornelius, *Legal Issues in Pediatrics*, in Ethical Issues in the Treatment of Children and Adolescents 195 (T. Silber, ed., Slack 1983).
44 *Id.* at 195–96.
45 *Id.* at 195.
46 American Medical Association Counsel on Ethical and Judicial Affairs, *Treatment Decisions for Seriously Ill Newborns*, American Medical Association Ceja Report I A-92 (1992).
47 Edwin N. Forman & Rosalind E. Ladd, Ethical Dilemmas in Pediatrics: A Case Study Approach 47 (Springer 1991).
48 *Id.*
49 Carol Ford, Abigail English & Garry Sigman, for the Society for Adolescent Medicine, *Confidential Health Care for Adolescents: Position Paper of the Society for Adolescent Medicine*, 35(1) J. Adolescent Health 1, 1 (2004).
50 428 U.S. 52 (1976).
51 *Bellotti v. Baird*, 443 U.S. 622.
52 Jennifer. C. Friedman, *Parental Notice in State Abortion Statutes: Filling the Gap in Constitutional Jurisprudence*, 29 Colum. Hum. Rights L. Rev. 437, 448 (1998).

53 12 Mass. App. Ct. 299 (cited in Katherine M. Waters, *Note: Judicial Consent to Abort: Assessing a Minor's Maturity*, 54 Geo. Wash. L. Rev. 90, 111 (November, 1985)).

54 *Id.*

55 Alan Guttmacher Institute, *Guttmacher Institute State Policies in Brief: Parental Involvement in Minors' Abortions* 2 (Sept. 1, 2005), http://www.guttmacher.org/statecenter/spibs/spib_PIMA.pdf (accessed Sept. 6, 2005).

56 *Id.*

57 *Id.*

58 *Id.*

59 *Id.*

60 Heather Boonstra & Elizabeth Nash, *Minors and the Right to Consent to Health Care*, 3(4) The Guttmacher Report on Public Policy 4, 5 (August 2000), http://www.guttmacher.org/pubs/tgr/03/4/gr030404.pdf (accessed Aug. 30, 2005).

61 *Id.*

62 431 U.S. 678 (1977).

63 Rozovsky, *supra* n. 9, at 277–78.

64 Rozovsky, *supra* n. 9, at 278.

65 *Id.*

66 Heather Boonstra & Elizabeth Nash, *Issues in Brief: Minors and the Right to Consent to Health Care, 2* The Guttmacher Report on Public Policy 1–6, 4 (August 2000), http://www.agi-usa.org/pubs/ib_minors_00.pdf (accessed Aug. 29, 2005).

67 Nancy. E. Walker, Catherine. M. Brooks & Lawrence. S. Wrightsman, Children's Rights in the United States: In Search of a National Policy 156 (Sage Publications 1999).

68 442 U.S. 584 (1979).

69 442 U.S. 585.

70 Rozovsky, *supra* n. 9, at 311.

71 442 U.S. 627–28.

72 45 C.F.R. 46.101–46.409.

73 Robert. J. Levine, *Research Involving Children: An Interpretation of the New Regulations*, 5:4 IRB: A Review of Human Subjects Research 1, 1 (July/August 1983).

74 The Nuremberg Code, in Trials of War Criminals Before the Nuremberg Military Tribunals Under Control Council Law No. 10, vol. 2, 181–82 (U.S. Government Printing Office 1949).

75 Susan E. Lederer & Michael A. Grodin, *Historical overview: Pediatric experimentation*, in Children as Research Subjects: Science, Ethics & Law 3, 16 (M. A. Grodin & L. H. Glantz, eds, Oxford University Press 1994) (citing Michael A. Grodin & Joel J. Alpert, *Children as Participants in Medical Research*, 35 Pediatric Clinics N.A. 1389 (1988)).

76 The World Medical Association, *The Helsinki Declaration: Ethical Principles for Medical Research Involving Human Subjects*, http://www.wma.net/e/policy/b3.htm (accessed Sept. 7, 2005).

77 45 C.F.R. 46.404–7.

78 45 C.F.R. 46.404–7.

79 45 C.F.R. 46.404.

80 45 C.F.R. 46.402b.

81 45 C.F.R. 46.405.

82 45 C.F.R. 46.406.

83 782 A.2d 807 (Md. Ct. of App. 2001, reconsideration denied Oct. 11, 2001).

84 45 C.F.R. 406.407.

85 45 C.F.R. 46.408.

86 228 A.D.2d 95 [1996].
87 228 A.D.2d 124.
88 91 N.Y.2d 860.
89 Rozovsky, *supra* n. 9, at 339.
90 *Id.* at 358.
91 *Id.*
92 Blustein, Levine & Dubler, *supra* n. 35, at 262.
93 *Id.* at 261.
94 *Id.* at 262.
95 *Id.* at 262.
96 Rozovsky, *supra* n. 9, at 359.
97 Rozovsky, *supra* n. 9, at 355–56.
98 375 Mass. 733 [1978].
99 375 Mass. 756.
100 *See* K. Pikunas, Presentation, *The Child's Right to Object to Psychiatric Hospitalization: A Survey of Michigan Judges and Hospital Administrators* (biennial meeting of the American Psychology-Law Society, Mar. 1994, Santa Fe, N.M.) (cited by Walker, Brooks & Wrightsman, *supra* n. 67, at 164).
101 Blustein, Levine & Dubler, *supra* n. 35, at 254.
102 *Supra* n. 2.
103 Walker, Brooks & Wrightsman, *supra* n. 67, at 12.

11 Health care decisions for the elderly

Marshall B. Kapp

Introduction

Many older persons regularly confront a variety of decisions regarding their health care (as well as other kinds of personal matters and financial concerns). The process of health care decision making takes place within a legal and ethical framework governed by the doctrine of informed consent. When older persons (referred to in this chapter as "patients" because of the health care focus) are involved, certain particular considerations regarding application of informed consent principles are more likely to arise, including the capacity to consent to or refuse diagnostic or therapeutic interventions, legal interventions available when decisional capacity is impaired, end of life treatment issues, long term care questions, and the participation in research activities by decisionally compromised human subjects. These topics are outlined briefly in this chapter.

Jurisprudence in the United States embraces the fundamental ethical principle of patient autonomy or self-determination.[1] This ethical commitment to permitting, indeed encouraging and perhaps even compelling,[2] individuals to make and express their own health care decisions has been transformed into the legally enforceable doctrine of informed consent. Under this precept, every mentally capable adult (with no upper age limit) has the right – within very broad parameters – to make personal decisions regarding his or her own body and health care, free of unwanted external interference.[3] In this construct, power ideally is shared in a partnership between an informed patient and an advising/counseling physician. In contrast, more traditional hierarchical models are predicated not on commitment to patient autonomy but rather on paternalistic assumptions that "Doctor knows best." A health care professional in the United States may be held liable for civil money damages for imposing a medical intervention without the knowledgeable, voluntary, and capable permission of the patient or the patient's surrogate.[4]

The current vitality of the informed consent doctrine was not always so strong in the United States, nor has it yet been universally adopted as the proper guiding cultural and ethical precept regarding decision making in medicine generally, or for older patients specifically. Many other countries now are at considerably earlier stages in their own evolutionary development regarding the doctrine of informed consent in the medical context.[5] For example, a patient's right to give or withhold consent to medical intervention, and the physician's corresponding responsibility, was not officially recognized in France until a ruling to that effect was issued by its highest court (la Cour de Cassation) on February 25, 1997.[6]

Courts in most U.S. jurisdictions analyze and characterize lack of informed consent claims under a negligence theory. The essence of a negligence-predicated claim in this arena is the breach of a fiduciary or trust relationship formed between the patient and physician. An important consequence of thinking about lack of informed consent as a matter of negligence (rather than as an instance of intentional battery, as earlier cases had held) is that a negligence rationale encompasses a broader range of medical interventions (e.g., drug prescribing, screening tests) than a battery theory (with its concentration on tangible physical touching) is designed to handle. A few commentators even have proposed that informed consent jurisprudence should categorize an unconsented-to medical intervention as a dignitary tort. This would recognize a compensable wrong whenever a patient's dignity is offended through insufficient information even when no tangible physical or mental damage has resulted and non-disclosure of the information in question did not affect the outcome of the patient's choice.[7]

Decisional capacity

Every adult is ethically and legally presumed to be capable of carrying out autonomous decision making. However, some patients (and older individuals are represented disproportionately in this group) may not personally possess the minimum level of cognitive and emotional capacity necessary to exercise autonomy in medical decision making.[8] In such circumstances, the ethical principle of beneficence, or doing good for others, translates into the legal concept of *parens patriae*. The *parens patriae* power is society's (i.e., the state's) inherent authority to act to protect individuals who are not able to protect themselves.

Pursuant to the states' *parens patriae* authority, the legal system has devised an array of mechanisms, discussed in the next section, for intervening (or for empowering private parties to intervene) in the lives of non-autonomous persons without their consent or even over their active objections. The trigger for moving from deference to an individual's autonomous decisions to reliance on some form of surrogate decision making for that individual is a determination that the person is not currently capable of engaging in a rational decision making process. That determination may take place in the context of a formal adjudication of incompetence by a court of law with appropriate jurisdiction. Much more frequently, though, extra-judicial assessments of incapacity are made by legal or health care professionals. Although these assessments by themselves carry no actual *de jure* or formal legal authority, health care professionals and others act on the basis of these judgments.

The strong weight of contemporary American bioethical theory and legal doctrine treats the evaluation of decisional capacity as a decision-specific matter, and this is consistent with a primary emphasis on maximizing personal autonomy. Under this approach, the inquiry ought to focus on whether the person under scrutiny currently has adequate capacity to make the particular decision on the agenda at that point in time, rather than on a more global, all-encompassing, and all-or-nothing assessment that was embodied earlier in U.S. law and that still characterizes statutes in some other jurisdictions. However, although the law in the United States now focuses on decision-specific capacity assessments, most guardianships continue to be ordered on a plenary or total basis. Courts' legislatively bestowed authority to impose guardianship on a partial or limited basis is used rarely in practice.[9]

In addition to focusing on decision-specific capacity assessments, the prevailing thought in the United States is that decisional incapacity is not always a permanent condition. For some (including some older persons), incapacity may be transitory, with cognitive and emotional abilities waxing and waning depending on such factors as when the person is asked to make a decision; the surrounding location and environment; the effect of medications; support or aggravation systems available; and the effects of temporary, treatable physical ailments. Thus, the evaluation of decisional capacity is something that should be revisited periodically for many individuals.

Legal interventions when capacity is impaired

The U.S. legal system provides competent individuals with opportunities to plan ahead for future scenarios in which decisions may need to be made but in which sufficient personal capacity to make them has been seriously compromised temporarily or permanently. These planning opportunities permit an individual capable of making decisions to maintain at least some degree of control, exercised prospectively, while obviating the need for court involvement to resolve intra-family or family/professional disagreements about how this person should be treated once severe impairment has occurred.

There are a number of voluntary legal mechanisms available for advance planning about financial matters. These include the durable power of attorney for financial affairs (authorizing a named agent to act as a surrogate decision-maker for the principal under specified circumstances), creation of *inter vivos* (living) trusts, joint ownership of property, and money management services. In the medical sphere, the major legal devices used for advance planning are the durable power of attorney for health care (in some jurisdictions called a health care proxy) and instruction directives, usually referred to as living wills or declarations.

The development of legal planning mechanisms designed to avoid unnecessary or premature judicial involvement reflects a core American social value that difficult, intimate decisions pertaining to persons with seriously compromised personal decisional capacity should be handled as much as possible by family, friends, and the health care team. There is a presumption, consistent with the fact that the implementation of these planning mechanisms ordinarily is not subject to any external oversight, that now-capable persons planning for a cognitively or emotionally impaired future must be able to trust the relatives, friends, and professionals to whom they are delegating the authority to advocate, represent, and make decisions. For their part, persons to whom such trust has been given are legally and ethically required to act in a fiduciary capacity focused on serving the impaired person's best interests.

Many individuals with decision making deficits have not engaged in voluntary advance medical planning in a timely fashion. This gap may be explained by an inability or unwillingness to place their trust in available others, as well as ignorance of possible alternatives, and frequently, just inertia. For such persons, society has relied on its inherent *parens patriae* power to establish several forms of surrogate decision making for the incapacitated person without that person's concurrence or even over that person's active objection. Statutes in every state allow courts, in response to petitions filed by interested parties (who usually do not have to be family members), to adjudicate a person to be mentally incompetent and appoint another person or agency to act as a guardian or conservator (terminology varies among jurisdictions) for the incompetent person.[10] A guardian has a fiduciary or trust responsibility to act in the best interests of the incapacitated person. As discussed earlier, the concept of decision-specific capacity has led state legislatures to create the mechanism of partial guardianship, with decision making authority granted by the court only to the extent that the person really needs a surrogate.[11] Nevertheless, most guardianship orders actually are still issued in global, all-encompassing terms.

In response to a financial grant incentive created by the federal Older Americans Act,[12] every state has legislatively developed its own adult protective services (APS) system.[13] An APS system, operating through local human services agencies, makes available to willing older persons a variety of coordinated health care and human service interventions designed to protect those persons from the dangers of abuse and neglect, including medical neglect. Moreover, state laws generally allow local APS agencies to impose beneficial services on unwilling recipients. With only a few exceptions, non-voluntary interventions of this type may be instituted for a very short period of time on an emergency basis, but must then be either discontinued or continued only under the authority of a court order. Such a court order requires a finding that the individual lacks an adequate level of capacity to accept or refuse the particular elements of care proposed and appoints a guardian to act as the surrogate decision-maker.

Health care decision making for "the unbefriended" represents a growing legal and ethical challenge.[14] This term applies to the increasing number of persons who are growing older and impaired in terms of decision making, but who have no suitable family members or friends available to act as formal or informal surrogate decision-makers and advocates for them. Neither unbefriended patients nor the health care professionals who wish to care for them are well served by the present rather limited array of planned and unplanned legal alternatives.[15]

End of life treatment issues

Decisions sometimes must be made about whether to begin, continue, withhold, or withdraw life-sustaining medical treatments (LSMTs) (chiefly, antibiotics, resuscitation, dialysis, artificial respiration, and artificial nutrition or hydration) for critically ill older patients. In the vast majority of such situations, a satisfactory resolution is reached through a process of discussion and negotiation involving the patient (when still able to participate), family or significant others, the physician, other members of the health care team, and perhaps some form of institutional or agency ethics committee. Most of the time, LSMT decisions are made and carried out without any formal intervention on the part of the legal system.

Sometimes, though, the informal or extrajudicial decision making process breaks down, and the parties go to court to obtain a judicial ruling. A body of case law has evolved since the groundbreaking *Quinlan* ruling,[16] which allowed a persistently vegetative woman's parents to consent to have her artificial respiration discontinued, was issued in New Jersey in 1976. The various courts confronting these issues have achieved a high, albeit not a total, degree of consensus on the major points. These well-publicized judicial decisions, in conjunction with statutes passed by Congress and the various state legislatures, have set the boundaries or parameters within which LSMT decisions may be made by and about dying patients, including those who are elderly.

There is little dispute today with the proposition that a decisionally capable adult (of any age) has a right to accept or refuse various forms of LSMT. This recognized right is predicated on the ethical principle of autonomy, the law of informed consent, and the liberty interest in the U.S. Constitution. Various state courts also have relied on provisions in state constitutions and statutes to support a competent patient's right to choose in this context.

Despite the apparent legal clarity on this point, there is a substantial body of data indicating that very often the contemporaneous or prospectively stated (for example, in an advance directive) wishes of patients regarding LSMT are not fully respected and implemented. In actuality, some critically ill patients receive more aggressive treatment than they say they want.[17] State advance directive statutes invariably excuse a health care provider who chooses not to implement a patient's (or surrogate's) express preferences concerning LSMT. In the same vein, courts have refused to hold health care providers legally liable for failing to follow a patient's or surrogate's instructions to withdraw or withhold particular forms of LSMT, on the grounds that providing life-prolonging intervention cannot ever be the proximate cause of legally compensable injuries.

When a critically ill patient is mentally or physically incapable of making and expressing contemporaneous decisions about LSMT and there has not been a timely executed advance directive, the customary practice has been for the health care team to confer and negotiate with, and generally to defer to, the wishes of the patient's available family members and additional significant others. This practice is based on the presumptions that families are most likely to know what decision the patient would make personally if he or she were decisionally capable at present and that families ordinarily act honestly in the best interests of their loved ones. A decision standard that attempts to implement what the patient's wishes most likely would have been is "substituted judgment" and is preferred as most consistent with the autonomy principle. The alternative, fall-back standard, used when substituted judgment is not feasible, is the best interests test.

A majority of states have formalized deference to families by enacting what have been generically termed "surrogate consent" statutes. These statutes codify usual practice by explicitly authorizing family members and selected others (in a stated priority order) to make LSMT decisions about a decisionally incapacitated person who has not executed an advance directive. States have placed surrogate consent provisions in specialized surrogate consent statutes, in a comprehensive health care decisions act, in an advance directives statute, or in a general informed consent statute. Surrogate consent statutes ordinarily specify that the surrogate is to make decisions first on the basis of the incapacitated patient's substituted judgment and, secondarily, on the basis of the patient's best interest. Some state statutes limit the kinds of decisions (for instance, not permitting surrogates to withdraw or withhold artificial forms of nutrition or hydration), while other statutes are all-inclusive.

Congress enacted the Patient Self-Determination Act (PSDA) in 1990.[18] Among other things, this legislation – passed in the aftermath of the U.S. Supreme Court's only decision to date on withholding or withdrawing LSMT from a patient[19] – requires all hospitals, nursing facilities, home health agencies, managed care organizations, and hospices participating in the Medicare and Medicaid programs to "maintain written policies and procedures with respect to all adult individuals receiving medical care by or through the provider or organization" and to make those policies and procedures easily available to their patients or patients' surrogates.

Many acute and long term care providers have created and implemented written protocols specifically regarding prospective physician orders to withhold attempts of particular kinds of LSMTs under specified circumstances.

Such "do not" orders are a variety of advance directive and ordinarily are written by the physician with the consultation and consent of a competent patient or the proxy for an incapacitated patient. Most attention has been concentrated on Do Not Resuscitate (DNR) orders to withhold basic and advanced cardiopulmonary resuscitation (CPR) in the eventuality of cardiac or respiratory arrest, but other forms of prospective instructions to limit LSMT, such as Do Not Hospitalize or Do Not Intubate orders, also may be entered. The PSDA requires covered health care providers and prepaid plans to adopt written DNR policies, as does the Joint Commission on Accreditation of Healthcare Organizations (JCAHO) for the facilities it accredits. Policies and procedures for withholding LSMT in the home also have been developed by many service providers.[20] Most states have passed statutes explicitly authorizing DNR or "No Code" orders to be applied in situations of cardiac or respiratory arrest taking place outside of a health care institution.

Health care providers' anxieties about potential criminal liability or professional disciplinary action (such as loss of license) have been blamed for widespread lapses in proper pain management and palliative care for dying patients. Although usually exaggerated, this anxiety has not been without some realistic foundation.[21] Since the mid-1990s, concerted academic, medical, and political efforts have been exerted to change the legal climate and providers' apprehensions, and therefore their behaviors, regarding the prescription of adequate quantities of medications (including opiates) to control the pain of terminally ill patients.[22] As a consequence, a majority of states have enacted statutes that explicitly allow physicians to prescribe controlled substances to alleviate severe or intractable pain. State medical boards have altered their policies and practices regarding the prescribing of controlled substances to encourage physicians to treat pain in dying patients more effectively. In addition, several families of deceased patients have brought civil malpractice lawsuits against physicians for inadequately treating the pain experienced by their dying relatives.

Sometimes, patients or their families request (or demand) forms of medical intervention that, in their physician's best professional judgment, are likely to be ineffective. The issue of whether a health care professional has a legal obligation to effectuate a patient's or family's (or other authorized surrogate's) demands for LSMT that the professional believes to be futile is unclear. This uncertainty persists despite the venerable legal maxim, *lex neminem cogil ad vana sue inutilia peragenda!* – "the law compels no one to do vain or useless things." Several states have attempted to define "futile" treatment statutorily, so as to relieve physicians from an obligation to provide it.[23] The American College of Emergency Physicians has issued a policy stating: "Physicians are under no ethical obligation to render treatments that they judge have no realistic likelihood of medical benefit to the patient."[24] According to the Society of Critical Care Medicine's Ethics Committee:

> Treatments that offer no physiologic benefit to the patient are futile and should never be offered. … Treatments in which the benefit is unlikely, uncertain, or controversial from the viewpoint of one or more of the appropriately involved decision-makers should not be labeled futile. … Treatments that are beneficial but extremely costly should be made available in a limited fashion, governed by principles of distributive justice.[25]

Long term care decisions

Older individuals who need ongoing help in carrying out their activities of daily living (ADLs) have available to them a broad array of housing alternatives in which to receive long term care services. Housing options range along a spectrum from remaining in one's own home ("aging in place") with formal (i.e., paid services provided by agencies or independent service providers) and/or informal (i.e., provided by families or friends, generally without financial compensation) assistance,[26] at one end, to taking up residence in a skilled nursing facility, at the other end, with various possibilities (including assisted living facilities) in between. As with other sorts of important life decisions, housing options are usually selected by the decisionally capable older individual, with surrogate decision making taking place when the individual cannot make autonomous choices.

When nursing home admission is involved, there may be substantial legal and ethical questions about the legitimate authority of surrogates to commit decisionally incapable individuals.[27] These issues may be exacerbated by the present push by both governmental service agencies and private geriatric service providers to keep even quite disabled individuals out of nursing homes if at all possible.[28]

There is currently a major effort, both internationally and in the United States, to enhance and expand the role of consumer choice, control, and direction regarding important aspects of publicly financed home- and community-based long term care (HCBLTC).[29] Justifications for consumer-directed long term care services include, among other things, individual empowerment, enhanced quality of life, more flexibility and responsiveness to needs, and greater consumer satisfaction with services received.

The paradigm shift away from extensive government regulation of the details of long term care delivery and financing and toward greater consumer choice and control over those matters, even when government is ultimately paying the bills, is premised on the existence of an autonomous consumer who is cognitively, physically, and emotionally able to act as an informed and voluntary decision-maker. In many situations, however, the one who needs long term care is not capable of independently taking on the ideal role of autonomous consumer. Under these circumstances, someone else must make choices on behalf of the care recipient or at least substantially help that person in making decisions.[30]

"A lurking question with all consumer direction is . . . how to handle the question of agency for people of any age who are incapable of directing their own care."[31] On one hand, there is a danger that persons with certain clinical diagnoses that rightly or wrongly raise questions about decisional capacity will experience discrimination by health plans or long term care providers refusing to market or sell their products directly to them. Such reluctance could stem from fear that purchase contracts entered into with such individuals may later be legally invalidated if challenged. Discrimination of this sort may violate the federal Americans with Disabilities Act (ADA)[32] and the Rehabilitation Act.[33] On the other hand, neglect of those who really lack the capacity to fend for themselves in a competitive marketplace must be avoided in a compassionate society that takes seriously its *parens patriae* obligation to safeguard the vulnerable.

Consumer direction in the HCBLTC context involves a variety of pragmatic questions: whether to use the services of a particular program, what specific services and how much of them to include in the service plan, who will provide those services, and when and where they will be delivered. A vital consumer role entails hiring, paying, scheduling, supervising, correcting problems with, and/or terminating one's home care worker(s). Accomplishing these functions successfully requires at least a certain amount of mental capacity. A realistic approach to the challenges presented lies, unclearly and uncertainly, somewhere in between the neatness of zealous consumer choice proponents who contend that *everyone* is a fully independent, capable consumer (or who are willing to quickly gloss over the concern that some may not be fully independent, capable consumers) and the absolute position held by firm opponents of consumer choice, who argue that *no one* except a government regulatory agency or its agent could be sufficiently capable of handling the complex details of defining and managing a HCBLTC service plan.

Research participation

When older individuals, particularly those with severe cognitive impairment, are recruited for enrollment as participants in biomedical, behavioral, and health services research protocols, a panoply of legal and ethical concerns arise. The issues are especially difficult when the proposed human participants are institutionalized as well as significantly mentally compromised.

Most (but not all) research conducted in the United States is regulated by federal law intended to protect the rights and welfare of potential human participants.[34] The Office of Human Research Protection (OHRP) within the Department of Health and Human Services (DHHS) has the power to suspend an institution's research activities involving human participants for deviation from applicable regulations and has exercised that authority at a number of renowned medical centers in the last decade. Research involving human participants also is regulated by state law in several jurisdictions.[35]

No particular legal restrictions apply exclusively to older research participants; hence, participation by older persons in research projects takes place within the same legal framework that governs research volunteers generally.[36] For decisionally incapacitated individuals, permission for research participation may be obtained from those persons who are authorized to make other kinds of decisions on behalf of the older person.[37] Federal regulations refer to the use of a legally authorized representative under applicable state law for making decisions about participation in research activities.[38]

However, a 1998 report by the National Bioethics Advisory Commission (NBAC) included several recommendations (none of which have been enacted into law yet) for explicitly protecting potential human research participants (across the entire adult age span) who have impaired capacity to personally consent to or refuse their own research participation. Among numerous other NBAC recommendations were the following:

- Institutional review board (IRB) membership should include at least two persons familiar with mental disorders.
- A special standing panel of DHHS (a "super" IRB) should be created to handle especially ethically vexing research protocols.
- Research using mentally compromised participants should be permitted only if the project could not be conducted using mentally healthy volunteers instead.
- For protocols exposing participants to more than minimal risk, there ought to be an independent assessment of each potential participant's capacity, and the protocol should detail the process of assessing decisional capacity in each potential participant.[39]

Conclusion

The legal doctrine of informed consent and the ethical principles underpinning it apply with full force to health care decisions made by and on behalf of older patients. The age of the patient, and associated physical or mental impairments or needs, may complicate application of the doctrine in particular cases. This chapter has attempted to elucidate some of the challenges arising in the application of the informed consent doctrine to the process of medical decision making when older, sometimes impaired, patients are involved.

Notes

1 *See generally* Carl E. Schneider, The Practice of Autonomy: Patients, Doctors, and Medical Decisions (Oxford University Press 1998).

2 *See generally* Jay Katz, The Silent World of Doctor and Patient (The Free Press, Collier McMillan 1984).

3 *See generally* Ruth R. Faden & Tom Beauchamp, A History and Theory of Informed Consent (Oxford University Press 1986); Jessica W. Berg, Paul S. Appelbaum, Lisa S. Parker & Charles W. Lidz, Informed Consent: Legal Theory and Clinical Practice (2d ed., Oxford University Press 2001).
4 *Canterbury v. Spence*, 464 F.2d 772 (D.C. Cir. 1972).
5 *See generally* Robert B. Leflar, *Informed Consent and Patients' Rights in Japan*, 33 Hous. L. Rev. 1 (1996); Richard Smith, *Informed Consent, Edging Forwards (and Backwards)*, 316 Brit. Med. J. 949 (1998).
6 C. Herve & M. Wolf, *Physician–Patient Relations: Right of Self Determination. Path across The Atlantic Regarding Medical Responsibility*, 27(27) Presse Med. 1387 (Sept. 19, 1998) (article is in French).
7 *See e.g.* Majorie Maguire Schultz, *From Informed Consent to Patient Choice: A New Protected Interest*, 95 Yale L. J. 219 (1985); David E. Seidelson, *Medical Malpractice Based on Lack of Informed Consent in "Full-Disclosure" Jurisdictions: The Enigmatic Affirmative Defense*, 29 Duq. L. Rev. 39 (1990).
8 Decision Making Capacity And Older Persons (Marshall Kapp, ed., Ethics, Law, and Aging Review, Vol. 10, Springer 2004).
9 Lawrence A. Frolik, *Promoting Judicial Acceptance and Use of Limited Guardianship*, 31 Stetson L. Rev. 735, 741 (2002).
10 Mary Joy Quinn, Guardianship of Adults 5–6 (Springer 2004).
11 *See e.g.* IDAHO Code {sec} 66–405(3) (2004); KY. Rev. Stat. Ann. {sec} 387.500(4) (2004); MICH. Stat. Ann. {sec} 330.1620 (2004).
12 Older Americans Act, 42 U.S.C. {sec} 3002 *et. seq.* (2004).
13 Joanne M. Otto, *The Role of Adult Protective Services in Addressing Abuse*, 24(2) Generations 33, 33 (2000); John J. Regan, *Intervention Through Adult Protective Services Programs*, 18(3) Gerontologist 250 (1978).
14 Naomi Karp & Erica Wood, Incapacitated and Alone: Health Care Decision-making for the Unbefriended Elderly (American Bar Association, Commission on Law and Aging 2003).
15 Marshall B. Kapp, *Surrogate Decision-Making for the Unbefriended: Social and Ethical Problem, Legal Solution?* 1(2) J. Ethics, L. & Aging 83, 83 (1995).
16 *In re Quinlan*, 355 A.2d 647 (N.J. 1976).
17 SUPPORT Principal Investigators, *A Controlled Trial to Improve Care for Seriously Ill Hospitalized Patients: The Study to Understand the Prognoses and Preferences for Outcomes and Risks of Treatments*, 274(20) JAMA 1591, 1594 (1995).
18 Patient Self-Determination Act, Pub. L. No. 101–508, 104 Stat. 1388 (1990).
19 *Cruzan v. Dir. Mo. Dep't. of Health*, 497 U.S. 261 (1990).
20 Marshall B. Kapp, *Problems and Protocols for Dying at Home in a High-Tech Environment, in* Bringing the Hospital Home: Ethical and Social Implications of High-tech Home Care 180 (John D. Arras, ed., Johns Hopkins University Press 1995).
21 Ann Alpers, *Criminal Act or Palliative Care? Prosecutions Involving the Care of the Dying*, 26(4) J.L. Med. & Ethics 308 (1998).
22 Symposium, *Improving the Treatment for Pain – Legal, Regulatory, and Research Perspectives*, 31(1) J. L. Med. & Ethics 15 (2003); Symposium, *The Undertreatment of Pain – Legal, Regulatory, and Research Perspectives and Solutions*, 29(1) J. L. Med. & Ethics 11, 11–12 (2001).
23 *See e.g.* MD. Code Ann., Health-Gen. § 5–601(n) (2004); N.Y. Pub. Health Law § 2961 (2004)("medically futile").
24 Am. Coll. of Emergency Physicians, *Nonbeneficial ("Futile") Emergency Medical Interventions*, 32(1) Annals Emergency Med. 126, 127 (1998).
25 Ethics Comm. of Soc'y of Critical Care Med., *Consensus Statement Regarding Futile and Other Possibly Inadvisable Treatments*, 25 Critical Care Med. 887, 888 (1997).

26 Symposium, *Family Caregiving: Current Challenges for a Time-Honored Practice*, 27(4) Generations 3 (2003–04).
27 Marshall B. Kapp, *The "Voluntary" Status of Nursing Facility Admissions: Legal, Practical and Public Policy Implications*, 24 N. Eng. J. on Crim. & Civ. Confinement 1 (1998); Marshall B. Kapp, *"A Place Like That": Advance Directives and Nursing Home Placement*, 4 Psychol., Pub. Pol'y & L. 805, 809–13 (1998).
28 Deinstitutionalizing Long-term Care: Making Legal Strides, Avoiding Policy Errors (Marshall B. Kapp, ed., Ethics, Law, and Aging Review, Vol. 11, Springer 2005).
29 Symposium, *Consumer Direction in Long-Term Care*, 24(3) Generations 3 (2000).
30 Marshall B. Kapp, *Health Care in the Marketplace: Implications for Decisionally Impaired Consumers and Their Surrogates and Advocates*, 24 S. Ill. U. L.J. 1, 35–49 (1999).
31 Rosalie A. Kane, Robert L. Kane & Richard C. Ladd, The Heart of Long-term Care 135 (Oxford University Press 1998).
32 Americans with Disabilities Act, 42 U.S.C. §§ 12011–213 (2004).
33 29 U.S.C. § 794 (2004).
34 45 C.F.R. pt. 46.101–409.
35 Marshall B. Kapp, *Protecting Human Participants in Long-Term Care Research: The Role of State Law and Policy*, 16 J. Aging & Soc. Pol'y 13, 17 (2004).
36 45 C.F.R. pt. 46.
37 45 C.F.R. § 46.102(c).
38 45 C.F.R. § 46.116.
39 National Bioethics Advisory Commission, *Research Involving Persons with Mental Disorders That May Affect Decisionmaking Capacity: Report And Recommendations of The National Bioethics Advisory Commission*, Vol. 1 (1998) http://www.georgetown.edu/research/nrcbl/nbac/capacity/TOC.htm (accessed Oct. 20, 2004).

12 Legal regulation of genetic testing

Balancing privacy and family interests

Loane Skene

Genetic information is widely regarded as a particularly sensitive form of personal information. The presence of a genetic mutation within a family is significant for family members as well as the individual. Those affected may suffer anxiety, fear, depression, guilt, "the stress of being the bearer of bad news in the family [and] disruption to family relationships."[1] Genetic information may influence life and health insurance, employment, loans, marriageability, reproductive choices, adoption, and entitlement to government services and law enforcement. Genetic information may inadvertently reveal details that were not sought or anticipated, such as non-paternity or consanguinity. It is conceivable that information may be disclosed to the police or the media.

Any genetic information obtained about a person requesting a test (an "inquirer") may indicate that blood relatives should also be monitored or tested. This is especially important if there are interventions available to cure or alleviate the medical condition, which may be extremely serious. Yet, the inquirer may be determined to keep the test results secret. Conversely, a genetic test may reveal information about third parties (blood relatives) even though they have not consented to being tested, may not want to be tested, and may not wish to know the results.

For all of these reasons, many people believe that there should be specific legislation to protect the privacy of genetic information, even from close relatives. This includes a right to decide whether to be tested or not, and to control the information about the test results, in particular to whom that information will be disclosed.

International instruments have focused on the need to obtain consent for a genetic test and to protect the privacy of genetic information. However, they have also acknowledged that information may be divulged in exceptional cases. For, example, the *International Declaration on Human Genetic Data*, Article 8(a) states that "[p]rior, free, informed and express consent ... should be obtained for the collection of human genetic data, human proteomic data or biological samples," though "[l]imitations on this principle of consent ... [may] be prescribed ... by domestic law" for "compelling reasons."[2]

Article 8(d) states that "genetic screening and testing of minors and adults not able to consent will normally only be ethically acceptable ... [for] his or her best interest" (i.e. not for the "interest" of others). The insertion of the word "normally" indicates that there may be exceptions. Article 14(b) states that "Human genetic data ... and biological samples linked to an identifiable person should not be disclosed or made accessible to third parties, in particular, employers, insurance companies, educational institutions *and the family* [emphasis added] without the person's express consent." However, Article 14(b) has a proviso, "except for an important public interest reason." These provisions, like those in genetic privacy legislation in the United States and other countries, illustrate the balance that must be struck between the protection of the privacy of particular individuals and the protection of other interests. Those interests may include the health of close blood relatives. This chapter argues that they should include the interests of family members, describing recent debates in Australia.

To date, the Australian regulatory approach, recently endorsed by the Australian Law Reform Commission (ALRC)[3] and the Australian Health Ethics Committee (AHEC), has been to reject "genetic essentialism." This is the notion that genetic information is so different from other types of personal information that it must be protected by specific legislation. Instead, the ALRC and the AHEC have recommended that the focus should be on existing privacy legislation, tightened if necessary to meet community concerns about genetic information. The ALRC and the AHEC have acknowledged that the restrictions usually imposed to protect the privacy of personal information may vary when considering the sharing of genetic information between close blood relatives. One possible reason for this reservation is that the Australian debates, more than those in other countries, have originated from and remained focused on the experience of doctors and genetic counselors in advising people affected by genetic conditions about their potential risks and options. Medical experts have recognized from the start that genetic diagnosis and treatment require a different approach from other types of medical procedures because they necessarily involve treating a family, not an individual patient. The law must therefore take a "familial" approach when considering the privacy of genetic information, as distinct from the "individual rights" approach that is common in western liberalism.

The familial aspect of diagnosis of genetic conditions

In Australia, the familial approach to the privacy of genetic information has originated from specialist medical knowledge of the process of diagnosing genetic conditions. First, genetic diagnosis is not always possible from a sample provided by one person. This is especially the case where there is no direct test for the gene itself and where a marker, or linkage, test is necessary.[4] Blood samples must be sought from several family members, "the more the better, in order to establish the inheritance patterns correctly."[5] Their genetic material is then compared, to establish linkage with a particular genetic marker.[6] "[T]he identification of most clinically significant genes will advance through a linkage testing phase";[7] and most molecular studies of families with genetic diseases initially involve this type of testing.[8] For example, before the gene for Huntington's disease was found, a test could not be done without a confirmed diagnosis of Huntington's disease in a family member and a comparison of the DNA marker of that person with those of other unaffected relatives.[9]

Linkage tests are now comparatively rare.[10] However, even after a gene has been isolated and can be detected directly with a single molecular test on blood or other tissue with a high degree of accuracy, it is still important to confirm the mutation in at least one other affected member of the family (the "index case").[11] This enables a "family-specific DNA test" to be developed which is then "available for predictive (100 per cent accurate) testing in at-risk family members of any age."[12] Testing of family members is also important in susceptibility testing. Testing for cancer susceptibility, for example, may require "a protracted search for the mutation or involve detailed linkage studies that require extensive collaboration among members of a family."[13]

Even if family members are not actually tested, the verification of a genetic diagnosis usually requires information from or about relatives: "a well-informed clinical diagnosis starts with a detailed interview that includes questions about first-, second-, and third-degree relatives. This is followed by the construction of a family pedigree."[14] The information to construct "the family pedigree" may come from living relatives, death registers, autopsy results, cancer or other registers,[15] medical records of relatives who have died,[16] deposits of stored tissue,[17] or other research studies.[18] Family members may not be prepared to consent to the provision of information or to be tested, and if access to the information cannot be obtained to verify test results it may not be possible to diagnose the inquirer correctly.

One principal lesson from starting with the medical aspects of genetic testing and genetic counselling and considering how they should be regulated has been the recognition that genetic information is significantly different from other types of personal health information. In particular, genetic information is of two types. It is *familial* to the extent that a mutation exists within a whole family. And it is also *individual*, to the extent that a particular family member is positive or negative for the mutation. While it is appropriate for the latter type of information to be kept confidential in the same way as any other personal information about an individual (such as their broken leg, mental illness, or HIV status), the familial information by its very nature has important implications for blood relatives' health care and reproductive decisions.

For that reason, there has, in my view, been a greater willingness in Australia than in other countries to recognize that people should not always be entitled to control who will have access to their genetic information and their excised tissue. People have a general right to privacy and confidentiality, and this has been strengthened by recent privacy legislation in Australia as in other countries. However, there may be circumstances in which people's right to control their own information – and their tissue from which information can be derived – is limited in the interests of others.

Because of the early recognition in Australia of the familial importance of genetic information, legislation like the Genetic Privacy and Non-Discrimination Acts that have been passed in many American states have not been enacted in Australia. Such legislation was proposed in a bill introduced into the Federal Parliament in Australia by the Australian Democrats in 1998 – the Genetic Privacy and Non-Discrimination Bill. It was not passed and the then leader of the party, Senator Natasha Stott-Despoja, later said that one of her aims in introducing the bill was to stimulate debate.

Regulatory approach in Australia

Instead, the regulation of genetic testing in Australia has come from "guidelines based on expert opinion."[19] The Victorian Anti-Cancer Council (now called the Victorian Cancer Council) established a multi-disciplinary Working Party in 1995 to consider ethical and legal issues in relation to genetic testing, especially testing for familial cancers.[20] The Working Party was chaired by the late Professor Emeritus Richard Lovell, AO, a retired professor of medicine, and its eleven members included four other medically qualified people: a clinical geneticist, a specialist in cancer genetics, a physician, and a hematologist/oncologist. The other members were a philosopher, a moral theologian, a layman, a laywoman, and a lawyer (the present author). The committee was also informed by presentations from practitioners with day-to-day experience of familial concerns. Its deliberations focused on the case of patients at risk of genetic conditions and their families. It specifically rejected "the language of individual patients' rights," preferring "an emphasis on wider responsibility and communal concerns."[21] It envisaged a proactive role for doctors and the sharing of patients' tissue and genetic information among blood relatives when necessary to provide good medical advice to all the relatives.[22]

The Committee's recommendations were endorsed by the National Health and Medical Research Council (NHMRC) and included in its Clinical Guidelines, *Familial Aspects of Cancer: A Guide to Clinical Practice*.[23] The NHMRC document describes the Committee's report as "guidelines based on expert opinion."[24] Paragraph 2.5, headed "Confidentiality and the family" states:

> The likelihood of relatives needing to share information on their family risk, including details of the relevant gene mutation, should be made clear early in the process of risk assessment.

> When, in the course of risk assessment, relatives of an inquirer need to be contacted, the identity of the inquirer and his or her risk status (including the result of any genetic test) should not be passed on to relatives without the inquirer's consent. ...
>
> In the exceptional situation where a patient or other inquirer objects to information on his or her genetic risk becoming known to relatives, it could still be possible for relatives to be advised that they may be at risk from a family cancer susceptibility, but without identifying the reluctant inquirer. For the purpose of their own genetic testing, the aim should also be to acquaint relatives with the specification of the gene mutation carried in their family.
>
> The best person to make initial contact with relatives will generally be the inquirer [but may be a doctor]. ... Whoever makes the initial approach, a letter simply advising relatives that there was information to hand, which they might wish to discuss with a doctor would be a discreet and sensitive way of broaching the matter.[25]

The Human Genetics Society of Australasia has prepared similar guidelines.[26] In particular these guidelines state that although a person's test results would not be given to anyone else without the person's written consent, they might be given to the person's next of kin after the person's death; that

> [t]he details of the mutation causing the disorder in the family can be made available to laboratories which have been asked to test other family members, or to genetic registers, where appropriate, providing that doing so does not reveal any individual's presymptomatic or predictive status;[27]

and that, after a test, the DNA will be the property of the testing laboratory.[28]

Recent ALRC–AHEC Inquiry into genetic privacy

The Australian Law Reform Commission (ALRC), together with the Australian Health Ethics Committee (AHEC) of the NHMRC, subsequently undertook a much more extensive investigation. The NHMRC is the major funding body for medical research in Australia[29] and it has played a leading role in the formulation of ethical principles for the conduct of medical research.[30] Medical practitioners have traditionally constituted the NHMRC's Committees and Working Parties have traditionally been constituted primarily by medical practitioners but they have also included representatives from other disciplines (lawyers, ministers of religion, and others, including community representatives). The starting point in each project has generally been the medical environment, either in clinical treatment or research. Additionally, guidelines and other recommendations produced by the Committees and Working Parties have been widely supported by the medical profession because so many doctors have been involved in their development. The involvement of the AHEC as a joint participant with the ALRC in the genetic privacy reference must also have influenced its recommendations, especially regarding the clinical use of genetic information.

The Terms of Reference given to the ALRC–AHEC Inquiry[31] required it to consider (*inter alia*) measures that may be needed to protect the privacy of genetic information.[32] This included the use of information and genetic material from which information could be obtained in clinical services, genetic databases (biobanks), and systematic health administration and research. The project considered a broad range of purposes for which private genetic information might be used and which might give rise to concern – employment; insurance; establishment of parentage or kinship, for example by immigration authorities; entitlement to services by reason of Aboriginality; and law enforcement. There was widespread community consultation – postcards and brochures were published about the issues, together with an Issues Paper[33] and a Discussion Paper;[34] there were 15 public forums, and over 200 targeted meetings; and more than 300 written submissions were received. The detailed final report had 1,158 pages and 144 recommendations.[35]

One significant finding throughout the consultation process was that, despite concerns about the potential contentious uses of genetic information, there were many people speaking at the public meetings and making submissions that were based on their own experience or on the experience of a family member suffering from a genetic condition.[36] When people at public meetings expressed fears about "mad scientists," eugenics, the potential misuse of genetic information, and commercialization and commodification of bodily material, members of families affected by genetic conditions would respond that the science should be allowed to proceed, seeing the direct benefit it may have for themselves as more important or concrete than the disadvantages.

As noted earlier, the general approach of the joint ALRC–AHEC Inquiry in its Report was to reject the notion of genetic essentialism. It concluded that genetic information is not so different from other types of personal health information that it warrants specific regulation (a Genetic Privacy Act). Genetic information is obviously "sensitive" information and has a high predictive value; but so do other medical tests. There is no reason why genetic privacy should not be protected in the same way as the privacy of other personal information.

In relation to the interests of blood relatives, the Inquiry called for more national debate on the tension between individual rights and family and community benefits. It stated that privacy legislation should be tightened to meet community concerns. For example, it should cover genetic samples as well as information and legislation has already been passed to this effect in the state of New South Wales.[37] But it also recognized that there may be circumstances in which genetic information should be disclosed to close family members who require it for their own health care or reproductive choice.[38] Recommendations 21-1 to 21-3 of the Report of the ALRC–AHEC Report, for example, are as follows:

> 21-1 The Commonwealth should amend the *Privacy Act 1988* (Cth) *(Privacy Act)* to permit a health professional to disclose genetic information about his or her patient to a genetic relative of that patient where the disclosure is necessary to lessen or prevent a serious threat to an individual's life, health, or safety, even where the threat is not imminent.
>
> 21-2 The National Health and Medical Research Council (NHMRC), in consultation with the Office of the Federal Privacy Commissioner, should develop guidelines for health professionals dealing with disclosure of genetic information to the genetic relatives of their patients. . . .
>
> 21-3 The Commonwealth should amend the *Privacy Act* to provide that an individual has a right to access genetic information about first-degree genetic relatives where such access is necessary to lessen or prevent a serious threat to the individual's life, health, or safety, even where the threat is not imminent. Where an organisation subject to the *Privacy Act* receives a request for access, the organisation should be obliged to seek consent, where practicable, before determining whether to provide access. The right of access should be exercisable only through a nominated medical practitioner or genetic counsellor and may be refused where providing access would have an unreasonable impact upon the privacy of the individual whose information is sought or other individuals.

Recommendation 8-4 is also important:

> The Commonwealth should amend the *Privacy Act* to provide that an individual has a right to access bodily samples of his or her first-degree genetic relatives, through a nominated medical practitioner, where access is necessary to lessen or prevent a serious threat to his or her life, health, or safety, even where the threat is not imminent. The right of access should be limited to a right to obtain access to part of the sample. Where an organisation subject to the *Privacy Act* receives a request for access, the organisation should be obliged to seek consent from the genetic relative, where practicable, before determining whether to provide access. Access may be refused where:
>
> (a) it is not physically possible to provide part of a sample;
>
> (b) providing part of a sample means that the remaining portion is insufficient for the purposes of the organisation retaining it;

(c) releasing a sample to an individual raises public health concerns; or

(d) providing access would have an unreasonable impact upon the privacy of the individual from whom the sample comes.

The principle that personal information may be divulged to avoid a serious risk to other people accords with other provisions in the Australian privacy legislation that allow disclosure when necessary to avoid a serious and imminent risk to a third party.[39] However, in my view the ALRC–AHEC recommendations go further, as they are not limited to "immediate" risks. This is significant because a genetic risk is not immediate as in the case of a life-threatening infection or a psychiatric patient armed with a weapon – the usual examples of situations in which it is justifiable to disclose information to protect other people.

The Inquiry also recommended that an independent standing committee be established (Human Genetics Commission of Australia) with broad-based membership – leading scientists and other professionals together with community members. Its role would be to provide high level advice to government, the community, regulatory authorities, employers, and others, not to be a regulatory body itself. It would provide a national forum for the co-ordination of policy and a watching brief over new issues as they emerge.

The openness of the ALRC–AHEC Inquiry to the sharing of genetic information between close blood relatives or their health professionals on a need-to-know basis has broad support in the medical profession. With advances in genetic knowledge, doctors and genetic counsellors commonly say "We treat families now, not individual patients." If people are better informed about the two types of genetic information – the familial and the individual aspect – there may be growing community support as well. For many, the primary concern is that third parties like employers, insurance companies, and government agencies will unfairly use genetic information to the disadvantage of the people concerned, not that others will find out about genetic conditions in their family. If their concerns can be safeguarded, people may acknowledge the health benefits of limited sharing of familial genetic information through genetic registers and between providers of clinical services, especially when they understand that the information that is shared in that way is the familial part of the genetic information and not their own genetic status. This will obviously only occur in rare circumstances when a person who has been tested refuses to have any information disclosed to relatives and they are at serious risk without that information. In the great majority of cases, people seeking a genetic test will be counselled concerning the need to share familial information with their relatives and most will agree to do so.

If a familial approach is adopted, it may require some rethinking concerning the "ownership" of excised genetic material[40] as well as the confidentiality of genetic information. This is an issue that has received little judicial attention in Australia to date, but I have argued in various publications that the law should not recognize a proprietary interest in favour of the person from whom excised tissue has been removed (though a limited proprietary interest may arise in favour of a third party by reason of work and skill expended on the material in research).[41] This issue was not within the Terms of Reference for the ALRC–AHEC Inquiry and is still under discussion.

Conclusion

From the start, Australian debates about the legal regulation of genetic testing have involved doctors and genetic counsellors, and they have focused on the clinical aspects of genetic conditions. There has been widespread community consultation in which many people suffering from genetic conditions and their families have urged that research should be continued. Although civil libertarians and others have been concerned about the sensitivity and potential abuse of genetic privacy, that has been balanced against the clinical advantages for families of sharing necessary genetic details, even if one family member objects to that course. In that regard, the Australian proposals are, in my view, distinctive and enlightened.

Notes

1 National Health and Medical Research Council (NHMRC), *Familial Aspects of Cancer, a Guide to Clinical Practice*, ch. 2 (1999), http://www.health.gov.au/nhmrc/publications/pdf/cp67.pdf (accessed Aug. 17, 2004) [hereinafter *Familial Aspects of Cancer*].
2 UNESCO, *International Declaration on Human Genetic Data* (Oct. 16, 2003), http://portal.unesco.org/en/ev.php-URL_ID=17720&URL_DO=DO_TOPIC&URL_SECTION=201.html (accessed Aug. 11, 2004).
3 Australian Law Reform Commission (ALRC), *Essentially Yours: The Protection of Human Genetic Information in Australia* (2003), http://www.austlii.edu.au/au/other/alrc/publications/reports/96/ (accessed Aug. 6, 2004). The recommendations in this report are discussed below.
4 Diseases in which a single test on an individual gives a result include sickle cell anaemia, phenylketonuria (PKU), and Tay-Sachs disease. Diseases requiring linkage tests include adult polycystic kidney disease and breast cancer (though most breast cancer is not familial).
5 Susan K. Miller, *To Catch a Killer Gene*, 1870 New Scientist 37, 41 (April 24, 1993).
6 Peter S. Harper, *Research Samples from Families with Genetic Diseases: A Proposed Code of Conduct*, 306 B.M.J. 1391 (1993).
7 Eric T. Juengst, *Priorities in Professional Ethics and Social Policy for Human Genetics*, 266 JAMA 1835, 1836 (1991).
8 Harper, *supra* n. 6, at 1391–92.
9 Gregory J. Meissen, R. H. Myers, C. A. Mastromauro, W. J. Koroshetz, K. W. Klinger, L. A. Farrer, P. A. Watkins, J. F. Gusella, E. D. Bird & J. B. Martin, *Predictive Testing for Huntington's Disease with the Use of a Linked DNA Marker*, 318 N. Eng. J. Med. 535, 535 (1988).

10 Bob Williamson, Director, Murdoch Children's Research Institute, Melbourne, says that linkage tests are "really a thing of the past"; personal communication, April 1998.

11 Leslie J. Sheffield, *DNA Diagnostic Tests: Presymptomatic and Prenatal*, 158 Med. J. Aust. 349, 349 (1993).

12 Finlay A. Macrae, *Screening for Colorectal Cancer*, 165 Med. J. Aust. 102, 104 (1996); *cf* Gillian Turner, W. Meagher, C. Willis & P. Colley, *Cascade Testing for Carrier Status in Cystic Fibrosis in a Large Family*, 159 Med. J. Aust. 163, 165 (1993). "The accurate method of testing [for cystic fibrosis] is to deduce the genotype of the proband by testing grandparents and then test the individual if the mutations can be identified." Cystic fibrosis requires "family specific DNA tests" because there are multiple mutations that cause the disease.

13 David E. C. Cole, S. Gallinger, D. R. McCready, B. Rosen, J. Engel & D. Malkin, *Genetic Counselling and Testing for Susceptibility to Breast, Ovarian and Colon Cancer. Where are We Today?* 154(2) Can. Med. Assoc. J. 149, 153 (1996); Bruce Ponder, *Genetic Testing for Cancer Risk*, 278 Science 1050, 1051 (1997).

14 Cole *et al., supra* n. 13, at 150. The clinical criteria for identifying a person at risk of breast, ovarian, or colon cancer require a family history in successive generations (at 152).

15 Doctors report cancer patients to cancer registers, either voluntarily, as in the United Kingdom, or by statute, as with some cancers in Australia.

16 Loane Skene & Julian Savulescu, *Who Has the Right to Access Medical Information from A Deceased Person? Ethical and Legal Perspectives*, 8 J. L. & Med. 81 (2000).

17 Loane Skene, *Ownership of Human Tissue and the Law*, 3 Nature Reviews Genetics (U.K.) 145, 146 (2002).

18 For example, "family genotyping of hereditary non-polyposis colorectal cancer syndrome is held by Australian research centres." *See* Macrae, *supra* n. 12, at 104.

19 *Familial Aspects of Cancer* (1999), *supra* n.1, ch. 2, at opening ¶.

20 Anti-Cancer Council of Victoria, Cancer Genetic Ethics Committee, *Ethics and Familial Cancers*, including proposed Guidelines on Ethical Aspects of Risk Assessment, Genetic Testing and Genetic Registers in Relation to Cancer (1996). Part of this report is reproduced in Chapter 2 of *Familial Aspects of Cancer* (1999), *supra* n. 1.

21 *Id.*

22 Another early Inquiry in the United Kingdom with a medical chair took a similar approach (the Bobrow Inquiry); Janet R. Richards & Martin Bobrow, *Ethical Issues in Clinical Genetics: A Report of A Joint Working Party of The College Committee on Ethical Issues in Medicine and The College Committee on Clinical Genetics*, 25(4) J. Royal College Phys. London 284 (1991). *See also* Nadeem Qureshi & John A. Raeburn, *Clinical Genetics Meets Primary Care*, 307 B.M.J. 816, 817 (1993).

23 *Familial Aspects of Cancer*, *supra* n. 1.

24 *Id.* at ch. 2, opening ¶.

25 *Id.* at ch. 2, § 2.5, emphasis added.

26 The Human Genetics Society of Australasia, *Guidelines for DNA Presymptomatic and Predictive Testing for Genetic Disorders* (2002), http://www.hgsa.com.au/policy/dnaptgd.html (accessed Aug. 17, 2004) [hereinafter *Guidelines*].

27 *Id.*

28 *Id.*

29 NHMRC, http://www.health.gov.au/nhmrc/ (accessed Aug. 11, 2004).

30 *See*, in particular, NHMRC, *National Statement on Ethical Conduct in Research Involving Human Subjects* (1999), http://www.nhmrc.gov.au/publications/humans/contents.htm (accessed Aug. 11, 2004). *See also*, in relation to genetic testing,

NHMRC, *Ethical Aspects of Human Genetic Testing – an Information Paper* (2000), http://www.health.gov.au/nhmrc/publications/pdf/e39.pdf (accessed Aug. 11, 2004); NHMRC, *Guidelines for Genetic Registers and Associated Genetic Material* (1999), http://www.nhmrc.gov.au/publications/pdf/e14.pdf (accessed Aug. 13, 2004).

31 ALRC, *supra* n. 3. This account of the Commission's work also draws upon a description by the President of the ALRC, Professor David Weisbrot, at the 15th World Congress on Medical Law in Sydney, Australia, August 4, 2004.

32 ALRC, *supra* n. 3, at 2(c)(xi).

33 ALRC, *Protection of Human Genetic Information* (2001), http://www.austlii.edu.au/au/other/alrc/publications/issues/26/ (accessed Aug. 6, 2004).

34 ALRC, *Protection of Human Genetic Information* (2002), http://www.austlii.edu.au/au/other/alrc/publications/dp/66/ (accessed Aug. 6, 2004).

35 *See supra* n. 3.

36 Weisbrot said that several hundred of the submissions to the Commission came from "ordinary members of the community," many of whom described their own experiences, saying that they "did not want other people to go through what we did." *See supra* n. 31.

37 Health Records and Information Privacy Act 2002 § 5(2); Privacy and Personal Information Protection Act 1998 § 4(2).

38 *See supra* n. 3, at 563–70, paras. 21.80 – 21.108.

39 *Privacy Act* 1988 (Cth) – National Privacy Principles, Schedule 3, 2.1(e)(i).

40 *Cf.* Human Genetics Society of Australasia, *Guidelines*, *supra* n. 26 and text in chapter at n. 28.

41 Loane Skene, *Arguments Against People "Owning" Their Own Bodies, Body Parts and Tissue*, 2 Macquarie L. J. 165 (2002); Loane Skene, *Proprietary Rights in Human Bodies, Body Parts and Tissue: Regulatory Contexts and Proposals for New Laws*, 22 Leg. Stud. 102, 102 (2002).

13 Assisted reproduction in Ireland

Deirdre Madden

Introduction

This chapter broadly describes the current legal context within which assisted human reproduction (AHR) treatment services are carried out in the Republic of Ireland. Given Ireland's proximity to the United Kingdom, both in geographical and jurisprudential terms, a brief synopsis of the regulation of AHR in the United Kingdom will also be given. Finally, the chapter will discuss the attempts at the European Union level to introduce some degree of harmonization in relation to bioethics generally, and the likelihood of achieving consensus between the European Union member states on AHR issues.

Brief history of abortion and other reproductive issues in Ireland

The history of the abortion debate in Ireland is not a happy one. "Anti-abortion rhetoric and the values underpinning it have been a dominant aspect of Irish society since political independence in 1922."[1] Through the influence of the Catholic Church, in both medical and political spheres, the Irish state, in its laws and particularly the 1937 Constitution, has enshrined a pronatalist policy in the legal system. The feminist ideology that had played an important role in the struggle for independence in the early decades of the twentieth century seemed to be overshadowed by religious dogma when it came to the drafting of the 1937 Constitution, *Bunreacht na hEireann*. In the Constitution, the state, heavily influenced by the Catholic Church, sought to exert control in the area of family and marriage.[2] "Mother and unpaid homemaker was portrayed as the appropriate role model for all Irish women."[3] This influence was seen in many different areas from the segregation of education, the imposition of a marriage bar in public service employment, the subordination of women to men in terms of property rights, and the prohibition of divorce.[4]

Article 41.2.1 of the 1937 Constitution provides explicit recognition of the importance to the state and the common good, of the support provided by the woman "by her life within the home." Art. 41.2.2 states that "the State shall, therefore, endeavour to ensure that mothers shall not be obliged by economic necessity to engage in labor to the neglect of their duties in the home." These provisions clearly demonstrate the influence of moral teaching on the political landscape in 1937, and help put the debate on reproductive rights in Ireland into context.

In relation to reproductive rights and freedoms, Irish women struggled for many years against the state to gain control of their fertility, as well as battling against the political and social ideology that denied them such freedom. The Catholic Church has traditionally been opposed to contraceptive measures and Irish official policy was not to encourage debate on such issues as sexuality and reproduction. Censorship legislation was enacted to prohibit advertisements, books, or periodicals relating to or advocating contraception or abortion. The legal prohibition of the sale or importation of contraceptives remained in place until the landmark Supreme Court case of *McGee v. Attorney General* in 1974.[5] In that case, a twenty-nine-year-old mother of four had been warned by her doctor that she would be at serious risk of death or paralysis if she became pregnant again, and he advised the use of contraceptives. When the plaintiff ordered these from England, the packet was intercepted by customs authorities and was confiscated. Mrs. McGee successfully brought an action against the state on grounds that her constitutional right to privacy had been violated, though this was based on her status as a married woman, as opposed to individual privacy. Two of the four majority judges relied on the United States Supreme Court case of *Griswold v. Connecticut*,[6] a reliance that caused some concern later to those who saw *Griswold* being invoked in *Roe v. Wade*[7] to recognize a right of privacy that was broad enough to encompass a woman's right to decide to terminate her pregnancy.

Legislation was passed in 1979 enabling, for the first time, contraceptives to be made available on prescription in Ireland for family planning or other medical reasons. However, the vast majority of pharmacists refused to stock them and contraceptives were instead supplied from family planning clinics in contravention of the law. Legislation continued to liberalize access to contraception throughout the 1980s and 1990s, and contraceptives are now widely available in Ireland.

This progressive move away from traditional Catholic dogma has not been seen in the context of abortion, where the position as enshrined by constitutional amendment in 1983 remains the same today.[8] Abortion was criminalized by the Offences against the Person Act in 1861, although there was some confusion regarding the wording of the legislation which seemed to envisage that there might be circumstances in which abortion could be lawful. The Act, together with the pervasive influence of the Catholic Church in Ireland and the refusal of the medical profession to take any position in violation of the Church's ethical stance, meant that abortions were not carried out in the jurisdiction, other than in a clandestine fashion. Irish women seeking abortions traveled to England from the 1930s onwards, the numbers increasing after the English Abortion Act in 1967.

In the late 1960s, women's groups began to campaign against state interference in their private lives, but the impetus for legal change did not come about through their pressure. Ironically, the position only changed in the early 1980s when some Roman Catholic groups began campaigning for a constitutional amendment protecting prenatal life. This was part of "a sexual ideology that also condemned contraception, extramarital sex, homosexuality, and divorce."[9] The debate on abortion was expanded to encompass the very nature of Irish identity with its traditional conservative values. Fears were expressed regarding the expansion of the right to privacy in the United States to include the right to abortion and, in order to prevent such a development happening in Ireland, it was argued that a specific constitutional provision should be inserted as a protective measure.

In 1983, "after a divisive and uninformed campaign characterised by a complete absence of principled political leadership, the Eighth Amendment to the Irish Constitution was adopted by a confused electorate."[10] The amendment added to Article 40.3 a further subsection – Article 40.3.3 – which states that "[t]he State acknowledges the right to life of the unborn and, with due regard to the equal right to life of the mother guarantees in its laws to respect, and, as far as practicable, by its laws to defend and vindicate that right." The recognition of equality between the right to life of the mother and fetus meant that, in the absence of legislation, in any conflict between those rights, the Supreme Court would have to decide which right took priority.

In 1986, the Society for the Protection of the Unborn Child (SPUC) sought an order preventing two women's health centers in Ireland from continuing to provide a non-directive counseling service to pregnant women that included information regarding the availability of abortion in England.[11] In the High Court, Hamilton, President of the High Court (hereinafter P.) held that "the right to life of the foetus, the unborn, is afforded statutory protection from the date of its conception." He went on to decide that the giving of information about abortion in England was unlawful, despite the fact that abortion was legal in England, and no Irish statute prohibited the giving of such information. The learned judge did not consider in his judgment the far-reaching implications of his chosen wording, particularly for post-coital contraception and IVF. His judgment was upheld by the Supreme Court, which held that the giving of information regarding abortion was assisting in the ultimate destruction of the life of the unborn.

In 1989, SPUC sought an injunction against student union officers in University College Dublin and Trinity College Dublin to prevent them from publishing or distributing a booklet for students containing the addresses and contact details of abortion clinics in England.[12] The Supreme Court granted the order sought, saying that there was no right given to a pregnant woman to receive information calculated to assist her in the accomplishment of intent to terminate protected unborn life.

The effect of these decisions was, according to Whitty, to legitimize an ideology that insisted that nothing could ever be done to prevent parenthood, regardless of the facts and circumstances. Ultimately the most important (and most difficult) decision on the interpretation of Article 40.3.3 arose out of the pregnancy of a fourteen-year-old suicidal girl.[13] The facts of the case, *Attorney General v. X*, were that the young girl had been sexually abused and raped by a family friend and had consequently become pregnant. The police were informed of this fact and that the girl, together with her parents, had decided to travel to England for an abortion. When the parents inquired, from England, about the possibility of retaining fetal tissue as evidence against the alleged rapist, legal opinion was sought on the matter from the Director of Public Prosecutions (DPP). The DPP then informed the Attorney General, who applied to the High Court for an injunction restraining X and her parents from arranging the abortion in Ireland or elsewhere, and restraining X from leaving the jurisdiction for nine months. The family returned to Ireland for the full hearing of the case. Evidence was given to the effect that X was in a serious psychological state and the damage to her of continuing the pregnancy would be devastating.

The High Court held that there was a real and imminent danger to the life of the unborn and that, although there was a risk that X might take her own life if she was prevented from having an abortion, this risk was much less than the certainty that the life of the unborn would be terminated if she was not prevented from traveling abroad. The Court also held that no right to travel abroad existed under European Community law if the purpose of the travel was to obtain an abortion.

The public backlash against this decision was unprecedented and ultimately the case was appealed to the Supreme Court. By a majority of four to one, the Court ruled that the injunction should be lifted. The majority retreated from the absolutist approach taken in the SPUC cases and held that where the rights to life of the mother and the fetus were in conflict, an approach favoring the right of the mother was permissible. The court held that where there is "a real and substantial risk to the life, as distinct from the health, of the mother, which can only be avoided by the termination of her pregnancy," abortion is justifiable. In this case X should not be enjoined from obtaining an abortion.

Following this case a constitutional amendment was passed to the effect that Article 40.3.3 does not limit freedom to travel between Ireland and another state, and a further amendment in 1992 ensured that Article 40.3.3 does not limit freedom to obtain information relating to services lawfully available in another state. Despite the fact that clear messages have been given from the courts that the legislature should enact legislation to deal with the impact of the *X* case, and despite a number of attempts to add further to Article 40.3.3, it remains in place in 2004 in the same form as it did in 1983. Today, Ireland has a high rate of unplanned pregnancies, and a high incidence of abortions obtained in other jurisdictions, and no legislation dealing with the issue. The social and political history of Ireland attempts to deal with the tension between freedom of choice and protection of unborn life; this history casts a long shadow over any future efforts to regulate AHR services.

Development of AHR services in Ireland

In vitro fertilization (IVF) was first introduced into the Republic of Ireland in 1987. At the present time there are nine clinics in operation in Ireland carrying out AHR services including IVF, insemination, and donor programs. It is estimated that over two thousand couples are treated annually in Irish clinics, and many more travel to the United Kingdom for treatment. There is a tax refund scheme in existence for the cost of the treatment and a drug payment scheme currently operated by the health boards for the cost of the drugs involved in IVF.

At the present time there is no legislation in effect in Ireland for the regulation of AHR treatments. There is no central regulatory authority with responsibility for collecting statistical data on the numbers of those being treated, nor is there any monitoring of the quality of the services provided by the clinics. The only existing regulation comes from the Irish Medical Council, a statutory body charged with responsibility for protecting the interests of the public when dealing with registered medical practitioners. The Council was established by the Medical Practitioners Act 1978 and commenced operation in April 1979. The principal roles of the Medical Council include: (1) assuring the quality of undergraduate education of doctors; (2) assuring the quality of postgraduate training of specialists; (3) registration of doctors; (4) disciplinary procedures; and (5) guidance on professional standards/ethical conduct.

The Medical Council publishes a *Guide to Ethical Conduct and Behaviour* every four to five years and these guidelines act as a self-imposed disciplinary code for registered medical practitioners. If these guidelines are contravened, practitioners may have their name erased from the Medical Register and would no longer be permitted to practice medicine in the state. The Council itself states that the Guide is simply an articulation of general principles of ethical conduct against which medical practitioners can measure their own behavior. However, the Guide may be indirectly incorporated into law through litigation. In the context of an action for medical negligence, a court could decide that although not of binding legal force in itself, departures from the Guide may constitute a breach of professional duty. It could also be argued that patients have an expectation that medical practitioners will follow the Guide, and this expectation may be deemed to form part of the implied contract between doctor and patient. In the absence of legislation dealing with AHR in Ireland, the Guide currently forms the only source of advice to doctors in this field and is heavily relied upon in practice. Therefore, it might be said that the Guide has a quasi-legal effect, despite protests to the contrary from the Council.

The tendency of the Medical Council has been to be extremely brief and broad in laying down general principles in relation to AHR. The most recent edition of the Guide (6th ed. 2004) provides that there is no objection to the preservation of sperm or ova to be used subsequently on behalf of those from whom they were originally taken. Doctors are advised that if they consider treating with donated gametes, they must pay particular attention to the safety issues involved, specifically the source of the donated gametes. They must also advise donors and recipients of the consequences of their involvement in such a treatment.

In relation to IVF, as well as setting out the need for thorough investigation and counseling, the Guide stipulates that "any fertilised ovum must be used for normal implantation and must not be deliberately destroyed." A new addition to the Guide in 2004 also states that "if couples have validly decided they do not wish to make use of their own fertilised ova, the potential for voluntary donation to other recipients may be considered."

The policy in relation to prohibition of embryo destruction is very much in keeping with the pro-life stance traditionally adopted by the Medical Council. Although embryo donation is now seen as a defensible practice in relation to surplus embryos, the question remains as to what may be done with embryos that are not used by the couple themselves in circumstances where they do not wish to donate those embryos. Regarding the possibility of donation for research, the Guide stipulates that the creation of embryos for research purposes is unethical and also states that the deliberate destruction of embryos is professional misconduct. If surplus embryos have been donated for research purposes, the ethical imperative is that they must not be subsequently used for reproduction and should be destroyed. As this is contrary to the Guide, it follows that embryo research is also impermissible under the terms of the Guide. Therefore, for those couples that choose not to donate, it would seem that the embryos must be stored indefinitely.

Legal issues arising in the specific Irish context

As has been outlined earlier, Ireland has had a troubled history of dealing with issues in the reproductive area and it is to be expected that in any attempt to grapple with the legal issues arising in AHR, similar strong divergences of opinion would be articulated. Although AHR has generally proved divisive in every jurisdiction in which it has arisen for public debate and regulation, there are some specific legal and constitutional tensions in the Irish context that are worth examining in more detail.

Given the constitutional backdrop against which AHR will be dealt with, one of the preliminary questions might be whether there is any feature of the Constitution that would enshrine in individuals an enforceable right to reproduce. Although the Irish courts have developed a strong jurisprudence in the vindication of personal rights, these have tended to remain in the area of negative or non-interference rights rather than positive rights that would incur the imposition of obligations on the state. There have been cases in which the state has been attacked for failure to provide educational services or housing,[14] but the courts have taken the view that where the vindication of personal rights would involve an adjudication of the fairness or otherwise of the administration of public resources, this would fall within the remit of the executive rather than the judiciary.[15] Therefore, while there might be scope for resisting state interference in procreational choices on grounds of a constitutional right to privacy, such as occurred in *McGee* described above, it does not appear likely that the courts would recognize a positive right to procreate that could be used by an individual or couple to oblige the state to provide AHR treatments.

It is also the case that if a couple attempted to resist state interference with a reproductive choice, the court might justify the interference on common good grounds. So, for example, a couple that chose to make an arrangement with a surrogate mother would not be likely to be successful, on constitutional rights arguments alone, in resisting regulation or interference. The state would argue that, despite the violation of personal privacy rights, prohibition or regulation of such arrangements is necessary on public policy grounds.

The most fundamental difficulty that any regulation of AHR will have to deal with in Ireland is undoubtedly the constitutional protection of the right to life of the unborn. As described above, Article 40.3.3 provides acknowledgment by the state of the right to life of the unborn and obliges the state to guarantee in its laws to respect, and as far as practicable, to defend and vindicate that right. The most significant word in the article for IVF purposes is "unborn." If this word is interpreted by the Irish Supreme Court to mean the fertilized ovum/embryo then the rights ascribed to the unborn in the Constitution, specifically the right to life, come into play. Thus, the state would be obliged to respect and, as far as practicable, vindicate such rights. This would cause difficulties in relation to the storage of embryos, and most certainly, in relation to embryo/stem cell research, as by facilitating storage and research the state could be seen as failing in its obligation to vindicate the embryos' right to life.[16]

On the other hand, if the word "unborn" were interpreted as extending only to the embryo *after* implantation in the uterus, then it would seem that embryo freezing and research would not violate the constitutional provisions. There is little guidance from the limited constitutional jurisprudence in existence in relation to this article. In the case of *Attorney General (SPUC) v. Open Door Counselling Ltd.*,[17] referred to above, Hamilton, Justice of the High Court (hereinafter J.) held that the Offences Against the Person Act 1861 protects the fetus in the womb, and "that protection dates from conception." However, it is not clear from the context whether conception means fertilization or implantation, a crucial distinction in relation to IVF.

In the *Attorney General v. X*,[18] the Supreme Court interpreted the constitutional provision to mean that termination of pregnancy was permissible only when it was established as a matter of probability that there was a real and substantial risk to the life of the mother if such termination were not effected. In relation to the question of when the constitutional protection begins, and therefore whether the pre-implantation embryo falls within the scope of the article, there is little to be gained from a reading of the judgments in the case. Given that the facts of the case pertained to an established pregnancy, the court did not have to consider the question as to whether or not the provision applied to the embryo prior to implantation. The language of the court relates to the "life of the infant in the womb," and Hederman J. (dissenting) states that "one cannot make distinctions between individual phases of unborn life before birth, or between unborn and born life." Unfortunately, it is far from clear from this case, or any other, to what extent, if any, the Court would apply the protection of Article 40.3.3 to the embryo outside the womb.

Academic commentators can only conclude that "it cannot be said with certainty whether the protection afforded by Article 40.3.3 to the 'unborn' applies from the moment of fertilization, the moment of implantation, or from some later date."[19] The Constitution Review Group agrees that definition is needed as to when the "unborn" acquires the protection of the law.[20] Their report states that the word "unborn" seems to imply "on the way to being born" or "capable of being born," but whether the Court would accept either of those definitions is as yet a moot point.

Sherlock argues that it is likely that the courts would hold the *in vitro* embryo to come within the protection of the Constitution and, if this were the case, it would rule out embryo research and embryo destruction. "It would also have implications for infertility treatments involving *in vitro* fertilisation (IVF) as it would undoubtedly require that all embryos produced would have to be placed in the woman's uterus."[21] However, it may also be argued that

> if the "unborn" means "not yet born" or "with the potential to be born" then, in the light of the biological development of the early embryo and the absence of potential in the pre-implantation embryo, it is likely that the embryo in the laboratory does not qualify for this constitutional protection.[22]

Ultimately, the meaning of the word will be interpreted by the Irish Supreme Court or clarified by constitutional referendum of the people.

Another question that arises is that of access to services. The Irish Constitution provides recognition for the family as "the natural and fundamental unit group of society," and pledges to guard with special care the institution of marriage on which the family is founded, and protect it against attack (Article 41.3.1). A question arises as to whether, if AHR treatment services were provided to single persons or same-sex couples, such a policy would be in keeping with this constitutional provision. A seemingly straightforward solution might be to restrict access to services to married couples, but this is not in line with current practices of treating unmarried couples, the Medical Council Guide (which no longer provides such a restriction), or equality law in Ireland.

Proponents of state interference in this area argue that it is the responsibility of the state to ensure that a child is born into a stable family relationship and home life. They point to the definition of marriage in the constitutional context as that given in *Murray v. Ireland*,[23] by Costello J. as "a partnership based on an irrevocable personal consent given by both spouses which establishes a unique and very special life-long relationship." This Christian concept of marriage would "appear to close off a line of argument that sought to extend [constitutional] protection to 'natural families.'"[24] However, the protection afforded by Article 41.2 of the Constitution (which refers to a woman's life within the home and obliges the state to endeavor to ensure that mothers are not compelled by economic necessity to work outside the home) does not appear to be confined to married women, and therefore it might be argued that a broader notion of the family might be developed to encompass those who choose not to marry.

A further complication is the Equal Status Act 2000, which prohibits discrimination in the provision of services (S.5 (1)), on the basis of, *inter alia*, marital status, race, gender, disability, and sexual orientation. There is no derogation given in the Act for AHR clinics and therefore it must be assumed that the Act currently applies to the provision of AHR treatment services. This means that clinics may not refuse to treat on the basis of, for example, marital status or sexual orientation, though discrimination will not be considered unlawful if made on clinical grounds (S.16 (2)(a)), such as, for example, age or health of the mother. Discrimination on grounds of disability may not be unlawful if the treatment of that person less favorably than other persons is deemed necessary to prevent harm to that person or others (S. 4 (4)). It remains to be seen whether complaints will be made against clinics under the provisions of this Act, and if so, what attitude the courts will take to the potential conflict with the constitutional protection of the marital family.

Assisted reproduction in the United Kingdom

The development of IVF techniques in Britain led to the birth in 1978 of Louise Brown, the world's first "test-tube baby." The British government set up a Committee of Inquiry into Human Fertilisation and Embryology, chaired by Baroness Warnock, which reported in 1984. The Warnock Report set out a range of issues and concerns arising from the rapid developments in AHR, and recommended statutory regulation of these treatment services. In the immediate aftermath of the Report, the Medical Research Council and the Royal College of Obstetricians and Gynaecologists set up a voluntary licensing system, the VLA (Voluntary Licensing Authority), later called the Interim Licensing Authority. This was a means by which infertility treatment and research could be patrolled from within the profession. This body existed until the British government acted on the Warnock Report's recommendations and passed the Human Fertilisation and Embryology Act in 1990.

The main thrust of this legislation was to set up a statutory regulatory authority, the Human Fertilisation and Embryology Authority (HFEA), which began regulating infertility clinics from August 1991. The HFEA licenses all British treatment clinics offering IVF or donor insemination; storing eggs, sperm, or embryos; or carrying out research on embryos. It produces a code of practice to guide clinics and obliges clinics to maintain adequate standards of good practice in relation to staff qualifications, embryo screening, and storage protocols. Quality control and safety are the main priorities of the HFEA.

It has been suggested that the Warnock Report itself was more of "an exercise in pragmatism than an exploration of the philosophy underpinning issues of reproductive choice."[25] Given the parliamentary support for embryo research in existence at the time of passing the Act, it has been argued that embryology was the main focus of public concern. It was perceived as crucial to facilitate embryo research by bringing it within a legitimating authority. Although the HFEA is sometimes criticized for its "lack of philosophical direction" Brazier asks whether this was ever in fact its brief: "Britain opted for a limited and pragmatic regulation of research and treatment focusing on ensuring public accountability on the part of both researchers and clinicians, facilitating medical and scientific progress and largely skating over fundamental questions of reproductive choice."[26]

The former Chairperson of the HFEA, Ruth Deech, asks "how was the humane treatment of infertile couples and the research appended to it, together with public fear and distrust, to be managed?"[27] This, it seems, is the nub of the work of the HFEA – managing the fertility business and allaying public fears of scientific progress. It has been described as the first attempt in English law to provide a comprehensive framework for making medical science democratically accountable.[28] The HFEA itself states that "underlying all its activities is the HFEA's determination to safeguard all relevant interests – patient, children, doctors and scientists, the wider public and future generations."[29]

An interesting issue which sparked considerable controversy and debate in Britain in recent years concerned the use of sperm taken from a comatose patient shortly before his death on the instructions of his wife, who wanted to use the sperm after the death of her husband in an attempt to become pregnant.[30] This was possible only with the written consent of the sperm provider. In this case, the Authority took a decision not to allow the sperm to be used by the man's widow due to the absence of written consent. The Authority also refused to allow the man's widow to export the sperm to Belgium for treatment there.

For the purposes of this chapter, it is interesting to note the argument made in relation to European law. It was provided under the legislation that a man could not consent to the export of his sperm unless the purpose for which the sperm is to be used abroad is a lawful procedure in the United Kingdom. It was accepted that in some states, such as Belgium and perhaps Greece, it was possible to carry out artificial insemination without the written consent of the donor. It was argued that the Authority was obliged to allow the treatment abroad as a matter of European Community law unless there was an objective justification for its refusal, and that by prohibiting the export of the sperm, it was infringing upon the right of the man's widow to seek medical treatment in another member state under Arts. 59 and 60 of the European Treaty. The Authority argued that it was not preventing the applicant from traveling to Belgium for artificial insemination (AI), but the court disagreed on the grounds that the applicant did not want AI, she wanted AI only with her husband's sperm, which is exactly what the authority was trying to prohibit her from doing. This argument on European law was ultimately successful, the court holding that the Authority had made their decision without regard for the cross-border rights of the applicant. The outcome of the case was to allow the export of the sperm to Belgium. A more recent development has been an amendment to the HFEA Act in order to facilitate the registration of children born in such circumstances with their deceased father named on the birth certificate.

There are many good features of the system, at least in theory. First, due to its status as a statutory body it has the ability to impose serious sanctions on those who do not comply with the provisions of the Act. This is intended to provide a clear deterrent to those who might otherwise be less than scrupulous in the provision of treatment services and embryo research. However, the lack of imposition of any sanctions for a number of years led to criticism of the Authority as an agency without "teeth."

Second, the Authority gives at least the appearance, if not the reality, of public involvement in the supervision of treatment services and research projects, which acts to reassure the public as to the activities sanctioned by the Authority. This transparency is thought by many to be essential to maintain confidence in the medical and scientific professions in the light of novel techniques being practiced and brought to public attention through the media. Another feature of this aspect of the Authority's work is that by disseminating information as to success rates and other new procedures offered by centers it acts to improve upon the knowledge available to members of the public as to the range of treatments available and the likely success of those treatments. This, however, may not always be positive as the publication of a league table of centers may only be of use if the parameters of success are clearly defined and reasonably understood.

Finally, the licensing process is used to impose rigorous qualitative standards in the centers in which treatment services are offered. This serves to reassure those undergoing treatments, which are of a highly personal and complex nature, that the team that is working with them to achieve a pregnancy is suitably qualified and experienced in the area. However, with a number of blunders having been reported in clinics in recent years, an investigation carried out at the behest of the Department of Health reveals that staff are overworked and under-resourced in this sector.[31]

On the negative side, criticism has been made of the role of the HFEA in acting as an arbiter of fundamental ethical issues on which there is no widespread agreement. Comment on Reproductive Ethics (CORE) complains that the HFEA is unduly influenced by scientists in the field and cedes too much control to clinics. In addition, CORE claims that those who have expressed reservations about some reproductive techniques are not represented on the Board of the HFEA, and consequently its work as a whole is compromised.[32] Other potential disadvantages of statutory regulation of AHR include the difficulties associated with definitional questions,[33] the danger of slippery slopes, and the imposition (through licence fees) of a tax on the infertile.[34]

Overview of assisted reproduction across the European Union

There is wide divergence across Europe on the acceptability and regulation of AHR techniques.[35] Many states have laws or statutes pertaining to AHR, most of which have a specific licensing body, such as Austria, Belgium, France, Germany, the Netherlands, and the United Kingdom. Some states, such as Portugal and Ireland, follow voluntary guidelines promulgated by medical or scientific societies.

In most countries a traditional heterosexual family (married or stable relationship) is preferred, and access to those outside of such units is generally limited.[36] Despite legislation having been passed in some countries in recent years to recognize the rights of homosexual couples, nonetheless there remains a reproductive tourism towards more liberal countries such as Belgium, Finland, Greece, and Spain.

Most European countries have guidelines or legislative provisions dealing with the issue of multiple pregnancies arising from embryo transfer. The generally accepted clinical guideline is to limit the number of embryos transferred to two, or in some cases, one. Embryo storage is permitted or used in all European countries with AHR programs, though the stage at which the embryos must be frozen varies, with Germany and Switzerland permitting preservation only at the pro-nuclear stage. The duration of storage varies from country to country, but the most commonly adopted period is five years.

In relation to donation of gametes, some countries, such as Austria and Norway, prohibit all gamete donation, whereas others such as Switzerland prohibit oocyte donation only. There is growing awareness, across all of the jurisdictions that permit gamete donation, of the interests and rights of donor-conceived children in relation to gaining access to identifying information about their genetic parents. However, at the present time only a small minority of states allow identifying information regarding donors to be revealed.

AHR treatments are invariably only provided with clear consent from those involved in the treatment. This system of consent also provides an assurance of legal responsibility for the resulting child. Although most clinicians would recognize the importance of safeguarding the welfare of the children to be born as a result of AHR, only Britain has obliged clinics to take this issue into account before treatment.

Often the most controversial AHR treatment is IVF surrogacy where a woman agrees to carry an embryo for a commissioning couple, and relinquish it to them on delivery. In most jurisdictions the birth mother is considered to be the legal mother, though legislative provisions have sometimes been introduced to specifically deal with the surrogacy situation. Several jurisdictions stipulate that no payment can be made to the surrogate mother.

Harmonization possibilities

It is commonly said that medical technology generally outstrips ethical and legal debate.[37] Part of the reason for this is that there exists no consensus about the complex ethical issues that arise, whether it be in relation to physician-assisted suicide and euthanasia, assisted reproduction techniques, genetic testing, cloning and stem cell research, or many more contentious issues. The challenge here is to obtain all the advantages of the technological revolution and avoid the disadvantages; to avoid becoming prisoners of progress, but to control the development and guide it in the directions we want.[38] Morgan argues that one of the problems here is trying to foresee unwanted consequences; another is agreeing upon which consequences are unwanted and how they are best avoided or minimized. One cause of apparent despair is that often societies have chosen, for a variety of reasons, to avoid attempts at reaching a moral consensus. In such a field, then, it may be argued that government sometimes acts wisely in refusing or failing to regulate in order to allow debate and discussion to proceed, and perhaps to encourage some moral consensus to emerge.

As European countries increasingly debate questions arising from issues such as death and dying, medical research, and reproductive genetics, it is apparent that general agreement is possible and that common approaches are desirable. Differences in legislative response will depend on permutations and nuances in tradition, religion, culture, economics, and wealth. Throughout the European Union, moral and legal pluralism reflecting these variations is evident – the Dutch introduced the first legislation worldwide to permit euthanasia; the English are the first to permit therapeutic cloning; the Swiss allow for the identity of genetic parents to be accessed by children born through assisted reproduction using donated sperm; the French government pays for four IVF attempts for infertile couples, and so on.

There are many difficulties that arise in trying to consider whether there is any consensus between European states on issues of medical law and ethics. In an analysis of the European regulation of this area, the different approaches may be described as ranging from prohibition, cautious regulation, liberal regulation, to laissez-faire approaches. The latter would include states that have adopted no legislative provisions but rely on the ethical guidelines of the medical profession.

Concern with and demand for reproductive medicine has become a global matter. Where technological development results in the blurring of national boundaries, the increasingly difficult task of one country insulating itself from events elsewhere in the world has given rise to the possibility of what Morgan calls "procreative tourism." Such divergence in opinion and incompatibility between laws of member states on reproductive issues would enable a citizen of one state that is seen as fairly restrictive to travel to another state where there are no legislative prohibitions on treatment or access to services.

There is also a provision in the European Treaty that obliges a member state to fund medical treatment that is not available in that state but available elsewhere in the European Union. However, while this may sound very promising for those who would like to avail themselves of more innovative techniques, there are many pre-conditions attached to this provision that often disqualify the individual from receiving the necessary funding. This means that those who travel to other states must do so usually at their own (considerable) expense.[39]

European Convention Of Bioethics

The European Union presently has no regulatory jurisdiction over research carried out privately in the E.U. member states, or concerning the "ethics" of member states. This does not, however, mean that decisions made by the European institutions cannot influence such matters on a political level. In the decade prior to 1990, the Council of Europe had been working through the Parliamentary Assembly and the Steering Committee on Bioethics, giving responses to advances in medicine and biology. In 1990 it was agreed to begin work on a framework convention to set out common general standards for the protection of the human person in the context of the development of the biomedical sciences. However, the European Convention for the Protection of Human Rights and Dignity of the Human Being with regard to the Application of Biology and Medicine (April 1997, known as the Oviedo Convention) has not proved popular among member states. The Convention contains provisions relating to, for example, equitable access to healthcare, prohibition of genetic discrimination, prohibition of sex selection for social reasons, and a prohibition on genetic modification other than for therapeutic purposes.

Significantly, the Convention does not contain any consensus as to the status of the embryo.[40] Article 18 deals with embryo research, but merely states that if such research is permissible under national law, the embryo must have adequate protection. It does not go on to set out the meaning of "adequate protection" or what these obligations entail for member states. This ambiguous expression has prevented some states from signing the Convention. As for some, such as Ireland, this expression conflicts with national constitutional provisions dealing with the protection of unborn life.

The starting point for the debate as to the status of the embryo and its protection should begin with a definition of the embryo. The term "embryo" is commonly used to describe the fertilized egg from the two-cell stage of development to the end of the eighth week, at which stage it becomes a fetus. In the context of the status of this entity, there is a marked division between those who are of the opinion that the embryo is a potential human person with consequent rights and protections applicable to it, and those who think that it is simply a cluster of cells. There is also a range of diverse views between these two opposite viewpoints. This is where the difference in cultural and religious perspectives becomes particularly evident.

Apart from religious influences, there is also the cultural divergence between member states to be accounted for. This would take into account the tradition in some states of encouraging public debate on matters of public importance, and education through the mass media including informative discussions and open forums involving members of the relevant interest groups who may express their concerns freely. Some states have traditionally taken a more paternalistic view of the role of medicine in society, taking the attitude that the professionals know best how to conduct their practice ethically. The argument is that doctors practicing reproductive medicine have the same concerns and ethical principles as any other member of the community and it is safe to leave it to professional bodies to self-regulate as to what treatments should and should not be available and to whom.

In each European country similar questions arise with respect to law, medicine, and bioethics. But there are differences of a philosophical, economic, and social nature, which are not easily bridged. The parallel between explosive political change within and across Europe and the rapid developments in biomedical sciences and their impacts on law, ethics, and human rights, give rise to many challenges. For example, what is the meaning of the right to life and how has this changed through the use of biotechnology? How should difficult issues be resolved, by tolerating moral pluralism or by attempting to reach one dominant approach? Should our laws be accommodating or antagonistic?

It is evident from the diversity of approaches taken to fertility and treatments offered for infertility that national influences tend to play an important role in determining both the way in which the issue is dealt with by the state and also the resolution of the problems encountered. However, due to the difficulties involved in taking local cultural factors into account, it is probably not feasible to produce a detailed set of guidelines to which all nations within Europe could subscribe. The most that could be gained from such an exercise, as has been undertaken in the Convention of 1997 referred to earlier, is a written confirmation of the lowest common denominators between the states that would not perhaps advance the ongoing debates on these topics. It also suffers from the difficulty that some states have not signed this Convention due perhaps to perceived national feeling or, in the case of Ireland, to constitutional difficulties in relation to protection of the unborn.

Perhaps this assortment of controls and ethical principles is in itself a characterization of a community of states but the danger of such contrasts is that it could lead to what has been described earlier as bioethical tourism. This may facilitate some people traveling to the Netherlands for euthanasia, to Britain for surrogate motherhood or therapeutic cloning, to Denmark for pre-implantation genetic diagnosis, and so on. The absence of regulation and participation in international conventions by some states may, in theory, leave the way open for research projects and treatments to be attempted in those jurisdictions at, perhaps, a high cost for those involved. Certainly for citizens of more restrictive regimes the benefits to be obtained by visiting another jurisdiction for treatment services must weigh heavily with them. The advantages of seeking consensus in Europe as to broad issues such as the prohibition of the commercialization of reproduction would be to provide protection for couples who are desperate enough to seize any chance offered to them, and to set boundaries to the development of embryo research on an international level.

Conclusion

The regulation of AHR and related therapies across the European Union reveals many areas of convergence and divergence. E.U. states are divided between legislation and non-legislative mechanisms, and between permissive and restrictive approaches. The stringency of the approach adopted does appear to be consistent within each state, so that, for example, those that are restrictive regarding embryo research are also restrictive regarding pre-implantation genetic diagnosis, and so on. Most states have adopted permissive legislation on abortion and pre-natal diagnosis, while cloning and germ-line gene therapy have attracted almost universal prohibition.

> Given the range and diversity of issues evoked by these technologies, it is perhaps not surprising to find that the E.U. states display such a marked divergence. The dangers of cross-border commuting or procreative tourism highlight the desirability of harmonizing regulation in this area, but the Council of Europe's aspirations concerning harmonization remain elusive.[41] Whether any attempts at harmonization in this area will ever achieve anything more than lip service to broad, arguably ineffective, principles remains to be seen.

Notes

1 Noel Whitty, *Law and the Regulation of Reproduction in Ireland: 1922–1992*, 43 U. Toronto L. J. 851 (1993).
2 Liam O'Dowd, *Church, State and Women: The Aftermath of Partition*, in Gender in Irish Society (Curtin *et al.* eds., Galway University Press 1987).
3 Whitty, *supra* n. 1, at 853.
4 *See generally*, Paul O'connor, Key Issues in Irish Family Law (Sweet & Maxwell Ltd. 1998).
5 [1974] I.R. 284.
6 381 U.S. 476 (1965).
7 410 U.S. 113 (1973).
8 For a historical perspective on the background to the 8th Amendment, *see* Whitty, *supra* n. 1, at 856–66.
9 Whitty, *supra* n. 1, at 863.
10 *Id.* at 865.
11 [1988] I.R. 593.
12 *SPUC Ltd. v. Grogan*, [1989] I.R. 753. *See also*, *SPUC Ltd. v. Coogan*, [1989] I.R. 734.
13 *Attorney General v. X*, [1992] 1 I.R. 1.
14 *O'Donoghue v. Minister for Health*, [1996] 2 I.R. 20; *Sinnott v. Minster for Education*, [2001] 2 I.R. 545; *O'Reilly v. Limerick Corporation*, [1989] I.L.R.M. 181.
15 *See* David Morgan, A Judgment Too Far? Judicial Activism and the Constitution 62–71 (Cork University Press 2001).
16 This section of the chapter is extracted from the following document: Deirdre Madden, *Assisted Reproduction in Ireland – a Legal Quagmire*, at http://www.ccels.cardiff.ac.uk/pubs/maddenpaper.pdf (accessed April 13, 2005).
17 [1988] I.R. 593.
18 [1992] 1 I.R. 1.
19 James Kingston, John Whelan & Ivana Bacik Abortion and the Law: An Irish Perspective 32 (Round Hall 1997).
20 *The Report of the Constitution Review Group* (Stationery Office 1996). *See also*, the *Green Paper on Abortion*, Government of Ireland (Stationery Office 1999), which suggests that exclusion of IVF from the protection of Article 40.3.3 could be anomalous.
21 Ann Sherlock, *The Right to Life of the Unborn and the Irish Constitution*, XXIV Ir. Jur. Rep. 13, 24 (1989).
22 Deirdre Madden, Medicine, Ethics and the Law ch. 6 ¶ 116 (Butterworths 2002).
23 [1985] I.R. 532.
24 John Kelly, The Irish Constitution 992 (Butterworths 1994). *See also* Michael Staines, *The Concept of "The Family" under The Irish Constitution*, 11 Ir. Jur. Rep. 223 (1976).
25 Margaret Brazier, *Regulating the Reproduction Business*, 7 Med. L. Rev. 166, 173 (1999).
26 *Id.*
27 Ruth Deech, *Infertility and Ethics*, 5 Child & Fam. L. Q. 337 (1997).
28 Jonathan Montgomery, *Rights, Restraints and Pragmatism: The Human Fertilisation and Embryology Act 1990*, 54 Mod. L. Rev. 524 (1991).
29 Human Fertilisation and Embryology Authority, 8th Annual Report and Accounts, 1 (The Stationery Office 1999), http://www.hfea.gov.uk/HFEAPublications/AnnualReport (accessed Sept. 30, 2005).
30 *R v. Human Fertilisation and Embryology Authority* (ex parte Blood), 2 All Engl.l. Rep. 687(1997). *See also*, Derek Morgan & Robert G. Lee, *In the Name of the Father? Ex parte Blood: Dealing with Novelty and Anomaly*, 60(6). 840, 841

(1997); Linda Delany & Kathy Doyle, *Fathers – Who Needs Them?* HFEA v Blood, Fam. Law 261 (1997).

31 Brian Toft, *Independent Review of the Circumstances Surrounding Four Adverse Events that Occurred in the Reproductive Medicine Units at the Leeds Teaching Hospitals NHS Trust, West Yorkshire*, (Department of Health 2004), at http://www.dh.gov.uk/assetRoot/04/08/43/58/04084358.pdf (accessed Sept. 28, 2005).

32 Stephanie Smith & Agneta Sutton, *The Human Fertilisation and Embryology Authority: A Critique of its First Reports (1992–94)*, (CORE 1995).

33 A number of cases have arisen in recent years in relation to the interpretation of the wording in the Act, including "embryo," "consent," and "treatment together." *See respectively: R (on the application of Bruno Quintavalle on behalf of Pro-Life Alliance) v. Secretary of State for Health*, [2001] 4 All E.R. 1013; *Evans v. Amicus Healthcare Ltd and others*, [2003] 4 All E.R. 903; *Leeds Teaching Hospitals NHS Trust v. Mr. and Mrs. A & others*, [2003] EWHC 259 (QB).

34 Derek Morgan & Robert Lee, Human Fertilisation And Embryology, Regulating the Reproductive Revolution 10 (Oxford University Press 2001).

35 For specific details of practices across 49 countries, see the following report: *Surveillance 2004 I.F.F.S. Questionnaire for Countries with Statutory, Voluntary, or No Guidelines for Assisted Reproductive Technology (ART)*, 81(5: Supp. 4) Fertility & Sterility 51 (2004).

36 *See* Darren Langdridge & Eric Blyth, *Regulation of Assisted Conception Services in Europe: Implications of the New Reproductive Technologies for "The Family,"* 23(1) J. Soc. Welfare & Fam. L. 45, 45 (2001).

37 One well-known depiction of the relationship between law and medicine is that given by Windeyer J. in *Mount Isa Mines v. Pusey*, [1970] 125 C.L.R. 383 at 395, where he said that law is seen as "marching with medicine but in the rear and limping a little."

38 Derek Morgan, Issues In Medical Law And Ethics (Cavendish Pub. Ltd. 2001).

39 *See generally*, Tamara Hervey, *Buy Baby: The European Union and Regulation of Human Reproduction*, 18 Oxford J. Leg. Stud. 207 (1998).

40 Deirdre Madden, *A Comparative Legal Analysis of IVF and the Status of Human Embryos*, Biosciences & L. 387, 388 (1998).

41 Calum Mackellar, Reproductive Medicine and Embryological Research – A European Handbook of Bioethical Legislation 1997–98 (European Bioethical Research 1998).

14 Canadian legal perspectives in bioethics

Bernard M. Dickens

The history of legal bioethics

The history of distinctive Canadian law regarding issues of bioethical concern is relatively short, although by the end of the twentieth century it had become quite intense. Until two landmark decisions of the Supreme Court of Canada on informed consent to medical care in 1980, in *Hopp v. Lepp*[1] and particularly *Reibl v. Hughes*,[2] the medical law of Canadian provinces in general followed principles of English law, although Québec retained an historical affiliation with French law. The Criminal Code of Canada, first adopted in 1892, which is federal and applies equally to all of the provinces, was an embodiment of English criminal law, often in its very language. Legal bioethics presented a particular instance of the more general critical observation of a leading Canadian legal academic in 1959, that:

> A perusal of Canadian law reports … conveys the impression that most of the opinions reported there are those of English judges applying English law in Canada, rather than those of Canadian judges developing Canadian law to meet Canadian needs with guidance of English precedents.[3]

Judgments of English courts remain frequently cited in Canadian courts considering bioethical matters, but are not invariably followed. On several occasions, indeed, English judgments have been explicitly rejected as representing inappropriate resolutions of contentious bioethical issues. Reciprocally, English courts considering Canadian judgments have pointed to how they differ from law prevailing in England,[4] showing the authenticity of a distinctive body of modern Canadian law on bioethics.

The Supreme Court's 1980 decisions on informed consent disfavored the pre-existing law that reflected English judgments, finding them excessively deferential to the medical profession, and adopted instead a patient-oriented approach developed in California.[5] Similarly, the Supreme Court's decision in 1988 that found the restrictive Criminal Code provisions on abortion unconstitutional[6] explicitly recognized the persuasive influence of a landmark judgment on abortion of the United States' Supreme Court.[7]

Nevertheless, Canadian medical law has not fallen under a strong U.S. influence. The provision and funding of health services in Canada follow a West European model of governmental responsibility rather than the free-market American approach, and since 1982 the terms and values of the Canadian Charter of Rights and Freedoms, a component of the Constitution of Canada,[8] have directed the country upon its own path. Canadian judgments commonly take account of courts in compatible English-speaking countries such as the United States, United Kingdom, Australia, and New Zealand, but they consciously develop the law according to their perceptions of the values that predominate in Canada.

Major court decisions

Many of the decisions discussed below are of the Supreme Court of Canada, the nation's highest court, whose judgments are binding on lower courts, although not on itself. Others are of provincial courts of appeal, binding only in their own province. A few are decisions of trial courts, and not of binding force at all. Those discussed are highly influential, endorsed by the respect and approval they have gained within the legal community of practicing and academic lawyers and judges. Some cases raise several issues of bioethical concern, but they are presented below by reference to key topics in the field of bioethics.

Informed consent

The two Supreme Court judgments of 1980 that marked development of a distinctive law regarding bioethics were significant because they addressed the core issue of informed consent.[9] A basic bioethical proposition is that patients cannot be treated without their adequately informed consent. The earlier law was based on the English-derived principle that a physician's duty to disclose information was measured by what other comparable physicians disclose.[10] Doctors were subject to a professional standard of conduct; a physician who did not give a patient information that comparable, responsible physicians would not have provided would satisfy this standard. In 1980, however, the Supreme Court ruled this unsatisfactory, since physicians considering what to disclose should direct themselves to what their patients need to know, rather than to what other physicians would decide to tell. Physicians' rights to control what patients may know and to apply their assessments of what patients can understand suggest that key decisions about treatment are made by physicians, not patients.

The Supreme Court rejected the medical paternalism of this approach, and established that decisions whether to have medical treatment are not themselves medical decisions, but personal decisions that patients make when informed of the available medical options, governed by their own personalities and preferences. The physician's role is to equip patients to make these decisions by providing material information about medical options and their medical and other implications, and the physician's recommendations. What a patient requires to know is determined initially according to what a reasonable, prudent person in the patient's general circumstances would want to know. Such information is amplified or refined by what the physician actually knows about what a particular patient may want to know. Thus, the information that should be disclosed according to the initial determination may be expanded in response to questions a patient asks, or decreased when a patient makes it evident that particular information is not relevant to his or her decision.

In *Reibl v. Hughes*,[11] for instance, a surgeon did not disclose the risk that surgery to forestall the high probability of the patient suffering a fatal or seriously disabling stroke in several years' time itself carried an irreducible fourteen percent risk of triggering an immediate stroke, which the patient unfortunately suffered. The patient agreed to the surgery in order to preserve his job and income, and was eighteen months short of entitlement to full disability insurance protection. The Court found that a reasonable, prudent patient would have postponed the surgery for that eighteen-month period, during which he would not have been at higher risk of suffering the stroke. The timing of the surgery should have been discussed with him in view of its immediate risks. The Court ruled that even inadequately informed but freely given consent negated any claim for non-consensual touching, described as assault in criminal law and battery in non-criminal or civil law, but that failure of proper disclosure of risk could constitute legal negligence. The physician was held negligent for inadequate disclosure of material information.

As against this, however, the Supreme Court has held that, even when information should in principle be disclosed, a patient cannot succeed in a claim of negligence if, on the particular facts of the case, the information not disclosed would not have influenced the patient's choice. In *Arndt v. Smith*,[12] a woman very much wanted to have a child, was skeptical of mainstream medicine and stated when pregnant that she did not want an ultrasound scan of her fetus. She suffered chickenpox in the second trimester of pregnancy, and was not informed that this presented a very small increased risk of serious injury to her fetus. The child was born with brain damage and related disabilities, and the woman claimed that the non-disclosure was negligent in denying her the option of abortion, which she would have taken. However, the Supreme Court upheld the decision of the trial court that it was improbable that this woman would have had an abortion, since she was very determined to have a child, the risk to the fetus was low, a second trimester abortion presents higher risk to a woman, and this woman had shown a disinclination to accept medical assessments and options. Accordingly, the Supreme Court's adoption in 1980 of a patient-oriented standard of disclosure has not necessarily favored patients who allege that they were not given information they were entitled to receive.

Confidentiality

In its origins, Canadian law on the bioethical duty of medical confidentiality is unremarkable, in that health service providers and institutions are routinely obliged to guard their patients' information against improper disclosure to third parties. The legal duty may arise directly from contracts for healthcare services made with patients, and indirectly when service providers are employed under contracts with hospitals and other health service institutions and agencies. In many of these contracts, the duty to maintain patients' confidences is an implied or unwritten term, rather than addressed in specific language. It is included, for instance, in the employee's contractual duty to act according to professional ethics. The duty also arises, irrespective of any parallel contractual obligations, under the general law of negligence, which is based on a legal duty of care to behave according to professional standards. If disclosures communicate false and harmful information or impressions, they may also fall under the law of defamation.

More distinctively, the Supreme Court of Canada has recognized a further foundation of the duty of confidentiality, in the law of fiduciary obligations. These arise in relations between unequal participants, particularly between physicians who undertake to care for patients on the basis of their private health-related information, and patients who have to be honest with physicians, for instance about their sexual behavior, addictions, and attitudes towards others, in order to receive proper diagnosis and treatment. The relationship of trust and dependency requires the more powerful party, the healthcare provider who possesses the power of medical and related knowledge, to act conscientiously as a guardian of the information the patient is induced and obliged to make available by confession and submission to medical examination.

In the 1992 Supreme Court of Canada case of *McInerney v. MacDonald*,[13] the Court drew an important distinction. This case involved a physician who had denied her patient's request for copies of medical records which this physician had received from the patient's previous physicians. The physician's reason for denying her patient's request was that it would be unethical to release these records without the consent of those physicians to whom the records belonged. The Court held that the materials by which physicians had recorded the patients' information, such as sheets of paper, X-ray plates, and computer data files, will usually be the property of the physicians, hospitals or other healthcare facilities that provide such materials for this purpose. However, the information itself represents a separate legal interest, which is owned by the patient from whom the information came. The physician has no ownership of that information, but only possession for the purposes of discharging duties owed to the patient. This does not necessarily oblige the physician to let the patient read the medical record. The physician who remains responsible for the patient's care cannot surrender possession of the patient's medical file, and is not necessarily obliged to give the patient a copy of it. The record may contain medical and related abbreviations, notations or observations that medically unqualified persons may not understand, or may harmfully misunderstand. The physician's duty of disclosure to the patient is to explain the meaning of the information, particularly in light of the patient's questions and concerns, or to provide a copy to a person or agency chosen by the patient through which the information in the medical record may be properly explained.

The Supreme Court of Canada recognized a limit or exception to the usual obligation of confidentiality in a 1999 case, blandly named *Smith v. Jones* in order not to disclose the true names of the parties.[14] A lawyer defending a man charged with a relatively minor sexual assault engaged a psychiatrist to examine the man for purposes of his defense against conviction and sentence. The psychiatrist became convinced from his examination that, on release, the man planned to pursue a career as a serial murderer. The man then pleaded guilty to the minor charge, so that no evidence was called in the case, and his lawyer did not use the psychiatrist's report at the sentence hearing. The psychiatrist commenced court proceedings against the man for a declaration that the psychiatrist was not bound by legal duties of confidentiality, arising from his and the lawyer's dealings with the accused man, and so could notify police authorities of his apprehension that, when the man completed sentence for the marginal offence, he would be a serious threat to commit murder. The Supreme Court ruled that the psychiatrist had a legal power, though not a duty, to breach confidentiality, provided that the perceived danger is of grave physical or psychological harm, that the risk is imminent, and that it is to adequately identifiable prospective victims. The Court found the conditions satisfied in this case.

Liability for prenatal injury

Recent cases show that there is no disposition in Canadian law to depart from the historic English legal provision of when the life of a human being commences. This is codified in the Criminal Code of Canada, section 223(1) of which provides that:

> A child becomes a human being ... when it has completely proceeded, in a living state, from the body of its mother whether or not (a) it has breathed, (b) it has an independent circulation, or (c) the navel string is severed.

The "born alive" condition of legal protection was endorsed by the Supreme Court of Canada in 1933,[15] and confirmed more recently. For instance in *Winnipeg Child and Family Services v. G.(D.F.)*,[16] a woman addicted to toxic glue sniffing, whose young children had been taken into care because she had been unable to provide for them, became pregnant.

A child welfare officer initiated proceedings for her to be involuntarily detained on the ground that her addiction rendered her mentally impaired and dangerous to herself or to another "person," meaning her unborn child. The Supreme Court upheld the Manitoba Court of Appeal decision, which had reversed the trial court's detention order. There was no evidence of her mental impairment or danger to herself, and the Court upheld the understanding that an unborn child is not in law considered to be a "person," which is equated with a human being.

A case of deliberate injury to an unborn child, resulting in a criminal charge, occurred in Ontario in 1996.[17] Close to full term in her pregnancy, a mother of two young children inserted a pellet rifle into her vagina and fired a pellet, which entered the brain of her unborn child. Two days later, she gave birth to a son, who required surgery about ninety hours later to preserve his life. Section 223(2) of the Criminal Code provides that "A person commits homicide when he causes injury to a child before or during its birth as a result of which the child dies after becoming a human being." Homicide includes murder and manslaughter, but, because the child did not die, the mother was charged with attempted murder. Since murder is the killing of a human being, attempted murder is the attempted killing of a human being. The defense successfully argued, however, that the attempt here was to kill a fetus, which is not a human being. The woman could not have been charged with an offence relating to abortion, since the Criminal Code prohibition had been declared unconstitutional in 1988 (See section on Abortion below).

Under the law of compensation or damages, however, children born alive can sue for prenatal injuries suffered *in utero*. The Supreme Court of Canada confirmed this in 1999, in a judgment in which an exception proved the rule. In *Dobson v. Dobson*,[18] a woman twenty-seven weeks pregnant was alleged to have driven negligently and caused an accident resulting in serious, permanent injuries to her child later delivered by caesarian section. The child, through a grandfather, sued his mother for compensation. The action was not liable to cause a rift between mother and child, since she had a motor vehicle insurance policy that would cover any compensation she became liable to pay, and an award would help her family to cope with financial costs of the son's disabilities; the defense to the claim was mounted primarily by her insurance company. It had long been accepted in Canada that children could sue their parents, and that children born alive could sue for injuries suffered *in utero*. The trial court and New Brunswick Court of Appeal held that this claim could proceed, since the mother owed a duty to exercise due care while driving to all persons liable to be directly injured. Had her negligence injured another woman's child *in utero* that was subsequently born alive, that child could sue her, and there was no legal barrier preventing her son from also suing her.

In a novel decision, the Supreme Court of Canada reversed this understanding of the law. It ruled that, as an exception to the general rule, a child cannot sue its own mother for injuries suffered during the pregnancy. The exception rests on three main grounds. First, "the existence of insurance is not an appropriate basis for the determination of tort liability between litigating parties."[19] Justice requires a distinction be drawn between those who may be legally liable and those who are not, but not between those who have insurance and those who do not. To permit those with insurance to be sued, when those without cannot be, is unjust. Second, a child's successful claim might result in scarce family resources being directed towards the injured child's care and away from care of other children and well-being of the family in general. The Court considered that "family harmony will be particularly important for the creation of a caring and nurturing environment for the injured child."[20] Third, most importantly, women's liability for their conduct when pregnant would subject them to intrusive interference in their lives and choices, on behalf of their fetuses, by family members, acquaintances, and strangers, a prospect the Court had already rejected in the *Winnipeg* case.[21] The Court reviewed many cases that might cause fetal injury, and concluded that "imposition of tort liability in those circumstances would significantly undermine the privacy and autonomy rights of women."[22]

Wrongful life, wrongful birth, and wrongful pregnancy

Claims alleging negligent performance of sterilization procedures resulting in childbirth are not unusual, but judgments are rarely appealed to the higher courts. Cases tend to turn on their facts rather than legal principles, and when principles are involved they tend to focus on informed consent and non-disclosure of risks that procedures might fail or fetuses be harmed by circumstances outside physicians' control.[23] The courts are usually strongly guided in this area by English higher courts, and cite them explicitly. For instance, in a 2001 case, it was alleged that an impaired child's injuries were caused by medication the defendant prescribed for the pregnant mother's epilepsy, and that, had she been informed of the risk to her fetus, she would have had an abortion. The Manitoba Court of Appeal upheld dismissal of the claim, characterizing it as a "wrongful life" action. In a decision on behalf of the Court, the judge said:

> Despite a valiant attempt by the plaintiffs' counsel to persuade me otherwise, I am unable to accept that an action for wrongful life should be recognized in Canada. I find the reasoning of the judges in [the English Court of Appeal][24] too compelling to do otherwise and I am unaware of any Canadian circumstances which would cause judges here to think differently.[25]

The wrongful life action is brought on behalf of an impaired child alleging that it should not have been conceived or, having been conceived, should have been aborted. The claim therefore triggers sensitivities about abortion and the sanctity of human life.

The Court distinguished this case in which, but for the alleged wrongful act of the physician in treating the mother, the child would not have been born at all, from other claims that a child's abnormalities have been directly caused by the wrongful act or omission of a physician or other defendant. A 1992 case found to be in this second category is *Cherry (Guardian ad litem of) v. Borsman*,[26] concerning the defendant physician injuring a fetus *in utero* during an attempt to perform an abortion. The British Columbia Court of Appeal found the action not to be for wrongful life, and upheld an award of damages. Further, in 1998 in *Webster v. Chapman*,[27] the child's claim was allowed for anomalies due to medication prescribed for the mother because, had the defendant physician consulted a specialist in time, the medication would have been discontinued. The contrast between the 1998 and 2001 cases, as explained by the Manitoba Court of Appeal, is that the medication in the 2001 case was necessary and proper for the mother's healthcare, so that any child she delivered would have been unavoidably affected by it. However, the distinction proposed between the judgments of the British Columbia and Manitoba Courts of Appeal in their 1992 and 2001 cases respectively is not clear beyond doubt, and a decision of the Supreme Court of Canada may be required to resolve any uncertainty.

Distinctions were also drawn in an Ontario trial court decision in a claim by parents that a negligently performed contraceptive sterilization resulted in the birth of a healthy child.[28] In a thorough comparative review of U.K., U.S., and Canadian law, the judge defined a "wrongful birth" case normally as "an action instituted by parents of a child who is born with birth defects as a result of a planned pregnancy," due to post-conception interference with "the mother's lawful right to terminate the pregnancy had an informed decision been available to her."[29] "Wrongful life" claims can be similar, but are advanced on behalf of the child when born with severe impairments. These children's claims for wrongful life can also be based on failed sterilization, improper genetic screening, or failed abortion and, as discussed above, are almost invariably rejected in Canada. In contrast are "wrongful pregnancy" claims, such as the one the trial judge was considering. These are claims for pre-conception errors, when parents allege that the defendant's negligence caused an unwanted pregnancy and birth, or unwanted pregnancy and the financial and emotional costs of abortion.

Wrongful pregnancy claims are now accepted in Canadian law, and the judge in the Ontario trial court addressed the issue of compensation. She awarded the parents damages for the discomforts, inconveniences, and expenses of pregnancy, labor, delivery, and re-sterilization, and for loss of income during confinement and parental leave after the child's birth. No damages were awarded for child-rearing costs, because the parents had an adequate income to bear them. However, the judge drew distinctions regarding different scenarios. She found that had the sterilization been sought not for contraceptive reasons but to prevent birth of a genetically or otherwise impaired child, and if, due to negligence, such a child had been born, damages would cover difference in cost between rearing that child and an unimpaired child. Further, had sterilization been sought because the family could not bear the financial costs of rearing a child or another child, damages would include child-rearing costs, even of a healthy child. That is, the reasons why sterilization is sought govern the damages recoverable if procedures are performed negligently.

Parental duties and powers

Parental duties to provide their children with medically indicated care are recognized by legislation in Canada. Provincial child welfare legislation requires parents to make adequate provision for their children's medical treatment, and section 215(1) of the Criminal Code of Canada declares that "[e]very one is under a legal duty (a) as a parent, foster parent, guardian or head of a family, to provide necessaries of life for a child under the age of sixteen years." The courts have long held that "necessaries" include medically indicated treatment.[30] More serious charges than failure to provide necessaries may be brought if children suffer serious harm or die. Parents have been charged with manslaughter, for instance, when their five-year-old diabetic child was not given insulin because of his parents' religious views and belief in faith-healing.[31]

Many cases arise in lower courts when parents who are Jehovah's Witnesses refuse consent to blood transfusions for their children. Courts have recognized adults' rights to decline such treatment for themselves.[32] However, when they decline indicated transfusion for their dependent children, physicians will inform governmental or quasi-governmental child welfare agencies, which will promptly initiate court proceedings under provincial law to have the children declared in need of protection and the agencies themselves appointed to consent to transfusion. When medical evidence shows transfusion necessary to preserve children's reasonable prospects of survival or good health, courts invariably grant declarations placing the children's medical care under the charge of the child welfare agencies. Transfusion is usually undertaken quickly, and parents rarely appeal to higher courts against these decisions.

Occasionally, however, parental decisions based not on religious grounds but perceptions of children's best interests prevail. In *Couture-Jacquet v. Montreal Children's Hospital*,[33] for instance, the Québec Court of Appeal reversed a lower court's order of medical treatment, requested by the hospital, when parents refused a fourth course of chemotherapy for a three-year-old child suffering pelvic cancer. The parents' evidence was that earlier treatment and side-effects caused the child severe distress and probably permanent damage, and the hospital accepted that the treatment afforded only a ten to twenty percent chance of arresting the disease. The Court was persuaded that the parental decision deserved respect.

Adolescents

Canadian law recognizes the historical concept of the "mature minor." Parental duties are recognized to care for their children up to sixteen years, and some provincial child welfare legislation sets a higher age such as eighteen years. However, courts tend to read legislation on parents' duties and legal minors' limited powers as subject to the general law. This provides that there is no fixed age below which minors cannot give legally effective consent to medical care that it is in their best interests to receive. Discussion of the issue has tended to center on adolescents' access without parental consent or knowledge to controversial medical treatments such as abortion and contraception, but the issue goes beyond to concern, for instance, blood transfusion, treatment for addiction, and mental health care.

In *C. (J.S.) v. Wren*,[34] a sixteen-year-old legal minor was found capable of requesting and consenting to an abortion, despite her parents' request for an injunction based on the claim that she had insufficient understanding of the spiritual aspects of the procedure. An adolescent's own profound religious convictions were considered sufficient to empower his independent choice, however, when a fifteen-year-old Jehovah's Witness cancer patient knowingly declined a possibly life-preserving blood transfusion.[35] In 1985, indeed, an Ontario Provincial Court found a twelve-year-old cancer patient who shared her parents' religious faith to possess a maturity beyond her years, and that she should be allowed to fight her disease without the transfusion she opposed and in dignity and peace.[36] Once the legal principle of the mature minor is recognized, each case turns on its own facts. One case, for instance, concerned a thirteen-year-old daughter of a Jehovah's Witness mother who, with her mother's support, refused to receive blood products to treat her aplastic anemia.[37] Her father was not of the same religious conviction, however, and supported the claim of the Children's Aid Society that the girl's decision be discounted since it did not express mature independence. The court agreed, and made an order of temporary wardship to enable an officer of the Society to approve treatment.

A Canadian court has tackled and perhaps resolved an issue that remains vexing in England, namely whether parents retain or must surrender power to give legally effective consent to medical treatment for their children when they become mature minors. As abortion cases show, a mature minor can consent to treatment over her parents' opposition. The blood transfusion cases raise the question, however, of whether parents can legally authorize transfusions that are opposed by their mature minor children for whose care transfusion is indicated. The English courts have approached the mature minor concept primarily as providing physicians with a defense, or "flak-jacket," when attacked by either a parent or a minor patient for administering treatment. They have held that legally protective consent can be provided by the parent of an opposed mature minor, or alternatively by such a minor despite parental opposition.[38] Physicians must take due account of a mature minor's preferences, and presumably would not undertake an abortion on the basis only of parental consent on a minor who opposed it, except perhaps for life-saving purposes. A blood transfusion might be feasible to administer to a disabled minor who opposed it on religious grounds, however, and an anorectic minor might be provided with nutritional supplements by minimally invasive means over objection.

In *Van Mol (Guardian ad litem of) v. Ashmore*,[39] parents of a sixteen-year-old legal minor consented to her cardiac surgery, which unfortunately resulted in her becoming paraplegic. Both the parents and the adolescent patient sued the surgeon for negligence, the patient suing on the ground that she had not given her informed consent to be exposed to this risk. The physician's defense to this claim was that her parents had provided legally effective consent. It was held, however, that she was a mature minor, that according to common law principles, discussion of the risk should have been conducted with her, and that, when she became mature enough to decide whether or not to have the surgery, her parents no longer had decision making capacity on her behalf. The majority of two of the three Court of Appeal judges interpreted the provincial legislation as consistent with these principles. They agreed that:

> ... once the required capacity to consent has been achieved by the young person reaching sufficient maturity, intelligence and capability to understanding, the discussions about the nature of the treatment, its gravity, the material risks and any special or unusual risks, and the decisions about undergoing treatment ... must all take place with and be made by the young person whose bodily integrity is to be invaded and whose life and health will be affected by the outcome. At that stage, the parent or guardian will no longer have any overriding right to give or withhold consent.[40]

They observed that these propositions of law are of long-standing duration, but added that:

> that is not to say that the parents need not be involved in the process of explanation, instruction and advice leading to the obtaining of the informed consent of the child. They should be involved as part of that process wherever possible.[41]

The reference to parental involvement "wherever possible" is also subject to the mature minor principle the Court's majority judgment upholds and elaborates. The mature minor is entitled to give or withhold autonomous consent not only to treatment, but also to disclosure of information about treatment to a third party. That is, capacity relates both to treatment and to confidentiality. Accordingly, parents' involvement depends on the willingness of mature minors to have their parents involved, which will usually be governed by the nature of the relationship between them.

Abortion

Since 1988, popular access to abortion in Canada has been under only ethical regulation. Abortion remains a medical procedure undertaken under the same provisions, for instance on medical practice, as any other medical procedure, but its criminal context was removed by the Supreme Court of Canada. Before the Court's January 1988 decision in *R. v. Morgentaler*,[42] the Criminal Code permitted abortion only when a therapeutic abortion committee certified that continuation of a pregnancy would or would be likely to endanger the woman's life or health. However, many hospitals were not qualified to establish such a committee, many that were qualified chose not to, and many committees declined to consider applications on behalf of women who resided outside their hospitals' catchment areas. No hospital was obliged to create a committee when eligible, and one province had no hospital that had constituted a committee, so that any woman in the province whose pregnancy endangered her life or her health was required to travel to another province. In that province, Prince Edward Island, which at that time had no bridge link to the mainland to ensure access when the ferry service could not operate, governments had defended the absence of provision for abortion services on grounds of ethics.

In 1988, however, five of seven sitting justices of the Supreme Court found that the promise in the Criminal Code to preserve women's lives and health through committee certification of necessary procedures was illusory and deceptive. The constitution and operation of therapeutic abortion committees were found arbitrary, inequitable, and prejudicial to women's health because of the delays caused in delivery of lawful care and the idiosyncratic criteria committees applied. Chief Justice Dickson for the Court's majority found a violation of the personal security guarantee of the Canadian Charter of Rights and Freedoms. He observed that:

> Forcing a woman, by threat of criminal sanction, to carry a foetus to term unless she meets certain criteria unrelated to her own priorities and aspirations, is a profound interference with a woman's body and thus a violation of security of the person.[43]

The Court accordingly declared the prohibitions of abortion contained in the Criminal Code to be inoperative. No replacement provisions have been enacted.

The result is that resort to abortion is now a matter only of ethical judgment. Women who would reject the procedure on ethical grounds before 1988 would presumably not change their attitude following the Court's judgment. However, many women with no ethical objections who would comply with a restrictive law now may exercise their ethical judgment on whether to continue or terminate an unplanned or hazardous pregnancy. The Supreme Court's judgment has therefore contributed to ethical decision making on this issue in Canada.

Both before and after the 1988 judgment, several men claiming to be fathers of unborn children sought injunctions to restrain scheduled abortions. Before 1988, many obtained interim injunctions to delay procedures for forty-eight hours or so, in order to determine whether legal indications and procedures had been satisfied, but no permanent injunctions were issued. Courts invariably accepted medical assessments that legal indications for abortion had been satisfied. In 1989, a Québec judge granted an interim injunction to restrain a woman from terminating a pregnancy when she ended cohabitation with her partner and, unusually, the Québec Court of Appeal upheld the injunction. The Court recognized that the Criminal Code prohibition of abortion had become inoperative, but interpreted the Québec Charter of Human Rights and Freedoms to afford a fetus status and protection as a "human being." Within two weeks, the Supreme Court of Canada reversed this decision, and ruled the injunction improper, since a fetus is not a "human being" as protected by the Québec Charter.[44]

During the Supreme Court hearing, the judges learned that the woman had gone to the United States earlier and terminated her pregnancy. The judges decided to deliver their unanimous judgment, however, perhaps lest another woman might be exposed to the psychological stress and risks of delayed abortion while subsequent proceedings moved through lower courts in order to reach the Supreme Court. Further, although the case originated under the provincial law of Québec, the Court placed its judgment in the wider setting of Anglo-Canadian law, which it fully reviewed. The judgment establishes a strong precedent, the Court observing that: "We have been unable to find a single decision in Quebec or elsewhere which would support the allegation of 'father's rights' necessary to support this injunction."[45] No further injunctions to restrain abortion at the request of putative fathers have been issued.

Sterilization

Modern and more historical experiences have caused Canadian courts to accept that actually and potentially oppressive sterilization for purposes of birth control is unacceptable. Individuals who possess the capacity and freedom to approve their own sterilization for contraceptive and other purposes may receive appropriate procedures. Further, when medical procedures that cause sterility are indicated to promote the health and well-being of minors and mentally impaired individuals incapable of giving their own legally effective consent, their legal guardians may consent. Such procedures include, for instance, removal of a diseased uterus and of cancerous testicles. However, when individuals cannot give their own competent consent to contraceptive or eugenic sterilization, guardians cannot give legally effective consent.

The shameful history of eugenic sterilization of institutionalized minors upon consent of a so-called Eugenics Board in the province of Alberta between the late 1920s and the early 1970s was recalled in the *Muir* case in 1996.[46] To its credit, the government of Alberta admitted that grave wrong had been done, declined to invoke the technical but complete defense the judge said was available under the statute that required proceedings to be commenced within a time limit, and resisted the claim only regarding how much compensation it should pay.

The government Ms. Muir sued was legal successor to all of the preceding governments dating back to when she was sterilized in 1959, at thirteen or fourteen years of age. The misconduct of the institutional authorities at that time has left modern courts apprehensive to permit sterilization of apparently mentally compromised individuals in any circumstances. The trial judge found that:

> the evidence establishes that the conduct of the government in labelling Ms. Muir a mental defective was high-handed and oppressive ... the government did not follow its own legislation, practices and procedures when it labelled Ms. Muir a moron. It ignored advice from an expert that Ms. Muir's problems were emotional, not mental; it ignored the services of social workers and psychologists who might have assisted in obtaining information about Ms. Muir's background; it failed to require compliance with the minimum standards which it had established – signature by a physician attesting to the validity of the admission information – and psychometric testing. Before admitting her to an institution where she would be sterilized and stigmatized, the government acknowledged that it had only cursory information.[47]

Recognizing that "the sterilization had a catastrophic impact on Ms. Muir," and that it had "changed, warped and haunted her life,"[48] the Court granted the maximum damages allowed by law for pain and suffering. However, punitive damages were considered inappropriate, although justifiable, because an early act of the defendant administration was to repeal the legislation under which sterilizations could be lawful, and in the present case the government had declined a defense that Ms. Muir's claim had been brought out of time. The judge observed that:

> This deliberate abandonment of a complete defence is in the nature of an apology. Indeed, it is more than an apology; it is an amendment – a

> real effort to make things right. As a matter of public policy, this and other governments should be encouraged to recognize historical wrongs and to make fair amends for them. They should not be punished for doing so.[49]

The oppression, mistreatment, and humiliation Ms. Muir had experienced since 1959 reinforced the caution the Supreme Court of Canada showed in 1986 in the case protectively named *Re. Eve*.[50] This concerned a mildly to moderately mentally impaired woman aged twenty-four in 1979 who suffered extreme expressive aphasia, which obstructed her communication of what she understood and thought. She was pleasant, affectionate, and capable of being attracted to and attracting young men. She had attended a school for mentally impaired adults, formed a close friendship with a male student, and had spoken of marriage. Her widowed mother aged fifty-nine was concerned that Eve might become pregnant, since it was not clear that she could cope with pregnancy and childbirth, and unlikely that she could rear a child. The mother considered that it would be better if Eve were sterilized, and sought a judicial declaration that, under provincial mental health legislation, the mother be authorized to consent to Eve's tubal ligation.

The trial judge reviewed the historic law under which the court could exercise the sovereign's protective jurisdiction over mentally impaired persons, the *parens patriae* jurisdiction, and concluded it could not authorize sterilization. On appeal, however, the appeal judges reversed this ruling, and authorized hysterectomy. On final appeal to the Supreme Court of Canada, the unanimous bench reinstated the trial judge's refusal of authorization, but on different grounds. The Court observed that the sterilization was not sought to treat a medical condition, but to spare Eve the alleged but unproven trauma of birth, and perhaps her mother the burden of caring for a grandchild. The Court reviewed U.S. cases, including those upholding legislation that implemented the eugenics movement in North America and invoked human rights to conclude that it was objectionable. The Court expressly recognized legality of sterilization that mentally capable persons request for themselves, but found that a medically non-indicated, irreversible, major surgical procedure of this nature could not be undertaken on an impaired person on a guardian's consent. Any legislation proposing to empower authorization of such a procedure would be reviewable under the Canadian Charter of Rights and Freedoms. None has been proposed.

HIV/AIDS

The landmark HIV/AIDS case is the Supreme Court of Canada's 1998 decision in *R. v. Cuerrier*.[51] This concerned a man who knew he was HIV-positive, and had been advised to use a condom in future intercourse, and tell partners of his HIV status. Nevertheless, he had unprotected sexual intercourse with two women. One asked if he had any infection, which he denied; and the other did not ask and he gave her no information of his HIV status. The women complained when they learned the truth, saying that they would not have had unprotected intercourse with him had they known. At the time of trial, neither had tested HIV-positive. The man was charged with committing aggravated assault, which requires proof of conduct that endangers life. The trial judge and British Columbia Court of Appeal applied the prevailing legal rule that assault consists in non-consensual touching, and found that both women understood the nature, quality, and risks of unprotected intercourse, and had consented. The prosecution appealed against his acquittal and dismissal of their appeal. Changes in the language of the Criminal Code in earlier years had left uncertainty about its modern meaning, including on consent negating assault in Section 265(3), which provides that: "For the purposes of this section, no consent is obtained where the complainant submits or does not resist by reason of . . . (c) fraud."

The Supreme Court addressed whether the intercourse in these circumstances was induced by fraud. The Court ruled that a first requirement of fraud is dishonesty, which includes non-disclosure of important facts. Since HIV infection can lead to devastating and fatal illness, the Court found that there is a positive duty to disclose HIV-positive status, even when not asked. The second requirement is actual harm, or the risk of harm. The Court found this present in unprotected intercourse, although not necessarily when a condom is carefully used. It found the accused man convictable, if the prosecution could show beyond reasonable doubt that either of the complainants, if informed of his HIV-positive status, would have refused to have unprotected intercourse with him. The trial court had not determined this since the judge ruled as a matter of law, upheld on appeal, that the women's *de facto* consent negated the alleged assault. The Supreme Court therefore sent the case back for a new trial on the basis of the law as interpreted by the Supreme Court.

Terminal care

Several recent authoritative judgments affecting end-of-life decisions have afforded Canadian law a coherent form. An initial case involved neither death nor a wish to die. In *Malette v. Shulman*[52] the Ontario Court of Appeal unanimously upheld an award of $20,000 in token damages for battery to a Jehovah's Witness who, taken to hospital unconscious and with heavy blood loss from a traffic injury, was transfused after her convictions were known. She carried a card explaining her religious rejection of blood transfusion and products. The defendant physician's explanation that he acted lest the patient may die was rejected, since a patient aware of that risk could lawfully take it. A competent young woman's wish to die was respected in the case of *Nancy B.*[53] The woman, age twenty-five, suffered an acute form of Guillain-Barré syndrome, and was totally disabled below her neck. She was dependent on artificial ventilation, but sued her hospital for an order that it be removed, so that she would be allowed to die. The Attorney-General of Québec intervened in the case, and supported the principle that mentally competent patients can decline unwanted treatment, even if they cannot survive without it. The judge did not order removal of ventilation, but declared that the patient's physician could lawfully comply with such a patient's request, and the patient was allowed to die.

In contrast, Sue Rodriguez, fearing the acute dependency and indignity of death from amyotrophic lateral sclerosis, sued for a judicial declaration that the Criminal Code prohibition of assisted suicide was unconstitutional.[54] She wanted to live until she found life unbearable, but anticipated that, by then, she would be unable to commit suicide unaided. Legislation in 1972 withdrew criminal penalties from attempted suicide, but giving assistance remains criminal. Each court up to and including the Supreme Court of Canada rejected her claim, although the last by a slender five to four majority. The majority upheld the criminal prohibition as defending vulnerable people who might be "assisted" to die when their wishes were unclear. The contrast with the *Nancy B.* case is that Nancy B. survived by artificial means and requested a natural death, whereas Sue Rodriguez could survive naturally and requested the right to die by artificial means. Nevertheless, four dissenting Supreme Court justices favored her claim to self-determination, finding vulnerable persons well protected by other criminal laws.

There is some fear among bioethicists that refusals to provide medical care on grounds of "futility" can shield discrimination, such as against disabled or elderly patients, and unwillingness to spend resources on hard-to-treat patients. A Manitoba trial judge in 1998 ordered removal of a Do Not Resuscitate order from the hospital chart of an elderly disabled patient at his wife's insistence, although the judge did not positively require resuscitation.[55] This caution may have deferred to the Manitoba Court of Appeal, which a little earlier had observed that "[t]here is no legal obligation on a medical doctor to take heroic measures to maintain the life of a patient in an irreversible vegetative state," adding that "[i]ndeed the opposite may be true."[56] In clear cases, courts may allow refusal of treatment of incompetent patients on grounds of futility, such as when a parent declined repeated chemotherapy for a child cancer patient.[57]

A 2001 case of enduring public controversy concerns a unanimous Supreme Court of Canada judgment upholding conviction for second degree murder, and the mandatory minimum sentence of life imprisonment and ten years before parole eligibility, of a father who deliberately killed his twelve-year-old severely disabled daughter whom he believed to face a future of unrelievable anguish.[58] The Court was "mindful of Mr. Latimer's good character and standing in the community, his tortured anxiety about [his daughter] Tracy's well-being, and his laudable perseverance as a caring and involved parent,"[59] and had initially described his action moderately as "an error in judgment."[60] The trial jury was sympathetic to the father, and recommended a more lenient sentence than the law allowed. The trial judge accepted the jury recommendation of two years' imprisonment, one year to be served before parole eligibility, as a "constitutional exemption" from the more severe punishment. The Saskatchewan Court of Appeal reversed the judge regarding the sentence, upholding the Criminal Code's minimum of life imprisonment. The Supreme Court upheld the conviction and the Court of Appeal on sentence. Public controversy is that many consider the minimum sentence required by law excessive on the facts of the case, and perhaps dysfunctional in being a deterrent to people disclosing suspicious cases of mercy killing or "compassionate homicide," and to juries convicting in such cases, while others are concerned that any lesser sentence would expose disabled people to vulnerability to be killed. The Supreme Court denied, and the prosecution did not allege, that the father killed his daughter primarily because she was disabled, and observed that the government's powers of executive clemency could accommodate any perception that the legal sentence was excessive.

Future prospects

An important 1997 Supreme Court of Canada judgment has implications for the ethics of healthcare delivery in Canada at the resource-allocation or macroethical level. In *Eldridge v. British Columbia (Attorney General)*,[61] several deaf people claimed violation of their right to non-discrimination secured by the Canadian Charter of Rights and Freedoms when provincial health facilities failed to provide sign-language translation. The Supreme Court held in 1990 that, in their day-to-day management, health facilities are not a branch of government, and so are not bound by the Charter.[62] The lower courts therefore dismissed the claim. However, the Supreme Court reversed their decisions, and distinguished between facilities' private functions, such as hiring staff and operating buildings, and their functions delegated by government, notably discharging the function assumed by government of providing reasonable access to necessary medical care. The Supreme Court held that government cannot evade its responsibilities under the Charter by delegating functions to private sector agencies such as hospitals, which in law are usually private corporations. The government is responsible to ensure observance of its duties, whether undertaken by government directly or delegated to hospitals or other private agencies. The Court therefore required the government to submit its plan to fund sign-language translation.

The financial costs in *Eldridge* were relatively trivial, but Charter rights can be limited, under section 1, when limitation is "demonstrably justified in a free and democratic society." After *Eldridge*, the Supreme Court recognized that "in some circumstances excessive cost may justify a refusal to accommodate those with disabilities,"[63] but cautioned against putting a low value on services that disabled people need. In *Cameron v. Nova Scotia (Attorney General)*,[64] provincial discrimination was alleged in failure to fund intracytoplasmic sperm injection (ICSI), a specialized form of *in vitro* fertilization required by some infertile couples. The Court found discrimination, but that it was demonstrably justified by the high cost of the procedure, and its limited success. In contrast, in the *Auton* case,[65] the trial court found that denial of appropriate treatment for autistic children, particularly pre-school-age children, was discriminatory and not justified. The judge required governmental funding, but, presuming governmental good will and compliance, refrained from making a mandatory order, or specifying what types of services should be funded.[66]

On the provincial government's unsuccessful appeal, the British Columbia Court of Appeal mandated delivery of a specific type of very costly treatment.[67] The provincial government's further appeal to the Supreme Court of Canada claimed, *inter alia*, that discharge of a legal duty of medical care should be determined by judicial deference to the province's assessment of clinical and budgetary considerations. The Supreme Court of Canada, without conceding any duty of deference, nevertheless reversed the lower courts' decisions,[68] finding that the provincial government was not obliged under its health insurance plan to deliver the treatment the children's parents sought. As non-medical, non-hospital-based treatment of a psychosocial nature, it was found to fall outside the legislated scheme of entitlement to medical care.

In a potentially important 2005 decision, the Supreme Court of Canada, again reversing provincial trial and appellate courts, found Québec legislation prohibiting private insurance and provision of services covered by the provincial health insurance plan to violate Québec's provincial Charter of Rights.[69] How far the judgment goes to authorize private insurance and provision of provincially insured services outside Québec remains unclear. The Court was divided by three judges to three on provincial compliance with the federal Canadian Charter of Rights and Freedoms, and suspended enforcement of its June 2005 ruling affecting Québec for a year, pending further argument. It therefore appears that the forthcoming years will show increasingly intensive litigation in this area, and through the Supreme Court, Canada will achieve an increasingly clear, although probably refined, understanding of the law at the macroethical level of health resource funding allocation and entitlement.

Notes

1 (1980), 112 Dominion Law Reports (3d) 67 (Sup. Ct. Can.).
2 (1980), 114 Dominion Law Reports (3d) 1 (Sup. Ct. Can.).
3 Horace E. Read, *The Judicial Process in Common Law Canada* 37 Canadian B. Rev. 265, 268 (1959).

4 *See e.g. Sidaway v. Bethlem Royal Hospital Governors* [1985] 1 All England Reports 643 (House of Lords); *Macfarlane v. Tayside Health Board* (1999), 4 All England Reports 961 (House of Lords).
5 *See Canterbury v. Spence* (1972), 464 Federal Reporter 2d 772 (D.C. Cir. Ct.); *Cobbs v. Grant* (1972), 502 Pacific Reporter 2d 1 (Calif. Sup. Ct.).
6 *R. v. Morgentaler* (1988), 44 Dominion Law Reports (4th) 385 (Sup. Ct. Can.).
7 *Roe v. Wade* (1973), 410 United States Reporter 113 (U.S. Sup. Ct.).
8 Constitution Act, 1982, Revised Statutes of Canada 1985, Appendix II, No. 44, Schedule B.
9 *Hopp v. Lepp*, *supra* n. 1; *Reibl v. Hughes*, *supra* n. 2.
10 *See Bolam v. Friern Hospital Management Committee*, [1957] 2 All England Reports 118 (Queen's Bench Division, High Court).
11 *Supra*, n. 2.
12 (1997), 148 Dominion Law Reports (4th) 48 (Sup. Ct. Can.).
13 (1992), 93 Dominion Law Reports (4th) 41 (Sup. Ct. Can.).
14 (1999) 169 Dominion Law Reports (4th) 385 (Sup. Ct. Can.).
15 *Montreal Tramways v. Léveillé* [1933] 4 Dominion Law Reports 337 (Sup. Ct. Can.).
16 (1997), 152 Dominion Law Reports (4th) 193 (Sup. Ct. Can.).
17 *R. v. Drummond* (1996), 143 Dominion Law Reports (4th) 368 (Ont. Ct. Provincial Div.).
18 (1999), 174 Dominion Law Reports (4th) 1 (Sup. Ct. Can.).
19 *Id.* at 31.
20 *Id.*
21 *See supra* n. 16.
22 *Supra* n. 16, at 20.
23 *See Arndt v. Smith*, *supra* n. 12.
24 *McKay v. Essex Area Health Authority* [1982] All England Reports 771 (Court of Appeal Civil Division).
25 *Lacroix (Litigation Guardian of) v. Dominique* (2001), 202 Dominion Law Reports (4th) 121 (Manitoba Court of Appeal).
26 (1992), 94 Dominion Law Reports (4th) 487 (British Columbia Court of Appeal).
27 (1998), 155 Dominion Law Reports (4th) 82 (Manitoba Court of Appeal).
28 *Kealey v. Berezowski* (1996), 136 Dominion Law Reports (4th) 708 (Ontario Court-General Division).
29 *Id.* at 723.
30 *R. v.Brooks* (1902), 5 Canadian Criminal Cases 372 (British Columbia Ct. App.).
31 *R. v. Tutton and Tutton* (1989), 48 Canadian Criminal Cases (3d) 129 (Sup. Ct. Can.).
32 *Malette v. Shulman* (1990), 67 Dominion Law Reports (4th) 321 (Ontario Ct. App.).
33 (1986), 28 Dominion Law Reports (4th) 22 (Québec Ct. App.).
34 (1987), 35 Dominion Law Reports (4th) 419 (Alberta Ct. App.).
35 *Walker (Litigation Guardian of) v. Region 2 Hospital Corporation* (1994), 116 Dominion Law Reports (4th) 476 (New Brunswick Ct. App.).
36 *Re. K. (L.D.)* (1985), 48 Reports of Family Law (2d) 164 (Ontario Prov. Ct.).
37 *H. (T.) v. Children's Aid Society of Metropolitan Toronto* (1996), 138 Dominion Law Reports (4th) 144 (Ontario General Division).
38 *Re. R.* [1991] 4 All England Reports 177 (Court of Appeal, Civil Division), *See* Lord Donaldson M.R. at 185.6.
39 (1999), 168 Dominion Law Reports (4th) 637 (British Columbia Court of Appeal).
40 *Id.* at 665.

41 *Id.* at 669.
42 (1988), 44 Dominion Law Reports (4th) 385 (Sup. Ct. Can.).
43 *Id.* at 402.
44 *Tremblay v. Daigle* (1989), 62 Dominion Law Reports (4th) 634 (Sup. Ct. Can.).
45 *Id.* at 665.
46 *Muir v. Alberta* (1996), 132 Dominion Law Reports (4th) 695 (Alberta Ct. of Queen's Bench).
47 *Id.* at 733.
48 *Id.* at 731.
49 *Id.* at 735.
50 *Re. Eve* (1986), 31 Dominion Law Reports (4th) 1 (Sup. Ct. Can.).
51 (1998), 127 Canadian Criminal Cases (3d) 1 (Sup. Ct. Can.).
52 (1990), 67 Dominion Law Reports (4th) 321 (Ont. Ct. App.).
53 *Nancy B. v. Hôtel-Dieu de Quebec* (1992), 86 Dominion Law Reports (4th) 385 (Que. Superior Ct.).
54 *Rodriguez v. British Columbia (Attorney-General)* (1993), 107 Dominion Law Reports (4th) 342 (Sup. Ct. Can.).
55 *Sawatzky v. Riverview Health Centre* (1998), 167 Dominion Law Reports (4th) 359 (Manitoba Queen's Bench).
56 *Child and Family Services of Central Manitoba v. L.(R.) and H.(S.L.)* (1997), 123 Manitoba Reports (2d) 135 (Manitoba Ct. App.) at 138.
57 *See Couture-Jacquet v. Montreal Children's Hospital, supra* n. 33.
58 *R. v. Latimer* (2001), 193 Dominion Law Reports (4th) 577 (Sup. Ct. Can.).
59 *Id.* at 608.
60 *Id.* at 585.
61 (1997), 151 Dominion Law Reports (4th) 577 (Sup. Ct. Can.).
62 *Stoffman v. Vancouver General Hospital* (1990), 76 Dominion Law Reports (4th) 700 (Sup. Ct. Can.).
63 *British Columbia (Superintendent of Motor Vehicles) v. British Columbia (Council of Human Rights)* (1999), 181 Dominion Law Reports (4th) 385 (Sup. Ct. Can.) at 401.
64 (1999), 177 Dominion Law Reports (4th) 611 (Nova Scotia Court of Appeal).
65 *Auton (Guardian ad litem of) v. British Columbia (Attorney-General)* (2000), 78 British Columbia Law Reports (3d) 55 (British Columbia Sup. Ct.).
66 *Auton (Guardian ad litem of) v. British Columbia (Attorney-General)* (2000), 84 British Columbia Law Reports (3d) 259 (British Columbia Sup. Ct.).
67 *Auton (Guardian ad litem of) v. British Columbia (Attorney-General)* (2002), 220 Dominion Law Reports (4th) 411 (British Columbia Court of Appeal).
68 *Auton (Guardian ad litem of) v. British Columbia (Attorney-General)* (2004), 245 Dominion Law Reports (4th) 1 (Supreme Court of Canada).
69 *Chaouilli v. Québec*, (2005) 254 Dominion Law Reports (4th) 577 (Supreme Court of Canada).

15 Bioethics and New Zealand health law

P. D. G. Skegg

General

New Zealand law still bears a fairly close family resemblance to the English law from which it developed. It also has a good deal in common with Canadian and Australian law. However, there are two respects in which New Zealand health law is now significantly different from the health law of other countries.

One is the relatively limited role of civil actions for damages for personal injuries. In the mid 1970s a statutory "accident" compensation scheme came into operation.[1] Since then, people entitled to claim under the successive statutory schemes have been barred by statute from bringing civil actions for compensatory damages for injuries compensable under the scheme. The effect of this "statutory bar" has varied with the scope of the statutory scheme. For example, in the mid 1980s a health practitioner's negligence which resulted in either physical or mental injuries would not give rise to an action for compensatory damages, as both forms of injury fell within the scope of the statutory scheme.[2] However, in the early 1990s the statutory scheme was changed in various ways, one of which involved ceasing to provide statutory compensation for many mental injuries that had previously been within the scope of the scheme.[3] In these cases, actions for compensatory damages became a possibility.[4]

The Injury Prevention, Rehabilitation, and Compensation Act 2001 now regulates the compensation scheme. In a health care context, compensation is available under the scheme where physical injury has resulted from the negligence of a health professional ("medical error"), and also where there has been an adverse consequence of (non-negligent) treatment, where the physical injury meets the statutory requirements of seriousness and severity ("medical mishap").[5]

A second distinctive element of New Zealand health law is the important role of Codes and Commissioners. In a health law context, they have helped fill some of gaps left by the accident compensation scheme and the related statutory bar on civil actions for compensatory damages.

The Health and Disability Commissioner Act 1994 provided for the appointment of a Health and Disability Commissioner.[6] It also provided for the Commissioner to have an important role in developing a Code of Health and Disability Services Consumers' Rights (which will be referred to in this chapter as the Code, or the Code of Rights).[7] The Act indicated what must and what may be included in the Code, and set out the consequences which may follow from a breach of the Code.

The Code itself is a form of delegated legislation, and the government rather than the Commissioner was responsible for its final form.[8] Clause 2 of the Code sets out ten "rights," and the headings give some indication of their content. They are as follows:

1 Right to be Treated with Respect;
2 Right to Freedom from Discrimination, Coercion, Harassment, and Exploitation;
3 Right to Dignity and Independence;
4 Right to Services of an Appropriate Standard;
5 Right to Effective Communication;
6 Right to be Fully Informed;
7 Right to Make An Informed Choice and Give Informed Consent;
8 Right to Support;
9 Rights in respect of Teaching or Research;
10 Right to Complain.

It is, however, necessary to stress that in law the detailed terms of the provisions are of much greater importance than the headings.[9]

Clause 2 of the Code, with the ten rights, does not stand alone. Crucial definitions are to be found in a later clause of the Code, and also in the Health and Disability Commissioner Act itself. Clause 3 of the Code is important. It provides that:

(1) A provider is not in breach of this Code if the provider has taken reasonable actions in the circumstances to give effect to the rights, and comply with the duties, in this Code.
(2) The onus is on the provider to prove that it took reasonable actions.
(3) For the purposes of this clause, "the circumstances" means all the relevant circumstances, including the consumer's clinical circumstances and the provider's resource constraints.[10]

The Code is a very important aspect of New Zealand health law: it is often the starting point for consideration of the legal rights of patients and the legal duties of doctors and others who provide health services. The Act which provided for it had the effect of creating a new form of civil liability, whereby damages (and other remedies) may sometimes be obtained in consequence of a breach of the Code.[11] However, a "statutory bar" applies, so damages cannot be obtained if an injury comes within the scope of the accident compensation scheme. Hence damages could in theory be recoverable, for breach of the Code, if a surgeon's receptionist spoke disrespectfully to a patient, but not if the surgeon unnecessarily and negligently amputated one of the patient's limbs.

In practice there are many obstacles to the recovery of damages for breach of the Code. Nevertheless, the Code has an importance in the relationship between health professionals and their patients which bears no relation to the rarity of damages being awarded for its breach. Doctors and others treat the investigations of the Health and Disability Commissioner and the resultant opinions very seriously indeed.

The Code of Rights does not deal with information privacy. The reason for this omission, which may surprise some, is that such matters were the subject of separate legislation. The Privacy Commissioner Act 1991 provided for the appointment of a Privacy Commissioner,[12] and this legislation was soon superseded by the more wide-ranging Privacy Act 1993.[13] This Privacy Act set out various "information privacy principles."[14] It stipulated the procedure for investigating alleged breaches of these principles and the civil remedies which could follow if breaches were proved to have occurred and harm resulted.[15] The Act also gave the Privacy Commissioner power to vary the application of the principles by issuing codes of practice in relation to particular activities.[16] This was done by the Health Information Privacy Code 1994.[17] Clause 5 of this Code sets out twelve detailed Health Information Privacy Rules.[18] Some indication of their scope may be gathered from the headings:

Rule 1 Purpose of Collection of Health Information
Rule 2 Source of Health Information
Rule 3 Collection of Health Information from Individual
Rule 4 Manner of Collection of Health Information
Rule 5 Storage and Security of Health Information
Rule 6 Access to Personal Health Information
Rule 7 Correction of Health Information
Rule 8 Accuracy etc of Health Information to be Checked before Use
Rule 9 Retention of Health Information
Rule 10 Limits on Use of Health Information
Rule 11 Limits on Disclosure of Health Information
Rule 12 Unique Identifiers[19]

The Health Information Privacy Code is by no means the sole source of law relating to the disclosure or use of patient information, but it is commonly the starting point for consideration of such issues. In the case of alleged breaches, the Privacy Commissioner has a role which is very similar to that of the Health and Disability Commissioner in relation to breaches of the Code of Rights.

Thus far, this account has focused on relatively new aspects of New Zealand law, which have set New Zealand apart from jurisdictions with which it otherwise has a good deal in common. However, in many respects the legal obligations on health professionals are similar to those in Australia, Canada, and England.

The greatest contribution of the Codes to New Zealand health law has not been in terms of content – although that contribution should not be minimized. It has been in the part they have played, in connection with the associated legislation, in providing a basis for the independent investigation of complaints and the consequences which can follow the completion of these investigations.

Reproduction

In New Zealand, professionals who provide assistance with reproductive services (e.g., donor insemination or IVF) are not permitted to refuse to provide services to anyone because of their age, marital status, or sexual orientation.[20]

New Zealand legislation has the effect of ensuring that gamete donors do not have to bear the responsibilities of parenthood in respect of children conceived with their gametes.[21] Beyond this, New Zealand has been very slow in enacting legislation in response to advances in assisted reproduction. Reports have been produced, and bills have been introduced into Parliament,[22] but new law has not yet resulted. In the interim, the National Ethics Committee on Assisted Human Reproduction provides ethical review of research and innovative treatments, and providers of assisted reproductive technologies are accredited through the Australian Reproductive Technology Accreditation Committee.

Surrogacy is not the subject of specific legislation, and only a handful of cases have reached the courts. Legislation prohibiting payments for adoption has not been construed to apply to surrogacy arrangements.[23] Once a child has been born, decisions are made on the basis of the usual "family" law principle that the welfare of the child is the paramount consideration.

There are not yet any express statutory restrictions on *ex utero* embryo experimentation in New Zealand. Prior to implantation, the general legal prohibition on attempts to procure a miscarriage does not apply, as "miscarriage" is defined as the destruction or death of an embryo or fetus *after implantation* (or the premature expulsion or removal of an embryo or fetus *after implantation*, otherwise than for the purpose of inducing the birth of a fetus believed to be viable or for removing a fetus that has died).[24]

The major abortion reforms of 1977 were preceded by a Royal Commission of Inquiry.[25] The reforms involved amendment of the relevant provisions of the Crimes Act, and also enactment of the Contraception, Sterilisation, and Abortion Act 1977. Part of the long title of the latter act stated that it was "to provide for the circumstances and procedures under which abortion may be authorised after having full regard to the rights of the unborn child."[26] However, regard to "the rights of the unborn child" is a not a striking characteristic of the law or of the way in which it is applied in practice.

In the case of a pregnancy of no more than twenty weeks' gestation, the main grounds for legally permitted abortion are that the person doing the act believes that "the continuance of the pregnancy would result in serious danger (not being danger normally attendant upon childbirth) to the life, or to the physical or mental health, of the woman or girl," or that "there is a substantial risk that the child, if born, would be so physically or mentally abnormal as to be seriously handicapped."[27] The first of these grounds, in particular, is often interpreted very liberally indeed by the medical practitioners who apply the law, and in practice it is almost impossible to challenge a certificate issued by a certifying consultant.[28] In many parts of the country, abortion is freely available early in pregnancy. Hence third or fourth year law students are often surprised to learn that there are any legal restrictions on abortion.

Later in pregnancy, abortion is less readily obtained. The only ground for lawful abortion in the case of a pregnancy of more that twenty weeks' gestation is that the person doing the act believed it to be necessary to "save the life" of the pregnant woman, or to prevent "serious permanent injury to her physical or mental health."[29] In practice, abortions are sometimes performed at this stage because the child would be seriously disabled (typically, with Down syndrome). Killings in the course of birth are only lawful if caused "by means employed in good faith for the preservation of the life of the mother."[30]

In most legal contexts, a child does not have any legal status until it is (fully) born alive.[31] However, a provision in the Children, Young Persons, and Their Families Act 1989, concerning the protective jurisdiction of the Family Court in relation to a "child" under the age of fourteen years, has been taken to extend to a child late in pregnancy.[32]

The only judicial authorization of caesarean operations has involved mothers who were already subject to a compulsory treatment order for their mental illness.[33] If an attempt was made to authorize such an intervention in the case of a pregnant woman of normal capacity, considerable weight would be given to the provision in the New Zealand Bill of Rights Act 1990 that "[e]veryone has the right to refuse to undergo any medical treatment."[34] Quite apart from that provision, judicial authorization or approval would be most unlikely.[35]

End of life

New Zealand law does not permit active euthanasia. It is murder to kill another person, meaning to do so. A person's consent to the "infliction of death" will not affect the criminal liability of anyone who is a party to the killing,[36] and the New Zealand courts have not developed a defense of necessity (or of duress of circumstances) in a way which would assist a person who provided active euthanasia. However, in practice, "mercy killers" have not been convicted of murder. Prosecutorial discretion can result in a lesser charge of assisting suicide,[37] or else a jury may bring in a conviction of manslaughter rather than murder.[38]

The prohibition of active euthanasia does not restrict the provision of pain-killing drugs to terminal patients, even though this may have the incidental effect of hastening death. There are several means by which a New Zealand court could avoid the conclusion that this was murder.[39]

In New Zealand law, there is no simple distinction to be drawn between active and passive euthanasia, the former being unlawful and the latter lawful. Sometimes there is a duty to provide life-prolonging treatment. Where there is such a duty (and no lawful excuse to fail to comply with it), then an omission to provide life-prolonging treatment could amount to murder if it was meant to cause death. In practice, a charge of manslaughter would be more likely to ensue if there was an omission to provide legally required treatment, and death resulted.

The "act"/"omission" distinction is not a simple one, especially in a jurisdiction where negligent acts are often characterized as omissions to do what the law requires. Fortunately, it is clear that the conduct of a responsible health provider in terminating artificial ventilation, or other means of prolonging a person's life, will be regarded as an omission.[40] This provides greater flexibility than if it were regarded as an act. Analyzed as an omission, criminal liability will not ensue unless there was a duty to continue to provide life-prolonging treatment (and no lawful excuse to omit to do so).

There are various statutory provisions which have the effect of imposing a duty to provide life-prolonging treatment[41] and there is also the possibility of common law duties providing the basis for a prosecution.[42] Even more important than the prima facie duties, in many circumstances, are the range of circumstances where there is a "lawful excuse" to omit to provide treatment. These are very extensive. One reasonably straightforward example is where a competent and informed patient refuses consent to life-prolonging treatment.[43] In the absence of any legal justification for treatment being provided without consent, there would then be a lawful excuse for omitting to provide treatment, even if death was the certain consequence.

There are many other circumstances where there will be a lawful excuse to withhold life-prolonging treatment. For example, the means of prolonging life may not be available (despite all reasonable efforts on the part of the provider), or there may be a good reason for the provider to make a limited resource available to some other patients instead. Alternatively, life-prolonging treatment may do more harm than good or may be pointless or in some other way may fail to achieve the objective for which it was commenced. In all these cases, there would usually be a lawful excuse to withdraw, or omit to continue, the life-prolonging treatment. The categories of lawful excuse are not closed. In practice it will be accepted that there is a lawful excuse to omit to prolong life when it is "good medical practice" to omit to prolong it. But these common exceptions to the rule should not obscure the rule itself. In many circumstances, someone who has undertaken the care of another will have a duty to provide (or to ensure that someone else provides) available and effective life-prolonging treatment which the patient wishes to receive.

In a few cases, courts have been approached while a patient's life was being maintained, and judges have agreed that life-prolonging treatment may be withheld or withdrawn. Three of these cases have involved adults.[44] *Shortland v. Northland Health Ltd.*, being a decision of the Court of Appeal, might have been expected to lay down some helpful general principles, but it barely did so.[45]

The Code of Rights provides that "[e]very consumer may use an advance directive in accordance with the common law."[46] This is consistent with the provision in the New Zealand Bill of Rights Act 1990 that "[e]veryone has the right to refuse to undergo any medical treatment."[47]

While competent and informed people may make a legally effective advance directive (in an attempt to ensure that effect is given to their wishes once they become incompetent), they might prefer to rely on the contemporaneous judgment of proxies they appointed to act on their behalf. There are, however, significant limits on the powers of people who hold an enduring power of attorney. They are precluded from refusing consent to the administering of any "standard medical treatment" to the (now incompetent) patient, or to any procedure intended "to save that person's life or to prevent serious damage to that person's health."[48] (This does not mean that such treatment must always be provided; simply that where it is omitted the legal justification for the omission cannot be any purported refusal of consent on the part of the person who holds an enduring power of attorney.)

New Zealand law does not define the point at which someone ceases to be a living human being, for the purpose of any particular rule of law.[49] The limited case law lends support to the view that New Zealand courts would accept that a person has died once it is established that brain stem death has occurred.[50] However, there is a good deal of inconsistency in practice. Organs are often removed from "brain dead" bodies while they are being maintained on ventilators (on the basis that the patient has died), but in other contexts doctors commonly wait until artificial ventilation has ceased before declaring such patients dead.

Research

The New Zealand Bill of Rights Act 1990 provides that "[e]very person has the right not to be subjected to medical or scientific experimentation without that person's consent."[51] The words "subjected to" could be taken to indicate that, in this context, "experimentation" excludes interventions intended to benefit the patient's health (although the courts do tend towards an extensive application of terms used in this Act). In law, this section is to be read in the light of an earlier provision which restricts the entities to which the Act applies,[52] and another which indicates that the specific provisions in the Act are subject to such "reasonable limits prescribed by law as can be demonstrably justified in a free and democratic society."[53]

Some New Zealand statutes appear to reflect a rather negative view of "experimentation," but this could result in the courts taking a narrow view of this term. The Protection of Personal and Property Rights Act 1988 provides that a welfare guardian (appointed by a court) or a person who holds an enduring power of attorney (appointed by the once competent person) does not have the power "[t]o consent to that [incompetent] person's taking part in any medical experiment other than one to be conducted for the purpose of saving that person's life or preventing serious damage to that person's health."[54] In practice, incompetent patients are unlikely to be denied access to experimental pain-relief measures in consequence of this limitation. However, the consent of the welfare guardian or attorney will not be the reason why the administration of the experimental pain relief would often be lawful.

There has been a good deal of controversy about the way in which New Zealand law, or ethics committees, or both, hinder some forms of medical research. The one relatively long-established statutory Ethics Committee is that of the Health Research Council.[55] More recently, the New Zealand Public Health and Disability Act 2000, section 16, required the Minister of Health to appoint a National Advisory Committee on Health and Disability Support Services Ethics. Its statutory duties are very extensive: it "must determine nationally consistent ethical standards across the health sector and provide scrutiny for national health research and health services."[56] In practice, the committee's terms of reference and funding will affect the extent to which it can carry out these duties. In recent years, proposals for medical research have been closely scrutinized by (for the most part) regional ethics committees, the majority of whose work has been taken up with examining research protocols. These committees have not been established by statute, although there is law relating to them and the government has issued a National Standard for Ethics Committees. Other ethics committees have been established by institutions (e.g., universities) to examine protocols for research involving human subjects.

New Zealand does not provide a strikingly friendly environment for biomedical research. A major reason for this has been the reaction to abuses which occurred in one of New Zealand's leading teaching hospitals. Ironically, some of this research had been approved by the one Institutional Review Board (to use North American terminology) that was functioning in New Zealand at the time. A Committee of Inquiry investigated this "unfortunate experiment."[57] It made many worthwhile recommendations, some of which have been implemented in full.

The allocation of limited resources

In a country in which a large proportion of major medical interventions are provided free of charge in state-funded institutions, it is not surprising that a great amount of attention has been given to the allocation of the inevitably limited resources. In 1991, the Minister of Health in the newly elected National Party Government issued a statement of Government Health Policy in which the concept of "core health services" played an important part. "Core health services" were defined as "health services to which we believe everyone should have access, on affordable terms and without unreasonable waiting time."[58] At one stage it seemed that the government proposed to enact legislation to ensure that these services were provided. In a section of the report headed "How the Core Might be Implemented and Enforced," it was said that

> [t]he list of core health services would be specified in general legislation, which would also specify penalties for [Regional Health Authorities (RHAs)] or health care plans which failed to provide core health services. The core would be enforced either through the general courts system or a specialist tribunal established by legislation, which would ensure that RHAs and health care plans did indeed provide core health services for all their clients. However, it would be the role of policy decisions, rather than legal decisions, to define what services fall within the scope of the core.
>
> The Government is currently considering establishing the Office of the Health Commissioner. This office might be a suitable place to locate responsibility for enforcement of the core.[59]

In 1992, the government set up a Core Services Committee, and later enacted legislation providing specifically for it.[60] However, it soon became apparent that there were very few services which should in all circumstances be excluded from the "core" – in the sense that they would never be available free of charge (or on "affordable terms") in publicly funded institutions. Furthermore, it became apparent that a vast expenditure of time, effort, and funds would be needed to detail the precise circumstances in which particular treatments should, or should not, be provided. Frequent revision of the lists would also be necessary, given medical advances. If the detailed criteria were linked to a legally enforceable right to services, a much increased proportion of the funds allocated by Parliament for Health would have been spent defending legal proceedings.

The committee did not attempt to detail "core" services, but focused on clarifying the circumstances in which particular services (especially high volume, high cost services such as coronary bypass grafts and joint replacements) should be provided within the publicly funded health system. This work led to a "points system" and then a "booking system," whereby patients would be assessed and booked for treatment within a specified time depending on the severity of their condition.[61] The approach has not been without its critics, but in some areas of medical practice it has led to greater fairness and openness. Judicial review is occasionally a possibility.[62]

In developing priority criteria, attention has had to be paid to the Human Rights Act 1993.[63] This makes it unlawful for anyone who provides services (to the public, or to any section of the public) to treat any one less favorably (in connection with the provision of those services) by reason of a prohibited grounds of discrimination.[64]

The prohibited grounds of discrimination include not only age, marital status, race, and sexual orientation, but also (among others) disability – which in the Act is defined in the following manner:

(i) Physical disability or impairment;
(ii) Physical illness;
(iii) Psychiatric illness;
(iv) Intellectual or psychological disability or impairment;
(v) Any other loss or abnormality of psychological, physiological, or anatomical structure or function;
(vi) Reliance on a guide dog, wheelchair, or other remedial means;
(vii) The presence in the body of organisms capable of causing illness.[65]

Although there is a partial exception relating to some of these grounds,[66] the Act has affected the provision of services, and the way in which any restrictions are expressed.[67]

It is not only direct discrimination which is outlawed by the Act. Section 65 provides that:

> Where any conduct, practice, requirement, or condition that is not apparently in contravention of any provision of this Part [of this Act] has the effect of treating a person or group of persons differently on one of the prohibited grounds of discrimination in a situation where such treatment would be unlawful under any provision of this Part other than this section, that conduct, practice, condition, or requirement shall be unlawful under that provision unless the person whose conduct or practice is in issue, or who imposes the condition or requirement, establishes good reason for it.[68]

The Code of Rights (discussed above) has the effect of adopting the anti-discrimination provisions of the Human Rights Act.[69] However, complaints to the Health and Disability Commissioner, about discrimination in the provision of health services, are likely to be referred to the Human Rights Commission for investigation. The Code of Rights is primarily concerned with the way in which services are provided, rather than with whether services were provided in the first place. In determining whether there has been a breach of the Code, providers' resource constraints are sometimes a relevant consideration.[70]

In some circumstances, the Crimes Act 1961 has the effect of making it an offense to omit to provide medical treatment – where death is caused, life endangered, or health permanently injured in consequence.[71]

Organ and tissue "donation"

New Zealand has very little law that deals specifically with the "living donors" of organs or tissue.[72] There is, however, a provision which helps ensure that those who provide blood remain donors, rather than become vendors.[73] There are no equivalent provisions relating to kidneys, as there has been no prospect of a trade in kidneys. Were it to become a real possibility, legislative prohibition would probably ensue.

In New Zealand as elsewhere, the language of "donors" is used in connection with bodies from which organs or tissue are removed (for transplantation, after death has occurred), even though the now-deceased person was not known to have indicated willingness that this be done. The relevant New Zealand law is to be found in the Human Tissue Act 1964, as amended.

That Act gives a crucial role to the "person lawfully in possession of the body of a deceased person" (hereinafter PLIPOB) – who, in the case of a body lying in a hospital ("hospital care institution"), is defined as the person "for the time being in charge" of the institution.[74] The law distinguishes between those cases where the now deceased person had, or had not, requested ("in writing at any time or orally in the presence of two or more witnesses during his last illness") that his or her body be used for therapeutic purposes, or for the purposes of medical education and research.[75] Where there is a relevant request, the PLIPOB may authorize the removal of a part of the body, for use in accordance with the request.[76] In law, there is no need to seek the agreement of a member of the family – although in practice this is done.

Where there is no relevant request, the PLIPOB may authorize the removal and use of parts of the body if "having made such reasonable enquiry as may be practicable" the PLIPOB has no reason to believe that there is a relevant objection.[77] There are two varieties of relevant objection. The first is an objection previously expressed (and not withdrawn) by the now-deceased person.[78] The other is an objection to the removal by the surviving spouse, or "any surviving relative" of the deceased person.[79] In law, the PLIPOB is free to authorize the removal of, say, a kidney for transplantation if, having made the required enquiry, the PLIPOB has no reason to believe that there is any relevant objection.[80] In practice, there is extreme reluctance to proceed without the agreement of a family member.

Pediatrics

New Zealand courts have often been called upon to resolve disputes about whether children should, or should not, be provided with particular medical treatments. Most of these children have been too young to decide for themselves.[81] The majority of cases have been ones in which health professionals considered treatment essential for the child's well being, but parents were opposed to its being provided. However, there has also been a case where parents were unwilling to agree to life-sustaining treatment being withheld, in circumstances where death was inevitable before long in any event and the treatment added to the child's suffering.[82] The outcome of these cases – which invariably result in the courts approving the response favored by the health professionals – might seem to indicate that parents have very little discretion about the treatment to be provided to their children. However, in the overwhelming majority of circumstances, parents' views are of crucial importance. It is only in a tiny minority of extreme cases that there is any legal challenge to the parents' refusal of consent. In practice, parents have considerable discretion about whether to take their children to a health care provider, which one they approach, and whether they adopt any course of action which is recommended.

In a New Zealand context, it is a slight oversimplification of the legal position to speak of the decision-making role of parents. In New Zealand law, the power to make decisions about the provision of medical treatment to a child is primarily that of the guardians[83] – who will usually, but by no means always, be the parents of the child. (Mothers are almost always guardians of the child, but unmarried fathers who were not in a de facto relationship with the mother at the time of birth are usually not guardians.)[84] In practice, hospital authorities are rarely in a position to be certain whether a particular person – especially a male – is, or is not, a guardian of the child. However, people claiming to be parents/guardians are usually regarded as such by health professionals. This practice is consistent with the policy behind the statutory provision which provides that if there is no guardian, or if no guardian can be found or is capable, then consent may be given by a person who has been acting in the place of a parent.[85]

In the late 1960s, New Zealand statute law was amended to make clear that people in their late teens (sixteen to nineteen) can consent to most medical procedures.[86] Unlike its English counterpart, the provision did not expressly preserve a child's common law capacity to consent, and it could have been taken to exclude this alternative. However, the consequences of this view would be so inconvenient, and so out of step with contemporary views about the decision-making capacity of many children of less than sixteen years of age, that it is unlikely to be accepted.[87] In practice, "*Gillick*-competent" children will usually be regarded as having the capacity to consent to some, even many, medical procedures.[88]

Concluding comment

In New Zealand, "bioethics" is commonly used as a synonym for biomedical ethics. However, the New Zealand Government is in the process of establishing a Bioethics Council, which will deal exclusively with matters outside the range of human biomedical ethics. A broader concept of bioethics is therefore likely to become established in New Zealand.[89]

Notes

1 Accident Compensation Act, 1972, effective from 1 April 1974.
2 Accident Compensation Act, 1982.
3 Accident Rehabilitation and Compensation Insurance Act, 1992.
4 *See L. v. Robinson* [2000] 3 NZLR 499.
5 NZ Legislation – Statutes, *Injury Prevention, Rehabilitation, and Compensation Act* 2001, http://www.legislation.govt.nz/browse_vw.asp?content-set=pal_statutes; *select* I, *select* Injury Prevention, Rehabilitation, and Compensation Act 2001 (accessed Oct. 31, 2005). For an account, *see* P. D. G. Skegg, *Compensation in the New Zealand Health Care Sector*, in No-fault Compensation System in the Health Care Sector (Tort & Insurance Law Series Vol. 8, Jos Dute, Michael Faure & Helmut Koziel, eds, Springer 2004).
6 HDC – Health and Disability Commissioner, *The Health and Disability Commissioner Act*, http://www.hdc.org.nz/theact.php (accessed Oct. 14, 2005).
7 *Id.*
8 Health and Disability Commissioner, *The HDC Code of Health and Disability Services Consumers' Rights Regulation 1996*, http://www.hdc.org.nz/page.php?page=theact&content=theact_thecodedetail (accessed Oct. 14, 2005) [hereinafter *HDC Code*].
9 For the text of these rights, *see id.*; For a wealth of related information to these rights, *see* HDC – Health and Disability Commissioner, http://www.hdc.org.nz/ (accessed Oct. 14, 2005).
10 *HDC Code, supra* n. 8, at http://www.hdc.org.nz/page.php?page=theact&content=theact_thecodedetail
11 *See* Health and Disability Commissioner Act 1994, *supra* n. 6, at http://www.hdc.org.nz/theact.php.
12 Privacy Commissioner Act 1991, http://knowledge-basket.co.nz/, or http://www.privacy.org.nz/top.html (accessed Dec. 15, 2005).
13 NZ Legislation – Statutes, *Privacy Act 1993*, http://www.legislation.govt.nz/browse_vw.asp?content-set=pal_statutes; *select* P,Q, *select* Privacy Act 1993 (accessed Oct. 31, 2005).
14 *Id.* at § 6.
15 *Id.* at Part VIII.
16 *Id.* at § 46.
17 For the amended text of that Code, *see Health Information Privacy Code 1994* (revised July 2000), http://www.privacy.org.nz/comply/HIPCWWW.pdf (accessed Oct. 31, 2005); For other relevant information to this, *see* Office of the Privacy Commissioner, New Zealand, *Health Information*, http://www.privacy.org.nz/shealthf.html (accessed Oct. 31, 2005).
18 Health Information Privacy Code 1994, *supra* n. 17.
19 *Id.*
20 NZ Legislation – Statutes, *Human Rights Act 1993*, http://www.legislation.govt.nz/browse_vw.asp?content-set=pal_statutes; *select* H, *select* Human Rights Act 1993 (accessed Oct. 31, 2005).

21 NZ Legislation – Statutes, *Status of Children Amendment Act, 1987*, http://www.knowledge-basket.co.nz (accessed Dec. 15, 2005).
22 Human Assisted Reproductive Technology Bill, 1996; Assisted Human Reproduction Bill, 1998.
23 *E.g.*, *Re. P (adoption: surrogacy)* [1990] NZFLR 385.
24 NZ Legislation – Statutes, *Crimes Act 1961*, § 182A, http://www.legislation.govt.nz/browse_vw.asp?content-set=pal_statutes; *select* C, *select* Crimes Act 1961 (accessed Nov. 1, 2005). *See also* NZ Legislation – Statutes, *Contraception, Sterilisation, and Abortion Act 1977*, § 2, http://www.legislation.govt.nz/browse_vw.asp?content-set=pal_statutes; *select* C, *select* Contraception, Sterilisation, and Abortion Act 1977 (accessed Nov. 1, 2005).
25 N.Z. Royal Comm'n on Contraception, Sterilisation, and Abortion, Contraception, Sterilisation, and Abortion in New Zealand: Report of the Royal Commission of Inquiry (Government Printer 1977).
26 *Contraception, Sterilisation, and Abortion Act 1977*, *supra* n. 24.
27 *Crimes Act 1961*, § 187A(1), *supra* n. 24.
28 *See Crimes Act 1961*, § 187A(4), *supra* n. 24; *Wall v. Livingston* [1982] 1 NZLR 734.
29 *Crimes Act 1961*, § 187A(3), *supra* n. 24.
30 *Crimes Act 1961*, § 182(2), *supra* n. 24; But also *see R v. Henderson* [1990] 3 NZLR 174.
31 *E.g.*, *Crimes Act 1961*, § 159(1), *supra* n. 24.
32 *E.g.*, In the matter of Baby P (an unborn child) [1995] NZFLR 577.
33 *See e.g.* In the Matter of V [1997] NZFLR 720 ("[W]ithout the intervention of birth by caesarean section both the mother and the baby would in the circumstances be placed at severe and avoidable risk.").
34 NZ Legislation – Statutes, *New Zealand Bill of Rights Act 1990*, § 11, http://www.legislation.govt.nz/browse_vw.asp?content-set=pal_statutes; *select* N, *select* New Zealand Bill of Rights Act 1990 (accessed Nov. 1, 2005). But also *see New Zealand Bill of Rights Act 1990*, §§ 3–6.
35 *See e.g. St George's Healthcare NHS Trust v. Fam 26* (Eng C.A. 1999).
36 *Crimes Act 1961*, § 63, *supra* n. 24.
37 *R v. Ruscoe* (1992) 8 CRNZ 68.
38 *R v. Stead* (1991) 7 CRNZ 291 (CA).
39 P. D. G. Skegg, *Pain-killing Drugs and the Law of Homicide*, 4(3) Otago Bioethics Report 8 (1995).
40 *Airedale NHS Trust v. Bland* [1993] A.C. 789, 866, 881–2. For the analysis to be adopted if death resulted from the intervention of an intruder, *see id.* 866; *Auckland Area Health Bd. v. Attorney-Gen.* [1993] 1 NZLR 235, 255.
41 *E.g.*, *Crimes Act 1961*, § 151, 157, *supra* n. 24.
42 *Cf. R v. Mwai* [1995] 3 NZLR 149.
43 *Auckland Area Health Bd. v. Attorney-Gen.* [1993] 1 NZLR 235, 245; *Airedale NHS Trust v. Bland* [1993] A.C. 789, 864 (1993).
44 *Auckland Area Health Bd. v. Attorney-Gen.* [1993] 1 NZLR 235 ("Re L"); *Re G* [1997] 2 NZLR 201; *Shortland v. Northland Health Ltd.* [1998] 1 NZLR 433.
45 *Shortland v. Northland Health Ltd.* [1998] 1 NZLR 433.
46 *HDC Code*, right 7(5), *supra* n. 8; For extensive definition of "advance directive" *see* clause 4 of the Code.
47 *New Zealand Bill of Rights Act 1990*, § 11, *supra* n. 34; But also *see New Zealand Bill of Rights Act 1990*, §§ 3–6; NZ Legislation – Statutes, *Mental Health (Compulsory Assessment and Treatment) Act 1992*, Part II, http://www.legislation.govt.nz/browse_vw.asp?content-set=pal_statutes; *select* M, *select* Mental Health (Compulsory Assessment and Treatment) Act 1992 (accessed Nov. 1, 2005).

48 NZ Legislation – Statutes, *Protection of Personal and Property Rights Act 1988*, § 18; *see also id.* §§ 94, 96, 98, http://www.legislation.govt.nz/browse_vw.asp?content-set=pal_statutes; *select* P,Q, *select* Protection of Personal and Property Rights Act 1988 (accessed Nov. 1, 2005).
49 *Cf. Crimes Act 1961*, s 159, *supra* n. 24.
50 *See e.g. Joe v Joe* [1985] 3 NZFLR 675, *Auckland Area Health Bd. v Attorney-Gen.* [1993] 1 NZLR 235, 246.
51 *New Zealand Bill of Rights Act 1990*, § 10, *supra* n. 34.
52 *Id.* at § 3.
53 *Id.* at § 5.
54 *Protection of Personal and Property Rights Act 1988*, § 18(1)(f); 98(4), *supra* n. 48.
55 NZ Legislation – Statutes, *Health Research Council Act 1990*, § 25, http://www.legislation.govt.nz/browse_vw.asp?content-set=pal_statutes; *select* H, *select* Health Research Council Act 1990 (accessed Nov. 1, 2005).
56 NZ Legislation – Statutes, *New Zealand Public Health and Disability Act, 2000*, § 16(2), http://www.legislation.govt.nz/browse_vw.asp?content-set=pal_statutes; *select* N, *select* New Zealand Public Health and Disability Act 2000 (accessed Nov. 1, 2005).
57 Comm. of Inquiry, Auckland, The Report of the Committee of Inquiry into Allegations Concerning the Treatment of Cervical Cancer at National Women's Hospital and into Other Related Matters 94 (1988).
58 Simon Upton, Your Health and the Public Health: A Statement of Government Health Policy, 75 (Ministry of Health 1991).
59 *Id.* at 86.
60 NZ Legislation – Statutes, *Health and Disability Services Act 1993*, § 6, http://www.knowledge-basket.co.nz (accessed Dec. 15, 2005).
61 *See e.g.* Benedict Hefford & Andrew Holmes, *Booking Systems for Elective Services: The New Zealand Experience*, 22(4) Austl. Health Rev. 61 (1999).
62 *See Shortland v. Northland Health Ltd., supra* n. 45.
63 *See generally* Ron J. Paterson, *Access to Health and Disability Services and the Human Rights Act*, 1(1) Hum. Rts. L. & Practice 5 (1995).
64 *Human Rights Act 1993*, § 44, *supra* n. 20.
65 *Id.* at § 21(1)(h).
66 *Id.* at § 52.
67 *Cf.* Core Services Comm., Core Health and Disability Support Services for 1993/94: First Report of the National Advisory Committee on Core Health and Disability Support Services 59 (1992).
68 *Human Rights Act 1993*, § 65, *supra* n. 20.
69 *HDC Code*, right 2, clause 4, *supra* n. 8.
70 *Id.* at clause 3(3).
71 *Crimes Act 1961*, § 151–2, 157, *supra* n. 24. *See also* §§ 150A, 160.
72 The Area Health Boards Act 1983 has been repealed, but this should not be taken to cast doubt on the acceptability of using living donors in some circumstances. *Cf. Crimes Act 1961*, § 61A, *supra* n. 24.
73 NZ Legislation – Statutes, *Health Act 1956*, § 92D(1), http://www.legislation.govt.nz/browse_vw.asp?content-set=pal_statutes; *select* H, *select* Health Act 1956 (accessed Nov. 1, 2005).
74 NZ Legislation – Statutes, *Human Tissue Act 1964*, § 2(2)(a), as amended, http://www.legislation.govt.nz/browse_vw.asp?content-set=pal_statutes; *select* H, *select* Human Tissue Act 1964(accessed Nov. 1, 2005).
75 *Id.* at § 3.
76 *Id.* at § 3(1).
77 *Id.* at § 3(2).
78 *Id.* at § 3(2)(a).

79 *Id.* at § 3(2)(b).
80 *Id.* at § 3.
81 *Eg., Re J (An Infant): B and B v. Dir.-Gen. of Soc. Welfare* [1996] 2 NZLR 134 (C.A.).
82 *Auckland Healthcare Services v. L* [1998] NZFLR 998.
83 *See* Guardianship Act, 1968, § 25(3), http://www.knowledge-basket.co.nz/gpacts/ (accessed Dec. 15, 2005).
84 *See generally id.* at §§ 6–8.
85 *Id.* at § 25(3)(b).
86 *Id.* at § 25(1)
87 But *see Auckland Healthcare Services Ltd v. Liu*, High Court, Auckland M812/96, 11 July 1996, Tompkins J; *cf. R v. Laufau*, High Court, Auckland T000759, Aug. 23, 2000, Potter J.
88 On *Gillick* competence, *see Gillick v. West Norfolk and Wisbech Area Health Authority* [1986] 1 A.C. 112. The view of a child's capacity which was adopted in this case was by no means a novelty in New Zealand. *See e.g.* P. D. G. Skegg, *Capacity of Minors to Consent to Medical Treatment on Themselves*, 4(8) Recent Law 295, 297–99 (1969); Ronald J. Paterson, *Consent of Medical Treatment by Minors*, J. Auckland Medico-Legal Soc. 70, 71–72 (1976).
89 For an account of the most recent developments in New Zealand health care law, see now Medical Law in New Zealand (P.D.G. Skegg and R.J. Patterson eds., Thomas Brookers, 2007).

16 Bioethics in the developing world[1]

Udo Schüklenk

Introduction

The majority of people on this planet live in countries defined as "developing."[2] This chapter identifies common themes that concern bioethicists in the developing world. Bioethics as a professional discipline exists in many developing countries. Bioethicists teach in many health sciences and humanities faculties in Africa, Asia, and Latin America. Countries such as Mexico have government appointed bioethics commissions not dissimilar to counterparts in North America or Western Europe. Indeed, professional journals dedicated exclusively to developing world bioethics have come into existence. Some of them, such as *Developing World Bioethics*,[3] are even supported by mainstream developed world publishers, while others, such as the Indian journal *Issues in Medical Ethics* continue to operate quite successfully on shoestring budgets. At the same time, otherwise excellent major textbooks on medicine and social justice ignore developing world issues nearly completely or look at them only from a U.S. American perspective.[4]

Who are the bioethicists working in the developing world, professionally speaking? Not unlike their Western colleagues, many have ventured into bioethics later in their careers. Initially, they started off in philosophy or politics/political science departments or on the medical faculties of tertiary institutions in their respective countries. Leading bioethicists in the Philippines, for instance, can be found in the philosophy and political science departments of Manila-based campuses of the University of the Philippines. It is fair to say that at the time of writing there is no straightforward career path available to budding bioethicists in developing countries, yet strides have been made by way of the development of undergraduate and postgraduate curricula.

International funding agencies such as the United States National Institutes of Health, the Wellcome Trust in the United Kingdom, and also the World Health Organization, to name a few, have made unilateral decisions to sponsor research ethics training programs. As a desirable consequence of this, research ethics competencies have dramatically improved in many parts of the developing world. This has come at a price, however. Budding bioethicists were (and are) invariably drawn to international funding available for this sort of activity. This has skewed the appearance of developing world bioethics in the international arena, and it has skewed the priorities bioethicists give in the work they undertake in their respective countries of origin. (For example, Argentinian bioethicists' contributions to congresses held by the International Association of Bioethics frequently have been related to research ethics.) I will return to this ongoing concern in the fourth part of this chapter.

In exploring these issues, it will become evident that laws, policies, and practices in the developed world affect the lives of persons in developing nations. Some of the most important bioethical issues in the developing world are the direct result of this circumstance. It is especially interesting to note the impact the laws of developed nations have on the lives of people in developing nations. We typically think of laws as affecting primarily persons who live in the jurisdiction covered under the law. However, in this chapter it will be evident that laws can cross boundaries and have significant effects on persons outside their jurisdiction. This is most evident in the case of intellectual property rights and access to essential drugs. The patent protections offered to pharmaceutical companies in developed nations make many drugs unaffordable and inaccessible in developing nations. The current availability of compulsory licensing in cases of public health emergencies is clearly insufficient in dealing with the health problems faced in the developing world.

It also will become evident that, while in developed nations there has been a tendency to legislate, regulate, and litigate bioethical issues, this has been less the case in developing nations. One does see evidence of regulation and legislation regarding some issues in developing nations, such as HIV/AIDS prevention. However, many of the bioethical issues that have been the subject of substantial government oversight and intervention in developed nations, such as informed consent, have received little legislative or judicial attention in the developing world.

What then are the issues that bioethicists in developing countries are primarily concerned about? I will divide my treatment of these issues in four main categories, each of which could be the subject of lengthier discussions in separate chapters: (1) clinical ethics; (2) policy issues; (3) research ethics; and (4) globalization and bioethics funding. The section on clinical ethics covers informed consent in the health care professional–patient relationship, infectious disease control, resource allocation issues, and organ donation/transplantation. The next section on policy issues discusses intellectual property rights (IPR) and access to essential drugs, as well as the 10/90 gap in research spending. Following this is the section on research ethics which is concerned with standards of care in clinical trials, reproductive health research on domestic violence, and benefit sharing in bioprospecting and genetic research. The fourth section concludes this chapter with a discussion of globalization and bioethics funding, particularly in regard to its impact on developing countries.

Clinical ethics

Informed consent in the health care professional–patient relationship

The health care professional–patient relationship in developing countries is not fundamentally different to that in developed countries. Issues such as informed consent, confidentiality, and truthfulness, as well as beginning and end-of-life decision making, affect patients in manners similar to developed countries, even though poverty and disparities in power relationships may make matters more difficult both on quantitative and qualitative levels in developing nations. However, because many developing countries are, among other issues, characterized by suboptimal levels of education, "short-cuts" with regard to informed consent are commonplace. Typically, the idea of paternalism is deployed to justify health care professionals making choices on behalf of patients that are deemed to be in the patient's best interest. As Gerald Dworkin rightly points out, we usually accept paternalistic decisions made by doctors on behalf of patients in cases of emergencies, incompetent patients (where no surrogate is immediately available), or when patients waive their right to be informed.[5] In developing countries, frequently, the second rationale is utilized to justify ignoring the informed consent requirement commonly accepted in medical ethics (and law) in the developed world. The argument is basically that the educational levels of the patients in question are so low as to make truly informed consent impossible. Truly informed consent here is understood as a patient becoming sufficiently informed about the matters at stake to be able to make her or his own autonomous choice about treatment options.[6] While this question ultimately is an empirical one that would probably have to be evaluated on a case-by-case basis, three observations are worth noting. First, we have empirical evidence that patients in developing countries are capable of understanding complex medical scenarios if those conveying the information use appropriate means of communication and take sufficient time to explain the issues at hand.[7] Second, the rationale – in my experience – is all too often used by doctors in poor public sector environments to "save time" and "treat more patients." This is a difficult issue to grapple with. It certainly is true that proper informed consent (as a process) requires time, and doctors in developing countries all too often are short on time because there are not enough health care professionals to satisfy the demand. Patients frequently arrive at the doorsteps of hospitals or clinics in the middle of the night to get a "good place" in the queue and so to have some chance of actually being seen by a doctor. Under such circumstances, a choice must be made between engaging in time-consuming informed consent processes versus treating as many patients as optimally as is feasible – obviously at a cost to the quality of the informed consent processes. Third, particularly when practiced in tertiary teaching hospitals by consultants and professors, short-cuts to the informed consent process are likely to damage the patient–health care professional relationship in the long term, because they are setting bad examples in the training of future health care professionals.

It has been argued that in the developing world people have different understanding of personal autonomy and that informed consent might not be such an important feature in the health care professional–patient relationship.[8] To some extent this argument has been discarded by demonstrating that the representatives of, for instance, African peoples hold the same values in high regard as the peoples in the so-called West.[9] For instance, human rights principles identical to the 1948 U.N. Declaration of Human Rights are expressed in the African Charter on Human and Peoples' Rights, ratified by the African heads of state in 1986.

Infectious disease control

AIDS, among other infectious diseases, has dramatically increased mortality across many parts of the developing world, most significantly so in sub-Saharan Africa. Prevalence of HIV in Southern Africa has reached staggering proportions, exceeding twenty-five percent of the population in some countries.[10] This has led to a serious challenge to the Hippocratic notion of confidentiality and privacy, namely that everything that transpires during a consultation remains between the doctor and the patient. Frequently, particularly so in rural areas, a family physician will treat not only one member of a family, but a husband, wife, children, grandparents, and other relatives. If the physician discovers during a consultation that, say, the wife has had a sexual partner other than her husband and has contracted HIV, does the physician have a moral obligation to inform the woman's husband? The discussion in the developed world has constructed this issue primarily as one of protecting confidentiality versus preventing harm to other parties. Some philosophers, such as H. Tristram Engelhardt, Jr., have argued, on utilitarian grounds, that the irreversible harm done to the doctor–patient relationship by breaking confidences would be so great as to outweigh the harm done by failing to warn people of their sex partner's HIV status.[11] Reportedly, in Asia it is common place to give lower priority to maintaining confidence, and health-related information is normally shared freely among family members.[12] In sub-Saharan Africa regulators have taken quite different views on the matter of HIV testing. In Botswana, for instance, the government has decided that the threat to society by HIV is so significant that to avoid getting tested in a public health facility one must explicitly opt out. Informed consent to testing is not sought. Those tested who turn out to be infected will receive state-of-the-art AIDS care, including access to essential AIDS drugs, free of charge.

Neighboring South Africa, with infection rates comparable to Botswana, has taken a different stance on this matter. South Africa's policies are in line with best developed-world standards, as far as HIV testing is concerned. Pre- and post-test counseling are required by law, and voluntary informed consent must be sought prior to testing. Guaranteed access to life-saving medication is not available at the time of writing. Despite this, the South African government's policy with regard to access to essential AIDS drugs has been nothing short of disastrous. It is characterized by a continuing denial of the true state of HIV/AIDS in the country and continuing ruminations by the country's President, Thabo Mbeki and his Health Minister, Manto Thabalala-Msimang, along the lines that HIV might not be the cause of AIDS, and essential AIDS drugs constitute a Western pharmaceutical industry conspiracy designed to poison poor Blacks.[13] The number of preventable deaths of Black South Africans that are a consequence of this policy exceed those suffered by Blacks during the racist apartheid decades by several magnitudes. Eurocentric as it may sound, it is probably fair to say that similarly eccentric behaviors would almost certainly not be tolerated by a more sophisticated European electorate. Ethical concerns have been expressed with regard to the professional behavior of U.S.-based scientists who went out of their way to convince a gullible African audience that HIV is not the cause of AIDS, and that, in fact, AIDS is not an infectious illness (implying that there was no need to use condoms in order to prevent AIDS).[14]

Openness about sexuality and sexual behaviors is not the norm in twenty-first century China, which makes HIV prevention programs suboptimal. As Yang-Guang Wang, a philosopher at the Chinese Academy of Social Sciences writes,

> The behaviour of homosexuals, drug users and prostitutes is often regarded as perverse, abnormal, impermissible or even disgusting. So their rights are often infringed upon. ... They are not treated as other persons. As a health professional phrased it: "their health should be protected, while their behaviour should be punished. How can those who are punished enjoy the same social, moral and legal status as other persons?"[15]

The ethical debates surrounding societal (religious etc.) hindrances to effective health promotion campaigns are not unique to developing countries and, for that reason, shall not be addressed in further detail here.[16] Given the much greater prevalence of infectious diseases in many developing countries, however, the consequence of permitting such hindrances to win the public relations wars are much greater in developing nations than in the developed world.

Resource allocation issues

Resource allocation issues are a common feature of managed care in the private and public sectors of health care delivery systems both in the developed and the developing world. In developing countries, of course, relatively and absolutely fewer resources are available to provide health care to the poor. Often one finds a two- or three-tier health delivery system, whereby the care provided to private sector patients is as good or even superior to what is provided to patients in any developed country. The opposite is true for the majority of citizens of developing world societies who have to rely on the public sector for health care. Philippines-based philosopher Peter A. Sy has proposed that the options of private versus public sector health care delivery should be discussed utilizing an ethical framework based on concepts of "power" and "justice." He defines power as "access to and control of resources."[17] Patients whose private health insurance runs out (or who never had any) depend on the suboptimal care that is provided in an overcrowded, underresourced public sector health care delivery system.

Ethical issues concerning resource allocation arise on at least two levels: First, is it acceptable for the private sector to "unload" patients who run out of private coverage onto the public sector? Health care here is essentially understood as an activity based on fee-for-service. This approach is very much libertarian in its outlook. Second, for-profit and not-for-profit private medical care organizations need to decide which services to provide, while aiming to ensure that membership fees remain competitive and generally affordable. Decisions such as these are, undoubtedly, dependent on normative choices that are essentially ethical in their nature.[18]

Public sector patients in developing nations find themselves confronted with resource allocation decisions that effectively shorten their lives because the necessary infrastructure, medication, and staff are unavailable when needed. Patients will be excluded from access to dialysis programs (and renal transplant programs) based on age or concomitant illnesses, despite the fact that they could clinically benefit from access. Deliberately or not, it is perhaps not insignificant that most developing countries that operate explicit resource allocation decision making policies are guided by utilitarian considerations, aiming to maximize the number of quality or disability adjusted life-years that can be saved within a given country's resource constraints.[19] It is troublesome that access to health-preserving means essentially depends on the resources individual patients have available. Given the lack of public sector infrastructure in most developing countries, the cut-off criteria are much lower than they are in the much better resourced health delivery services such as the National Health Service in the United Kingdom. Hence, resource allocation decisions and the criteria used to make such decisions are of a much more explosive nature.

Organ donation/transplantation

The ethical issues resulting from the possibility of organ donation are significant and have been debated in the developed world for decades.[20] In developing countries the issues discussed are similar but usually the emphasis is on the possibility that impoverished people are being exploited as live organ donors for rich people in their own country or in the developed world. Argentina law professor Eduardo Rivera Lopez argues that we should be less concerned about the fact that people try to sell their organs and more concerned about the "forms of exploitation and inequality that generate this practice."[21] Abul Fadl Mohsin Ebrahim discusses how Islamic legal scholars have dealt with the ethical challenge posed to prospective Muslim organ donors in the Qur'an. The ethical challenge posed is that Muslims believe that whatever they possess has been given to them by their God and that it could constitute arguably a breach of God's trust to give consent to the removal of body parts.[22] I am not so much interested in engaging (or competent to engage) the theological pursuit of this issue but in noting the fact that a religion that is predominant in many developing countries aims to find ways to alleviate human suffering and to identify rationales within its authoritative scriptures permitting organ transplantation. This, to some extent, contradicts the picture of Islam that is frequently painted in the West, whereby it is seen as a monolithic ideology unmovable by the human condition. For instance, the argument has been advanced that an organ donation must be just that, a donation. Realizing that this fails to generate sufficient numbers of organs to meet the demand, Islamic scholars have sought pragmatic solutions within the religious framework given in the Qur'an. For instance, a senior Islamic scholar suggested during a health care ethics conference hosted by the United Arab Emirates in 2002, that nothing would prevent the recipient of the donation from offering a gift to the donor in order to express her or his gratitude. This "gift" could well be in the form of cash. Efforts have been made in Latin American countries to establish ethical criteria and operating procedures for the allocation of scarce transplant organs.[23]

Not only are people moving across borders seamlessly in unprecedented numbers, but so are human organs destined for organ transplantation. Ethical issues discussed in this context have to do with the fundamental concern of the exploitation of impoverished organ donors in the developing world. Commercial organ sales resulting in organ transfers (for payment) from developing world sources to developed world recipients are of concern because of the economic power differential between the parties to the contract. Similarly, doctors' participation in such contracts has been criticized as incompatible with doctors' professional obligations. Professionalism, in its historic religious derivation, means essentially to profess publicly to serve the public good. Arguably, access to life-saving organs based exclusively on a given prospective patient's capacity to pay is incompatible with professional duties so understood. Equitable access as a fundamental requirement of the principle of distributive justice is not guaranteed under such circumstances, despite frequently equal needs on the part of those requiring transplant organs. Evidence has begun to accumulate that at least some "donors" had no substantial understanding of the implications of their decision, nor were even aware of their "donation." It has also been reported that organs were stolen from deceased patients, as well as from impoverished patients. The latter had come to hospitals for care and left them with less than their full set of organs.[24] Reportedly, the Turkish Interior Ministry warned after the major 1999 earthquake that groups were roaming the country in search of children orphaned by the earthquake to kidnap them and remove organs for sale.[25] In South Africa, at the time of writing, a major criminal investigation is under way, aiming to unearth the involvement of local doctors in international organ trafficking. An Israeli recipient of a kidney had his travel document seized, pending the outcome of the investigation.[26] Many such reports and evidence have been accumulated by University of California at Berkeley anthropology professor Nancy Sheper-Hughes. She reports that,

> [t]he business of organ transplants is conducted in a transnational space. Elements of both legal and illegal trade in blood and solid organs exist in some parts of the world. Between 1983 and 1988, 131 patients from three renal units in the United Arab Emirates and Oman traveled to Bombay, India where they purchased, through local brokers, kidneys from living donors. The donors were from urban shanty towns outside Bombay who were compensated between $2,000 and $3,000 for a kidney. This ghoulish trade was widely publicized in an Indian news weekly, but treated as well in a Lancet article analyzing the high mortality among the Arab recipients of purchased Indian kidneys (Salahudeen *et al.* 1990). Where there is a legal market in the sale of blood or organs, one can be almost certain of an illegal black-market [*sic*] replete with human rights abuses.[27]

Policy issues

Many policy issues have a bearing on the health care delivery and the health care research sectors. I have chosen only two for this chapter. Another issue to look for in the literature is the poaching of health care professionals from developing countries to developed countries. Effectively, developing countries train doctors and nurses (and subsidize their education) only to see them subsequently poached by agencies in the developed world. This undoubtedly is an ethical issue which should be addressed by policy makers.[28]

Intellectual property rights (IPR) and access to essential drugs

The issue of IPR and affordable access to essential drugs in the developing world has been of concern to treatment access activists, United Nations organizations, as well as bioethicists for some time. At the heart of the ethical debate is the following issue: poor people in developing countries have no means to afford patented life-saving drugs, the patents of which are owned by Western pharmaceutical companies. The industry argues that it must charge high prices for its products to recover hundreds of millions of Euros or U.S. Dollars in research and development costs. Different views have been expressed by professionals writing on this issue. Some have argued that developing countries must significantly increase their own investment in drug research and development and stop being free-riders prior to getting a seat at the negotiating table for drug prices.[29] Others have held that developing nations' governments are entitled to disregard intellectual property rights in cases of public health emergencies.[30] This stance is in line with requirements laid out in the Trade-Related Aspects of Intellectual Property Rights (TRIPS) agreement of the World Trade Organization and therefore in line with currently binding international trade regimes.[31] One of the reasons even industry-friendly organizations such as the World Trade Organization support the idea of compulsory licensing of essential drugs in public health emergencies is that one of the major ethical rationales for patent protection is a public interest-based argument. It is in the public's best interest to see patents protected, so goes the argument, because otherwise industry has no incentive to invest in drug research and development. This, in turn, would deprive the public of needed remedies against diseases. This same interest-based argument has been utilized successfully in the debate on IPR and public health emergencies, where an international consensus has emerged that permits compulsory licensing if certain well-defined public health-related criteria are met.

The 10/90 gap in research spending

According to the Global Forum for Health Research, "every year more than U.S. $70 billion is spent on health research and development by the public and private sectors. An estimated 10 % of this is used for research into 90 % of the world's health problems. This is what is called the 10/90 gap."[32] The issue of neglected diseases research is obviously of central importance to people living in developing countries.[33] A team of researchers from Doctors without Borders reviewed the situation in a 2002 Lancet publication and concluded that "despite an ever-increasing need for safe, effective, and affordable medicines for the treatment of these [tropical] diseases, drug development has virtually stopped."[34] International discussions about how to address these challenges in a just manner have been going on for some time but without any satisfactory solutions at the time of writing.[35] New trade frameworks for health care research and development (R&D) have, for instance, been proposed by the United States-based Consumer Project Technology. James Love of Consumer Project Technology argues that "trade agreements should be reframed to focus on standards for sharing the costs of R&D" and that we "need business models for financing R&D that do not depend on marketing monopolies for approved products."[36] The ethical question that arises in this context is simple: whose responsibility is it to ensure that the world's disease burdens determine research priorities? The current situation, where the markets determine what is likely to maximize shareholder values of pharmaceutical multinationals, results in millions of preventable deaths among the world's poor. That mainstream bioethics is paying insufficient attention to these crucial ethical issues has more recently been criticized by health care professionals rather than conceded by bioethicists themselves.[37] For instance, the Global Forum for Ethics in Health Research, an annual gathering of research ethics specialists sponsored by the United States National Institutes of Health, has so far avoided addressing this problem.

Research ethics

Standards of care in a trial

An acrimonious and lengthy international debate on the ethically appropriate standards of care provided in clinical trials in developing countries was triggered by an AIDS trial that took place in South Africa, among other countries. The trial in question was responding to a perceived need in developing countries to investigate a potentially affordable medication that might reduce the transmission of HIV from a pregnant infected woman to her offspring. Before the trial started, a trial undertaken only in developed countries had established that twenty-five percent of HIV-infected pregnant women who use no antiretroviral medication transmit the virus to their offspring, but less then eight percent of those who used a particular regime of the drug zidovudine do. Not unexpectedly, this trial regime soon became the gold standard for mother-to-child-transmission (MTCT) prevention in the developed world. Unfortunately, this drug regime proved to be unaffordable for the majority of infected women in developing countries. The developing world trial aimed at testing a cheaper yet effective MTCT regime. In order to do so, the investigators sought to establish not whether a lower dosage was as efficient as the higher one provided in the developed world, but whether it was more efficient than doing nothing. In other words, the test regime was matched against the local standard of care. Because the developed world standard of care was unaffordable to developing country public health systems, the local standard of care was effectively no drug at all, and hence, the test regime was matched against a placebo control.

The trial regime was quickly denounced by many in international medical[38] and bioethics[39] journals, because it violated a standard provision of the world's pivotal research ethics guideline, the World Medical Association's Declaration of Helsinki. The Declaration of Helsinki would have required the developing world investigators to compare their trial regime against the existing gold standard of HIV MTCT prevention, that is, the locally unaffordable regime. High profile defenders of the trial in question argued that the Helsinki Declaration was not a particularly useful ethical yardstick against which to hold the developing world-based trial. They proposed to adjust the Declaration to the realities of developing world health care.[40] At the heart of their analysis were two ethical arguments. The first argument was that women in the trials in question were no worse off by virtue of their trial participation. The participating pregnant women would not have had access to antiretrovirals at all in the public health care sector of their countries. Hence, those in the placebo arm were not in any way worse off, while those in the active agent arm were almost certainly better off. The second argument states, in a nutshell, that the Helsinki requirement to test a new experimental agent always against the best proven diagnostic and therapeutic method of treatment is preventing useful research in developing countries. If one always has to test a new agent against the best medication that exists somewhere in the world, no matter whether people in a given location can access or afford it, one would not be able to investigate cheaper treatment regimes that could actually make a difference in a developing country.

The counter arguments employed question the need to develop cheaper drugs, asking whether there is such a thing as a natural (in the sense of: not subjected to human choices) price for any given medication. Proponents of this point of view argue that the prices people pay for essential drugs are the result of pricing decisions made by major multinational pharmaceutical corporations. If it is possible to remove the patent protection of essential AIDS drugs, and hence their high price tag, the need to develop cheaper AIDS drugs for developing countries may well all but disappear. Arguably, however, this in itself does not solve other issues such as lack of systems for the delivery of antiretroviral drugs in many developing countries. The successful provision of such treatment regimes also depends on performing blood work routinely to check blood counts and maintaining satisfactory levels of nutrition. Still, it is widely accepted that the drug price is one of the primary hindrances of poor peoples' access to essential AIDS drugs. One might even argue that prices for diagnostic instruments could be subjected to a critique similar of that deployed against high prices for patented drugs.

Two other interrelated issues need to be looked at. Both have to do with standards of care. First: what standards of care can participants reasonably expect after a trial has concluded? Second: what standards of care are ethically required for people who contract HIV during preventative vaccine or microbicide trials? Preventative vaccine or microbicide trials are designed to test whether a vaccine candidate or a microbicide is capable of reducing the number of HIV infections transmitted in a given cohort of patients. As no preventative agent currently exists it is legitimate to compare the candidate agents against a placebo control. Invariably, in any given clinical trial there are a number of participants who labor under a therapeutic misconception. The patients believe, despite the genuinely best efforts by the investigators to inform them otherwise, that they are receiving a working preventative agent against HIV. If such participants become infected as a consequence of risk-taking triggered or influenced by the therapeutic misconception, their situation has worsened as a consequence of their trial participation. The question then is whether or not one should accept the UNAIDS view that an infection acquired under such circumstances does not constitute a trial-related injury that should be subject to compensation. The policy implications of this question obviously go far beyond AIDS research and affect all prevention trials.

The experiences of people conducting trials around the world suggest that these questions are being answered quite differently. The investigators in Thai HIV preventative vaccine trials seem to agree that infections acquired during the course of the trial should not be seen as a trial-related injury. Authorities in that country decided that anyone who would become infected during the trial should not receive anything other than what is available through the public health delivery system. This does not extend to the provision of antiretrovirals and other essential AIDS drugs. In South Africa two pivotal research ethics committees withdrew approval for preventative vaccine trials because the committees considered unacceptable the investigators' intention not to provide essential AIDS drugs to trial participants who become infected.

Clearly then, decision-makers in various parts of the world have taken different ethical stances on this matter. Interestingly, the ethical evaluation of this question is once again strongly influenced by economic factors. If a given investigator has to find the additional funds to guarantee life-long treatment (or, as South African ethics committees suggested, treatment for as long as there is therapeutic benefit to be gained) with essential AIDS drugs, the investigator may well decide not to proceed with the trial at all. In turn, this could severely increase the time it takes to develop a preventative HIV vaccine. More lives might be lost in the medium to long term if this were a consequence of demands pertaining to standards of care to be provided to failures in preventative trials. Arguably, microbicide trials might be even more negatively affected because historically it has been difficult for those wanting to investigate such agents to find the funding required to conduct the research. Investigators have pointed out that in the preventative trials undertaken so far, despite some possible infections due to a therapeutic misconception, overall the number of infections was below what it would have been in the trial population had the trial not taken place. They argue, quite persuasively, that this was a result of their trial-related counseling regarding safe sex. While this argument may well satisfy some, it may not satisfy those who believe that each individual who is worse off as a result of trial participation should be adequately cared for and ought to receive essential AIDS drugs even if these are not available through the public health delivery system.

Reproductive health research on domestic violence

Domestic violence, including rape (mostly directed against women and children) has reached epidemic proportions in some developing countries, including certainly many Southern African ones.[41] Researching the phenomenon is an important step on the road towards reducing (if not eliminating) the problem. In the process, researchers as well as research participants may well come across information that is psychologically disturbing. Researchers also might find evidence of a criminal act (e.g., rape or incest). As one investigator put it quite poignantly to a Nicaraguan interviewer, "The image of these stories affects you, to see how these women suffer, and especially the feeling that no one supports them, these are experiences that you never forget."[42] Detailed international guidelines have evolved, mostly produced by women conducting such vital, if difficult, research.[43] Stories are told of researchers entering "into lengthy negotiations to purchase a chicken from an inquisitive husband [in Zimbabwe] of a respondent, so that the respondent could be interviewed in private."[44] Perhaps, in light of the comments made below in the fourth section, it is not entirely coincidental that discussions about this matter take place in medical journals and specialist publications such as *Reproductive Health Matters* but not in mainstream bioethics journals. This is not to say that individual bioethicists are not interested or engaged in these issues,[45] but by and large reproductive health research is ignored in favor of "sexier" topics such as the ethics of stem cell research.

Benefit sharing in bioprospecting and genetics research

It is widely accepted internationally that if you use people in developing countries for clinical research purposes, or if you use their human or non-human genetic resources (including their traditional knowledges), there must be some appreciable benefit flowing back to them.[46] Non-human genetic materials could be plants that are utilized for therapeutic purposes. Traditional knowledge could be indigenous peoples' knowledge of such plants' therapeutic properties.[47] For instance, the U.N. Convention on Biological Diversity (CBD) requires that the benefits of non-human genetic resources be shared. The Secretariat of the Convention explains the ethical rationale behind this:

> An important part of the biodiversity debate involves access to and sharing of the benefits arising out of the commercial and other utilization of genetic material, such as pharmaceutical products. Most of the world's biodiversity is found in developing countries, which consider it

> a resource for fueling their economic and social development. Historically, plant genetic resources were collected for commercial use outside their region of origin or as inputs in plant breeding. Foreign bioprospectors have searched for natural substances to develop new commercial products, such as drugs. Often, the products would be sold and protected by patents or other intellectual property rights, without fair benefits to the source countries. The treaty recognizes national sovereignty over all genetic resources, and provides that access to valuable biological resources be carried out on "mutually agreed terms", and subject to "prior informed consent" of the country of origin.[48]

Some bioethicists have suggested that the typical North American response to such challenges, namely improved informed consent procedures and the like, is missing the point, because the response ignores the more fundamental problems with the commodification of human bodies.[49]

Arguably, benefit sharing as a policy strategy is problematic even if one agrees in principle that impoverished, indigenous communities should not be exploited and that they should be assisted in improving their living conditions. The currently accepted concept of intellectual property protection requires clearly defined originators and owners of knowledge, whereas the concept of community membership is fluid and indigenous knowledge is, by its very nature, open, with the originator(s) lost in the mists of time. The representation of an already nebulous entity, such as a community, in benefit sharing negotiations further complicates matters and is open to abuse. If benefit sharing is to be used to improve access to essential health services and other resources, it has been argued that representative governments themselves should negotiate the terms and the distribution of benefits.

Human genetic material constitutes a different case, because the owner is clearly identifiable and for that reason alone a stronger case in favor of compensation for those who enable such research by means of contributing their genetic material can be made.

Globalization and the ethics of funding bioethics

In recent years the funding of bioethics-related research projects as well as bioethics centers (and concomitant potential conflicts of interest arising on the funded institution's side) has led to debate among professionals in the developed world.[50] However, the arguably negative impact of developed world funding for developing world bioethics activities has not received much attention yet, despite obvious problems. Major funding agencies in the United States (namely the National Institutes of Health – NIH) as well as in Europe (the Wellcome Trust) fund bioethicists prepared to spend their time thinking about research ethics. While research ethics is an important field within bioethics, the survey of other topics in this contribution shows that there are many other issues, some more important than research ethics, to be addressed in developing countries. Yet, sadly, critical intelligence is lured with generous U.S and E.U. funding from those areas of inquiry (and teaching) to the comparably less problematic (politically less sensitive) field of research ethics. While developed world bioethicists openly discuss potential conflicts of interests that come with decisions to accept funding from certain sources, discussion among developing world bioethicists about this issue is more muted because the dependency on those sources of funding is much greater. In South Africa, where I worked for five years, only my unit provided comprehensive general bioethics programs on undergraduate and postgraduate levels (the latter designed to build local capacity in the field). All other medical school-based bioethics units specialized in research training programs due to funding priorities laid down by the U.S. NIH. Clearly, there are only so many research ethics specialists needed in the country and on the continent, yet this does not seem to be of any concern to U.S. and E.U. funding agencies.

What should be of greater concern to bioethicists and their funding agencies both in the developed and developing world are undoubtedly the ethical implications of globalization for the health care sector in the widest sense, including issues such as international patent regimes and equitable access to affordable medication. The implications of the current operational trade frameworks for the developing world's poor (and increasingly the developed world's poor) as far as health care is concerned, have not been researched to any appreciable extent by professional bioethicists. This is partly due to the fact that funders of bioethical research seem to have no interest in supporting such much-needed critical analyses. Bioethics remains still, to a large extent, true to its roots in North American liberalism; hence, the focus remains on informed consent and autonomy while very little attention is given to the socio-economic context in which health care is delivered in the developed and developing world alike.

Notes

1 Sections of this manuscript ("Standards of Care in a Trial" and "Benefit Sharing in Bioprospecting and Genetics Research") rely heavily on two previously published manuscripts: Udo Schüklenk, *AIDS: Bioethics and Public Policy*, 1(1) New Review Of Bioethics 127 (2003); and Udo Schüklenk & Anita Kleinsmidt, *North-South Benefit Sharing Arrangements in Bioprospecting and Genetic Research: A Critical Ethical and Legal Analysis*, 3 Developing World Bioethics 122 (2006). I owe a great deal of gratitude to Richard E. Ashcroft who read the manuscript and made detailed comments, many of which triggered changes. The editors of this book drew to my attention important links between ethical debates and the law. This is reflected in a paragraph added to the Introduction. For any remaining mistakes I remain solely responsible.

2 The World Bank Group, *Data and Statistics: Country Groups*, www.worldbank.org/data/countryclass/classgroups.htm (accessed Sept. 20, 2005).

3 Declaring a potential conflict of interest: I am a founding and current Co-Editor of this journal.

4 For example, *see* Rosamond Rhodes, Margaret P. Battin & Anita Silvers (eds), Medicine and Social Justice (Oxford University Press 2002).
5 Gerald Dworkin, The Theory and Practice of Autonomy (Cambridge University Press 1988).
6 Ruth R. Faden & Tom L. Beauchamp, A History and Theory of Informed Consent (Oxford University Press 1986).
7 Q. Abdool Karim, S. S. Abdool Karim, H. M. Coovadia & M. Susser, *Informed Consent for HIV testing in a South African Hospital: Is It Truly Informed and Truly Voluntary?* 88(4) American Journal Of Public Health 637 (1998).
8 E. Maxine Ankrah & Lawrence O. Gostin, *Ethical and Legal Considerations of the HIV Epidemic in Africa*, in Aids in Africa (Max Essex, Souleymane Mboup & Phyllis J. Kanki (eds), Raven Press 1994); Nicholas A. Christakis, *The Ethical Design of An AIDS Vaccine Trial in Africa – Another Look*, 18(3) Hastings Center Report 31 (1988).
9 Udo Schüklenk, Vichai Chokevivat, Carlos Del Rio, Segun Gbadegesin & Carlos Magis, *AIDS: Ethical Issues in The Developing World*, in A Companion to Bioethics (Helga Kuhse & Peter Singer (eds), Oxford 1998).
10 Alan Whiteside, Tony Barnett, Gavin George & Anton A. Van Niekerk, *Through a Glass Darkly: Data and Uncertainty in the AIDS Debate*, 3(1) Developing World Bioethics 49 (2003).
11 H. Tristam Englehardt, Jr., The Foundations of Bioethics (Oxford University Press 1986).
12 Angeles Tan Alora & Josephine M. Lumitao (eds), Beyond a Western Bioethics: Voices from the Developing World (Georgetown University Press 2001).
13 Udo Schüklenk, *Professional Responsibilities of Biomedical Scientists in Public Discourse*, 30 J. Med. Ethics 53 (2004).
14 *Id.*
15 Yan-Guang Wang, *Ethical Dilemmas Facing China in HIV Prevention*, 11(3–4) Bioethics 323, 325 (1997).
16 *See e.g.* Loretta M. Kopelman, *If HIV/AIDS is Punishment, Who is Bad?* 27(2) J. med. & phil. 231 (2002).
17 *See e.g.* Peter A. Sy, *Welfarism vs "Free Enterprise": Considerations of Power and Justice in the Philippine Healthcare System*, 17(5–6) Bioethics 555, 555 (2003).
18 Friedrich Breyer, Hartmuth Kliemt & Felix. Thiele (eds), Rationing in Medicine: Ethical, Legal and Practical Aspects (Springer 2002).
19 John Mckie, Peter Singer, Helga Kuhse & Jeff Richardson, The Allocation of Health Care Resources: An Ethical Evaluation of the 'QALY' Approach (Ashgate 1998).
20 *See e.g.* the special issue of this U.S.-based journal: 29(6) Hastings Center Report (1999).
21 Eduardo R. Lopez, *What is Exactly Wrong with Selling Your Body Parts?* in Bioethics: Latin American Perspectives 153 (Arleen L. F. Salles & María. J. Bertomeu (eds), Rodopi 2001).
22 A. F. Mohsin Ebrahim, *Organ Transplantation: Contemporary Sunni Muslim Legal and Ethical Perspectives* 9 Bioethics 291 (1995).
23 Maria G. De Ortuzar, *Interdisciplinary Ethics Committees for Determining Criteria for Organ Distribution*, in Bioethics: Latin American Perspectives 171 (Arleen L. F. Salles & María. J. Bertomeu (eds), Rodopi 2001).
24 Anonymous, *Officials Probe Turkish Organ Theft*, Associated Press (Sept. 17, 1999).
25 Anonymous, *Turkish Officials Say Quake Children Stolen for Their Organs*, Bloomberg (Sept. 1, 1999).
26 Anonymous, *Organ Trafficking: Manto "Shocked."* SAPA (Dec. 8, 2003), http://iafrica.com/news/sa/45524.htm (accessed Jan. 4, 2005).

27 Nancy Sheper-Hughes, *Organ Stealing: Fact, Fantasy, Conspiracy or Urban Legend?* http://sunsite.berkeley.edu/biotech/organswatch/pages/theftoflife2.html (accessed Jan. 4, 2005); A. K. Salahudeen, H. F. Woods & A. Pingle, *High Mortality among Recipients of Bought Living-Unrelated Donor Kidneys*, 336(8717) The Lancet 725 (1990).

28 Richard Ashcroft alerts me to the fact that some policy makers are doing just this. *See* Department of Health (United Kingdom), *Code of Practice for NHS Employers Involved in The International Recruitment of Healthcare Professionals* (2001), http://www.dh.gov.uk/PublicationsAndStatistics/Publications/Publications PolicyAndGuidance/PublicationsPolicyAndGuidanceArticle/fs/en?CONTENT_ID =4006781&chk=UU0hur (accessed Jan. 15, 2005).

29 David B. Resnik, *Developing Drugs for the Developing World: An Economic, Legal, Moral and Political Dilemma*, 1(1) Developing World Bioethics 11 (2001).

30 Dan W. Brock, *Some Questions about The Moral Responsibilities of Drug Companies in Developing Countries*, 1(1) Developing World Bioethics 33 (2001); Norman Daniels, *Social Responsibility and Global Pharmaceutical Companies*, 1(1) Developing World Bioethics 38 (2001).

31 Udo Schüklenk & Richard E. Ashcroft, *Affordable Access to Essential Medication in Developing Countries: Conflicts Between Ethical and Economic Imperatives*, 27(2) J. Med. & Phil. 179 (2002).

32 Louis J. Currat, *Health Research, Health Development, Poverty and Global Security*, in The 10/90 Report on Health Research (2001–02) 1, 3 (Sheila Davey (ed.), Global Forum for Health/WHO), http://www.globalforumhealth.org/filesupld/35.pdf (accessed Oct. 28, 2005).

33 Drugs for Neglected Diseases Working Group/Médecins Sans Frontières, *Fatal Imbalance: The Crisis in Research and Development for Drugs in Neglected Diseases* (MSF 2001), http://www.accessmed-msf.org/documents/fatal_imbalance_2001.pdf (accessed Sept. 26, 2005).

34 Patrice Trouiller, Piero Olliaro, Els Torreele, James Orbinski, Richard Laing & Nathan Ford, *Drug Development for Neglected Diseases: A Deficient Market and A Public-health Policy Failure*, 359(9324) The Lancet 2188 (2002), http://www.doctorswithoutborders.org/publications/opedsarticles/miltefosine_06–2002.cfm (accessed Oct. 28, 2005).

35 Tim Hubbard & James Love, *A New Trade Framework for Global Healthcare R&D*, 2(2) Plos Biology 147 (2004), http://biology.plosjournals.org/archive/1545–7885/2/2/pdf/10.1371_journal.pbio.0020052-L.pdf (accessed Sept. 29, 2005).

36 James Love, *A New Trade Framework for Global Healthcare R&D* (Dec. 4, 2003), http://www.earthinstitute.columbia.edu/cgsd/documents/love_000.pdf (accessed Apr. 30, 2004).

37 Paul Farmer & Nicole G. Campos, *Rethinking Medical Ethics: A View from Below*, 4(1) Developing World Bioethics 17 (2004).

38 *See e.g.* Peter Lurie & Sidney M. Wolfe, *Unethical Trials of Interventions to Reduce Perinatal Transmission of HIV in Developing Countries*, 337(12) New Eng. J. Med. 853 (1997).

39 *See e.g.* Udo Schüklenk & Richard E. Ashcroft, *International Research Ethics*, 14(2) Bioethics 158 (2000).

40 Robert J. Levine, *The Need to Revise the Declaration of Helsinki*, 341(7) New Eng. J. Med. 531 (1999).

41 *See e.g.* Charlotte Watts, Erica Keogh, Mavis Ndlovu & Rudo Kwaramba, *Withholding Sex and Forced Sex: Dimensions of Violence Against Zimbabwean Women*, 6(12) Reproductive Health Matters 57 (1998); Ademola J. Ajuwon, Iwalola Akin-Jimoh, Benjamin Oladapo Olley & Olagoke Akintola, *Perceptions of Sexual Coercion: Learning from Young People in Ibadan, Nigeria*, 9(17) Reproductive Health Matters 128 (2001); Rachel Jewkes, Charlotte Watts,

Naeema Abrahams, Loveday Penn-Kekana & Claudia García-Moreno, *Ethical and Methodological Issues in Conducting Research on Gender-Based Violence in Southern Africa*, 8(15) Reproductive Health Matters 93 (2000).

42 Mary Ellsberg & Lori Heise, *Bearing Witness: Ethics in Domestic Violence Research*, 359(9317) Lancet 1599 (2002).

43 WHO, *Putting Women First: Ethical and Safety Recommendations for Research on Domestic Violence Against Women* (WHO 2000). Mary Ellsberg, Lori Heise, Rodolfo Pena, Sonia Agurto & Anna Winkvist, *Researching Domestic Violence Against Women: Methodological and Ethical Considerations*, 32(1) Studies in Family Planning 1 (2001).

44 Ellsberg & Heise, *supra* n. 42.

45 Ruth Macklin is one exception. *See e.g.* her book Against Relativism (Oxford University Press 1999); *See also* Rebecca J. Cook, Bernard M. Dickens & Mahmoud F. Fathalla (eds), Reproductive Health and Human Rights: Integrating Medicine, Ethics, and Law (Oxford University Press 2003).

46 Reidar K. Lie, Ezekiel Emanuel, Christine Grady & David Wendler, *The Standard of Care Debate: The Declaration of Helsinki versus the International Consensus Opinion*, 30 J. Med. Ethics 190 (2004); Udo Schüklenk, *The Standard of Care Debate: Against the Myth of an "International Consensus Opinion,"* 30 J. Med. Ethics 194 (2004).

47 Udo Schüklenk & Anita Kleinsmidt, *supra* n.l.

48 Secretariat of the Convention on Biological Diversity. *Sustaining Life on Earth: How the Convention on Biological Diversity Promotes Nature and Human Well-being* (UNEP 2000), http://www.biodiv.org/doc/publications/cbd-sustain-en.pdf. (accessed Sept. 26, 2005).

49 Donna Dickenson, *Consent, Commodification and Benefit-Sharing in Genetic Research*, 4(2) Developing World Bioethics 109 (2004).

50 Udo Schüklenk & Jason Lott, *Bioethics and (Public) Policy Advice*, in Bioethics in a Small World (Felix Thiele & Richard E. Ashcroft (eds), Springer 2005).

Index

Cases

For Product Safety Concerns and Information please contact our EU
representative GPSR@taylorandfrancis.com
Taylor & Francis Verlag GmbH, Kaufingerstraße 24, 80331 München, Germany

www.ingramcontent.com/pod-product-compliance
Ingram Content Group UK Ltd.
Pitfield, Milton Keynes, MK11 3LW, UK
UKHW022012180926
475701UK00003B/326
9780415607513